A M E R I C   L E G E:

                              ribes

A compilation of works and essays

in honor of the first fifty years of

American Indian College of the Assemblies of God

in Phoenix, Arizona:

1957–2007.

Editors
Joseph J. Saggio & Jim Dempsey

Foreword by George O. Wood

GPH™

Printed by
Gospel Publishing House
Springfield, Missouri

This book was published in part through the generosity of a grant from
the General Council Fund for Pentecostal Distinctives.

Printed by Gospel Publishing House, 1445 North Boonville Avenue, Springfield, Missouri 65802.

Visit American Indian College's Web site at www.aicag.edu

Cover design, photo editing, graphic layout, and artwork by Sue Comer.

Photos supplied by American Indian College Office of Institutional Research

Scripture quotations from the Holy Bible are as follows and were used by permission:

King James Version (KJV)

Scripture taken from the New King James Version. Copyright © 1982 by Thomas Nelson, Inc. Used by permission. All rights reserved.

THE HOLY BIBLE, NEW INTERNATIONAL VERSION ® NIV ®. Copyright © 1973, 1978, 1984 by International Bible Society ®. Used by permission of Zondervan. All rights reserved.

Scripture taken from THE MESSAGE. Copyright © 1993, 1994, 1995, 1996, 2000, 2001, 2002. Used by permission of NavPress Publishing Group.

Library of Congress Cataloging-in-Publication Data

Saggio, Joseph J., editor

American Indian College: A Witness to the Tribes

Includes bibliographical references, names index, and a photo index

ISBN: 978-1-60585-167-9

1. American Indian College   2. Assemblies of God - Education - History
3. Bible Colleges – Arizona – Phoenix   4. Native American Higher Education
– United States
5. Christian Higher Education – United States

I. Dempsey, Jim

LD 1761 A4S2 2008
378.071

Printed in the United States of America

Dedicated to the enduring legacy of
Alta M. and Clarence Washburn
as well as the countless others
who saw fit to answer the clarion call
—becoming witnesses to the tribes,
and who tenaciously believed
that Native people should be empowered
to reach their own and others
for the cause of the gospel of Jesus Christ . . .
to the many Native leaders
and others
who have been prepared
for Christian service at this institution
and whose impact can only
be measured in eternity

TABLE OF CONTENTS

Samuel Ware and Miracle (VanZant) Johnson

FOREWORD

Moses, the Psalmist in Psalm 90:12—perhaps aware of the fleeting nature of this earthly journey—calls upon the Lord to "Teach us to number our days aright, that we may gain a heart of wisdom" (NIV). On September 23, 2007, American Indian College in Phoenix, Arizona, celebrated its fiftieth anniversary as an institution dedicated to "equip[ping] Native American students for Christian service, emphasizing Biblical truths and academic excellence within a Christian community." For over half a century this institution—which has undergone several name changes as well as a refining of its strategic purpose—has sought to remain true to its historic moorings and core values. Although time has transformed the cultural landscape in many ways, AIC has striven to remain relevant without compromising the Pentecostal values and vision of its missionary founder, Rev. Alta M. Washburn.

As a unique institution poised to serve American Indians and Alaska Natives at this strategic juncture of history, I believe it is fitting that AIC seeks to "number its days." How might they do this you ask? First, the college needs to number its days in order to assess the institution's aggregate accomplishments and strategic purpose in light of the past fifty years. At the time of this writing, AIC has been in operation more than 18,250 days. During that time 1,396 students[1] have passed through its doors and been impacted by dozens of faculty, staff, and administrators seeking to infuse them with a sense of mission to reach the lost—both to their own people, but also to wherever else the Lord may direct. Also during that time, numerous lifelong friendships (and many marital partnerships!) have also been forged with results that will need an eternal perspective to truly appreciate.

From 1957 to 2007, 488 degrees or diplomas[2] have been conferred symbolizing not only the acquisition of propositional knowledge, but much more importantly, transformational learning that equips graduates to raise up a new generation of disciples and build up strong churches that will reach Native America—as well as the world—for Christ. In the past half century, senior pastors, church staff members, military chaplains, tribal leaders, K-12 educators, principals, and even college professors and administrators have emerged from the ranks of AIC alumni.

Although the enrollment and graduation numbers may seem quite small by the standards of most colleges and universities, as you read the following chapters you will see that despite the small size of the college's enrollment, this has been overshadowed by its big heart for missions and great vision for the future. We too can join our voices in asking, "Who despises the day of small things?" (Zechariah 4:10, NIV). As you consider the accounts contained in this volume, you will be blessed by the personal accounts of administrators, faculty members, college staff, board members, and most importantly alumni who informally relate how they have been profoundly impacted by the Pentecostal nurturing, cultural relevancy, and academic formation of American Indian College.

Secondly, as AIC seeks to number its days I believe the college must also evaluate where the future is leading. No institution of higher learning can afford the luxury of resting on its laurels. We live in a world that is moving at warp speed. Globalization, non-traditional forms of learning, and rapid developments in information technology have impacted the entire landscape of American higher education. With the looming specter of increasing postmodernism on the horizon, as a twenty-first century Pentecostal Bible college, AIC has a responsibility to ask itself the hard questions: Are we still relevant? Can this institution continue to serve the needs of Native Americans and others living in a postmodern world—while yet still holding to the biblical values espoused since 1957 by its founder? What will our legacy be? Finally, what might this college look like in another fifty years? These questions (and many others) are posed throughout this book.

I am firmly convinced that you will be greatly edified and encouraged as you read the accounts contained in this work. The real life accounts of many different people, interwoven into one volume, provide a richly textured snapshot of the first fifty years of AIC's history. Moreover, you will be challenged and inspired by the dedication, talent, and spiritual vitality of the entire AIC community that have been a part of this institution for over fifty years—making it truly a witness to the tribes!

Dr. George O. Wood
General Superintendent
The General Council of the Assemblies of God
Springfield, Missouri
USA

NOTES

1 See American Indian College: 2008 Self-Study Report, p.7.

2 Ibid.

From our earliest beginnings on Washington Street in 1957...

to

Beautiful present-day campus on 15th Avenue

PREFACE

Fifty years ago one of God's choice servants had a vision that became a mandate from the Lord—establish a Bible school that would serve as a means to equip Native American leaders for the Harvest field. Following this vision and becoming obedient to that mandate, Rev. Alta M. Washburn and her husband, Clarence, established All Tribes Indian Bible School in 1957 here in Phoenix, Arizona. Although it began with little fanfare in the traditional sense of the word, we believe that something was truly released in the heavenly realm when All Tribes Indian Bible School was founded. The Lord's blessing has been evident upon this place over the past fifty years even in the most difficult of times. We can be truly grateful that the Washburns established a precedent of persevering and remaining steadfastly committed to the task at hand.

As you read through the various essays and works contained within this volume we trust that you will see the following themes evident: faithfulness, steadfastness, and the power of God's Holy Spirit to empower for Christian service. If you are looking for a purely historical work about the history of American Indian College of the Assemblies of God since its inception in 1957, you may be disappointed with this book. Although many historical events related to the college are chronicled within these pages, the primary thrust has not been to document history, but rather to capture the stories behind the history—if you will, the heart and soul of these events. You will note an air of informality in these pages as key participants share their experiences in their own words and in their own unique ways. In other words, this book may not have the polished feel that some historical works possess, but we do hope that it will inspire readers to glorify God for what He has done in the past fifty years.

We have sought to compile a broad-based collection of previously published as well as new material about the college and

P
R
E
F
A
C
E

its impact on Native American ministry within the Assemblies of God and beyond, as well as firsthand accounts from alumni, faculty, staff, administration, and Board of Regents members on how they have been impacted by American Indian College (under all of its various name changes). As the only regionally accredited Pentecostal Bible college in the United States with a specific educational mission of preparing Native Americans for ministry, we believe that our broad-based constituency has a richly textured story to tell. We desire above all else for their voices to be heard and are deeply appreciative that we have the privilege of printing this book through our own denominational publishing house, Gospel Publishing House.

In 2006 we sent our proposal for this book to our General Council executive officers including (then) General Superintendent Thomas E. Trask, (then) Assistant Superintendent Charles T. Crabtree, (then) General Secretary (now General Superintendent) George O. Wood, (then) General Treasurer James K. Bridges, Executive Director of World Missions L. John Bueno, and (then) Executive Director of U.S. Missions (now Assistant General Superintendent) L. Alton Garrison. We wish to express our grateful appreciation to our executive leadership for providing a generous grant from the General Council Fund for Pentecostal Distinctives. Their generous investment has assisted in part the publication of this work as well as helped to underwrite our Jubilee: Fifty Years of Native Pentecost celebration, commemorating the first fifty years of AIC's existence (1957–2007). Their trust in our efforts to boldly declare our continuing allegiance to the college's Pentecostal heritage is also gratefully acknowledged.

President James V. Comer has been enormously supportive of the idea of this book from its inception. His help in assisting us with obtaining the grant that has helped to fund this project is deeply appreciated. Sue Comer provided us with the graphic arts and layout design that has given us a finished product that we can proud of. Words cannot express our appreciation for the countless hours that she gave to this project—in the midst of all of her other projects—to make this dream come true.

Professor Emerita Alma F. Thomas has been a blessing to us

xii   AMERICAN INDIAN COLLEGE: A Witness to the Tribes by prayerfully saturating this work with prayer and by sharing her invaluable memories of the early days of this institution. Although a lifetime of activity has slowed her down physically, she has remained a steadfast prayer warrior and advocate for the college and especially for the Native people whom she dearly loves.

J. D. Lopez, Kerrie DeClay, Natashia Atcitty, and especially Kristin DeGarmo are students who assisted with some of the typing, scanning, and other clerical tasks. Longtime staff member M. Nadine Waldrop assisted with fact-checking, especially in the various appendices. John S. Rose, Katherine Rose, and Peggy Gray assisted with cataloging information.

We wish to also thank Darrin J. Rodgers, director of the Flower Pentecostal Heritage Center in Springfield, Missouri, for advising us and advocating on our behalf to Gospel Publishing House to work with us in printing this publication.

To the many students, faculty, staff, administrators, MAPS volunteers, and board members who have richly blessed our lives and ministry as missionary educators, we greatly appreciate your efforts and validation in this enterprise.

To our spouses and children, we thank you for putting up with the long hours that we spent poring over manuscripts, constantly editing and rewriting, as well as the other myriad tasks associated with launching a work such as this. We owe you big time!

Finally, and we believe most importantly, to our Lord and Savior Jesus Christ whom we gratefully serve with the first fruits of our labors, we are grateful that You have seen fit to place us in this corner of your vineyard to serve representative students from the over 700 Indian nations throughout the United States and Canada. Our prayer is that they may fulfill the biblical mandate to "teach all nations" and truly become *witnesses to the tribes!*

Joseph J. Saggio
Phoenix, Arizona

Jim Dempsey
Phoenix, Arizona

A WORD TO THE READER

Over the years the institution presently known as American Indian College of the Assemblies of God (AIC) located in Phoenix, Arizona, has undergone a number of name changes. Moreover, the school has also had two different locations, eighteen miles apart. From 1957 to 1972, the school—then known as All Tribes Bible School (ATBS)—was located at 4123 E. Washington Street in downtown Phoenix. From its inauspicious beginnings at that location it evolved from a local church Bible training center to a regional Bible institute of the Assemblies of God, renamed the American Indian Bible Institute (AIBI) in 1965.

By 1968, a new ten-acre site for the campus was purchased in the north Phoenix neighborhood where the college is presently located at 10020 N. Fifteenth Avenue, several blocks south of Peoria Avenue and a few blocks north of Hatcher. AIBI took up residence at the new location in 1972 after completion of the multipurpose building now known as the Washburn Dormitory, named in honor of Alta W. Washburn, founder of the school. In 1982 the school was renamed the American Indian Bible College (AIBC). In 1994 the name was changed again to American Indian College of the Assemblies of God (AIC) to reflect the addition of more degree programs to supplement the curriculum in Bible and Ministry. Over the years, the campus has added additional buildings as well as strengthened its academic infrastructure in response to the school's growth and continuing development as a Bible college.

Because of the various names of the school over the years, the reader could easily become confused so we have sought to clarify the various names which all refer to the same institution, albeit during different time periods:

All Tribes Bible School (ATBS) (1957-1965)[1]
American Indian Bible Institute (AIBI) (1965-1982)
American Indian Bible College (AIBC) (1982-1994)
American Indian College of the Assemblies of God (AIC) (1994-Present)

The reader should note throughout this work that the various essay authors will often refer to the college by the name (or initials) that they came to know the school by during their time here as a student, faculty member, administrator, or board member. These names (or initials) all stand for the same school, and we have respected the authors' desires to remember and cherish their alma mater by the name they grew to love!

NOTES

1   Early records from the school show the initials ATBS standing for "All Tribes Bible School" as well as "All Tribes Indian Bible School." Interestingly, the earliest flyer advertising the school even refers to it as "All Tribes Indian Bible Training School." During the early years of the school while ATBS was a ministry of All Tribes Assembly of God, the name had yet to be officially standardized and was apparently subject to change based on conversational usage. Once the school was incorporated as American Indian Bible Institute in 1965 as a regional institute of the Assemblies of God, the name became a consistent means of identifying the school.

The Case for an
INDIAN BIBLE COLLEGE

Joseph J. Saggio

There's no doubt about it—she was a visionary! As I've spent more than a dozen years serving the students at American Indian College of the Assemblies of God (AIC), I've been impressed by the passionate vision of Rev. Alta M. Washburn and her husband, Clarence, in founding an institution that would eventually become the first regionally accredited Pentecostal Bible college for Native Americans in the United States. Long before the original All Tribes Indian Bible School (ATBS) was planted at 4123 East Washington Street in Phoenix, Arizona, the Washburns were already successful missionary pastors who developed strong, vibrant churches wherever they went. Theirs was a faith ministry in that they both depended greatly on the Lord of the Harvest to help send them the means and personnel by which they could accomplish their missionary calling in each church they served. Like so many Pentecostal pioneers, the Washburns saw a need that could only be met through God's providence; thus they took on a task so large that unless God was in it—it couldn't possibly succeed. Yet it has—because God has been in it!

In 1957 Sister Washburn responded to the need to create a Bible school where Native students could be trained with God's Word in an environment where their heritage would be nurtured and celebrated. This need became painfully apparent in the late 1950s when an unscrupulous evangelist began to wreak havoc in some of the Indian Assemblies of God churches by promoting false doctrine and boasting that he would steal their flocks in order to bolster his own ministry. Alta Washburn reported:

> As I saw what was happening to our people in Phoenix and
> other Indian folks coming from the reservation to attend the
> evangelist's meeting, I was driven to my knees in travailing
> prayer and fasting. As I prayed, the Lord impressed me that
> a means to indoctrinate the people into the truth of the Word
> and following Christ, not a man, was desperately needed.
> The solution seemed to be immediately clear: establish a
> Bible school right here at [Phoenix] All Tribes Assembly.[1]

So began a journey that has now lasted over fifty years—
and should the Lord delay His return, it will continue for many
more. Indeed, Alta Washburn was way ahead of her time in her
thinking in that she saw the need for the development of indigenous ministry principles among Native people before many of
her contemporaries did. In spite of their vision and foresight,
the Washburns were not without criticism, but thankfully they
were blessed to have many who supported their vision to create a Pentecostal Bible college for Native Americans. I need not
mention that this great Pentecostal pioneer never even had the
opportunity to finish high school herself, yet she persisted in her
vision and calling. Nor did Alta Washburn allow the fact that
she was a woman deter her from assuming the role of an educational leader at a time when such a thing was unheard of. Alta
Washburn truly believed that in Christ: "There is neither Jew nor
Greek, there is neither bond nor free, there is neither male nor
female: for ye are all one in Christ Jesus" (Galatians 3:28, KJV).

Washburn also passionately believed that successful ministry
by Native Americans to Native Americans must be empowered by
the Holy Spirit. The atmosphere at the college has always been Pentecostal in both doctrine and practice. The story of Jacob Escalante,
originally recounted in Trail to the Tribes, illustrates the important
role that the baptism in the Holy Spirit played in the life of students
at the Bible college. After having graduated from ATBS in 1962, this
Native evangelist still had not received the Baptism. Nevertheless,
he was determined to remain at the Bible school until he was bap-

tized in the Spirit in order to be empowered for ministry. Washburn recounts Escalante's determination to receive the infilling of the Holy Spirit with the initial evidence of speaking in tongues:

> *We started a revival immediately following the graduation of the 1962 class. On Sunday night after the altar call, Jake made his way to the back of the platform as he had done so many times before to tarry for the Baptism of the Holy Spirit. His knees had hardly touched the floor when he began to speak in a beautiful heavenly language. It was a glorious experience of the Spirit's infilling.[2]*

In more recent times, I remember about ten years ago during an altar service in chapel a female Navajo student approached another woman who was a tribal member of the Ute Nation. The Navajo student thanked the Ute woman for praying in Navajo—a prayer that truly blessed her! In absolute surprise, the Ute student replied that she did not speak Navajo at all, but that she was praying in her heavenly language. Evidently as the Ute student was praying in tongues, she found herself praying in Navajo—a totally different language that she was completely unfamiliar with. Needless to say, this created quite a delightful stir throughout the campus when this became known.

Since 1957, dedicated staff, faculty, administrators, students, MAPS volunteers, and board members have faithfully and sacrificially carried out the mission and purpose of this school. Throughout the rest of this book you will hear some of their stories—accounts that come straight from the hearts of many of the key players who have been instrumental in advancing the original call and ministry of the Washburns.

As a missionary educator and researcher I've followed Native American issues in higher education with a passionate interest for more than a decade. I've seen that this institution has helped to fill a unique niche in American higher education since its inception. This is especially important since Native Americans have been determined to be the most at risk group in American higher education.[3] The reasons for this are many (and could easily fill several additional volumes) and include reservation schools lacking qualified faculty and appropriate instructional technology, poverty, English language learning (ELL) problems, and a great cultural gulf existing between historic Native core values and those of mainstream American society.[4] In short, many Native students benefit from the unique type of educational culture that AIC is able to provide. The educational culture of this Bible college includes an environment that celebrates the diverse ethnic core of students that compose our campus community. Underscoring this educational philosophy is a biblical understanding of the need to reach American Indians and Alaska Natives with the gospel of Jesus Christ by raising up Spirit-filled indigenous leaders who can be readily equipped to reach their own people—as well as go wherever the Lord directs them.

Consider this, AIC was not the first attempt to create an institution of higher learning for American Indians and Alaska Natives. In fact, the very first attempt to create such an institution was Harvard College established by Puritan ministers in 1636 to serve the spiritual and educational needs of the Massachusetts colony. By 1650, Harvard had enlarged its original charter so that it could also serve the Native people in that region. In 1665, Caleb Cheeshateaumuck, an Algonquian Indian from Martha's Vineyard, became one of Harvard's first Native graduates. Fluent in several languages, Caleb was a brilliant student. Sadly, he died shortly after his graduation and was never able to use his education.[5] In fact, throughout the colonial era, the Indian Charity School (now Dartmouth College), the college of New Jersey (now Princeton), as well as the college of William and Mary—all had (at least in part) historic missions to educate Native Americans for ministry.[6] Although these schools have become top-tier educational institutions, educating Native students for ministry is no longer a priority for them.

The AG has long been concerned about the increasing secularization of American higher education and its departure from its earlier established academic mission of educating ministers for the gospel. Even before the first General Council convened in

Hot Springs, Arkansas, in 1914, there was already a core group of Pentecostal leaders who saw the enduring merits of Christian higher education. In fact, from 1908–1914, D. C. O. Opperman, a former school system principal from Illinois turned preacher, operated at least eight short-term Bible schools in Mississippi, Texas, Missouri, Alabama, Iowa, and Arkansas. Although opposed by some, Opperman and other early Pentecostal pioneers (including W. F. Carothers, Andrew Fraser, T. K. Leonard, J. Roswell Flower, and Ralph Riggs) keenly recognized the need for a biblically literate and Spirit-empowered ministry.[7] These men knew that for the burgeoning Pentecostal movement to find its way it must develop a corps of qualified leaders who were grounded in our Pentecostal distinctives.

Since there was no existing Bible college within the AG in 1914, some denominational leaders encouraged men and women who were called of God to ministry to affiliate with an available "full gospel" school. Early non-AG Pentecostal schools that nonetheless had unofficial endorsement included Bethel Bible Institute in Newark, New Jersey; Elim Bible School in Rochester, New York; and Beulah Heights Missionary Training School in North Bergen, New Jersey.

By 1920, the fledgling AG fellowship established two Bible colleges in California: Glad Tidings Bible Institute (today Bethany University located in Scotts Valley) and Southern California Bible College (today Vanguard University of Southern California and located in Costa Mesa) were in operation in San Francisco and Pasadena, California, respectively. In 1922, the General Council of the AG established Central Bible Institute (CBI), now known as Central Bible College and located on fifteen acres of land it had acquired in north Springfield, Missouri. Such was the beginning of Bible college education within the AG.[8] In the years to follow a number of other institutions were to be established to serve the growing constituency of the General Council.[9]

Still, it would be many years before an institution would be founded that would have a unique mission to serve American Indian students. In fact, a 1952 article in the *Pentecostal Evangel* features the story of the late Pentecostal Navajo church pioneer

Rev. Charles E. Lee in which he tells of his educational formation at (then) Central Bible Institute.[10] A 1951 graduate of CBI,
Lee was one of the earliest Native Christian leaders to graduate
from an AG Bible college. He went on to a highly successful ministry as the founding pastor of Mesa View AG (now Four Cor-
ners Community Church) in Shiprock, New Mexico, serving for
thirty-six years, followed by several years as a faculty member
and board of regents member here at American Indian College.

Just a few short years after Lee's graduation from CBI, God
would place it in the heart of Rev. Alta Washburn to establish All
Tribes Bible School in downtown Phoenix to meet the unique educational and spiritual needs of Native American men and women,
providing an education in an environment that affirmed their
ethnic and cultural heritage. Opening on September 23, 1957, to
inauspicious beginnings, the school has striven to remain faithful to its original moorings, although today the curriculum has
expanded to include elementary education and business—as well
as a major in Christian ministry to prepare full-time ministers.

Therefore, we can rejoice because the Washburns had vision to
serve American Indian and Alaska Native students—and that vision
persists to this day! Although AIC remains a small Bible college, it
continues to be committed to equipping students for the harvest.
Indeed, the need is greater than ever before! Consider the following:

▶ The 2003 U.S. Census indicates over 4.4 million people
self-identified as American Indian or Alaska Native in the
United States, representing 1.5% of the total U.S. population, yet they make up only 1.0% of the college-going
population, meaning that Native Americans are not pro-
portionately represented in American higher education.[11]

▶ American Indians and Alaska Natives are less likely
to be enrolled in a college or university than their
white, Asian/Pacific Islander, and African-American
peers. They are also only one-third as likely to receive
a bachelor's degree as their white counterparts.[12]

▶ In a study conducted in 2000, American Indian College students reported that the spiritual climate of this college along with supportive faculty members, the development of positive life experiences, and a positive institutional culture has helped them to remain in college past the pivotal first year.[13]

▶ According to Rev. John E. Maracle (Mohawk, Wolf Clan), President of the Native American Fellowship of the Assemblies of God, and Executive Presbyter, Ethnic Fellowships of the Assemblies of God, only about 5% of Native Americans know Jesus Christ as their Lord and Savior.[14]

▶ In the Great Commission found in Matthew 28:18-20, we are commanded to take Christ's gospel to "every nation"—and that includes the over 701 Indian nations residing throughout North America.

Clearly, AIC is still needed and continues to play a vital role in equipping Native leaders. Although AIC has always welcomed students of any ethnicity, its distinct mission continues to remain: *Equip[ping] Native American students for Christian service, emphasizing Biblical truths and academic excellence within a Christian community.* Today AIC alumni can be found serving as leaders within our fellowship, senior pastors, youth pastors, homeless advocates, as well as educators in K-12 and higher education, tribal office workers, and in various other roles throughout the United States—and beyond. As former AIC president, Rev. Jim H. Lopez is fond of saying, "The sun never sets on an AIC graduate."[15]

AIC has not been without its share of struggles and difficulties, yet this school has always shown an amazing resilience to survive—and even thrive—in a constantly changing economy. When financial times have been tough (and they often have been), the entire campus community has pulled together and found creative ways to keep the doors open. Because AIC operates under the auspices of the AG Division of U.S. Missions, the bulk of the college's personnel tirelessly raise and maintain their own support in an ongoing attempt to keep costs affordable for our students. We've always had a heart for the harvest as well. In addition to regular outreaches to reservations and rural and urban Native communities, AIC students and faculty have in recent years pursued ministry opportunities in Mexico, Belize, Honduras, the Philippines, India, and even Outer Mongolia. For the past fifteen years at Christmas time, AIC students under the capable direction of Rev. Betty J. Hanna, longtime AIC instructor, reach out to the local Phoenix community through their Birthday Party for Jesus. Over the years, this outreach has yielded hundreds of decisions for Christ and has endeared AIC's students to the local community. In fact, just this past year was the largest one in the college's history, with over 400 people coming on to our campus to hear the good news of Jesus Christ!

In retrospect, I am firmly persuaded that only eternity will reveal the profound impact that this Bible college, located in the heart of the southwestern United States, has had on the hundreds of students who have passed through its doors over the past half-century. I am further convinced that the aggregate accomplishments of our students and alumni over the past five decades clearly underscores that AIC continues to make a strong case for the need of a Pentecostal Bible college for American Indians. American Indian College has been—and continues to be—a witness to the tribes!

NOTES

1 Alta M. Washburn, *Trail to the Tribes* (Prescott, AZ, 1990), 48.

2 Ibid., 59.

3 D.P. Benjamin, S. Chambers, G. Reiterman, "A Focus on American Indian College Persistence," *Journal of American Indian Education* 32 (Winter 1993): 24–30.

4 Ibid. See also W. G. Demmert, "Indian Nations at Risk," in *Educating a New Majority*, Laura I. Rendón and Richard Hope, eds. (San Francisco: Jossey Bass Publishers, 1996), 237–242; C. R. Colbert, "The Academic Progress of American Indian and Alaska Native Students at Arizona State University: A Longitudinal Six-Year Trend of the 1989, 1990, and 1991 Cohorts" (PhD diss, Arizona State University, 1999).

5 Bobby Wright and William G. Tierney, "American Indians in Higher Education: A History of Cultural Conflict," *Change* 23 (March/April 1991): 11–18.

6 Joseph J. Saggio, "Native American Christian Higher Education: Challenges and Opportunities for the Twenty-First Century," *Christian Higher Education: A Journal of Applied Research and Practice*, 3 (Winter 2004): 329-347.

7 William W. Menzies, *Anointed to Serve* (Springfield, MO: Gospel Publishing House, 1971), 88. See also Barry H. Corey, *From Opposition to Opening*. (Springfield, MO: Evangel University Press, 2005), 25-28.

8 Menzies, 88-89; Edith L. Blumhofer, *The Assemblies of God: A Chapter in the Story of American Pentecostalism*, vol. 1, *To 1941* (Springfield, MO: Gospel Publishing House, 1989), 314–317.

9 Today there are nineteen institutions of higher learning officially endorsed by the General Council of the Assemblies of God. They are (in alphabetical order): American Indian College of the Assemblies of God, Assemblies of God Theological Seminary, Bethany University, Caribbean Theological College, Central Bible College, Evangel University, Global University, Latin American Bible Institute–California, Latin American Bible Institute–Texas, Native American Bible College, North Central University, Northwest University, Southeastern University, Southwestern Assemblies of God University, Trinity Bible College, Valley Forge Christian College, Vanguard University of Southern California, Western Bible College, and Zion Bible College.

10 "Charlie Lee's Testimony," *Pentecostal Evangel*, No. 1997 (17 August 1952): 10–11.

11 National Center for Education Statistics. U.S. Department of Education Institute of Education Sciences NCES 2005-108. *Status and Trends in the Education of American Indians and Alaska Natives*: 2, 96. Available at http://nces.ed.gov/pubs2005/2005108.pdf (accessed 11/26/2006).

12 Ibid., 98, 106.

13 Joseph J. Saggio, *Experiences Affecting Post-Freshman Retention of American Indian/Alaskan Native Students at a Bible College* (PhD diss., Arizona State University, 2000). See also Joseph J. Saggio and Laura I. Rendón, "Persistence Among American Indians and Alaska Natives at a Bible College: The Importance of Family, Spirituality, and Validation," *Christian Higher Education: A Journal of Applied Research and Practice*, 3 (Summer 2004): 223–240.

14 I have heard Rev. Maracle use this particular statistic on several different occasions when speaking to various audiences about the important need of evangelizing Native Americans.

15 I have heard Rev. Lopez use this expression several times in both chapel services and faculty/staff meetings during his tenure as President of American Indian College.

EDITORS' NOTE:

Alta M. Washburn's autobiography *Trail to the Tribes*, originally released just after her death in 1990, is introduced in this first section by a new introduction, especially written for *American Indian College: A Witness to the Tribes* by Alta Washburn's longtime friend and colleague Alma F. Thomas. Out of print since its first and only release nearly twenty years ago, this exciting story, covering more than fifty years in the life of Rev. Alta M. Washburn, will provide the reader with important background for understanding the establishment and primary educational mission of American Indian College as well as some of the other ministry achievements in her life.

In *Trail to the Tribes* you will see the lifelong ministry and passion that Alta Washburn had towards Native Americans, especially those tribes residing in the southwestern United States. This remarkable woman never went past the eighth grade in school, yet along with her husband Clarence, was a successful missionary pastor and church planter, and perhaps most remarkably, the founder of All Tribes Bible School, today known as the American Indian College of the Assemblies of God.

One final note, in order to preserve as much as possible the original content and flavor of this work, the editors have chosen to do minimal editing, even though the reader may notice that some terminology is dated and perhaps offensive by contemporary standards.

PART ONE ▲▲▲

Trail to the Tribes

Introduction to *Trail to the Tribes*
Alma F. Thomas

Trail to the Tribes
Alta M. Washburn

▲

Alta & Clarence Washburn

Ethel Smoker

All Tribes Bible School during 1965–1966 school year with the first Speed-the-Light bus

Introduction to TRAIL to the TRIBES

Introduction by Alma F. Thomas
Professor Emerita, American Indian College

In early 1956, Rev. Alta M. Washburn—at that time pastoring All Tribes Assembly of God in Phoenix with her husband, Clarence—saw the need to create a Bible institute to equip Native Americans from Phoenix (and the surrounding reservation communities) for the work of the ministry. After spending much time in prayer, she and Clarence realized that the Lord had clearly laid this mantle upon them to establish the school.

Shortly thereafter, Leslie Sampson, one of the Sampson brothers (Pima Indians saved under the ministry of the Washburns), approached Sister Washburn after having returned as a student from one of the other Assemblies of God Bible colleges. He shared with her that he had a difficult time there because he was part of a tiny minority of non-Anglo students who felt academically unprepared for the challenging curriculum. In frustration, Leslie questioned Sister Washburn,

"Why can't we Indians have our own Bible school? We can preach in our language, but we need a place where we Indians can study the Word together; a place where we have more in common than in a school where most of the students are Anglos." [1]

Sister Washburn sensed that Leslie's heartfelt appeal was another confirmation that God was definitely leading her, as well as the workers and helpers at All Tribes Assembly of God. She was so sure of this vision and call to initiate plans for building a school that she did not wait long to start making those plans. In *Trail to the Tribes* Alta M. Washburn further recounts:

> *I began to dream, talk, write, and pray about the Bible school. The burden consumed me. The very thought of it excited my spirit because I knew I was moving in the center of God's will. Even though my burden was not shared by everyone, the congregation of All Tribes Assembly did share it with me.*
>
> *I felt led to write about the vision for the school to Brother C. M. Ward who was then pastoring in California.*
>
> *"Sister Washburn", he wrote back, "Keep yelling about that Bible school. Someone will hear you."* [2]

Of course, this brief quote can only give the reader a snapshot of the birthing of All Tribes Bible School—you'll need to read *Trail to the Tribes*, which follows this introduction, to get a better picture.

Realizing that the existing facilities of the All Tribes Assembly were insufficient to meet the needs of a Bible school, Brother Washburn and some helpers erected a small block building located behind the church sanctuary. This building was used as a dormitory to house female students and also served as the dining room and kitchen. A small lounge was located at the entrance to the building, which included a sitting area and a small library and a beautiful wall painting created by Cherokee evangelist Rev. John McPherson. A wood structure was located at the rear of the church property and was used to house male students. It was all a very primitive and simple beginning, but it was overshadowed by the Lord's presence as He met daily with students, faculty, administration, and staff in a demonstration of blessings, as well as an awareness of His presence. There was no doubt in the minds of those who experienced those early years that we had the Lord's approval of all the efforts and love poured into the initial establishment of this Bible school.

From that humble beginning the school grew and developed, experiencing a number of transitions, evidenced in part by the name changes over the years: All Tribes Bible School (its original name), American Indian Bible Institute, American Indian Bible College, and now American Indian College of the Assemblies of God. Today the school has moved from its original location on East Washington Street and is now a regionally accredited college on a ten-acre campus located eighteen miles away in a north Phoenix neighborhood at 10020 N. Fifteenth Avenue. American Indian College now offers two associate degrees: one in business and the other in Christian ministry. The college also offers two bachelor's degrees: one in Christian ministry and the other in elementary education.

In retrospect it was an honor for me to have served as a faculty member at the college for many years. I had the privilege of teaching in each phase of the school's history beginning in the early 1960s up until 2001, when I retired from classroom teaching. Perhaps the greatest honor for my late husband, Lonnie, and I was to have set under the mentorship of Alta Washburn, who taught and modeled how to minister to Native Americans, and to be inspired by her sincere desire to see the students adequately equipped to minister God's Word to their fellow tribal members and families. The graduates inherited Sister Washburn's vision and burden for the gospel to reach these first Americans.

Before her death in 1990, Sister Washburn was able to see and be aware that a number of graduates from the school were then serving in various Native communities throughout Arizona and other states. One example is the ministry of a couple who met here at the Bible school, married after graduation, and began immediately ministering in Native churches throughout Arizona. The woman's maiden name is Geraldine Moses, an Apache, her husband Vernon Poncho is an Alabama–Coushatta Indian from south Texas. Together they have pastored in Arizona and Oklahoma and are now, at the time of this writing, back in Arizona pastoring on the San Carlos Apache reservation at Bylas. Sister Washburn knew this couple well and was blessed to know that they have been so active in ministry since their graduation.

On my last visit with Alta Washburn, just before her passing, I vividly remember her telling me, and also stating in her autobiography:

> *I have spent so much time reflecting over these forty-two years God has given us to minister the gospel to Native Americans. We feel no regrets, only wish we could have many more years to work in this great Harvest for the Lord. Clarence and I are consoled by the knowledge that our vision is perpetuated by those whom our lives have touched.*[3]

At the close of the book she wrote: "Oh, how I would love to step over on some cloud and watch them go in [to heaven], especially those with whom we had the great honor and joy to share the gospel. Maranatha!"[4]

She was such a great example to me of total dedication and commitment, giving American Indians the opportunity to know Jesus as their Savior. She was a great friend and I loved her dearly.

NOTES

1 See Alta M. Washburn, *Trail to the Tribes* (Prescott, AZ, 1990), 48.

2 Ibid., 49.

3 Ibid., 100.

4 Ibid., 101.

Trail to the
TRIBES
▲▲▲

Alta M. Washburn

"Jesus is my exceeding great reward."

" Lord hold me fast

to that which drew me first,

when the cross was my whole attraction,

and I wanted nothing more."

-Anonymous-

These sayings have undergirded me through all my Christian life and ministry.
-Alta Washburn-

DEDICATION

I lovingly dedicate this book to my beloved husband and co-worker, Clarence, and my family, particularly our son, Thomas, who greatly helped us in our early years in American Indian missionary work.

This dedication also includes all the loyal colaborers the Lord sent to assist us. And last, but not least, I dedicate this book to all my dear Indian friends throughout the United States and Canada.

FOREWORD

As I read this book, I believe its outstanding feature is the relating of the ease with which Sister Alta Washburn was able to find the will of God. Hers was a life led entirely by the Spirit of God; certainly an interesting and profitable life for the Kingdom of God among the American Indians. And, one must realize there is only one Clarence Washburn, a devoted husband, always willing to make the moves Sister Washburn felt were in God's perfect will.

It was in God's perfect timing that the Washburns came to Phoenix when they did. From her pioneering ministry to the Indians in the Phoenix area, scores of Indians from urban Phoenix to surrounding reservations began to hear the full gospel message for the first time. Particular mention should be made of her numerous visits to patients in the Phoenix Indian Hospital which provided contacts for outreach on those reservations.

Students going out from the All Tribes Bible School established by Sister Washburn in 1957 to their own reservations generated many invitations we received in the Arizona Assemblies of God District office when I was superintendent to send missionaries to establish missions there. Directly and indirectly, Sister Washburn's ministry became the source for much of Indian mission work in Arizona.

During my tenure as superintendent, Gayle Lewis was director of Home Missions at our Assemblies of God headquarters in Springfield, Missouri. We both realized the importance of establishing some guidelines and qualifications for future missionaries who would go into those reservations to minister. As a result, we developed a standard by which each missionary would be evaluated. We also stipulated that no missionary should come to the American Indian mission field without financial support.

Sister Alta Washburn and her dedicated husband have been an inestimable blessing to the state of Arizona in answering God's call to share the Good News of the gospel with the American Indians. May God send us many more missionaries with the same perseverance, burden and dedication.

I salute you, Brother and Sister Washburn, for your contribution to the enlargement of God's Kingdom among Native Americans.

J.K. Gressett
Phoenix, Arizona January 1990

The Salt River Canyon, Arizona

AMERICAN INDIAN COLLEGE: A Witness to the Tribes

As I lay cringing on the floorboard of the car, I was petrified with fear. In my mind I could visualize our car slipping off the treacherous road into the Salt River Canyon in northern Arizona, a canyon so deep it looked like a bottomless pit to me. Huge boulders and mountains covered with jagged rocks rose on every side. The narrow two-lane road curved, climbed, and descended precariously.

On this trip across the dreadful canyon from San Carlos to White River to visit my sister and family, my husband and sons stopped at every viewing point to look down into that abyss.

They urged me to view the scenery with them, but I could not move from my refuge. Crying and moaning because of my terror, I made my lamentation to the Lord.

"Oh, Lord, what are we doing here? This country is so strange and terrifying. And, Lord, I'm not sure the Indian people will accept us. How can I preach to them when I can't speak their language? I'm frightened and discouraged, Lord. Please strengthen and increase my faith right now, Lord."

Satan's taunts were instantly silenced by the still small voice of the Lord as He spoke His assurance into my spirit:

"My call will never change for you. You are called to preach the gospel to the American Indians who will accept and listen to you. Do not fear, take new courage, and trust me completely."

I immediately sat up in the car, dried my eyes, and sensed a calm settling over me. I had heard from my Lord. Nothing could keep me from obeying Him and fulfilling His call on my life.

MY ROOTS

The beautiful Ohio River divides identical twin mountains in Ohio and West Virginia, the Switzerland of America. There Indian warriors first beheld the placid and tumbling river. They called it *ohio*—"beautiful" in their language. The four letters named the beauty of the river as well as that of the whole state of West Virginia, the state of my birth. Ohio was the state of my spiritual birth.

For many miles along the great Ohio River and across the bordering states were coal, steel, clay, and salt mines. Great thundering trains moved in and out between every little hill and mountain, lacing a pattern through the leafy shadows of flowers and trees. My home lay in a valley nestled between verdant hills. I loved West Virginia in spite of coal soot, spring floods, and long dark winter days.

Even though we lived in a mining community, we were not a mining family. However, one time my husband was enticed to try mining because of the good pay it offered. He had worked for one week when a cave-in occurred in the tunnel where he was working. When he heard the walls of the mine shaft cracking, he ran for his life to the entrance of the tunnel. The cave-in covered his loading car and knocked him down just as he reached the entrance. He managed to crawl to safety, but that was the last day he ever entered a mining tunnel.

The miners' lives followed a routine of coming out of the tunnels at the end of a long hard day, blackened with coal dust and eager to reach the comfort and warmth of their homes.

Within a short time, they bathed, shaved, and sat on their front porches. In the winter when they could not enjoy their porches, they would relax with the daily paper while their wives put the finishing touches on the evening meal. Bedtime came early for most of those hardworking miners as their day started at sunrise. Some would go into the cities to visit a saloon or attend a vaudeville or a dance.

Most miners were family men who knew the importance of following Christian principles. On Sundays they took their families to worship in the little white box-type churches with spires reaching high above other village buildings.

An elderly friend of mine told me about his childhood experience of a typical Sunday in one of the mining community churches. He said the children were encouraged to eat a hearty breakfast so they would not be in a hurry to leave church for the noon meal. Because the churches always seemed to be so cold in the frigid winter months, they bundled up in their mackinaws, boots, stocking caps, and mittens. In summer they sat dripping wet with sweat. No matter how uncomfortable, they sat erect and motionless in a row like fence posts.

"On Sundays as we filed into our pews," said the old gentleman, "I managed to sit on the last seat in the corner. I wanted to observe an industrious spider going up and down that corner wall. I thought that spider was the most active bit of life in that church.

"During the summer months with doors open, flies swarmed everywhere. Every Sunday I saw that spider setting his trap for a juicy fly for his dinner. I actually looked forward to going to church so I could watch him devour his full course meal before the church service was over. No one ever seemed to notice me watching the spider.

"However, one Sunday, a hornet flew into the building. It zoomed over everyone's heads and buzzed the pastor behind the pulpit. I watched with intense interest as that spider began to set his trap for a more sumptuous meal than a fly. Yet, I thought, that hornet has power, maybe too much for that spider. But my doubts disappeared as I heard the hornet's last zing; then silence. Everyone had their eyes on the preacher, but my eyes were glued to that spider with his meal firmly snagged in his web. I was so overcome with the spider's success, I jumped off my seat and shouted, "Got'cha!" I think every member of my family grabbed me at once and firmly set me back in my corner. My fun was over."

The old gentleman ended his little story with this spiritual application. "My experience observing that spider made me think there should be more action in the churches. They were lifeless in those days and needed more of the life that spider had. I felt God had given me a parable based on that childhood experience."

He was right. Those communities were in need of a move of God.

THE MOVE BEGINS

World War I was in full fury. From the mines and from every walk of life, America's brave men spread around the world fighting to defend our nation's freedom. Many young soldiers encountered God in foxholes and actual combat. If a soldier knew one scripture verse in the hour of danger and death, he quoted and embraced it. Numbers of young men surrendered their lives to Christ and answered the call to the ministry in those adverse circumstances. A move of God for spreading the gospel around the world was birthed in the hearts of young soldiers fighting for their homeland.

At home in the United States, winds of revival moved in great force. City churches suddenly became alive spiritually. The revival spirit spread to the countryside where camp meetings were held under brush arbor sanctuaries. Even the Apostle Paul's trade of tent making began to flourish as many evangelists ordered tents to use in evangelistic campaigns. They hauled and set up those tents in any city, town, or community where they could find a vacant lot or field.

This new move of God was not readily received by some churches and men of the cloth. Those clergymen seemed to draw their clerical robes tighter as they heard of and in some cases, observed the unconventional methods of worship the followers of this "move" demonstrated. However, multitudes of their members, spiritually starved for something real from God, were attracted to those non-traditional meetings. They drifted from their denominational churches into the new spiritual dimension.

Young men who had experienced a spiritual conversion while fighting in World War I returned home. After the war they found their places in the new spiritual move toward God. Many of them were filled with the Holy Spirit and began to launch out in the ministry.

In 1931, one such young man came to Clarksburg, West Virginia, and set up a large tent for gospel meetings. The people of the surrounding communities as well as townspeople flocked to hear him preach. Scores were saved and the move began to gain momentum.

It was in that meeting my mother's sisters and their families were converted. They immediately began to take turns witnessing to my mother, pleading with her to accept the Lord. They spoke eloquently of the guilt of sin, Christ's righteousness, and the judgment to come. They also witnessed to my husband and me. But we scorned, ridiculed, and hated them. We felt uncomfortable around them because their spiritual light revealed the darkness in our own lives.

We were not to remain in this spiritual darkness much longer. At this time I was a twenty-five-year-old wife and mother, crippled, paralyzed, and near death as a result of complications from a severe case of scarlet fever. Fortified with travailing prayer for my salvation, my aunt witnessed to me. Her unwavering attention to my physical and spiritual needs convinced me I was a sinner and needed forgiveness. On my bed of affliction I finally surrendered my life to the Lord. Not only was I saved, but my crippled and paralyzed limbs instantly received the touch of God. I was totally healed!

What a day to be remembered when I arose from the bed that had long held me prisoner. More glorious was my deliverance from the bondage of sin. Not only does that day in 1931 mark the date of my salvation and healing, but it was the day I heard God call me to be a missionary. Little did I know what the future held for me.

As the months passed, I learned of another experience called the baptism in the Holy Spirit. I was told, "It will give you power in your life. Just pray and ask God to fill you, and He will."

"That simple?" I questioned. "Then I will ask."

Six months after I was converted, God filled me with the Holy Spirit as I sought Him in prayer in my home. I felt spiritually equipped to obey God's call on my life, but I knew so little of the Bible. How could I preach or teach if I did not know how to minister the Word?

Since I had the responsibility of a homemaker, there was no possibility of my going to Bible school. My despair over my lack of knowledge of the Bible did not subside until the pastor of our church in Clarksburg gave a prophecy in a service. It spoke directly to me:

> "There is someone in our midst called of God to minister for Him. This person will be in active work for the Lord in a short time."

The director of our young people's group, the Christ Ambassadors, inspired me. He said if I would give myself to concentrated study of the Bible along with prayer, the Holy Spirit would enlighten the Scriptures to me. Daily, in every available portion of time, I hungrily devoured the Bible. The Holy Spirit helped me and anointed my study. I hid God's Word in my heart. I knew it would be there for me to use when the doors of ministry would open. And open they would. I had that witness in my heart.

A short time later, our church youth director resigned and moved to another town. Our pastor asked if I would like to assume the duties of the president. He assured me that he thought I was fully competent to fill the position. My joy was boundless! God was beginning to open the door. A few months later a lady evangelist, whom we had entertained in our home, greatly encouraged me. She advised me to take the Bible correspondence course "The Word of Life," published by the Foursquare Church, and she would pay the fee. God helped me to finish the course, which greatly strengthened my working knowledge of the Bible.

That same year, while on vacation in West Virginia, I visited a tent revival with one of my cousins.

"Isn't this a nice tent?" I whispered to her. "I would surely like to have one so I could preach some tent revivals in our area."

"Well, you probably can have one", my cousin replied. "See that elderly man sitting on the platform? He's a millionaire, and he gives tents to many evangelists for revival meetings all over the country. Let him know you would like to have one. Ask him." I took her advice.

Two weeks after I returned home, our local freight depot called to say there was a very large shipment for me. There it was, a tent and all the needed equipment. My evangelism days were soon to begin.

As the years passed, God helped me to care for my little family and set up the tent in many towns and communities to preach the gospel. All praise and glory to Him for the many souls who found the Lord in those meetings.

The Clarksburg tent revival closed, leaving many Spirit-filled believers who formed a nucleus that developed into a powerful witness for Christ in that community. Many accounts of other tent meetings were spread throughout the state by those who witnessed and "tasted" of God's spiritual outpouring. One such meeting was conducted by a former World War I soldier whom God had healed of a serious throat injury caused from breathing mustard gas during the war. God had called him into action. His ministry reached many parts of Ohio.

A railroader had gone to California and returned with a blazing testimony of God's outpouring of the Holy Spirit on Azusa Street. Out of that testimony many Ohio valley churches were started. They grew into powerhouses for God, reaching scores of souls in their communities. The Martins Ferry church, which later became my home church, was mightily affected by this railroader's testimony.

The mining towns became alive to the Holy Spirit, accepting the witness of those who had been touched by the Holy Spirit's power. In the caverns of the earth, miners witnessed to their fellow workers while on their jobs. Many went door-to-door to witness and distribute gospel tracts.

We moved to Salineville, Ohio, a little town a few miles east of the Ohio River. There we found a storefront mission with an Assemblies of God sign above the door.

The church's facility had become too small for the growing congregation, making it necessary to move their meetings out on the streets or wherever they could find a place. They played music, gave out little sacks of popcorn, and gave rousing testimonies of their experiences, the baptism in the Holy Spirit, and divine healing. They taught about such attention-getting topics as the rapture of the Church and sometimes spoke in tongues in the street meetings. Their zealous witnessing had a great impact on that community. Conviction rested on the listeners, and, one by one, they began to kneel on those streets, accepting Jesus as their Savior.

▼▼▼

Ernest Marshall, a miner, and his wife, Ethel, also lived in Salineville. He was a hardworking miner who always enjoyed a relaxing evening. Sometimes he and his wife would take a walk to the business section of town. One evening as they were walking at leisure, they heard music coming from a little group of people standing on the sidewalk. The music sounded attractive to them, so they stopped to listen. When the musicians stopped playing, one of the members of the group testified of salvation and God's willingness and power to heal any sickness or affliction. As the Marshalls walked home, they discussed what they had heard and seen and wondered at the strange religion of those people from the Pentecostal Assemblies of God church.

That little group of witnesses never dreamed how far-reaching their testimonies would be. Nor did they ever realize how many missionaries would carry the gospel around the world as a result of their burden to share their testimonies on that street sanctuary.

The next day, Ernest was seriously injured in an accident in the mine and was rushed to the hospital near death. The examining doctors gave little hope of his survival because of his extensive injuries.

In spite of his serious condition, Ernest remained conscious. Remembering the people they had heard on the street, he asked his wife, "Ethel, remember how we heard those people preaching and singing on the street that Jesus could heal people? Will you have them come pray for me right away?"

The little group of believers came, and God came with them! After they prayed for Ernest's healing, he and his wife both gave their hearts to the Lord, and he was miraculously healed. Every broken bone in his body was instantly set in place without medical assistance!

▲

Fred Beadle, also a resident of Salineville, was saved and healed as a result of a similar mine accident. These men and their families became close friends. They began to witness to anyone who would listen to their testimonies of salvation and healing.

Simultaneously, these men and their wives felt a burden for American Indians. Because it seemed the Lord was leading them to Arizona, they made a trip to visit San Carlos on the Apache Reservation. The visit intensified their burden. Now they knew what God wanted them to do.

When they returned to Salineville, both families sold their homes, gathered equipment for a simple lifestyle on the reservation, and returned to San Carlos. They were determined to establish a mission among the Apache, who at this time were not receptive to the white man in their midst.

The White Mountain Apache Reservation covers 2,854 square miles of rugged country covered with forests and laced with streams and rivers. Even though the scenery was beautiful, it was the domain of the Apache, known for their savage warfare. White settlers and other Indian tribes feared the Apache's famous chief, Geronimo. He passed on his tradition of terror beyond the borders of Arizona and beyond the years of his life. In his time, people from Mexico brought caravans of food and supplies into Arizona. Many times this chief and his warriors waylaid them in the mountain passes. They ravaged the wagons and killed the drivers.

When the Marshalls and Beadles arrived in Apache-land, they started gospel meetings. They were hindered by the fighting and killings among the Apache and by the witchcraft and superstitions of the medicine men who held captivating power over the Indians.

Later on, however, it became evident there was a greater power than that of the medicine men and their pagan rituals. These two missionary families were in this unfriendly land at God's command fully equipped with the two-edged sword, the Word of God. With this weapon of warfare and the power of the Holy Spirit, they were able to battle against powers standing in the way of the gospel.

Shortly after their arrival in San Carlos, the missionaries put up a little mission building. They built it on the location of the present San Carlos Assembly of God church. Fire destroyed one of the two original buildings. One is now used as a parsonage.

In those early days, missionaries had no church sponsors or missions boards to back them financially. When the Beadles' money ran out, they returned to Salineville and sold their farm for enough money to return to San Carlos for the second time. In time, that money ran out. They would again travel back to their home penniless.

When the Beadles returned to Salineville, Dewie Beadle worked in the mines. He bought another home for his family and remained there until 1947. Again the call became so strong to return to the Apaches that he sold the family possessions in order to finance their third trip to the reservation.

The consecration of these missionary families began to bring results. They labored faithfully in spite of all hardships and opposition. The gospel began to take root, and God sent His Holy Spirit to confirm His word. Apaches began to accept Jesus as their Savior and be baptized in the Holy Spirit according to Acts 2:4.

The Apaches witnessed many miracles that further confirmed the gospel's power. Sick bodies healed demonstrated to the medicine men there was a power much greater than their own. One medicine man came to the altar, took off his hat, feathers, and shirt, all representing his witchcraft powers. He declared to all present that the power of God was the real power. He burned all his fetishes and ritual paraphernalia. Then he was baptized before all his people as testimony of turning from his pagan ways and totally surrendering to the Lord.

As the revival fires continued to burn, the saved and Spirit-filled Apaches carried their testimonies to their relatives and friends around the village. Their zeal and newfound joy prepared them for true discipleship.

The missionaries and believers extended their ministry to Bylas, a nearby Apache village. News of God's work in San Carlos spread to Whiteriver, an Apache village one hundred miles over the mountains.

By this time the San Carlos mission was fifteen years old and was the first established Assemblies of God Indian church in Arizona. It was officially set in order in 1947 at the time Mrs. Marshall resigned as pastor.

▲▲▲

Fifteen years had passed since the little store frontchurch in Ohio gave birth to four pioneer missionaries to the American Indians. Now the congregation worshiped in a nice facility on a main street in Salineville. The congregation continued to be a praying missionary-minded assembly. Dedicated men and women who pastored this church accepted the call to missions in lands beyond the seas and in the homeland. Others stepped through the door to the ranks in glory and are reaping the fruits of their labors.

The church board invited me to accept the pastorate of the Salineville church after the resignation of their pastor, Milton Kimble. I accepted the pastorate for I felt it was in God's will.

While pastoring this church, I met the Dewie Beadles, who continually requested prayer for the American Indians in our services. Something always gripped my heart when I heard those requests. Since my deathbed experience and healing in 1931, I had felt an intense burden and call to Indians. However, I thought I would sometime go to the country and people of India. Because of this burden, I had given much study to that land, its customs and people.

Since my mother's family had American Indian ancestors, I always felt an attachment to Indians. Now, hearing requests for prayer so often, something began to tug at my heart. The Beadles' impassioned prayers and burden for these people intensified my spiritual interest. I found my heart joining theirs as we spent more and more time talking together about our shared burden.

During my pastorate in Salineville, I had invited my dear friend Daena Cargnel to conduct an evangelistic meeting in our church. She agreed with the understanding that I would preach a revival for her in Utica, New York. Later while preaching that meeting I received from God what I had been waiting to hear. He came to me, confirming His call upon my life, in a vivid visitation of His presence.

"Now is the time for you to take the gospel to the American Indians," He said. "You know now where they are. Go home and prepare yourself. Tell your husband and your church, and I will make the way plain for you."

With this commission from the Lord, an intense love for American Indians flooded my soul. Now that I had a confirmation of my call from God, I knew I must take the next step—a step of faith.

The next morning I shared this experience with the Cargnels. They felt a witness that this was truly God placing His divine call and will upon my life. They encouraged me to obey that call, trust His guidance, and have faith.

Many things now flooded my mind and heart. Many questions had to be answered. How could I tell my church congregation? How could I tell my husband? And how could he understand my burden? Could I expect him to leave all he had worked so hard to accomplish and go to an unknown land? But had not the Lord just reminded me that the American Indian mission field was no longer an unknown place?

Arriving back in Salineville from New York, I prayed earnestly and pondered all that had happened. I weighed every detail, but I could not settle on an easy way to tell my husband. Little did I know that God was already resolving the problem in His providential way.

Clarence worked twenty-five miles from our home in Salineville. Since he worked nights, he could call me on his lunch hour. One evening when he called, he surprised me by asking if I would like for us to have a travel trailer to use when we attended the state camp meetings. Before I thought, I answered, "Oh, yes, that would be ideal for us to use on the mission field."

He was startled by my response. After some hesitation, he reminded me that it would be quite difficult to take a trailer to India. Now was my opportunity to tell him about my call to the American Indians. I couldn't hold back my burden any longer from him. "Alta, you had better pray about this," came his expected response. "Would you leave your pastorate, your mother, and the nice house I have just remodeled for you?" I did not need to ponder before answering him. I told him I would be willing to leave it all to follow the call the Lord placed on my life in 1931.

Clarence's answer remained the same, "You had better pray much about this, Alta."

I felt my greatest challenge was to pray my husband out of his lifetime job, even though it seemed unfair to him. But I knew I was moving in God's will and set my heart to see this prayer answered.

My sister and brother-in—law, the Ted Johnsons, were graduating from North Central Bible Institute in Minneapolis, Minnesota. They were coming home to Ohio to prepare for missionary work in Africa. I wrote and asked them to take me to Arizona before they left for Africa.

At the time I was writing, God had spoken to my brother-in-law in a dream. He saw an Apache camp in the Arizona White Mountains and Apache women in their native dress asking him to bring them the gospel. We had never discussed Indian missions ,nor had I ever shared my missionary burden with them. This turn of events confirmed our shared call to the Indian people. Ted immediately answered my letter saying they would be glad to take me to Arizona. Even though I had not told all this to my husband, I sensed God's divine will in the developing circumstances.

The time came when I had to tell Clarence my plans. He seemed troubled. This, obviously, caused me great distress. The pull between two loyalties—my call to Indian missions and my husband's feelings and welfare—were difficult emotions to handle. However, God was working!

Clarence called me from his job one evening after I had told him of my planned trip to Arizona with the Johnsons. He told me not to answer Ted's letter. That was all he would say. This left me troubled. I knew he could put his foot down, and I, as a dutiful wife, knew I could not blatantly defy him. For me, wrestling with this situation was like Jacob petitioning God to protect him from his brother Esau. I, too, prevailed until the dawn as Jacob did when he wrestled with the angel. My travail in prayer was gloriously answered in a way more than I could ever have dreamed!

When my husband came home that early morning, his words were music to my ears! "Don't plan on your trip to Arizona with the Johnsons," he said. "We will sell our house and all go together." My joy was unbounded. Surely God does do exceedingly and abundantly above all we could ever hope for.

This happened in the spring of 1947. There were many details to work out, and some circumstances made the move questionable. When my husband's boss heard Clarence planned to resign from his job, he offered him a raise in pay, extra time off from the job, and daytime work. Even though the offer was attractive, Clarence was firm in his decision. He informed his boss we were definitely moving to Arizona.

One major concern we had was our two widowed mothers, who lived in two houses we owned in the city where Clarence worked. Little did we realize God was already taking care of this situation in an unexpected manner. My mother came for a visit with us in Salineville, where she met and married a widowed deacon from our church. My mother-in-law came for their June wedding and met another widowed deacon and became his bride in August.

All the circumstances seemed to be made-to-order, making it evident to us that God had directed each of our lives in accordance with His divine plan.

When the Johnsons came in May 1947, we had the travel trailer all ready for the trip to Arizona. Our property had not sold yet, however. We sold our furniture and had given away many possessions we felt we would not need in Arizona. While sitting on packing crates, we hoped and prayed every day a buyer would release us from our real estate.

Because we did not want the Johnsons to be delayed any longer, we urged them to take our trailer and go on to Arizona to fulfill their mission assignment. We knew God would make a way for us to follow soon.

One day while waiting on the sale of our property, I listened to Kathryn Kuhlman's radio program. A farmer had requested prayer that his farm would sell. She asked the farmer what day he would like for the buyer to come. She was specific, so he set the day. Of course, all this caught my undivided attention because of our similar situation. A few days later while listening to Sister Kuhlman's program, I heard her announce that a buyer purchased the farm the exact day the farmer specified to sell.

I was so inspired in hearing of that miracle I wrote Sister Kuhlman asking her to pray for God to send us a buyer on the following Friday at noon. I could not have been more specific. As God did for the farmer, He sent a buyer exactly at noon on that particular Friday. God was working out all the details. Now we were actually released to begin our journey to Arizona.

Imagine our joy when Thomas, one of our married sons, and his wife, Vida, told us they would like to make the trip to Arizona with us. Our youngest son, Floyd, was a schoolboy at this time. So now we had two of our three sons with us. This was an added blessing and made the separation from home much easier.

We attended the Ohio camp meeting with the Beadles in those waiting summer months of 1947. This dedicated couple decided to join us on the trip. This would make the third time they had sold a home and gone to the people and land of their calling. Since they could orient us on what to expect when we arrived in Indian territory, we were delighted they would be going with us.

Before we left for Arizona, Earl Bond, our Ohio district superintendent, contacted the Home Missions Department requesting an official appointment application for me. We both realized I needed some recognition and approval from headquarters before launching out into Indian missions. I was sent a foreign missions application because they had not yet been prepared for home missionaries. The appointment was soon granted. This made me the first officially appointed missionary to American Indians. We were now ready to obey our call and begin another chapter in our lives.

I was assigned to assume the pastorate of the San Carlos Apache Mission. Sister Marshall, who had pioneered the mission with her husband (now deceased), had resigned after fifteen years of ministry there.

The Beadles arrived at San Carlos with their trailer house before we did and welcomed us when we arrived. Getting acquainted with the Apaches was made much easier for us since the Beadles knew them and were familiar with their culture. Although we felt uncomfortable in this strange environment, the Beadles calmed our apprehension by assuring us there was nothing to fear.

We parked our trailer near the Beadles and busied ourselves getting settled. Our young son, Floyd, began watching closely to see some "wild" Indians, but none came around that first day. He went to bed disappointed because he thought surely he would see Indians hiding behind rocks and trees shooting with their bows and arrows.

The first night after we had gone to bed, we heard a loud BOOM BOOM coming from drums in the distance. The dreadful noise was accompanied by loud shouts and chants. It all sounded much too close. We hurried to the windows and peeked through the curtains. Across the clearing a campfire blazed and half naked people, their bodies covered with strange designs, leaped and jumped to the drumbeats. Their hooded masks identified them as Apache devil dancers. They were having a "sing" for a dying woman lying on a blanket beside the fire. There was no sound sleep for us that night nor the following two nights, for the ceremonies continued that long. Finally, on the third night, the drums were silent. The woman had died.

Mixed emotions filled our hearts, as we were now in the land of our calling. Our inquisitiveness about our surroundings had ceased. We no longer looked for Indians hiding behind trees and rocks, nor was our son playing cowboys and Indians any longer.

This was the real thing. We realized we had to prepare ourselves with God's help for a transition to this strange environment and people.

Did doubts arise? Had we followed a lark in being there?

No.

Was the call real?

Oh, yes.

God's perfect will was never in doubt.

Since we had not seen my sister, Jean, and brother-in-law, the Ted Johnsons, since we arrived, we decided to make a trip over the treacherous Salt River Canyon road to their mission at White River in the White Mountains. As I mentioned in the first chapter, traveling that road was a harrowing experience for me. I was greatly relieved when we finally reached my sister's house.

What a happy reunion to see the Johnsons again. Jean had always seemed more like a daughter to me since she was only three years older than our oldest son. Here we were, a family united, in a land that seemed as far from home as India or Africa. Our visit was filled with reminiscing about home, our loved ones, and our shared calls to the Indian people.

There was no church building in Whiteriver, so Jean, Ted, and the Roy Suhis, whom they were assisting, set up a tent by the river for their services. It was winter and snow had accumulated on the tent, but they didn't seem to mind that there wasn't a more comfortable, warm place to worship. When Jean asked me to preach for them I answered, "I don't know how to preach in the Apache language."

"Of course not," she said, "but we'll get you an interpreter, and it will be just like preaching in Ohio."

I consented, but an uneasy feeling began to surge over me. I lay in bed that night pleading with God to help me with the sermon and to remove my fears.

The tent was full of Apache Indians when the service started the next day. They didn't look so wild, I thought. They just appeared to be anxiously waiting, like Cornelius and his household waited to hear the gospel from Paul. A huge Apache cowboy interpreted for me. As I proceeded into my sermon, entitled "The Right and Wrong Trails to Heaven," I noticed tears in the cowboy's eyes.

He began to cry and leaned against a tent pole, saying, "I'm lost. I've been on the wrong trail all my life. Pray, pray for me." That man and his whole family were saved in that service. At the writing of this book, four generations of the man's family are saved and working for the Lord.

As we drove down the mountain roads back to San Carlos, the Holy Spirit whispered into my soul, "Now, did I not tell you that God would make a way for you to reach these people with the gospel and they would accept you and your ministry?"

After our visit with the Johnsons in Whiteriver, it seemed that as every difficult time arose for us in our ministry with the Apaches, I would feel the Holy Spirit reminding me of that confirmation and assurance of my call. Clarence and I both felt strength to continue on in spite of each obstacle Satan put before us.

While I was still living in Ohio and praying much about the call to the Arizona Indians, I had a vision of a long, long road that I was to travel. It was a clear, smooth road as far as I could see. However, at the end, which I knew was Arizona, a great black cloud settled over the road. In this vision I was aware there would be difficult times ahead, but I was conscious that God would be an "ever present help in time of need." I did not tell my husband or sons about my vision because I did not want them to have any doubts about our being in Arizona.

Memory of that vision came back to me after we had been at San Carlos for a short time. Although the church had many Christian believers, I soon faced problems both among the church members and from outside sources. I wondered why my mission board had not informed me of trials I would face in this Indian country. But even if I had known, I would not have rejected God's call. I faced trials in that Apache church I had never faced in all my previous pastoral ministry. But, thank God, the Beadles, with all their experience and exposure to the unique problems in pastoring American Indians, were there to comfort and encourage me. Numerous times we travailed together in prayer in the midst of the hardest times, and each time God always confirmed His call and Word. God sent some of the greatest miracles of my ministry during our months in San Carlos.

I had never encountered such jealousy as I saw among the Indian women. A man would sometimes desert his wife and children, then take one or more wives for himself. The deserted wife would hide in the dark and throw rocks at the ex-husband's family wickiup. Even worse, she might burn it down. In angry desperation she might pour gasoline over her own body and set herself on fire. She felt she was getting revenge on her husband by performing such a violent, and in most cases, fatal act.

On one such occasion I was called to the hospital to visit a woman who had set herself on fire. She was lying under an oxygen tent dying of third degree burns over most of her body. I ministered to her but knew she would soon expire. Her body showed no sign of life. But immediately after I finished praying, her eyes opened. She said she had seen an angel and all her pain was gone. Her burns began to heal and she improved rapidly. Her miraculous recovery amazed the doctors. The woman gave her heart to the Lord and became a dedicated Christian.

The spirit of Geronimo, the infamous Apache chief of the 1800s, prevailed over the Apache reservations long after he died. Fierce fighting continued between tribes as well as individuals. The women were the most vicious in fighting over their men. They would lunge at each other, taking a deadlock grip on the long hair of the other. Often a woman held on so tenaciously, she came away with a handful of hair and a piece of scalp attached!

Sometimes those terrible incidents happened during a church service right in the middle of my sermon. We had a mixture of acts of violence and demonstrations of God's miracle-working power in our services. I always wondered why when I was under a heavy anointing of the Holy Spirit those things happened. But, inevitably, God's power would begin to move and settle the disturbances.

In one particular Sunday service I was stopped in the middle of my sermon by a large Apache man rushing through the doors brandishing a gun. He pointed that gun straight at me! Before I could gain my composure, he saw his wife and baby sitting near where he was standing. He lunged at his wife, grabbed her by the hair, and hit her on the jaw. The force of his blow caused her to lose her hold on the baby, and the child landed halfway down the aisle. At that moment the doors flew open as two Apache policemen ran in and apprehended the man. He had escaped from jail and had come to the church to kill his wife. Even though the mother and child were injured, they survived the ordeal. We all praised the Lord together for His divine protection for us.

When the Apaches entered the church, they always went to the altar first to pray before they found a place to sit. As a result of this, I felt the presence of the Lord and His anointing in each service. As I heard them praying, I would hear the Apache word *enesuit*, for "missionary." Knowing they were praying for me made it easier to preach and minister to them.

On one memorable Sunday morning, God had already set the stage and preparation for a great miracle for that service. I was preaching on an all-powerful God who could do anything, anywhere, anytime. Little did I realize that my sermon was about to be proven. The presence of the Lord was so radiant, I felt the doors should be locked to hinder any intrusion into that hallowed presence. But, of course, we don't lock doors during church services.

During the sermon, the front doors burst open, and a woman ran toward me carrying a baby. She literally threw the baby into my arms. The baby's little body was cold and stiff in death. She had just taken it from the hospital morgue and was on her way to the cemetery for its burial. Reckless faith, however, directed her to the church. She wanted us to pray her baby would live again! There I stood holding that little corpse. This had to be possibly the greatest challenge of my ministry. But had I not just preached that nothing is impossible with God? I suddenly realized that I was agonizing before God for the little dead infant as I did when I lay dying as a cripple in 1931. Somehow those travailing prayers always seemed to penetrate through the barriers of hell and reach God's throne.

As I prayed, I began to feel warmth return to that little body and the rigid little limbs become limp and movable. I handed that baby restored to life into its mother's arms. All of us in that Sunday service were overcome with the knowledge that we had actually beheld the resurrection power of the Lord. I didn't even attempt to finish my sermon or pray the closing prayer. God had already placed His divine benediction on that service! Little did I know that I would again be confronted with a spiritual challenge concerning that child in later years.

Eighteen years later in Phoenix, I answered a knock on our parsonage door. There stood an Apache lady, whom I did not recognize, and a young man.

"Sister Washburn," she said, "you remember my boy, don't you?" Noticing the blank expression on my face, she continued, "Yes, you know my boy. He's the one that died in San Carlos when he was a baby. You prayed for him and he lived."

Of course, I remembered. How could I ever forget that momentous day?

"Today I bring him back to you for prayer," she said. "I want you to bless him. He's in the army now and leaves for the Vietnam war tomorrow. I want you to pray God will bring him back home safely."

I was overcome with emotion at that moment and wept and prayed for that young man. Faith in God's divine protection assured me he would return safely. Later I heard he had returned to San Carlos after the war without any battle injuries.

▲▲▲

God was moving in a phenomenal way in Whiteriver. An old Catholic church building was given to the Suhis and Johnsons. They tore it down and used the materials to build a church. No mission board sponsored their efforts, and very little finances were available for their personal needs. Ted received a small disability check from the army that supplied their bare necessities.

Troublesome times besieged them because of witchcraft, demon powers, and rejection by some of the Indians. But they knew they were in the will of God and refused to let Satan win in his on-slaught against them.

Many times my sister and I would compare our experiences, hardships, dangers, and victories. We shed tears together; then suddenly we would lift our heads, rejoice and laugh together, and remember some of the situations we had encountered. God was our deliverer, strength, and ever-present help in times of our need.

When our time of visiting was over, we would jokingly tell each other, "I go now. I be back." This was an expression used by the Apache medicine man when he showed his displeasure with us. He wanted us to live in fear of his curses and threats. They were useless. Satan, who empowered that medicine man, could not touch us. We were surrounded by the all-powerful and protective covering of God's holy presence.

▲▲▲

The Apache reservations are well-known as cattle country. The stock roams free on the high plateaus and mountainous ter-rain of the tribal rangelands. Once each year the Apache cowboys have a mammoth roundup of cattle to be sold or auctioned off at public sales.

My sister, Jean, shared the following account of one of the roundups in which they were involved during their ministry in Whiteriver.

"We knew roundup time had started because we heard the rumbling of thousands of hooves as the cattle were driven into the roundup corrals. The sky turned hazy from the dust kicked up by the cattle.

"It was now time for us missionaries to rush about, gather our musical instruments, saddlebags, supplies, and stuff every pocket with gospel tracts and scripture portions. We hurried to the stockyards before the cattle and drivers arrived.

"The chuckwagon arrived first to begin preparing food for

the hungry cowboys, who had been on the trail a long time. The air was charged with frenzied excitement as Indians, missionaries, and the Apache cowboys moved about. It reminded me of a county fair.

"We missionaries were welcomed to eat with the cowboy crew and Apaches. Huge steaming pots of beef, potatoes, plenty of gravy, and pancake-sized biscuits provided a sumptuous meal. After being filled with such a satisfying feast, the cowboys lay around drinking coffee, resting and talking about the cattle drive. Even though we could not understand their language, we could tell by their actions they were glad the drive was over.

"Soon we gathered our guitars, accordions, and banjos and started singing gospel songs and hymns. The cool night's breeze, the starry, moonlit sky, outlines of the White Mountains visible in the distance, and the gentle lowing of cattle provided a perfect setting in which we worshiped the Great Creator and shared His Word with those tired cowboys.

"As we began to sing, the people all joined in, clapping their hands to songs such as 'Power in the Blood' or 'When the Saints Go Marching In'. One song always requested was 'The Old Rugged Cross.'

"Soon the musical instruments were laid aside, and one of the missionaries opened the Bible to minister. The preaching was powerful but as gentle as a fisherman drawing in his net. By this time, the cowboys had removed their dusty, trail-worn hats. We detected an atmosphere of reverence for God's holy presence. We knew conviction of the Holy Spirit rested heavily upon the hearts of those Apache cowboys and others gathered in that tribal stockyards. Many Apache souls were saved that night.

"In other roundups cowboys were born into the kingdom of God as they heard of His story of love for all men.

"I count those roundup times as some of the most cherished and remembered experiences of our ministry among the Apaches."

San Carlos and Whiteriver were the only Assembly of God Indian churches in Arizona in those early days in the 1940s. Our visits with the Johnsons were rare because of the one hundred miles between us and terrible roads we had to travel through the canyons. Going to the post office to receive letters, especially from home, and the visitors who occasionally came our way were the highlights of any day.

One day a letter came from Brother Fred Vogler, who was then our home missions director in Springfield. He wrote that the department was planning a regional missions convocation and would like to have the meeting in our church in San Carlos. We were excited to hear the news because the meeting would provide an opportunity for us to meet other missionaries.

The convocation was a great success. We met, among others, Mildred Charles, a pioneer missionary from California. George Effman, Jr., and John McPherson also came from California. Charlie Lee, a young Navajo minister from New Mexico, and Dick Boni, one of our own Apache preachers, attended. And what a privilege to have Fred Vogler, whom we missionaries called our "great white father," to minister to us.

I was particularly blessed in that meeting because district officials from the Arizona Assemblies of God came and gave me a hearty welcome to the district as an Indian missionary.

After the convention, dark storm clouds of discouragement and trials began to settle over us at San Carlos. Any effort of progress in the church seemed to be blocked. A shortage of funds for our own personal needs became a serious concern, for which we had no ready solution. Part of the money from the sale of our property in Ohio was used to purchase our trailer and truck. Now the money we had left was diminishing rapidly.

We remembered that the home missions headquarters in Springfield had told us the American Indian mission field was wide open, but there was no established support fund for missionaries. We realized we would have to be responsible for our support, but we did not know we would find ourselves in such dire circumstances so soon after coming to Arizona.

The San Carlos church did have a tithe fund, which they regularly deposited in the bank, but they had not yet realized their need to support their pastors. My sermons on pastoral support seemed to fall on deaf ears.

Clarence applied for a job at one of the nearby copper mines but failed his eye test. Naturally, he remembered he left a lifetime job in Ohio where they never required an eye test. Finally, he told me in desperation that he knew nothing else to do but go to Phoenix and look for employment.

My first thought was I would have to leave my church in San Carlos. It was a trying time for us. We never realized when we came to Arizona we would be facing such obstacles. Yet the call remained firm.

When my husband and our son Thomas left for Phoenix I was distraught because I knew they would have to cross that terrible Salt River Canyon. I cried, "Oh, God, they will never make it. They will fall off that narrow road and I will never see my husband again."

I was convinced only the Holy Spirit could get them through those canyons alive.

My daughter-in-law and I spent three days in prayer and fasting for their safety. Our concern for their employment was not as intense as our travailing before God for their safe return. I wondered if God thought my prayer was stupid, but I know He heard my heart's cry.

Our men did return safely and announced they had both found jobs. Leaving San Carlos would not be easy. We would have to leave the church with the Beadles, but clouds of depression and discouragement began to lift. The prospect of moving along another trail in our lives held excitement and challenge.

Many times I climbed the mountain behind the church, looked out over the village, and wept for the people. I regretted I was not able to do more for them. Love flooded my soul for the Apaches, and the burden for them continued even after we left.

I realize now that had those dark clouds not settled over us in San Carlos, we possibly would not have found the central trail God wanted us to travel—a trail which would lead to many other Indian tribes.

Clarence told me when he returned from Phoenix many Indians lived in the great Valley of the Sun. That stimulated my desire to go. I felt a tug at my heart. God was leading us on a new trail of ministry for Him.

Today a beautiful highway with guard rails and lookout points traverses the Salt River Canyon. That was not the case when we began our trip to Phoenix. That road was only a dirt trail switching back and forth like a corkscrew. We prayed no one would come from the opposite direction until we had safely climbed to the top of the canyon.

One fear I had materialized. Climbing out of the canyon, our old truck labored under pulling the trailer weighted down with all our earthly possessions. Finally it balked and refused to go any further. We were stuck in a place called Devil's Canyon. I felt it was appropriately named to catch poor wayfaring travelers!

Our son drove to Globe, Arizona, to get a wrecker to tow us out of the canyon. When we reached the top of the canyon wall and began descending to the desert, I was elated and shouted for joy at the promise of reaching safety.

Clarence found a good job with the Trailways Bus Lines doing the same kind of work he did in Ohio. We traded our trailer for a little house on Twentieth Street in Phoenix. Jack enrolled in a trade school and our young son, Floyd, attended a nearby elementary school. After our families were settled, we began looking around for those Indians Clarence had told me about.

On our first visit to First Assembly of God church, an invitation to testify gave us an opportunity to tell the people about our burden for American Indians. We also told them of our desire to pursue a ministry among them in the Phoenix area. The pastor, Rev. Claude Wood, told us we were welcome to begin services for Indians in their church. Grateful for his invitation, we felt doors were beginning to open.

Not only were there multitudes of desert Indians living on nearby reservations, thousands of Indians from many tribes had moved to Phoenix. The Indian Hospital, Phoenix Indian High School, job training, and work opportunities attracted them.

The next Sunday after our first visit to First Assembly we brought ten high school students from the government Indian school. They were a beautiful sight to me, filling a whole row of seats in front of us. Brother Wood preached a powerful message on the soon coming of Jesus. When he gave the congregation an invitation to receive Christ and be ready for His coming, all ten students raised their hands for salvation and filed out of the pew to the altar for prayer. My cup of joy overflowed!

The following Sunday we brought five more students to church. They were not only saved but filled with the Holy Spirit. Revival broke out in that church Sunday after Sunday as Indian students responded to the invitation to accept Jesus as their Savior.

Mamie Rice, an Apache lady who lives in Prescott, Arizona, and the mother of David Rice, one of our Arizona Assemblies of God ministers, was one of the students saved in those services. Others included Pauline Miles and the Antonio Kessey daughters and sons. Then Indian adults and children began to attend. Many of the Indian children who were saved and Spirit-filled prophesied under the anointing of the Holy Spirit to their families and neighbors about their need to repent and be saved. Because of God using those children, many of those Indian adults broke before the Lord, crying out for mercy and forgiveness.

The Indian people responded to the power of the Holy Spirit in a more demonstrative way than I had witnessed in my ministry among Anglos. I sometimes feared it was a wave of "wild fire." But it was not. Their type of worship was due to a genuine move of God, not only in the church services but also in their homes.

An early part of our ministry in Phoenix was begun in the Indian hospital. We witnessed numerous miracles and healings among the Indian patients, who came from various tribes and reservations.

God's healing power was present when I prayed for the first lady I visited in the hospital. She was a victim of rheumatic fever. Her body lay in a crippled fetal position. As I talked to her about Jesus' love for sinners and His healing power, tears filled her eyes and ran down on her pillow. She readily accepted Jesus as her Savior, was healed and soon able to walk.

One day when I visited this lady, I met her mother. Her daughter had witnessed to her about her experiences of salvation and healing.

When I entered the room, she introduced me and said to her mother, "This is the woman I was telling you about. You should invite her to come to our house and pray for all of you to get saved. You know all of you really need to get right with God."

Later, the mother, Zula McGinnis, a Maricopa Indian married to a black man, invited me to their home on Eleventh Street for a service. The whole family attended. It was some of the children from this family who were saved in our services at First Assembly. They had faithfully prophesied and witnessed to their family. They had planted the seed in those adult hearts, which prepared them for the preaching and receiving of the Word.

Eventually, Brother and Sister McGinnis and the whole McGinnis family were saved. It was in the home of their son-in-law and daughter, the Richard McCloskey family, that the All Tribes Indian Assembly actually began.

Easter Sunday afternoon in 1948, a happy crowd met with us in First Assembly's education building. We celebrated the first public service of the Phoenix All Tribes Assembly of God.

Until this time, our ministry centered around the Indians living in the city and the Indian students in the government school.

As the ministry grew, the Indian converts became burdened for their relatives living on Indian reservations in areas around Phoenix. We began to concentrate our prayers for those unsaved kin and their neighbors on the reservations.

Some of the new converts were introduced into personal ministry when they accompanied me on visits to the Indian hospital.

We went from room to room praying for the sick.

Once we visited a lady who lay swathed in bandages and wore a neck brace. Her neck had been broken in a car accident. I told her the simple story of salvation and healing. She accepted the Lord as Savior. We told her we would continue to pray for her complete healing from her injuries. On another visit, I inquired about her and was told she had already gone home. She had been miraculously healed.

A short time later this same lady invited me to come to her home in Laveen, a community located on the northwestern part of the Gila River Reservation, to hold a gospel service. She wanted her family and neighbors to hear about Jesus.

In that first service in her home, she held up the heavy neck brace before the people and told them how God had healed her. That testimony had an impressive effect on her family and neighbors. In that service and others that followed, many Indians from that reservation were saved. The Co-op Indian Assembly and Laveen Indian Assembly of God churches stand on that reservation as a memorial of that lady's healing and opening her home to the gospel.

Another hospital healing occurred when we visited a lady with severe head injuries received in a fight with another woman. After we witnessed and prayed for her, she was saved and healed. She asked us to have a meeting in her home on the Salt River Reservation. From that initial service, a strong, active Assembly of God church stands today.

Our visits to the Indian hospital provided the basis for our contacts with the American Indians. Those contacts opened up a way to pioneer the gospel outreach points on the various reservations. In my heart, I know God providentially led me to the Indian hospital soon after our move to Phoenix.

By this time the annex that Phoenix First Assembly of God church allowed us to use for our services overflowed. We could see the handwriting on the wall; we must have a church home for the Indian people. For several services, the Lord spoke to me: "Step into the waters. I will carry you through." Did that message from the Lord mean that we were to launch out by faith and build or buy a church building?

We had no reserve funds, and I questioned in my heart how I could possibly think of building without any money. Then the Lord impressed me to go back to Ohio to raise funds for the church. I had many friends and pastors who would allow me to present our need to their congregations. We found a facility at 4123 East Washington, on the eastern side of the city near the reservation Indians. We felt the Lord directed us to that suitable location.

The Pentecostal Church of God who owned and used the building had moved to another location. They priced it to us at $10,000. That seemed a staggering amount in those days. The son-in-law of a friend of mine served on their church board. My friend suggested to him that he request the church board reduce the price to $5,000 for an Indian mission. The board generously agreed. But then the money had to be raised.

When I approached my husband about a trip to Ohio in our old Hudson car, he objected strongly. He reminded me of the length of the trip. He doubted the old car would make it that far. I believed him because he was a mechanic, but I could not accept his negative reply, especially after God had given me His directive. Prayer was my only recourse. Right off I reminded God, as if He didn't already know, of the car's mechanical ills. I even went into detail about different parts of the car Clarence said were too worn-out to be trusted. I continued to remind God that since He had all power in heaven and in earth, He could surely "heal" that old car.

While I dried my tears, the Lord spoke to my spirit, "Do not worry. If you are willing to go on this trip, I will go with you. The trip will be safe and successful."

That was all I needed, for I had heard from my Lord again.

I told Clarence that God had made it clear I was to make the trip and He would go with me. He said no more but began right away to repair and revitalize that old Hudson. He had learned long ago when I declared I had heard directly from the Lord, he should object no longer and acquiesce to my wishes.

Vida, my daughter-in—law, said she would care for the house and cook for Clarence. So, I left for Ohio along with my ten-year-old son, Floyd, and a young man I had known in Ohio. He lived in California at this time and offered to drive for me. As we drove out of Phoenix, I had no apprehensions. I knew God was riding right beside us in that car. The trip was trouble-free. Of course it was; God said it would be!

What a joy it was to see my dear mother and friends from the Salineville church again. The first night at my mother's home was a very special night. After I had gone to bed, I felt the Lord's presence hovering over me, and it seemed I was walking in a garden of fragrant flowers. That experience was the crowning point of my trip because I knew it was God's confirmation of his blessings on my itinerary.

When I came downstairs the next morning to Mother's delicious breakfast with West Virginia hot biscuits, I was conscious the presence of God was still with me. As she passed me a cup of coffee across the table, I was suddenly aware of that presence close between us. I heard His words in my spirit say, "You have believed me, now ask what you want and I will grant it to you." Overcome with emotion, I stood to my feet and raised my hands in praise.

My mother was visibly moved by my sudden mood of worship in her kitchen. She asked, "Alta, what has happened?"

I told her how the Lord had visited me in the night and assured me of His promise to be with me. Now, at that moment in her kitchen, He reassured me of that promise.

Before we finished breakfast, one of the former members of the Salineville Assembly of God called to invite me to dinner at her home that night. What a pleasure to again sit at her table and enjoy red raspberries drenched in real country cream. I feasted on her delicious food, but our fellowship in the Lord was even sweeter. As I left her home that night, she gave me three one-hundred-dollar bills. That was my first offering for the new church.

Early in my itinerary I mailed one thousand dollars in offerings to Clarence. Before he opened the letter, he thought I was writing home for money. His first reaction was the old Hudson car had broken down somewhere on the itinerary and I needed money for repairs. However, instead of asking for money, I was sending money home for the down payment on the church. During the remainder of the itinerary, I raised another thousand dollars.

On the trouble-free trip back to Phoenix, the Lord still traveled along as an unseen passenger. The old Hudson purred along over the highways. As we traveled, I was reminded of the familiar promise in Psalms 91:4:(KJV) "He shall cover thee with His feathers, and under His wings shalt thou trust." Too numerous to count were the times I had leaned hard upon that promise.

During this time, J. K. Gressett, our Arizona Assemblies of God superintendent, attended a Home Missions seminar in Springfield, Missouri. While there he asked for a loan for us. Since the board selling the church wanted cash, we needed $3,000 to add to the $2,000 I had already raised. The loan was approved and we wasted no time in paying off that $5,000.

It was a great celebration day when we moved into our own building. From our first service at 4123 East Washington Street, the church was filled to capacity with our Indian congregation and many visitors.

▲▲▲

I received an invitation to join nine foreign missionaries in a series of missions conventions in California. Our first convention was held in C. M. Ward's church in Bakersfield. The offerings from the conventions were distributed between the ten of us. Each of us had a project, and mine was to pay off our church loan.

To my dismay, some of the Indian missionaries criticized me for using convention money to pay off our church loan. I never did understand their objections.

At a missions convocation at our All Tribes Assembly, J. K. Gressett, Fred Vogler, and G. F. Lewis, who had been my superintendent in Ohio, settled the dispute. They stated there was no regulation against how we spent the convention offerings.

During that convocation we accommodated guests in our church quarters. While I washed dishes after one of the meals we had served our guests, my sister told me about the negative attitudes toward me. I was so distressed, I actually fainted right there in my kitchen.

My husband rebuked me for being affected by the criticism. Clarence never felt a call to pulpit ministry, but he ministered to me in my many times of discouragement. Had it not been for his love, encouragement, exhortation, and standing by me, I doubt if I could have accomplished much for the Lord. In the truest sense, he was my pastor.

On this occasion he did not try to soothe me, but said, "Alta, what a time for you to act like this. It doesn't matter who's mad at you. You've done nothing wrong. You've preached to others to be strong in the face of adversity; now practice what you've preached."

That did it! I fell before the Lord and began to pray for His grace. I asked God to help me let nothing deter me from what I knew was His will.

In 1949 there were three established Assemblies of God Indian churches in the state. They were San Carlos, the Whiteriver church with its building program complete, and our All Tribes Church in Phoenix. At that time a missionary was pioneering a mission among the Papagos in Sells.

There were no full gospel outreaches among the Navajos or Hopi tribes in northern Arizona or New Mexico except for an independent work started in Farmington, New Mexico. A Navajo family had been saved in our church and returned to Gallup, New Mexico. They began witnessing about salvation and the Pentecostal experience of the baptism in the Holy Spirit. Thirty people were saved as a result of their witnessing. Later an Assembly of God church was established in Gallup by this family.

The Ted Johnsons went from Whiteriver to Bylas to pioneer a mission work among the Apaches. After the Bylas church was established, they opened the first full gospel mission among the

Navajos and Hopis at Tuba City, located on the western side of the Navajo Reservation. They used a hogan for their church and proudly hung the sign "Assembly of God Church" above the door.

Ted bought a small generator light plant and, in a unique manner, hauled it around on a baby buggy. He spread the invitation, "Come to our hogan church and see lights turned on that are not lanterns."

Electric lights were an oddity to the people at that time. Their curiosity enticed them into the hogan church where many heard the gospel for the first time. Through the anointed ministry of the Johnsons, a number of Navajo and Hopi Indians were saved. The Johnsons also held services in the Navajo village of Moenave and the Hopi village of Moenkopi.

As years passed, dedicated missionaries pioneered other Navajo missions on the vast Navajo reservation. Missionaries came and went, but those who stayed endured the hardships of reservation living. The zealous soul winners worked hard and laid the foundation for strong, progressive Assemblies of God churches in that area.

Phoenix All Tribes Assembly continued to branch out on all the surrounding Indian reservations with the gospel. Several of our young people felt a call to preach. They started their ministry holding revivals on the Indian reservations in a tent we had purchased. Some of them attended Assemblies of God Bible schools and became ordained Assemblies of God ministers.

Three old Phoenix city buses were given to us to transport the city and reservation Indians and students from the Bureau of Indian Affairs (BIA) Indian High School to our services. God supplied us with bus drivers from Phoenix First Assembly of God. A Pima Indian man from Salt River and Clarence also drove the buses. We began Sunday with an afternoon Sunday School and service. All except the students came prepared to remain over for the night service.

It was not unusual for our night services to last until the early morning hours. God moved among the Indian people in Holy Ghost power. They were slain in the Spirit, lost in worship, praising, crying, and laughing; all totally consumed in God's holy presence.

We opened an outstation at Laveen, twenty-five miles southwest of Phoenix on the Gila River Indian Reservation. A large mesquite tree with its sheltering branches provided us with an outdoor sanctuary. Later we put up a tent at Casa Blanca on the same reservation. Later an Assemblies of God church was established there.

We started outstation services at San Tan, also on the Gila River reservation; Guadalupe, a Yaqui village adjoining Phoenix on the south; and Salt River, a Pima reservation located east of Scottsdale.

All Tribes Assembly gave a nucleus of people to help start each new mission. Dedicated ministers who had worked with us became their pastors.

As we gave some of our members to the churches, God gave, and He kept adding, Indian people to our congregation. We never suffered in any way from "mothering" those new churches. Actually, we were tremendously blessed in many ways because we fulfilled what God wanted us to do for Him. As a cell of an organism divides, it multiplies. We proved that fact true at All Tribes Assembly.

As I related about our beginnings at First Assembly of God in Phoenix, our first converts were students from the Indian school. Over the years we continued to bring the students to our services by bus or to conduct classes for them on the school campus.

This ministry to the government school students was like a pastorate in itself. That released-time ministry had far-reaching results. On our itineraries, we came across former students living as far away as New York state. They were involved in various phases of Christian service, in full-time ministries, and as workers in local Indian churches. I will always be grateful that the Lord opened that ministry for us forty years ago. Only God knows the dividends the spiritual investment in those young lives will yield.

The Presbyterians operated a Bible school for Indian students near the government's Phoenix Indian High School. Some of their students from the Plains tribes attended our services at First Assembly of God. Two of the married couples who were living on the Bible school campus received the baptism in the Holy Spirit when they worshiped with us. They went back to the campus and shared their full gospel experience with their fellow students. As a result, prayer meetings were held, and a number of the students also received the baptism in the Holy Spirit.

The boldness of these couples as they told about their Pentecostal experience caused no small stir among the administrators and faculty. The school dean and principal admonished and warned them that speaking in tongues was of the devil. They further warned them not to attend our services anymore or to "practice the ways of the devil." The students ignored the stern rebukes of the school leaders and continued to worship as led by the Holy Spirit.

Finally, those students were expelled and told, "Pack your belongings and go over there to those Pentecostals. We can't have you spreading that kind of doctrine and worship on this campus."

By this time we had moved into our church on East Washington. When they came, I was in a missions convention in California. The expelled students poured out their hearts to my husband about their plight. They had no place to go and no money for a trip back to their reservation in Montana. Even though they had very little in material things or funds, they had "joy unspeakable" and were "full of glory."

Clarence bought them a large sack of beans, potatoes, eggs and gallons of milk for their children. He also gave them a place to sleep in the church. While they waited for money from their relatives in Montana for their trip home, they spent their time in prayer and praising the Lord. When they returned to their reservation in the northern plains, they carried testimonies of their Pentecostal experience wherever they went. We later heard that God had anointed their witnessing and preaching with signs following. Their ministry initially helped to open the door for the

Pentecostal message to reach the Plains Indians on those northern reservations.

Soon after we moved to Phoenix and were doing hospital visitation work in the Phoenix Indian Hospital, we ministered to a little Apache girl named Pauline. She had suffered burns on her hand and needed skin grafts. Her fingers were drawn and the palm of the hand was decaying. Since she had come from the White Mountain Apache Reservation two hundred miles from Phoenix, her family was seldom able to visit her. Because of her condition and loneliness, I wanted to do something for her.

My opportunity came one day when I visited her. She told me a minister had brought her a catechism to study, but she found it too difficult to understand. When she saw him coming to see her, she hid in the restroom. She was ashamed to tell him she had not studied. I told her I had a story she would understand. As I told her about Jesus and His love for those who hurt and need a friend, she accepted His love and was saved in that hospital room.

Not long after Pauline gave her heart and life to Jesus, she was released from the hospital. Her hand appeared to be healed, and we knew God had touched her. We brought her and her few earthly belongings to our home. She became our first foster Indian daughter.

Pauline lived with us until she married our Sunday School superintendent and accompanied him when he went into the army. Each baby born to that couple was brought to Phoenix for us to name. After four sons, God blessed the family with a baby girl. We named her Rea Joice because of the joy her birth brought to the family.

A total of seventeen girls and seven boys came into our home as foster children. Because we want them to be kept in remembrance, I am listing them by name. The girls were Pauline, Peggy, Oreta, Linda, Dorris, Vangie, Susan, Mary, Rosena, Nandla, Delores, Elvira, Betty and the four girls each named Rose. The young men were Virgil, Alvin, Lyman, Rupert, Ralston, Gerry, and Gabriel. We also opened our home and hearts to Yemani and Zerezghi, who were from Ethiopia.

Each of those young people needed loving physical and spiritual care. It was our privilege to do what we could to meet those needs. They were our sons and daughters in the Lord, and we loved them dearly.

All of them accepted the Lord as their Savior before they left our home. Most are now married and several are in the ministry. Even though they have gone in many different directions, God in heaven watches over each one.

THE PIMA GIANTS

One day when I was visiting on the Salt River Indian reservation, I knocked on the door of a little adobe house. A large woman opened the door, and a little girl was hidden in the folds of her dress. The one-room house was dark inside. However, I thought I saw a huge man and heard unfriendly voices coming from the darkness. After I greeted the woman, I told her I was inviting children on the reservation to attend our Vacation Bible School at All Tribes Assembly. Even though the woman did not respond, I told her our church bus would stop for the little girl the next morning. There was no promise that she would be ready—only silence. The sound of the gruff voices inside increased as the woman quickly closed the door. I stood before the closed door, wondering at the strange forebodings of that house.

The next day, much to my surprise, the little girl came running out of the house and boarded the church bus. She was shining clean in a freshly ironed dress, and her long black hair was combed and tied in neat braids. She told me her name was Julienne and that she had five brothers. I remembered that brief glimpse I had of one of them before the door was closed and thought he had to be the biggest man I had ever seen. I learned the gruff voices I heard came from the brothers telling their mother not to let me in the house. It was evident they did not want any preachers anywhere close to them or their home.

Even though I did not know how little Julienne was able to convince her mother and brothers to let her continue coming to church, she never missed a service after that first visit. She would sing the songs she learned and show her Sunday School lessons to her brothers.

When the Pima "giants" reinforced their order that no preacher was to come into their house, little Julienne bravely told them, "Sister Washburn is not a preacher; she's a missionary. And that's different."

On the closing night of our VBS, all the children had parts in the program. Many of the friends and family members came to see the children perform—all except Julienne's giant brothers. The program was a great success and many of the people continued to attend All Tribes Assembly.

Since Pimas love to sing, they were attracted to our lively song services. Even though they weren't sure what they were singing about at that time, they enjoyed singing the choruses and hymns. But not much later they did know, because they began kneeling at the altars and confessing Christ as their Savior.

Our Sunday School classes and worship services met on Sunday afternoons rather than Sunday mornings. The buses had to go several miles one way to bring in the Indians for services. So we decided to save time and gasoline by serving a simple meal of pinto beans and tortillas after our afternoon service. Following the meal, the people enjoyed a time of fellowship together. The evening service started with the youth in charge, and the regular service followed. It was a good arrangement and lasted the many years our church was located at 4123 East Washington. Even though some criticized our feeding the people, we felt it kept them coming to church so the conviction of the Holy Spirit would eventually bring them to Calvary. And that is exactly what happened.

Since the women were not home on Sundays to prepare meals, the men folk would come to church about mealtime to eat. The Pima men, especially the Sampsons, were not in a happy frame of mind since they had to drive several miles into the city to get a meal. We were always glad to feed them because we had no desire to upset them any further. We were also hoping and praying they would stay over for our night service. And they did. At first they stood by the entrance doors to hear the singing. Soon they began to slip in and sit in the back pews.

Before long the Sampson brothers were brought to their

knees at our altar under the conviction of the Holy Spirit. They wept tears of repentance, their massive bodies quivering as they sobbed out their confessions of sin before the Lord. What an impact their salvation made on our congregation and on the people of the Salt River Reservation. Notorious for their drinking and fighting, they had now become as gentle as babes. Each one was filled with the Holy Spirit, which made their testimonies even more effective.

It wasn't an easy task to baptize them in water. Some of them stood well over six feet tall and weighed as much as four hundred pounds. But God helped me, and our congregation resounded in praise as each one arose from that baptistry, dead to their old life of sin and alive unto God.

When the Sampson brothers began to obey God's call for evangelizing, we did not have a Bible school to teach them the Word of God and to train them in practical aspects of the ministry. However, we did the best we could in teaching them the basics of the gospel.

Because their call was so intense, they were eager to learn all they could. A burden to see Indian people come out of their bondage of sin and tribal religions made the brothers anxious to carry the message of salvation to them. Soon we sent them out from All Tribes Assembly to fulfill their calls to evangelism.

Eventually we sent three of the brothers, Virgil, Leslie, and Clifford, to Southwestern Bible Institute in Waxahachie, Texas. The adjustment to the school and being away from home was not easy for them. Clifford and Leslie remained for several semesters, but Virgil continued on for the three years and earned his Bible school diploma.

More practical experience was provided for them when they accompanied me on some of my itineraries and missions conventions. The brothers blessed the congregations when they gave their testimonies of deliverance from their violent lives of sin.

On one of our trips to the northeastern states, we ministered in the Seneca Indian assembly in Lawton, New York. While I visited my son in Rochester, New York, the brothers stayed on the reservation and conducted a successful revival for that Indian assembly. They were talented musicians and played their guitars like professionals. The missionary was so impressed with their ministry, he took them to Canada with him to minister in a camp meeting.

The contacts they made in Canada at that time had far reaching results. In later years when we opened All Tribes Bible School in Phoenix, students came from New York, and later from British Columbia and the Yukon territory in Canada, where the brothers had evangelized.

Single life for the Sampson brothers did not last long. Virgil married Eunice Buchanan, missionary pastor of the Papago Assembly of God in Sells, Arizona. The other brothers all married girls who were students in All Tribes Bible School.

PITCHING A TENT ON THE TRAIL

We held our first tent revival at Lehi, a Pima village on the Salt River Indian Reservation located a few miles from Phoenix. The Sampson brothers were the evangelists and musicians. Each night lively singing drew the crowds. Many Mormons attended, and some were related to the brothers. The people sat spellbound as they heard those men, known as the reservation drunks and fighters, tell how God forgave their sins and changed their lives. Each brother made an impassioned plea for the listening Pimas to give their hearts to Jesus. Their testimonies had a tremendous impact. Scores of Pimas were saved. Most of them were Mormons and gave their personal testimonies of being set free from the Mormon cult.

The tent-meeting services were not all singing, preaching, and shouting, however. We experienced attacks of satanic opposition. Occasionally we had to call for the tribal police to control the area around the tent. Fighting outside the tent disturbed our services.

One night something ablaze with fire was thrown on top of the tent. The tribal medicine men were upset when they saw the Pimas who had been followers of the traditional religion praying at the altar. They considered the "white man's religion" a threat to their pagan worship. Little did they realize we brought a message of salvation and hope to those Pimas that their religion could not offer. We emphasized that the gospel is not just for the white man but for all mankind. Peter wrote that Jesus is "not willing that any should perish, but that all should come to repentance" (2 Peter 3:9, KJV).

That summer dust storms made the camp meeting difficult. Swirls of dust blew around us with such fierceness that the evangelist was almost obscured from view. Strong desert winds posed a threat to the tent as it swayed in the gusts. All the men tenaciously hung onto the ropes and poles to hold it down.

Unrelenting heat produced temperatures of 100 degrees and higher during our night services. Those desert temperatures rarely went below 90-95 degrees even in the "coolest" time of the night. Plenty of drinking water and water-soaked towels to cover our shoulders and laps provided our only cooling system. Regardless of what some might call obstacles, no one complained. Each night souls came to Jesus. We felt no discomfort could compare to the joy of our seeing souls born into His Kingdom.

TRAILS INTO SPANISH LANDS

Guadalupe is a small village of Mexicans and Yaqui Indians only a few miles from our All Tribes Assembly. The Yaquis migrated to that area many years ago from across the border of Mexico. A lady who was interested in the welfare of the tribe donated several acres of land for their village. Having a burden for the Yaquis, I visited Guadalupe to see if we could start an outstation there.

We received permission and started services under a large tamarisk tree. I used a Mexican lady as my interpreter. The majority of the Yaquis did not understand English. Even though they had their own language, they were fluent in Spanish.

As at Lehi, our lively music attracted the people. They had never heard singing like ours before.

Since the Yaquis were Mexican Indians, the federal government did not, at that time, recognize them as an American Indian tribe. For that reason they did not qualify for government assistance, not even medical care. When I heard of their status, my burden for them intensified. I wanted desperately to help them.

We collected clothing, blankets, and food from every available source to distribute to them when they came to the services. The items were not given to coax the people to come but to express a heart of love and compassion. Many years later I started the Second Mile Ministries (which will be mentioned later in this book) in Guadalupe.

As the Guadalupe congregation grew, we moved from the tamarisk tree to an old barracks building. But it eventually became too small. We had to find or build something larger and permanent.

Our son Floyd had recently returned from a tour of duty in the army. When he learned of our need for Guadalupe, he gave us enough money to buy a plot of land on the main street of the village. Now we had the property but no money to build a church.

At a camp meeting in southern California, I met a man who was interested in financially assisting a Spanish mission. Upon learning about our need at Guadalupe, he readily committed himself to donate funds for the building.

The next need for Guadalupe was a Spanish-speaking pastor for the congregation. I made two trips into Mexico in search of a native pastor, but none of the Mexican ministers I met felt he could leave his country or congregations.

In my quest for a pastor, I met a Christian lady who, in the natural, would not be a likely candidate for the Guadalupe church. She was not Mexican nor could she speak Spanish. Her name was Mary Booher. However, she and her husband, Al, had a burden for Guadalupe and offered themselves as pastors. Strongly impressed that they were God's choice, I felt relieved that the congregation now had a pastor. Sister Booher studied the Spanish language and became fluent enough in the language that she could minister to the people. The Boohers remained as dedicated pastors of the Guadalupe Assembly of God for twelve years.

TRAILS INTO BOBCAT COUNTRY

Bordered on the south by the rugged Estrella Mountains, the Indian village of Laveen and surrounding community was home to Papago and Maricopa Indians. While visiting in that area, we went to the little adobe house of the lady who had been healed of a broken neck in the Indian hospital. Her invitation to hold gospel meetings on that reservation opened another door for us. Her testimony had a profound effect on the people there. She was burdened for the Indian people, many of whom were her own relatives.

No adobe house was large enough to house the people. The only option was to conduct our meetings under a large mesquite tree. We made benches out of long boards and hung lanterns from the tree limbs. The people came, heard the gospel message, moved under conviction to our crude altars made of boards, and accepted Jesus as their Savior. Both the Co-op and Laveen Indian Assemblies of God were later established with a nucleus of people saved in that outreach ministry.

On several of our visits to the reservation, we saw bobcats race across the road in front of our car. Seeing those animals so numerous and close made us glad for the security of our vehicle.

Not only bobcats, but rattle snakes, gila monsters, scorpions and centipedes infested the area. One evening I noticed something moving on a lady's blanket. I screamed, but she merely shook the blanket and out ran a large centipede. Those creatures terrified me, but the Indian people, so accustomed to sharing their habitat with them, showed no alarm.

ALL TRIBES INDIAN BIBLE TRAINING SCHOOL

ASSEMBLIES OF GOD
4123 E. Washington St.
Phoenix, Arizona

School Staff
D. E. Gribling
Harold Grant
Ruth Gardner

Board of Education
V. E. Shores   L. E. Davis
J. K. Gressett, Mrs. L. E. Davis
A. M. Washburn, Virginia Kridler

Opening --- September 23, 1957
Classes --- Mon. thru. Fri. 1:00 - 4:00 P.M.

FIRST SEMESTER
1. Bible, Birdseye View
2. Life of Christ (1)
3. Gospels
4. Personal Work
5. Old Testament
6. Knowing the Doctrines
7. We Believe

SECOND SEMESTER
1. New Testament
2. Author and Origin
3. Romans and Epistles
4. Life of Christ (2) & Acts
5. Ages and Dispensations
6. Successful Pastor
7. Pastoral Theology

* *

The objective of this Bible Training School program is to train the native Indian worker in sound Bible Doctrines that they may in turn go out to reach their own tribes in the native language, thereby spreading the Gospel quickly to every kindred, tribe and tongue.

It is our desire that upon completion of the school term that all students return to their respective reservations and mission churches to work with their missionaries; to be guided into useful Bible men and women, native pastors, evangelists.

May the students of this school ever keep in mind the high calling of Christ to be a SOUL WINNER not in work alone but in every day living with their fellow students and the world. God has given you, the American Indian, the call, the ability and the last day challenge to reach your own people and prepare them for His soon coming. You will again have the opportunity to become leaders and chiefs to bring your own people into the Kingdom of God.

Christian students desiring enrollment in the Indian Training School will be considered upon recommendation of their missionaries or pastors. Application blanks are to be filled out and signed by them.

Housing facilities will be made available as far as possible. Single men and women living in the dormitories will be able to eat in the dining room. Meal tickets can be purchased at a very small fee.

Assistance will be given those seeking employment to help make their way. Early contact should be made with the school by those wishing to find part time work. Address correspondence to Alta M. Washburn, Supervisor or Virginia Kridler, Secretary, using the above address.

* *

IMPORTANT INFORMATION

Tuition: $20.00 per year
Books: 12.00 per year
Room and Board: 5.00 per week
Total Entrance Fee: 52.00
(This includes tuition, books
and 4 weeks room and board.)

Please bring:
Personal Items
Street Clothes
Large foot locker (2 keys)
Pen
Alarm Clock

The original flyer advertising the opening of the Bible school on September 23, 1957.

An evangelist came to Phoenix with a big tent and set it up on Washington Avenue not far from our church. He had a vendetta against the Assemblies of God and boasted he would empty every Indian assembly of its congregation and draw them to his newly formed organization.

This boast did materialize on the Apache Reservation at Whiteriver and San Carlos. Those Assembly of God churches literally lost their congregations to the magnetic pull of the evangelist. He urged them to follow him rather than remain faithful to their own churches. It was a ministry based on the man rather than the pure gospel.

Obviously I was troubled when I learned that the evangelist was conducting his Phoenix crusade so close to us. My concern was deepened as I witnessed those who had great experiences in the Lord fall into the evangelist's subtle traps. During his meeting at Whiteriver, I was invited for a visit to see for myself what was happening. Only two faithful families remained in the Whiteriver Assembly. Such a pathetic sight!

I was asked to preach in their Sunday morning service. Some of those who had been swayed over to the tent meeting came that Sunday morning. Their actions were intolerable and disgusting. They screamed, jumped, bounced up and down on the benches, and stood in the aisles dancing in the most grotesque way. It was total chaos!

When some of the families returned to the Assembly church in San Carlos after the tent meetings, I was told their fleshy demonstrations were the same. The San Carlos missionary pastor was unable to control the people in the services. He became so overcome with frustration and despair that he suffered a nervous breakdown and had to resign as pastor.

As I saw what was happening to our people in Phoenix and other Indian folks coming from the reservation to attend the evangelist's meeting, I was driven to my knees in travailing prayer and fasting. As I prayed, the Lord impressed me that a means to indoctrinate the people into the truth of the Word and following Christ, not a man, was desperately needed. The solution seemed to be immediately made clear: establish a Bible school right here at All Tribes Assembly.

After the witness from the Lord about the need for the Bible school, one of the Sampson brothers returned from Southwestern Bible College. He told me how it was difficult to adjust to the college there.

"Sister Washburn," he questioned, "why can't we Indians have our own Bible school? We can preach in our language but we need a place where we can study the Word together, a place where we have more in common than in a school where most of the students are Anglos."

That heartfelt appeal was another confirmation that God was leading us into a great challenge for Him. I was determined to obey the Lord and see the answer He was making clear to me.

Our Phoenix Ministers' Association was called together to meet with a Brother Lindsay, who brought official affidavits that gave information about splits and divisions in many churches in other states brought about by the tent evangelist's influence. The documents also stated he had been arrested and incarcerated for infractions of state laws. This news troubled all of us. The chairman of our association told us that before we left that meeting we should earnestly seek God for the solution to the dilemma we all faced. We pastors began to intercede for our congregations to be spared from exploitation by the evangelist.

Plainly the Lord spoke to me, "There came a bear and a lion, and there came Goliath who roared against the camp of Israel. What did David do? He arose in the name of the Lord God of Israel. He laid hold of the bear, the lion, and Goliath. He did more than pray. He attacked them and prevailed."

As I left that meeting I was more assured than ever that God would help us build a Bible school for American Indians. There they could learn to fight the good fight of faith with sound Bible doctrine against the bears, the lions, and the Goliaths who might come against them.

I began to dream, talk, write, and pray about the Bible school. The burden consumed me. The very thought of it excited my spirit because I knew I was moving in the center of God's will. Even though my burden was not shared by everyone, the congregation of All Tribes Assembly did share it with me.

I felt led to write about our vision for the school to Brother C. M. Ward, who was then pastoring in California.

"Sister Washburn," he wrote back, "keep yelling about that Bible school. Someone will hear you."

That letter tremendously boosted my morale.

Perhaps knowing that not all the missionaries could see the need for the school compounded my burden. They feared that if they sent their young people to Phoenix to attend school, the students would not want to return to reservation life. Obviously, there would be much more to see, do, and learn about in the city. And there was more exposure to conveniences they did not have at home.

Later, however, the missionaries' attitudes changed. They began sending their young people to the school and encouraged them to study so each student could become a "workman that needeth not to be ashamed, rightly dividing the word of truth" (2 Timothy 2:15, KJV). Few of those students remained in the city after their training because they were anxious to go back to work for the Lord in their local churches on the reservations.

The first ray of hope came when I received a phone call from Brother J. K. Gressett, then the superintendent of the Arizona Assemblies of God. He had good news for me.

A church in Houston, Texas, wanted an Indian project to sponsor. Brother Gressett asked if we had any needs the Texas church could help with.

"Oh, yes, Brother Gressett," I quickly responded. "I want to start on the Bible school as soon as possible. Maybe they would like to help us with the project."

"I'll call them today and let them know what you need," he replied. "We'll see what they have to say."

There were times I was not sure Brother Gressett thought the

Bible school could even be a possibility because of so many things involved. True, there would be many obstacles. But his telephone call encouraged me. I knew he wanted to help us see the school become a reality. He and other district leaders assisted us greatly in building and establishing the school. I will always be grateful to them.

The pastor of First Assembly of God in Houston, Texas, told Brother Gressett they would be happy for us to come and present our burden and need for the school. At Brother Gressett's suggestion, we took some of our young Indian preachers with us. The church gave us a warm welcome and listened intently to our presentation. They contributed enough funds for the concrete floor, plumbing, and part of the masonry blocks for the walls.

Soon the time came for the groundbreaking ceremony on the land behind our All Tribes Assembly. At my request, Brother Gressett preached the dedication message. It was a masterpiece. He spoke about Nehemiah and his men rebuilding the walls of Jerusalem. He emphasized how they refused to let any hindrances or opposition stop their progress. I absorbed every word he preached because his message related to our situation perfectly. I knew there was opposition, but I could not let it deter us from building the school.

Later when Brother Gressett informed me the opposition was increasing, I reminded him of his sermon.

"Brother Gressett," I said, "your message about Nehemiah rebuilding the wall has been my inspiration. I could no more stop what God has told me to do than Nehemiah could stop building on that wall."

We built in troublesome times. But knowing that God was with us and that the building would soon provide a place for Indian adults to study God's Word, we moved ahead with our commission. The scripture "The weapons of our warfare are not carnal, but mighty through God to the pulling down of strong holds" (2 Corinthians 10:4, KJV) motivated us to press ahead.

I had drawn the plans for the building, which consisted of dormitory rooms, reception room, classrooms, dining room, kitchen, and utility rooms. My husband, who had expertise in construction, drew my plans up to scale. They were approved by the city zoning commission without any problems.

Everything was ready to start construction. The congregation of All Tribes Church contributed labor and funds for the foundation. The men of the church worked diligently along with several pastors of local Assemblies of God churches.

During this time, it was necessary for me to take time out from my pastoral duties to itinerate to raise funds for the building. Based on my husband's wise counsel, we refrained from borrowing money, even though I considered it an option.

"Alta, this is God's project," Clarence reminded me. "I don't think we should go into debt for it. He will provide the money we need as we need it. You wait and see."

His faith encouraged me when my faith began to waiver. Many times he admonished me to exercise patience when I thought the construction was moving too slowly.

When we exhausted all our funds, we stopped the men from working and called them and the people together to petition God to supply more money for the materials. Each time we met that crisis, the funds came in from the most unexpected sources.

One Sunday we asked the congregation to join us in prayer for an amount needed. During the evening service, the telephone rang. Clarence rushed to answer it and was pleasantly surprised to hear the voice of Brother Lindsay, pastor of First Assembly of God in Covina, California.

"Brother Washburn," Brother Lindsay said, "we have raised $1,600 in our service today for your Bible school building. I've put the check in the mail, and you should receive it soon."

Words could not express the elation we all shared when my husband came back in the church and told us about the $1,600. As the months passed, the Covina Assembly contributed more financial assistance as well as furnishings and food.

The year the Southern California District of the Assemblies of God moved into their new Big Bear campground facilities, they gave us all their beds, bedding, and linens from the old campground.

That contribution gave us a good start in furnishing the dormitory rooms.

The Weatherfords, dear friends from Covina First Assembly, came to Phoenix with a truckload of supplies, including a deep freeze and food for our cupboards. They remained faithful helpers with us for many years.

Another church in California gave us a whole central heating and cooling system. Sister Halvorson, Southern California District Women's Ministries president, presented all our classroom equipment from that district's WM ladies.

Other contributions included a walk-in refrigerator from the Orange County, California, Women's Ministries. A Brother Bryant from St. Louis, Missouri, gave us ovens for our kitchen, and the Scio and Clutter Pottery Companies of Ohio donated dishes and cookware.

Our own Indian people gave beautiful handicrafts and rugs for our reception room. Brother John McPherson of Sacramento, California, painted a beautiful mural on one of the reception room walls.

Each day as we saw the building moving toward completion, and every needed item supplied, any doubts about the project being in God's will were erased. We beheld the hand of God hovering over all the activities, and we knew He was honoring our faith. My burden to see Indians taught sound Bible doctrine was coming to fruition.

During the summer of 1957, I had the opportunity to introduce All Tribes Bible School at various Indian camp meetings in Arizona, New Mexico, Nevada, and northern California. A number of Indian young people showed an interest in enrolling in ATBS. However, a few of the missionary pastors were still reluctant to encourage them. I was asked to share my burden with them. My emphasis was on how the "Goliaths" were apostasizing the Indian youth and not preaching sound doctrine. My further appeal that God could use young Indian "Davids" to rise up and become warriors for the Lord. This could be attained by training in sound Bible doctrine the school would provide.

The missionaries' attitudes began to change. They saw the value of the school and how it would benefit prospective students as well as Indian churches.

At last we were ready for the official opening of All Tribes Bible School in September of 1957. For that first term God sent us three capable and dedicated teachers who were willing to teach without any salary. Before school opened, I knew God had already commissioned our first teachers.

They were Lois Carruthers, who had taught in a Bible school in Hawaii, Virginia Kridler, and Ruth Gardiner. All these ladies were Bible college graduates. In years to follow, God continued to send us qualified faculty and staff.

Before any of the students arrived, Ethel Smoker, a Klamath Indian from Wichapec, California, and Avelena, a local Apache girl, were so excited about attending ATBS they came early to enroll. They helped me get everything ready for the opening of the school.

Ethel Smoker was one of our first graduates. She later married a Navajo student, David Maloney. They returned to her church in California to assist in the ministry there.

Thirty-two students enrolled the first semester. Twelve of them came from the Sampson family. Over a period of several years, we enrolled thirty-two students from the Sampson family.

Students from Apache, Navajo, Pima, and Papago tribes also came that first year. In the 1958–59 school year, students attended from as far away as British Columbia, Hawaii, Montreal, and nine other states in the United States. Word traveled far and wide that a Bible training school for American Indians had opened in Phoenix.

It was my privilege as president of the school to minister to the students in the morning chapel services. My messages were mainly on how to exercise faith. Since most of the students came to ATBS entirely on faith, and I endeavored to practice it myself, it seemed to be a timely topic. The life of faith was a new concept to most of the students. My exhortation to them was that God sets forth His covenant by saying, "If you will, I will. If you will not, then I am not obligated to you."

Obviously, the married students had to rely more heavily upon God to supply their needs. Most of them had two or more children.

For example, when Alvin's wife, Juanita, needed dental work done, Alvin did not have money for the dentist's fee. But he tried hard to trust the Lord for the money.

Each day he said, "Sister Washburn, I still don't have a job. I'm trying to believe God will meet the need. But how can we keep that dental appointment for Juanita if I don't have the money to pay the bill?"

We kept agreeing together as we prayed that the money would be there on time. The appointment day came. I saw Alvin walking toward me with a dejected countenance. The appointment was only hours away. We met in the hall, and he had only time to say, "I thought you told me—" when the entrance door opened and a complete stranger stood in the doorway.

"I just came in from Canada," the man said as he introduced himself. "I felt the Lord would have me come visit your school and give a contribution to help one of your students."

Alvin and I looked at each other, remembering how we discussed that God works on His own schedule and is never late.

The man's gift went to Alvin and Juanita to pay her dental bill. Enough money was left for Alvin to buy a new tire for his car and some groceries. His testimony in chapel the next morning stimulated the other students to trust God for their needs also.

Another student, Elvira, was going to work with only enough money for her bus fare. How could she get back to school after work, she questioned. It was too far to walk. While waiting for the bus, she shuffled her feet around and casually glanced down. She saw something glistening in the sun. It was some coins, just enough for another day's bus fare. The next day, more coins were found, enough to pay her bus fare until she received her paycheck. Strange and unbelievable? Yes. But our God is greater than any improbability or impossibility.

Another incident that showed God's providential care happened to me. I lacked one hundred dollars to pay a certain bill. Although

I never divulged all my financial needs in our chapel services, I would often mention a special prayer request to the student body. I shared this unspoken request with them. But I prayed specifically that from somewhere, somehow I could get that one hundred dollars. Sister Helen Rickey joined me in prayer for the need since she, now my bookkeeper and secretary, knew about it.

Later, as I looked for a certain receipt in my files, there, tucked in among other papers, was a one hundred dollar bill. Then I remembered I had laid the money back to pay a certain bill. However, I had already paid it. Sister Rickey and I had a time rejoicing in the school office that day!

We charged the students $1 a day, only a token payment on the cost of the school's operating expenses. No money came from the tribes for the students' education in those days or from parents who were practically all living far below the poverty level. But we trusted God to meet each day's need, and He never failed us. There was never a meal without enough food on the tables. It would take an entire book to tell all the marvelous ways the Lord supplied food and funds for the school.

Our students, who came from many different tribes, all had tastes and desires for different kinds of foods. The Pimas and Papago were happy with the pinto beans, tortillas, and chilies we often served. The Navajos loved their mutton stew; the northwestern and Canadian tribes longed for fish; the Apache ate beef; and the Plains Indian students relished wild game. Naturally, we had no way of knowing how God would send in those different foods, but He had a way.

"Some of you hunt wild game for the sport of it," I wrote to all the Arizona Assemblies of God ministers one fall, "but we could really use the meat. We will pray that you will bag a big buck elk or deer if you will share some of its meat with our students. Our Plains Indian students would be ever so grateful."

That letter and our prayers paid off! Our freezers were soon stocked with generous portions of deer and elk.

The Navajos were asking for mutton. How were we going to come up with a ewe or lamb? Mutton was much too expensive to buy in the market. But God had an answer to our dilemma. A local minister called to tell us he had two lambs he had bought as gifts for his children. The lambs had outgrown their pet stage and he had to dispose of them. Would we like to have them? That question was easy to answer. Later, after a meal of mutton stew, the Navajo student's appetite for mutton had been appeased.

Someone called to have us pick up forty live chickens. The students wasted no time in dressing and preparing those chickens for a fried chicken feast.

Friends who owned a meat locker wanted it emptied before deer season and offered its contents to us. From it we were well supplied with salmon, fish of all kinds, and other good food items. Our northeastern students were pleased to have salmon again.

A beekeeper delivered a truckload of honey to us. We hastened to find recipes using honey in any shape, form, or fashion.

St. John's Food Bank had opened a building in Phoenix to distribute fresh vegetables in season as well as bread and bakery products to needy individuals and non-profit organizations. They generously shared those items with us.

The only food contributions our students didn't relish were sauerkraut we made from a truckload of cabbage given to us and oysters shipped to us from friends in Galveston, Texas.

Days came, however, when our faith was tested to the point of near despair. I recall writing in a newsletter:

> "A cold winter in Phoenix, most unusual. Students had a siege of the mumps and flu. Hardest month ever to pay bills. Fewest contributions for the work. The washer broke down. The refrigerator. The car. The record player. Had leak in the roof and I lost my Scofield Bible. We turned the sheets and patched the blankets and added pinto beans for breakfast."

On one occasion when our cupboards were low on supplies, God laid it on my heart to suggest to Sister Lois Gribling, our Arizona District Women's Ministries director, to ask the WM groups throughout the state to help us with our food needs. My idea was that a Harvest Rally at the Thanksgiving season would be an appropriate time for them to bring gifts of food for ATBS. She agreed, and we had a great rally at the church. The ladies' generosity was an inestimable blessing in that first rally, and even today, many years later, they continue to bring their food items to fill the Bible school's cupboards.

I carried many responsibilities in those first years at All Tribes Bible School. Pastoring the church, doing all the preaching and most of the visitation, raising funds, supervising each department of the school, counseling with students, and keeping the books on the school and church exhausted me. Before we secured a cook, I did all the cooking and bread baking. God gave me added strength and wisdom from day-to-day to accomplish all that needed to be done. Capable and dedicated staff members came to help as the workload increased.

Cooks were always hard to find because we could not pay a salary. Those who came had to have some support of their own. But they came, dedicated and called to share in the burden and vision for the school. It was also necessary for the faculty members to have their own support. Most of them were Indian missionaries appointed by the Assemblies of God and had raised support from their home districts.

Those teachers willingly gave of their time, talent, and knowledge of the Bible. Many times they went beyond the call of duty to see the school accomplish what God intended for it. Words could never express my gratitude and appreciation for all those who stood by me and shared my burden throughout those early Bible school years.

Two lady staff members whom I must mention are Rose Chase and Helen Rickey. Rose came to help with the cooking and soon became dean of women as well as school nurse. What a blessing she was to me during my times of illness and recuperation!

I met Helen Rickey at an Arizona camp meeting the summer before ATBS opened. When I told her about the school, she offered to come as full-time cook. Later, after we secured additional help for the kitchen, she assisted me with the office work and served as editor of the school newspaper. She and her husband, Dee, came to live on our campus and remained as valuable helpers for many years.

Both Helen and Rose traveled with me at different times when I was itinerating to raise funds for the school and to recruit prospective students. I have fond memories of both these two dear sisters in the Lord. They sustained and helped me during trying times like Hur and Aaron when they held up Moses' hands in the Israelites' battle with the Amalekites.

On a trip to the East, three of our students, Lyman, Leslie, and Mary, accompanied us and held a revival in Oka, Canada. As a result of that meeting, four Mohawk young people from one family enrolled at ATBS. Their brother, Roger Cree, later came to Arizona to pastor the Papago church in Sells. Years later, he became president of another Indian Bible school located in North Carolina.

Several married men enrolled in the first years of ATBS. Joe Ellis, a Navajo man with a family of ten, lived in a remote area of the Navajo Reservation. During the week he worked at a government job in northeastern California and drove to his home on weekends. He preached to his Navajo neighbors on his days at home.

Joe heard about the Bible school and wrote a letter asking to enroll. I answered that I could see no way he could attend classes and find employment that would meet the needs of his large family. However, my letter did not deter him. His next letter told of his intense burden for his Navajo people to be saved and his awareness that he could not adequately preach to them without more knowledge of the Bible. After that appeal we could not refuse him admission.

The Lord knew Joe's needs and supplied him with a job having a sufficient salary to provide for his family. Soon they joined him in Phoenix. He spent four years attending night classes at ATBS and graduated with academic honors.

Jake Escalante, a married man with a family of ten, from the Papago Reservation, enrolled in ATBS. He also found a good job. He completed his Bible training in four years attending the night classes.

Although he felt a compelling burden to return to his reservation to preach the gospel after his graduation, he told us, "I can't leave yet even though I have graduated. I haven't been filled with the Holy Spirit. I wouldn't be able to preach to my Papago people in their spiritual darkness without the power of the Holy Spirit. My people are controlled by Catholicism mixed with our own tribal religion. My preaching could not penetrate that darkness. No, I will not go until I have been baptized in the Holy Spirit."

We started a revival immediately following the graduation of the 1962 class. On Sunday night after the altar call, Jake made his way to the back of the platform, as he had done so many times before, to tarry for the baptism of the Holy Spirit. His knees had hardly touched the floor when he began to speak in a beautiful heavenly language. It was a glorious experience of the Spirit's infilling.

"Well, now that God has given me the power I need to preach His Word," Jake exclaimed, "I'll quit my job tomorrow and move my family back to Sells."

In a short time, Jake had moved his family to the pastorate of an Indian Assembly of God near Yuma, Arizona. Down through the years he has ministered to his Papago people as well as other tribes in southwestern Arizona and across the Colorado River in California. For a time, he was an official for the Papago tribe.

As I ponder the path on which God led those men, as well as others, I marvel at God's providence: how he led them, blessed them, provided for them, and used them to build His Kingdom.

In organizing the Bible school, I had to consider the curriculum, job descriptions for staff and faculty members, and guidelines and rules for the academic and social life of the students. I anticipated the attraction of the opposite sexes to each other. Love, courtship, and marriage between the students would be cause for much concern. What guidelines should I establish for those social relationships?

I studied the catalogs of Bible colleges of the Assemblies of God and consulted with the Ted Johnsons, who had been students at North Central Bible College. They told me about the college's strict social and dating rules. Would the same rules work at ATBS?

After much prayer and research, I set up rules I felt would be workable and acceptable to the students. The "love factor" and Cupid would be permanent residents at ATBS! We needed to be prepared.

Cupid did not waste time. The first school year, Ethel Smoker met David, a handsome Navajo student. They fell in love, completed their three year program, and married after graduation. Clifford Sampson and Laverne Salem were attracted to each other soon after they enrolled. Mary, one of my foster daughters, and Herman Hoffman fell in love. Pat Cunningham and George Garcia soon became a twosome after their enrollment. These couples married after their graduation.

The dating rules we established were strict, but the couples willingly complied. They were glad for any opportunity to spend some time together, even though that time was controlled. Only in a chaperoned student group did we allow any off-campus dating.

In most cases, we did not allow couples to marry until after their graduation. After couples became engaged, faculty members and I counseled them about the importance of placing God as the highest priority in their lives. We did not discourage them about marriage, but we tried to show them that God always has a right person and time for marriage.

As the years have passed, the majority of those couples who married in the early years of the Bible school are still working for the Lord in some phase of gospel ministry.

Too numerous to mention are all the miracles God performed throughout our years at All Tribes Bible School. Yes, there were the hardships, trials, and agonizing travail in intercessory prayer for many critical needs. But our God was always with us, and His grace was sufficient for whatever we had to face. Tragedy the first and second school years, as well as years that followed, tested our faith. They were times when all of us—faculty, staff, and students—were drawn together in a bond of love, concern, and intercessory prayer. In those times we affirmed that God was our "everpresent help in time of need."

The Wickenburg Cowboy

Joe, a Hualapai Indian, was a cowboy working the range north of Wickenburg in the Kingman mountains. He was an older, rather shy cowpuncher who shared a bunkhouse with other cowboys who worked for the same ranch. Those fellows were loud, boisterous, talkative, and gifted at telling tall tales. Joe kept to himself and did not enter into their social time in the evenings in the bunkhouse. On the trail he was the same, doing his job riding the fences, rounding up stray cattle, or taking care of a sickly calf.

The cowboys thought Joe was strange because he didn't care about telling or listening to their off-color stories. What he really enjoyed was watching the life and movement of nature about him: the quail, roadrunners, owls, and the soaring eagle. He felt a part of it all as he rode the trails. In the evening, the blending of the sunset colors made him a little melancholy. A feeling of loneliness would come over him, and he would talk to his horse or even to himself.

One evening while he was relaxing outside in the twilight, loneliness seemed to engulf him. He raised his hands and his voice to the sky and cried, "Oh, Great Spirit, where are you?" Suddenly, he heard a voice so near he looked around to see who was speaking. The voice out of the air said, "Joe, I am right here with you and have been all the time. I want you to believe in Me and know Who I am. I am God, your Father, and Jesus, your Savior."

Joe's spirit responded immediately and he began to lift his voice in praise to God, and in his heart he accepted the invitation to know Jesus as his Savior.

And then Joe began to speak in a language that was neither his native Hualapai nor English but one he had never heard before. He was filled with ecstasy as he continued to speak in this beautiful language. As he went back to the bunkhouse, the language subsided but the glorious presence of the Holy Spirit did not leave him. He didn't tell anyone about his experience but kept questioning in his heart how he could speak in such a beautiful language. All night as he lay in his bunk he knew he had to find the answer. Suddenly, he had the answer. There was someone in his home village who could help him.

The next morning Joe asked his foreman for a few days off so he could make a trip back to his home reservation near Peach Springs. Without any hesitation, the foreman gave him permission to go, knowing Joe was trustworthy and would return to his job when he said he would.

Since Joe had been raised a devout Catholic, he felt sure his priest at the mission could help him. In anticipation of learning more about the experience he had the night before, he wasted no time in going to the mission as soon as he reached his village.

The priest greeted him warmly and said, "Joe, I have never seen you looking so happy. Tell me, what has happened that has brought you such joy."

Joe quickly explained all that happened to him, thinking the priest would also share in his joy. But, instead, he was surprised to hear the priest say, "Joe, what you have told me is not good. An evil spirit has come upon you that has made you feel this way and made you talk in that devilish language. Come, I will pray for you to be delivered from these demons that have taken control of you."

Joe stood still, crushed in his heart because the priest to whom he had gone many times for prayer and counsel did not share his joy.

Again, he heard a voice speak comforting words into his spirit, "Joe, I am still right here with you. Follow me, and I will lead you to someone who will help you."

Rather than follow the priest into the mission, Joe mounted his horse. He knew exactly where to go. He remembered Maria, an old lady who always sat with a black book in her lap. She always tried to get people to read with her. People from the reservation shunned her because she appeared to be too religious. But during times of tragedy, sickness, or trouble, they sought her out for prayer.

When Joe reached Lady Maria's place, she was outside cooking tortillas over an open fire. She was glad to see Joe and greeted him warmly saying, "Joe, Joe, you have come back home. You look so happy. Come, tell me why you look so happy."

After Joe shared his story, Lady Maria told him that all he had told her was in the black book.

"Joe," she said, "my eyes are so bad now I can't read anymore. Here, read these verses in my black book. They will tell you everything that has happened to you."

"Joe," she continued after a pause, "I heard there is a school in Phoenix that teaches Indians about the Bible. They can tell you about that strange language you talked. They make preachers there. They can answer your questions better than I can."

After the coaxing from Lady Maria, Joe left his horse with her and caught the next bus to Phoenix.

I was in the reception room of the Bible school on Sunday morning when Joe walked into the building. After he introduced himself, he poured out the account of his experience on the range. He also told me about Lady Maria and how she had encouraged him to seek our help to answer all the questions in his heart.

Several students and I prayed for Joe after explaining from Acts 2:4 about his infilling in the Holy Spirit. We told him that the voice he heard from God was an assurance that no matter where he was, as long as he served the Lord, He would never leave him nor forsake him.

Joe spent a few days with us at the school and enjoyed the fellowship, Bible study, and worship. As he left, we all knew that as he rode the range, he wouldn't feel lonely again but always be aware that a "friend that sticketh closer than a brother" (Proverbs 18:24) would be with him.

All Tribes Church in the 1960s

Salt River Assembly of God in the 1960s

▼▼▼

We were in a revival at All Tribes Church during Christmas of the first school year. Gifts were piled around the platform in the colorfully decorated sanctuary. Many churches and W.M. groups had sent gifts for the students. Each service of that revival was so charged with the power of the Holy Spirit that some of the people fell prostrate on the floor. One service lasted into the early morning hours. Before everyone left, the students wanted to pray for the friends who had sent the Christmas gifts.

While they were praying, Henry, one of the Sampson brothers, but even larger than the others, was clothed in the Holy Spirit's power. He began to walk among the people prophesying and speaking in tongues. When a visiting Shoshone family walked into the church, they stopped and listened intently to Henry speaking in tongues. After he finished, they told us Henry had spoken in the Shoshone language about the wonders of the Lord. We all rejoiced at the manifestation of God moving among us.

The service was finally dismissed, and Henry drove to Scottsdale to pick up his niece, Paulita, from her night job. She was a student at ATBS and worked part-time.

At a street intersection in Scottsdale, two intoxicated Arizona State University students ran a stop sign and plunged into Henry's car. Paulita was thrown from the car, but her little girl, whom Henry had brought with him from the church, was killed instantly. Henry died soon after the accident in the hospital. The driver of the ambulance, whom we knew, told us later that as he was driving the victims to the hospital, Henry spoke in tongues continually.

When the family arrived at the hospital, the nurse on duty when Henry was brought into the emergency room was amazed when she heard he was Pima.

"I don't understand," she said. "I'm Pima also, but that language he was talking was not Pima or English."

One of the family members told her that Henry had been speaking in a heavenly language. Even in his death, Henry was a testimony of the power of God.

We had a double funeral for Henry and Paulita's little girl. It was a sad time, especially for the many unsaved Sampson family members. By contrast, it was a time of rejoicing for the saved family members. They knew Henry and his little niece were with Jesus and they would see them again.

Paulita lay near death in a body cast. The doctors gave no hope for her recovery. They told us that if she lived, she would never walk again. In their negative prognosis, those doctors did not take God's healing power into account.

Months later Lyman accompanied me as my driver on an itinerary in the East. He and I attended a Kathryn Kuhlman meeting. We claimed Paulita's healing in that service. Soon word came to us from Phoenix that she had been instantly healed of all her injuries. The doctor's prognosis was wrong indeed! She was walking again. No distance or time can affect our God's healing power.

The two students who had caused the accident sustained serious injuries and were taken to the hospital in Scottsdale. The parents of both the young men came from out of state to be with them. Shortly after the accident, Virgil, Leslie, and Willard Sampson went to visit the boys.

When they and their parents saw the "giants" come in the room, they were terrified. Knowing the three brothers were relatives of the dead and injured, they did not know what to expect. They were certain they had come for revenge.

"Don't be afraid," said one of the Sampsons as they walked up to the student's beds. "You did cause the deaths of our brother and niece and our sister's injuries. But we didn't come to harm you. We came to pray for you. We want to tell you about Jesus, that He can save you from your sins and make you well again." Imagine the surprise and relief of both the boys and their parents when they heard those words. Only eternity will reveal the effect of the love and concern those Sampson brothers had on them in that hospital room that day.

An insurance settlement of several thousand dollars was awarded to the Sampson family as a result of the deaths. Their tithe paid to the church and school supplied funds enough to carry the school through financially for the rest of that school year.

At the close of the 1958-59 school year, the Sampson evangelists prepared for a full summer's ministry in revivals and camp meetings. Clifford, Leslie, and Alvin Sampson along with a new team member, Herman Hoffman, were invited to conduct a revival in Denver, Colorado.

While traveling through New Mexico, they had a terrible car accident. Alvin was killed instantly and the others were injured. Juanita, Alvin's wife, and the children were staying with us at the time. Only the Spirit of peace and the grace of God sustained Juanita through that time of sorrow. Alvin was a dedicated young man, full of zeal and love for the ministry. We missed him but knew he was at perfect peace in God's presence.

The insurance money from that accident was tithed to the church and school and again, although we wished it could have come from another source, helped to meet many needs.

During the summer months of 1963 it was necessary for me to travel in the interest of the school, speaking at Indian camp meetings and churches. Hilda Cree and I traveled to Ohio, Pennsylvania, New York, and Canada. Response in the services was excellent in both Anglo and Indian churches. We visited reservations in New York and in Hilda's hometown of Oka, Canada.

Hilda's little Volkswagen bug climbed the mountain roads without difficulty. In the hundreds of miles covered that summer, we never encountered any mechanical problems or accidents. We were grateful for God's overshadowing protection.

After we returned home to Phoenix for the opening of the fall school term, I suffered an injured shoulder and broken arm in an automobile accident. The doctors placed me in a swinging arm and body cast. I had to sleep sitting up in a chair, and from that encumbered position, I discharged my duties as school administrator for several months.

Peter's encouragement in 1 Peter 4:12 (KJV) seemed appropriate: "Beloved, think it not strange concerning the fiery trial which is to try you, as though some strange thing happened unto you."

Surely that scripture verse had some application to the chain of events in my life at that point. For no sooner had my body casts been removed than I developed a serious bout of pneumonia.

I have often wondered how I would have made it through those trying times without Rose Chase, our efficient and caring school nurse. God always has that certain person there when most needed.

I will long remember that winter. The faculty and staff made every effort and worked extra hours to stand by me and see the school move smoothly through that fall term.

Physical therapy on my shoulder and arm after the casts were removed limited any traveling for me that year. The congregation of All Tribes Assembly regretted my physical impairment, but they were glad to have their pastor home more than usual. No pastor could have had a more faithful and loving congregation, and only God knows how much my pastoral love went out to them.

Unfortunately, the American Indian of today is compared to the stereotype that television gives him in the wild western movies. He is pictured as savage, unfeeling, and unmerciful. Nothing could be further from the truth. Little do people who hold this concept realize that Native Americans can love and care for others as much as, if not more than, any other race or nationality. When Christ comes into their hearts, those traits become even more evident and forceful.

In August, only a few days from the opening of the 1964 school term, I became the victim of another accident. This one was freakish but more serious than the automobile accident.

The little apartment we occupied behind the church sanctuary had two bedrooms. My husband and I shared the larger one, even though it was considered small by most standards. We had a visitor from out of state and gave her our bedroom. Clarence and I slept on the bunk bed in the smaller bedroom. We slept well the first night, but when I stepped down to the step stool the next morning, it broke with me, throwing me into the door. The impact of the fall seriously injured my lungs. Clarence and Sister Chase immediately called for an ambulance. I and those around me questioned why those physical trials were being heaped upon me. However, through it all, I was assured God was still there for me and would bring me through that crisis as He had so many times before.

I lay in a critical condition in the hospital for three months. Eventually, surgery was performed on my lungs to extricate fluid that had accumulated too fast. The surgery was successful, but complete healing did not come until Brother Richard Jeffery prayed for me. The healing virtue of Jesus availed again. My lungs were totally healed, and I was able to go back to my duties at the church and school.

Even though I was extremely weak in body, the God who stands behind His promise of strength for our day did just that for me. That was my promise for each day of my recuperation period.

In my absence, problems had developed among the faculty and staff. Indeed my physical problems were small in comparison to this burden. My heart ached because I loved all these people. I was distressed to see a rift in the rapport they had with one another, and with me. As always, I laid the problem before the Lord. God moved, and the situation eased. Once again congeniality, cooperation, and peace prevailed among ~~~ school workers. Blessed Peace~~~~

Students harvesting fruit and vegetables

Belle Kennedy, Deer Kennedy, and Noreen Eddy

During my times of intercession before the Lord, I would look back to ten years of glorious fulfillment of all God had asked me to accomplish for His glory. The faces of so many friends came before me, friends who had added their concern and prayers with those of our All Tribes congregation. I knew there were multitudes of prayer partners all over the nation interceding for me and our missionary endeavors.

Fondly, I remembered the little Indian boys and girls and young men led to the Lord in our services under the mesquite trees. So many of them are now ordained and out evangelizing or pastoring churches in various places across the nation.

The realization that the previous crusades that had spread false doctrine among the Indian people were subsiding was a boost to my spiritual morale. The Lord reminded me how the Indian people had become more spiritually stable because of their foundation in sound Bible doctrine. They were taking initiative in leadership and responsibilities in the church. I was beginning to see the indigenous principle develop among them. Was not this what we missionaries had been praying, working, and planning for?

The vision God gave me in 1954 for the Bible school had never dimmed, nor had I ever doubted the far-reaching potential of the Native American.

In 1965, I began to sense that God was giving me a new directive and new trails to travel. He wanted me to resign as president of ATBS. The burden of being pastor/administrator had taken its physical toll on me. Emotions welled up within me. How could I give up something so precious as seeing young Indian people come year after year to the school for Bible training? But I knew I was hearing from God. Such a difficult decision to make; nonetheless, my heart told me this was God's will.

I submitted my resignation as president of All Tribes Bible School at the close of the 1965 school year. I turned the school over to the Division of Home Missions of the Assemblies of God. They appointed a board of directors, who chose a new president.

The board placed the reigns of leadership into the capable hands of Donald Ramsey to begin the 1966 school term. Brother Ramsey possessed all the academic credentials, spiritual qualities, and standards necessary to lead the school on to achieve the goals God had placed in my heart many years before. How great is our God! His guiding hand providentially puts everything in place for the furtherance of His kingdom on earth. And I knew the Bible school would continue to be an important factor in His Kingdom by spreading the gospel among the Indian tribes of the western hemisphere.

My dear friend Helen Rickey, the school secretary, graphically wrote our sentiments when the school was transferred to the Division of Home Missions:

"As I look back, I see this infant in his cradleboard,
struggling to hold onto life.
He begins to crawl. Pulls to his feet.
Gains strength to stand...
May our little papoose grow to great stature and
always be 'meet for the Master's use.'
Goodbye, little All Tribes Bible School;
we wish you Godspeed."

Under Brother Ramsey's administration, the school outgrew its facilities on East Washington Street. In time, a ten-acre plot in north Phoenix was acquired for the building of the new campus. The school had now attained institute status under the Department of Education of the Assemblies of God. Officially, it was now called American Indian Bible Institute.

Don Ramsey served AIBI as president from 1966–1978. He directed the building of a multipurpose facility. Later, he built the chapel, named after a true champion of the school, Rev. Clyde Henson.

Simon Peter, a beloved and respected Cherokee Indian minister, served the school as president following Brother Ramsey's resignation, from July 1978 until his death from cancer in March 1979.

Carl Collins, an educator and pastor from North Carolina, was chosen to become the next president. Under his leadership, the institute began to develop academically by adding several new departments to its curriculum. Enrollment began to increase to near 100.

During Brother Collin's leadership, another building was erected, the Gannon Memorial Dormitory for women. The Jimmy Swaggart Ministries generously donated $176,000 toward its building costs.

It was during Brother Collin's tenure as president that he and other administrators and faculty began the process of pursuing collegiate accreditation for the institute.

In 1987 Brother Collins resigned to become the pastor of the All Tribes Assembly in Phoenix. My heart is warmed knowing that that congregation is in the loving pastoral care of Carl and Alice Collins.

The progress of the school since the early days when it was just an idea, then a reality, is awesome. From its fledgling beginnings on East Washington Street—a most unlikely location for a school of any kind—God set the school on its divine schedule. To God be the glory for all the men and women who shared my vision of sending out laborers to the Native American harvest.

Many times I wondered if I would ever see the building and establishing of the school become a reality, see the first graduation class, or see the first graduate ordained into the ministry. Now that I have seen all these come to pass, I join the apostle Paul in saying, "I was not disobedient unto the heavenly vision" (Acts 26:19, KJV).

In concluding this chapter, I express how privileged and honored my husband and I were to have been invited to be the guest speakers at the twenty-fifth anniversary of the school in 1982. Several years have passed since that time. American Indian Bible College has now reached its thirty-second birthday and achieved its status as a fully accredited college.

My continual prayer will be that the graduates going out from American Indian Bible College will be diligent warriors of the Cross, obediently traveling every trail on which God may lead them. In my heart, I know AIBC will provide all its students a place of learning and the preparedness they will need to carry the message of the cross of Jesus to lost souls wherever they go on that trail. To God be all the praise!

After the transfer of the All Tribes Bible School and church property to the Division of Home Missions was finalized, we began searching for a new location for All Tribes Church. Prospects looked favorable for us to purchase one of two unused church facilities in downtown Phoenix. Since most of the city Indian people lived in the inner city, that was where we wanted to locate. We wanted to buy the larger of the two buildings, but we didn't have enough money. We had to settle for the smaller building on East Fillmore Street.

Moving into the new location did not diminish the blessings and presence of God in our services. The Lord transferred His blessings from the old property on East Washington to our new place. Revival fires burned, and souls were saved. We started a bus outreach and radio program, which helped bring in new people each service. Even though our auditorium was crowded, the people continued to come.

We never gave up praying that God would give us that larger building. Each time we passed it and saw the For Sale sign, we claimed it for the Lord.

The For Sale sign was removed when a wealthy family bought it to establish their own church. Naturally, all of us at All Tribes felt the loss, for we had faith God would give us that church. For three years we prayed God would help us accumulate enough funds to buy it. We did not understand this disappointment. On the other hand, had not God said that we should cast all our cares on Him? Furthermore, He said, "Trust in the Lord with all thine heart; and lean not unto thine own understanding" (Proverbs 3:5, KJV). God's delays are not His denials.

One day I read an article on the front page of the newspaper saying a rift had developed among members of the family-owned church. The pastor led one group and his brother-in-law led the other. Soon, both groups offered to sell us the property.

Even though we wanted to buy the property, there were many complications. Each group claimed to hold the legal title. One group offered to sell us the property at a reasonable price, one we could now afford. However, I told them they must meet with our Arizona Assemblies of God officials before we could make a decision.

The night before the arranged meeting, I had a disturbing dream in which I saw three men meeting with our district brethren. One of them was an attorney. In the dream the Lord spoke to me that no papers should be signed at the meeting. I was troubled. Should I tell the brethren about the dream?

Clarence, with his wise counsel, admonished me to let the Lord take care of it. He said, "Alta, don't you know God can give those brethren discernment whether they should sign the contract to buy the property from those people?"

As always, his wisdom gave me the guidance I needed. I kept the dream to myself.

At the appointed time we all met at the district office. As in my dream, the three men appeared representing the first group. Also, as I remembered from my dream, the attorney did most of the talking. After his presentation, he laid the contract papers on the desk for the officials' signatures.

Silently I prayed, "Dear, God, don't let them sign that contract."

As I waited for what seemed an eternity, our district superintendent calmly informed the committee from the church, "We appreciate your generous offer, but we will have to present this matter to our district board of directors for their decision."

The attorney, not willing to accept that response, angrily stated that the offer stood for that time or never. In his outrage, he told the brethren they would bulldoze the church and build apartments on the property. All three men stomped out of the room. How relieved I was that those papers were not signed! Furthermore, I was not sure I would want the property if we had to deal with that committee. Yet we continued to pray that God's will would be done in His own time.

The newspapers continued to carry stories about the bitter feuding between the two factions of the church. They wrote of violence, court orders, and lawsuits. One group sued to retrieve all the tithes they had paid into the church. They felt the pastor should return every penny. However, the judge told them that tithes were paid to God and he certainly would not bring the case before God! In due time the case was settled in favor of the pastor and his group. The attorney was later imprisoned for six years for embezzling church funds.

One day another story in our daily newspaper caught my attention. The article and a map showed where a new interstate freeway was proposed for downtown Phoenix. Looking closely at the map, we noticed that the freeway was routed right through our present Fillmore Street church property. Sometimes we felt we were going through one turmoil after another. People were calling and expressing regret that we would lose our church because of the proposed freeway. However, we knew God was working out His will in the midst of the turmoil. Soon we were approached by the Arizona Highway Department. They offered us the exact amount for the church property we had prayed for so we could buy the larger church.

Now that all the legal problems were settled and we had cash in hand, we bought the property on the corner of East McKinley and Ninth Street. For seven years we prayed God would preserve the property for us until we could raise the money. God's providence prevailed!

The sanctuary had a seating capacity of 400 and had blond wood church pews, light green carpeting, a Hammond organ, piano, and a complete public address system. Downstairs were classrooms, a nursery, and a lounge. A large annex behind the main building had a fellowship hall, kitchen, and upstairs office rooms. The property also included a red brick parsonage. With anticipation, I planned to redecorate it and make it comfortable for our living quarters.

Before we left the Fillmore location, the Donald Keeters from

Ohio came to assist me at the church. They had been involved with David Wilkerson in Teen Challenge ministries in New York. Through my dear friend Daena Cargnel, I heard about them. She had met them while holding an evangelistic meeting in their home church and was impressed with their dedication and talents. She told them of our need of helpers at All Tribes Assembly.

The Keeters, feeling a strong interest in Indian missionary work, began praying for God's will. Soon I received a letter from them saying they planned a trip to Arizona to observe the Indian work.

They arrived during our summer camp meeting at Casa Blanca, 35 miles south of Phoenix. In that desert setting, the heat ranged from 108 to 115 degrees. There was no type of cooling system, of course, so it was quite an experience for the Keeters. I was interested to see how they would react.

Camp meeting was a time of excitement and expectancy. The Indian people enjoyed building their little shade houses out of branches, which provided temporary shelter during the meetings. Each sponsoring Indian church cooked one large meal a day, which mostly consisted of pinto beans, tortillas, squash, chili peppers, and black coffee.

In most services the preaching was under a tent. To combat the heat as much as possible, we laid large wet towels across our laps and shoulders. Our wet clothing didn't matter; it was important to keep as cool as we could. Large jugs of water were absolute necessities. During high winds the men strong-armed the tent poles to keep the tent from blowing down.

Those desert Indian people never complained about the heat, flies, bugs, scorpions, or the ever-present sand, which blew into everything during the meeting. The desert was home and they were accustomed to its environment. They had Jesus in their hearts, good Christian fellowship and plenty of food. What more could they ask?

When Brother Keeter volunteered to drive the church van, I felt that traveling the hot dusty roads of the reservation and Phoenix city streets would provide an excellent trial run for him. How would he cope with the heat, the silent Indian passengers, and the late hours driving the people back to their homes after the night services?

Usually Indian people do not communicate much with strangers. But that was not the case with the Keeters. The van passengers entered right in conversation and joined the Keeters in singing choruses as they rode along.

The Indians and their missionary pastors involved in the camp meeting readily accepted the Keeters. I was pleased with what I observed and had a witness in my heart that God was sending the Keeters to help us at All Tribes Assembly.

Though the first day of the camp meeting went well for the Keeters, the heat and the strange diet of beans and tortillas took their toll on Brother Keeter. He never complained, but he didn't fare so well. Back in Phoenix after the second day of the camp meeting, my husband commented he had serious doubts about Brother Keeter. He felt he would be unable to cope with the strenuous regimen we followed in Indian missions. He said he didn't expect them to return to Arizona after they left for Ohio, but I knew they would, and they did.

In a Sunday morning service while we were still at the Fill-more Street property, the Holy Spirit moved in a phenomenal way. A Navajo couple had dedicated themselves to return to their reser-vation as evangelists. We rejoiced as we laid hands on them, com-mitting them to the Lord's service. Anticipation of soon moving into our new church location also generated more jubilant wor-ship. The congregation faithfully prayed for the building. Now they were visibly expressing their joy and sharing in the fruits of their faith.

Feeling weary that Sunday afternoon, I lay down to rest be-fore the evening service. A deep sleep came over me as the Lord revealed himself to me in a vision. I could feel His awesome pres-ence hovering over my bed. He said, "If you will take my Word se-riously, I will send you to the ends of the earth to carry the gospel to searching and needy people." When I awoke from that vision, I knew exactly what God's message meant. It related directly to let-ters I had received from one of my foster sons, Gabriel Ochoa, who was serving in the United States armed forces in Ethiopia.

Gabriel had come to us as a young teenager who needed a home. He was of Yaqui parentage from Guadalupe. After finish-ing high school, he joined the army. Before he was sent to overseas duty in Ethiopia, it was my privilege to perform his marriage to Grace, a lovely Christian Hispanic girl. The trip to Ethiopia was their honeymoon.

Gabriel had played the piano and organ for our services at All Tribes Assembly. In Ethiopia, he rented a piano for his own enjoy-ment and to sing gospel songs with Grace. The strains of music coming from their house stirred the curiosity of some Ethiopian young men living near the army base.

Recognizing they had a great opportunity to witness to those young men about the Lord, Gabriel and Grace invited them to their home for a time of fellowship and listening to their gospel singing.

What they had hoped for, happened. The young men became visibly affected by the music. Conviction of their sins and the power of the Holy Spirit rested upon them. They wept and called on God—not Allah—for forgiveness. Having received salvation, they experienced a spirit of worship. Some of them were filled with the Holy Spirit according to Acts 2:4.

Gabriel and Grace knew there was no preacher or missionary available who could help them guide this congregation of zealous young men. Because the men knew the Koran, the Islamic written guide, did not contain the true Word of God, they were eager to understand the Bible. For days some of them stayed in Gabriel and Grace's home searching the Scriptures and asking questions.

Because of the cultural taboos of Islam, the women were not permitted to attend the gatherings with the men. However, the men related their experiences to their wives and other women in the privacy of their homes as well as were asking questions about the gospel that Gabriel and Grace could not answer, so these two young men were faced with a dilemma.

So Gabriel's letters began coming to me. He pleaded with me to come to Ethiopia and help with his fledgling congregation.

In answering his letters, I casually wrote that the only way I would ever be able to go to Ethiopia would be like Phillip: to be spirited there supernaturally. I thought Gabriel and Grace were just homesick and used what was developing as a reason to urge me to visit them.

When I awoke from my vision, I realized what God meant when He said I should be serious about what He wanted me to do. He was calling me to Ethiopia!

What was I to do? Here we were, almost ready to move into our new church facilities and God called me to Africa! What could I ever tell my congregation and my husband? That afternoon Clarence had already left to pick up the city Indians for the night service when I awoke. Before the service, my sister came

Trail to the Tribes

into the apartment for a brief visit. Bursting with emotion I told her about the vision. I said, "You know, Imogean, that I have never told God no to anything He has called me to do or any place He has called me to go. But Ethiopia! How can I tell Clarence? What will he say? What shall I do?"

My sister, from whom I had sought counsel many times, had no answer for me. Her words of encouragement, however, bolstered my faith. I had to believe that God would somehow, someway give me the wisdom and grace I needed. I must make this new commission from God known to my dear husband and congregation. God would handle it!

Brother Keeter led the worship in the evening service. Messages in tongues and interpretations came forth related to God's call that I had received in my vision. Each message pertained to the mission field. The congregation rejoiced because they thought the messages were directed to the young Navajo couple. Only my sister and I knew that God, through the ministry of the Holy Spirit, was actually confirming my call to Ethiopia.

God's calls upon my life had disrupted our lives over and over again. They necessitated Clarence leaving good jobs and our moving out of homes we had built or remodeled. My dear husband never complained. He accepted my calls as if they were his own. We had pursued unknown trails together, never divided in our objectives but always in total agreement in God's purpose for our lives. That unity and God's grace always sustained us in difficult times.

When Clarence returned after taking the people home, I told him everything: the vision, the Holy Spirit's confirmation, and Gabriel's appeals for me to go to Ethiopia.

"Do you think the Keeters will take the pastorate when you go? Will they take the responsibility of moving the church to the new location?" he asked.

I must admit, I did not expect his agreeable response without some initial questions. Again, this dear, gentle man the Lord had given me knew God had made His will known to me. And we were both to obey His will.

"I don't know, Clarence," I replied. "Let's ask them now."

When we approached the Keeters, they said they would gladly accept the pastorate while I was away and handle everything involved in moving to our McKinley Street property. We rejoiced and praised God together for His guidance and will for our lives.

Clarence and I now had serious matters to discuss, decisions to make, and plans for my travel to Ethiopia to consider. He was apprehensive of my traveling alone and suggested I contact a travel agency to place me in a tour group for security.

My friend Daena Cargnel told me about a group going to Africa and the Middle East. I contacted the tour leader to see if I could join his tour but leave it in Israel and go to Ethiopia. He told me no arrangement could be made for that type of diversion from the tour.

I waited and prayed, not only for the routing and schedule for the trip but the money for the fare. At that time we did not have the several hundred dollars needed for the plane tickets, lodging, and other necessities for the trip. Nonetheless, I knew God had called me, and I was ready to go. He would supply the need.

We had sold some lots for which we were paid $25 a month through a title company. While praying and waiting on God for the trip money, we received a check for $250 from the company. It seemed the owner had sold the lots and would be paying off the balance he owed us. Clarence and I recognized this was God's way of supplying my fare and expense money for my trip.

Paul's words in Philippians 4:19 (KJV), "My God shall supply all your need according to his riches in glory by Christ Jesus," were my source of faith.

A few days later I received a telephone call from the tour group leader in Ohio saying he had reconsidered my request. Two other missionaries joining the group wanted to break with the tour and go on to Nairobi in Kenya, East Africa. He said he could make the arrangements for the three of us to follow our desired itineraries. Oh, the wonders of how God's mighty hand moves circumstances and hearts of men to accomplish His will!

God had shown me this was the time to resign as pastor of All Tribes Assembly. For twenty-five years I had pastored that Indian congregation. Each member was close to my heart. I will never forget the emotional experience of my resignation.

The Sunday I resigned, I looked into the faces of the people. I well remembered each one's conversion, and thrilled at their spiritual growth. Even today, I often find myself remembering all those dear people and the great times we had worshiping and working together. Telling them farewell at that time was heartwrenching, but I had no doubt about God's will for me. I must follow the longest trail I had ever traveled, and it would take me to the farthest side of the earth.

▲▲▲

Our tour group flew from New York to Egypt, our first sightseeing stop.

After a good night's rest and a quick breakfast the next morning, we were promptly taken to our rendezvous with our transportation for the day—the camels. My first impression of those beasts was their height. They were so tall! Fear and apprehension swept over me when I realized I would have to mount one of those animals for my day's travels.

When the camel assigned to me was made to kneel down, his driver assisted me up on its back. The driver urged me to hold tight to the saddle horn as the camel began to rise. By the time I had figured out what the driver was trying to tell me in his broken English, the camel lunged up and forward. I held so tightly to that saddle horn my knuckles turned white. If I had not, I would have been thrown over the beast's head. As our caravan moved ahead, I began to have misgivings about my comfort and safety on that animal.

We rode those camels all day in unrelenting blowing sand. It made me think of the dust storms on our Arizona desert. Only, in Arizona, I would not be riding on the back of a grumpy, lunging animal. I was glad I had purchased a head wrap to protect me from the sun and dust, even though it made me look like an Arab.

Seeing the Pyramids was worth all the hassle we went through to reach them on our camel-pace journey. We marveled at early man's skill and power to erect those magnificent monuments.

Our tour spent several days visiting the tombs of the ancient monarchs of Egypt, the Sphinx, the silver mines, the perfume parlors, and shops. I hardly realized I was seeing all the wonders of that ancient country.

The next day we flew to Tel Aviv and Jerusalem. We visited Golan Heights, which had been laid waste by the Six Day War between Israel and Egypt. Other sights of interest were the Samaritan Inn, Masada, Solomon's stables, and Lazarus' tomb. I was privileged to minister to the tour group when we visited the Garden of Gethsemane, Mount Calvary, Christ's empty tomb, and on the ship on the Sea of Galilee.

Our visit to the Upper Room where Jesus and His disciples partook of the Last Supper was a blessed experience for me. Some believe the 120 disciples received the baptism in the Holy Spirit there on the Day of Pentecost. Uniquely, there were exactly 120 people in our tour. Some of our group received the Holy Spirit according to Acts 2:4 in that room. Also, some were baptized in the Jordan River at the place where John the Baptist baptized Jesus.

Choice memories will always remain with me of that time in my life when I actually saw the places where my Savior walked, talked, and ministered.

The evening before our departure from Jerusalem, we attended a banquet held in our honor at the Saint George Hotel. The tables were laid with exquisite linen tablecloths, silver, and china. A great silver platter holding a roasted lamb adorned the center of the table. Our appetites diminished; we were tired of mutton, mutton, and more mutton. It seemed to always be the main meat dish on every menu in every restaurant where we ate.

After our meal, it was my honor to be the banquet speaker. What a joy to share God's Word and tell how He had led me, and was leading me, in winning souls for Him! After I sat down, a man sitting near me handed me a one hundred dollar bill. That gift went a long way toward meeting my travel expenses.

The other two missionaries had already left the tour for Nairobi. My plane for Addis Ababa was scheduled to leave at 11:00 PM at the Tel Aviv airport forty miles away. The tour guide assured me someone would take me without delay. Soon, an Arab driving a large black limousine taxi came for me. Sitting in the back seat, I felt relieved to be on the way to the airport. I also tried to calm my nerves and fears. Traveling in the dead of night with an Arab taxi driver didn't help.

When we had gone about twenty miles, he pulled over to the side of the road. My fears escalated. Why was he stopping in the middle of the desert? Was he going to rob me and leave me stranded in this wilderness? Fearful questions raced through my mind. But he evidently only needed to relieve himself, for he was gone just a short time. Yet my apprehensions did not subside until we reached the airport.

To increase my qualms, I learned the plane to Addis Ababa, which connected with the plane to Asmira, my destination, had already departed. I was told that another plane would leave at 2:00 AM the next morning. I never liked waiting, but there was no alternative. In spite of my difficulty in understanding the flight calls and reading the schedules in a foreign language, God helped me get on the right plane at the departure time.

As soon as we were airborne, a violent rainstorm erupted around us. The plane bounced up and down and from side to side. Rain poured off the wings of the plane like a small Niagara Falls. Again my mind was besieged with disturbing questions. Would the storm cause the plane to crash?

The pilots safely navigated the plane through the storm to the Addis Ababa airport. I was relieved. But my relief was short-lived. The airline announced the Asmira flight was delayed until morning because of the storm. As distressed as I was, I welcomed the hotel accommodations we were given for the night by the airlines.

Some months before I made the trip to Ethiopia, I had a witness in my spirit that Satan would try to kill me on my journey. Knowing my life was being divinely protected by my guardian angel and the power of God, I paid no heed to that witness. However, the next morning I was shocked at the accuracy of that witness. The original flight to Addis Ababa had crashed in the storm. The announcement reported there were no survivors. Had that Arab taxi driver not made his stop in the desert, I would have been on that flight. In my heart I felt I could join David when he declared his assurance of God's protection in Psalm 34:7 (KJV), "The angel of the Lord encampeth round about them that fear him, and delivereth them."

Before leaving Addis Ababa on my flight to Asmira, I called Gabriel and Grace to let them know why I had not arrived as originally scheduled. They had heard of the plane crash and were sure I was one of the victims. Their voices on the phone reflected their surprise and joy to learn I was still alive and would soon join them.

I told them I would take a taxi to their home when I arrived in Asmira, but they exclaimed, "Oh, no, don't take a taxi! The driver will think you are a rich white woman, rob you, and take you for your last ride. We'll come for you."

Later while riding in their comfortable vehicle, I noticed the kind of taxis used in Asmira: wooden carts drawn by water buffaloes! How glad I was I didn't insist on the taxi ride.

Our reunion was filled with rejoicing, embracing, and asking questions about each one's welfare. It had been quite a long time since we had seen each other. Some of their converts they brought with them also gave me a warm welcome. After my eventful trip from Tel Aviv, I felt comfortable and safe again.

Asmira had just had a great celebration for Haile Selassie, the ruler of Ethiopia at that time. It was a celebration I was glad to have missed. Six hundred people were massacred at a nearby village by communist rebels. Ethiopia was in the midst of a bloody revolution. Army tanks and soldiers occupied every street. The tense atmosphere of the city caused uneasiness in all of us.

The U. S. Army personnel were housed in magnificent homes of Italian architecture. Gabriel and Grace lived in one of those stately homes, surrounded by other mansions occupied by army personnel. Yet, in spite of all the grandeur, military guards patrolled the rooftops of the buildings. High iron or stone walls surrounded the courtyards. Windows had three shutters. One was a steel-louvered shutter that came down from the high ceilings and locked inside. All windows, doors, and gates were securely locked before dark.

No one would open a door for anyone after all had been made secure. Seeing that situation made me understand a little better the parable of the man awakened at midnight and asked to lend his neighbor three loaves of bread to feed his guests. The man was reluctant to accommodate his neighbor and said, "Trouble me not: the door is now shut [locked]. . ." (Luke 11:7, KJV).

A question plagued me as I observed the tight security and government unrest among the people. How could we have a revival in this locked-up place and war-torn city?

When he heard of my consternation and doubts, Gabriel assured me he had made arrangements for the use of a meeting hall in downtown Asmira. He urged me not to worry. Even though he was restricted to where he could go in the city, the meeting site would be safe.

When we arrived at the meeting hall for our first service, I noticed no women were present. The hall was filled with Ethiopian men. The same security was maintained for our meetings as on the army base. Security guards were placed outside the entrance, and all windows were covered with the same steel-louvered shutters. Strangely, I felt no fear but filled with God's peace, for I knew He was right there with us in that place.

As I stood before those men to minister, they reminded me of the people in Cornelius' household, eager to hear the gospel.

Two young college students were my interpreters. As God anointed me when I preached, those young interpreters were also anointed. The expressions on the faces of the Ethiopians told me the Word from the Lord was reaching their hearts.

God overshadowed each service with His presence and power. Scores of young men were gloriously saved and filled with the Holy Spirit. My only regret was that women could not attend, but

I trusted that those men who were saved would share their experiences with the women in their lives.

One of the interpreters continued with the services after I left Asmira and eventually became pastor of that thriving, growing body of Ethiopian men.

After I arrived back in Phoenix, letters from Gabriel told me that more than a thousand had been saved. He enclosed photos of men with their families. My question had been answered: those men did share the gospel with their families.

Later when the communists took over the government of Ethiopia, all churches were machine-gunned and destroyed. Christians who escaped being killed or captured by the communists had to go underground or escape to refugee camps in neighboring countries. My two young interpreters, Zerezghi and Yemane, were barely able to escape before their church and scores of members were machine gunned. Later they were able to flee Ethiopia and come to the United States.

We took Zerezghi and Yemane into our home as our own sons and saw them develop into fine professional Christian men. Zerezghi's fiancee, Alyonish, was not able to escape with him but came to the States five years later. Both young men completed their college education after coming to the United States. Zerezghi and Alyonish married and are now teaching in a Christian school. Yemane is a professor at Harvard University.

As I think back over my experience in Ethiopia and all those precious souls either killed, imprisoned, or scattered into other countries, I am comforted. I know the deceased are with Jesus, and that He was an ever present help in time of need to the living. For me, my comfort is in saying with Paul, "I was not disobedient unto the heavenly vision" (Acts 26:19, KJV).

Before I left for Ethiopia, we had moved to a beautiful mountain area near Prescott, Arizona, eighty-five miles north of Phoenix. Even though God led us to locate in Prescott, we found His guidance difficult to understand. Later God showed us that this trail and a small Yavapai Indian reservation near Prescott were a definite part of His plan for us.

When I arrived home from Africa, a raging fire was consuming hundreds of acres of beautiful Ponderosa pines near our Prescott home. We called on God to place a hedge of protection around our mountain home against the fire. Dense smoke all around us made breathing difficult. Hundreds of firefighters moved up and down the mountain trails. Slurry planes steadily flew overhead to dump fire-extinguishing fluids on the blazing forest. Living on the edge of that fire was a harrowing experience.

We prayed not only for our protection but for homes in the direct path of the fire. We prayed for families who had already lost their dwellings to the blazing inferno. Trusting God to protect us, we went to bed. The next morning we rejoiced to hear the fire had been contained. The little forest animals that had been our daily visitors were either killed by the fire or fled to another area. We missed them.

In the high altitude of Ethiopia, I had suffered some distress in my right ear. After returning home, the pain continued until I lost the hearing in that ear. One day, physically weakened by the ordeal, I desperately petitioned God for healing. Going into much detail, I informed God of my discouragement, weakness, and pain, as if He didn't already know of my plight.

Then, in the quietness of my spirit, I heard the Lord say, "I know about your weakness and pain. Have faith; I will heal and strengthen you, for I have set before you an open door of ministry in this place."

Suddenly, renewed strength filled my body, and I literally

bounded out of my bed. I was spiritually soaring. Once again I had heard God's call to travel another trail for Him. But where? Here in Prescott? I was full of questions. Yet I had long ago learned to have faith and confidence in His guidance.

Near the Yavapai Indian Reservation was a little Indian Assembly of God church. When Clarence and I started attending the services, the pastor cordially welcomed us. Some of the Yavapai Apache Indian members had been saved in our All Tribes Assembly in Phoenix years before. Joy filled my heart to know they were continuing their walk with the Lord.

As we continued to attend the Indian mission, I felt my strength return day by day. Worshiping with the congregation and pastor also gave me a spiritual uplift.

The people worshiped in a creaky, unsafe old building. It appeared to me that the floor might collapse into the basement or the roof might cave in. Of course, my fears were exaggerated.

One Sunday the pastor challenged the congregation to start a building fund. The people responded favorably and began giving their small offerings to the fund, and the pastor, who was secularly employed, was a generous contributor.

In another Sunday morning service, God spoke through a message in tongues and interpretation:

"Hear and obey my voice. I will direct and bless you as you proceed with my work in this place."

Thinking the Holy Spirit was confirming God's will upon the pastor and the building plans, I rejoiced in God's approval on the people's efforts. Later, however, I learned I was not listening or thinking with my spiritual ears and mind.

That Sunday afternoon the pastor came for a visit. After our greetings, the pastor initiated the conversation. "Sister Washburn, did the Holy Spirit speak to you this morning through the message and interpretation?"

Stunned for a moment by his question, I answered, "No, Pastor, I was not aware He was. I thought the message was directed to you because it seemed to confirm your plans for the new building."

"I know He wasn't speaking to me", he replied, "because I had already planned to resign the church soon. My job takes so much of my time, I felt I should resign. Sister Washburn, would you consider accepting the pastorate?"

My memory promptly took me back to the day God said He would open a door of ministry in Prescott for me. Could this be that door?

After much seeking God for His will, we knew the pastorate of the Prescott Indian church was that open door. We gave the pastor our affirmative answer. He soon resigned and we accepted the pastorate. The congregation was as anxious to start planning for the new building as we were. Tearing down the old building would be the first project.

As Clarence and a Christian brother were demolishing the old building a roof beam broke, throwing Clarence to the floor. Instantly, the brother began praying for a miracle as Clarence lay on the floor. That prayer touched God's healing power. Clarence stood to his feet and came home. Although he didn't seem to be injured, we took him to the hospital for X-rays.

To confirm the miracle, the doctor found three broken bones in Clarence's leg which had perfectly set together. Unbelievable as it was, the doctor said the healing must have occurred when Clarence arose from his fall and walked to the car. As a precaution against any rebreaking of the bones, the doctor put a cast on Clarence's leg up to the hip.

Clarence never missed a day working on the building in spite of the injury, nor did he have any pain. How great is our God of miracles! He had performed numerous miracles for me. Now He had given Clarence his own miracle.

The building was soon finished and dedicated to the Lord. We praised the Lord that funds and helpers had always been available when needed. Almost two years later, in 1974, the Prescott All Tribes Assembly of God was set in order with the Arizona Assemblies of God district as a completely indigenous church. It provided salaries for me, the assistant pastor, and paid all the church expenses. This was the first time I had received a pastoral salary since I resigned my pastorate in Ohio in 1947. In the previous twenty-five years of pastoring an Indian church, my husband willingly provided funds from his own salary to meet my needs as well as those of the church.

Toward the end of four enjoyable years at Prescott, Clarence became seriously ill. Our doctor advised him to move to a lower elevation. Was God now leading us back to the desert? What ministry awaited us there?

Clanrence Washburn

After our move back to Phoenix, Clarence soon regained his health in the warmth and lower altitude of the desert valley.

Before we moved, we started watching Trinity Broadcasting Network, Channel 21, a Christian TV station based in Phoenix. On one of the trips to the doctor in Phoenix, I suggested to Clarence that we visit the new station. After we toured the facility, the director asked me to join their staff of telephone counselors. I sensed that invitation was in God's plan for me. I readily agreed.

Telephone counseling was rewarding: talking with people with various needs, leading them to the Lord, and praying with them. The network's outreach ministry went to many foreign countries. On one occasion I was privileged to go as a member of the crusade staff to Guatemala City, Guatemala. Eighty thousand people stood shoulder to shoulder to hear the gospel in that crusade. My joy was to share in ministering to those poor, needy, physically and spiritually hurting natives. Another part of a counselor's work was to participate in prayer groups and personal counseling in crusades in churches and auditoriums in the United States.

An effective ministry of Channel 21 was His Hand Extended, an outreach supplying food, clothing, and household furnishings to the needy in the Phoenix area. When I was requested to direct that department, I accepted the position. I felt comfortable with the opportunity to minister materially to the needy because of my years of similar ministry to the American Indians.

We received a tremendous response to our weekly appeals and those made on the telethon broadcast twice yearly. The viewing public gave generously of items for us to distribute to the needy. Not only did we minister to their material needs, but God gave us multiplied opportunities to minister to their spiritual needs. At Christmas we had an abundance of toys for the children and gifts for shut-ins.

Clarence and I continued with His Hand Extended ministry for six years after moving back to Phoenix. In addition to our involvement five days a week at Channel 21, I pastored a group of Pimas in an outreach ministry ten miles east of Phoenix. We named our congregation Trinity Assembly of God. Some members were Pima Indians who had attended All Tribes Church in Phoenix many years before.

Eventually, because of the rapid growth and heavy workload of His Hand Extended, Clarence and I felt we should resign. Even though we thoroughly enjoyed the work, the physical responsibility became too much for us. God helped us to organize and develop the ministry, but we had a witness it was time to turn it over to someone else. We will always cherish the friendships we made with the staff at Channel 21. They were our support base in prayer and finances in our outreach work among the Pimas.

After we resigned from the Trinity Broadcasting Network, I accepted the pastorate of the Indian assembly on the Salt River Pima Reservation. Attendance had declined, members scattered, and most were not attending any church. The majority had been members of Phoenix All Tribes Assembly in years gone by. I had been burdened then for seven years. With God's help and much prayer, I was determined to do all I could to regather the scattered congregation. We merged the Trinity Assembly I had pioneered while working at TBN with the Salt River church.

The buildings needed repair and another building was needed. In time, God helped us complete the repairs. We purchased new pews, installed a baptistery, and added new classrooms.

Former members began to return. Revivals, camp meetings, and added membership encouraged and uplifted all of us. The church had once again become a strong, productive, and soul-winning congregation.

In 1984, after seven years pastoring the Salt River church, I felt it was time to resign. God's commission to regather, revive, and re-establish the Salt River Assembly was accomplished through His power, guidance, and strength.

▼▼▼

After my resignation as pastor of Salt River Assembly, we waited until the end of the summer for the new pastor, Roger Cree, to arrive. He had served as president of Eastern Bible Institute in North Carolina for several years. The church was blessed to have Brother Cree and his family become their spiritual shepherds.

At the conclusion of the first service after the Cree's arrival, we went to the altar for prayer. No sooner had I knelt at the altar then I once again heard the voice of the Lord. It was a strange message.

"From today forth," came God's message, "you will be ministering for me in your own home. You will counsel and pray for those whom I will send to you or who will call you by phone."

That was all He said. Soon my new commission became clear to me. My telephone began to ring with calls from distant places. A familiar voice of some dear Indian who had been a member of one of our Indian congregations would call asking for prayer, counsel, or encouragement. It was not uncommon for me to spend hours praying and ministering in our home for an Indian in urgent need of spiritual help.

We continued to contribute food and clothing to the needy after we left Channel 21. Markets and food banks liberally gave us food for Second Miles Ministries, our assistance organization for the needy. With our car loaded to capacity with food and clothing, Clarence and I traveled to Indian reservations near Phoenix. We distributed items to as many as 250 people a week. My husband willingly gave his time for Second Mile Ministries. He was in good health and had recuperated completely from his previous illnesses.

I was not as fortunate. My health seemed to decline, but daily I claimed God's promise "As thy days, so shall they strength be" (Deuteronomy 33:25, KJV).

Early in 1985, the superintendent of the Arizona district of the Assemblies of God asked me to accept the pastorate of the Yaqui Indian Assembly in Guadalupe. I have already told how we started an outstation work there as an outreach of All Tribes Assembly. In fact, Guadalupe was our second outreach. Now I was asked to become its pastor after all these years. Doubts flooded my mind when I considered my age of 79, how tired I was physically, and how long the trails had been. Was I able to get an affirmative answer?

I could never close a door that God had opened for me, nor could I close this one. Had I not proved many times that God's strength and grace sustained me in spite of obstacles to fulfilling His will? Yes, I would accept the pastorate.

The Yaqui village assembly had been struck with a crisis. It was as if a mother's love and burden welled up in my heart for the affected and hurting people in that little church. My initial reaction was a consuming desire to restore what had been pulled apart by the church's internal problems. After a few months of ministry, we rejoiced to see a unified and growing congregation. The church once again became a lighthouse to the community of Guadalupe.

In September 1985 I resigned the pastorate of the Yaqui church. We bought a home in Camp Verde, Arizona, a town near a Yavapai Apache Reservation. Evidence of the trails we traveled are ever before us. Brother McCloskey, in whose home the Phoenix All Tribes Assembly began, lives here. From those first services in his home, many who were saved are now propagating the gospel across the nation.

From classes we conducted as an outreach of All Tribes Assembly among students in the Indian government school in Phoenix, many were saved. A number of them are now active in the ministry or in their local churches. I think particularly of the Clarks, Navajo students in that school. They pioneered the Indian Assembly in Gallup, New Mexico, after their marriage and graduation from the Phoenix Indian High School.

Hundreds of students have gone out from the All Tribes Bible School, which is now American Indian Bible College. They continue to evangelize, pastor, and carry leadership positions among their Indian people. Their trails have touched literally thousands of Native Americans with the gospel.

As I conclude this book, it is now 1989. I have spent much time reflecting over these past forty-two years God has given us to minister the gospel to Native Americans. We feel no regrets, only a wish that we could have many more years to work in this great harvest for the Lord. Clarence and I are consoled by the knowledge that our vision is perpetuated by those whom our lives have touched. They are sowing seeds of the gospel until Jesus returns for His Bride. Hallelujah!

Trails, trails, trails—no, they will never end until we hear the clarion call to every kindred, tribe, and nation, the call to come up higher into His Holy Presence. Oh, how I would love to step over on some cloud and watch them go in, especially those with whom we had the great honor to share the gospel. All glory and praise to our Savior, Lord, and soon coming King! Maranatha!

ACKNOWLEDGEMENTS

Words would not adequately express my appreciation for all the valuable help the following people gave to us in our years of Indian ministries, particularly those who assisted us in the All Tribes Bible School and All Tribes Assembly of God Church.

I wish to thank Alma Thomas who edited and typed the manuscript for this book and Pauline Dunn for her assistance in the editing.

Rose Chase
Ollie Dingman
Ruth Gardner
Lucille Greathouse
Betty Hanna
Harold Hansen
Jack Ireland
Mrs. T. L. Johnson
Mrs. Gay Keeter
Joe Lack
Mrs. Joe Leichty
Marcia McCorkle
Helen Rickey
Virgil Sampson
Jan Stewart
Lonnie Thomas
Vida Washburn
Barbara Willoughby

William Comstock
Hilda Cree Garcia
Lois Carruthers
Rose Grant
Joe Hanna
Mable Holland
T.L. Johnson
Donald Keeter
Virginia Kridler
Joseph Leichty
Eva McClintock
Dee Rickey
Eunice Sampson
Caleb Smith
Alma Thomas
Thomas Washburn
Wallace Weatherford

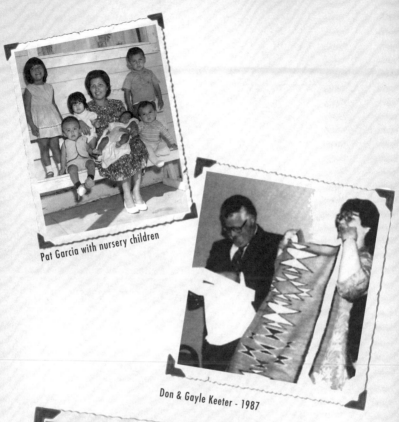

Pat Garcia with nursery children

Don & Gayle Keeter - 1987

front row, left to right: Helen Rickey, Clarence Washburn, Alta Washburn, Virginia Kridler
back row, left to right: Dee Rickey, Lois Carruthers, Rose Chase, Ruth Gardner, Harold Hanson

PART TWO ▲▲▲

Board Reflections

T. Ray Rachels

Rodger A. Cree, Sr.

Curtis W. Ringness

Marvin B. Begay

AIBI Board of Directors, 1968–1969

T. Ray Rachels and Don and Virginia Ramsey at the 2000 Dedication Ceremony of Ramsey Cafeteria

AIC Board Meeting Spring 2007

Front: Stephen Harris, T. Ray Rachels, Tommy Crider, James Comer - Middle: Robert Slaton, Becky Dickenson, Priscilla Taylor, Betty Owens, Irving Terry, Sandra Ticeahkie, Marvin Begay, Back: Don George, Ed Bradford, Larry Moore, Dennis Hodges, Frank Cargill, David Cole, John Maracle, Donald Bogue, David DeGarmo, Charley Odell, Doug York, Vince Roubideaux, Tommy Carpenter

Board Reflections ▲▲▲

T. RAY RACHELS

Board of Regents Chair, American Indian College
Superintendent, Southern California District Council of the Assemblies of God

I remember watching a skilled Native American artist weaving an intricate pattern. The overall beauty was even more remarkable when you got close up and could see the tiny details that made it truly unique. American Indian College in Phoenix, Arizona, is like that, a beautiful story of a vision and a mission, but the little details reveal the miracles. Glancing over the names of the buildings reminded me of pennies that Assemblies of God women from all over the western United States have collected. Those pennies helped buy those buildings. A penny—small and insignificant, but an integral part of the big picture!

Another detail I learned recently is that the state of Missouri, home to our General Council Assemblies of God headquarters, is named after a Native American tribe. The name is thought to mean "People of the big canoes." I like that! Canoes take people places and people take Jesus with them. And big canoes take more people!

So I looked up how to make a canoe. At the top of the instruction page was an all caps message: NOTE: THIS IS NOT A ONE PERSON JOB! It's a big job, and American Indian College is a big canoe that many builders have labored on, and we want to remember that as we mark the achievement of fifty years of equipping Native American students to carry the gospel to every tribe and every nation.

The wonderful campus in Phoenix, Arizona, is a testimony to God's provision and the people who have made it happen. The names of the buildings speak of the past builders: Ramsey Cafeteria, the Clyde Henson Memorial Chapel, and the Dorothy Cummings Library. That list is still growing!

A quick look at the AIC Web site points to AIC's success. It is poised for the future, expanding in 2005 to become an approved branch campus featuring the Master of Arts program in Christian Ministries offered by the Assemblies of God Theological Seminary (AGTS) based in Springfield, Missouri. That success reminds me of legendary coaching giant and winner of an incredible ten NCAA basketball titles for UCLA—The "Wizard of Westwood," John Wooden.

Wooden had a rule for his players. When you make a basket, immediately look for the teammate who either passed you the ball or who blocked out your opponent, allowing you to score, and point him out: he's the one who made possible your score. Somebody was responsible for helping you put the ball in the basket. Who was it? Point that person out! It's a way of saying thanks, and it was one of Wooden's unbending rules. If you don't point and say thanks, you don't play.

That's the reason, even when they became NBA pros, you could always tell the players coached by Wooden: they were the ones pointing toward the teammate who had helped them score or make the play.

Wooden's goal was to create teamwork, to build a team, and to promote team spirit, and he did it through making sure his players recognized the contributions of those whose work made possible their score, whose unselfishness allowed them to succeed.

"The main ingredient to stardom," said Wooden, "is the rest of the team."

When Raymond Berry was head coach for the NFL's New England Patriots, he took Polaroid snapshots of all the ball boys who helped the team.

Then he asked each ball boy to sign his name on his picture.

At a team meeting, Berry passed out the photos and told his players to learn the names that went with the faces:

"The boys know who you are," said Berry. "I want you to know them. Every person who contributes to the success of this team is important."

Lou Holtz, South Carolina University football coach, had a way of getting the same thought across. At the initial team meeting of his first year coaching at the University of Minnesota, Holtz distributed T-shirts with the word "team" printed on them in big block letters. Underneath, in tiny print, was the word "me."

The ministry, as well, is no place for lone rangers, or ball hogs, or for having a case of spotlight fever. "Servant" is the operative word for Christ-followers.

"He must increase, but I must decrease," said John the Baptist of Jesus (John 3:30, NKJV).

"Follow my example, as I follow the example of Christ," said the apostle Paul to Timothy (1 Corinthians 11:1, NIV).

"We then, as workers together with Him . . . ," said Paul to the Corinthians (2 Corinthians 6:1, NKJV).

Pointing to Jesus, of course, is the most elementary step in Christian leadership. He's the One who always passes to you the divine advantage for ministry.

Pointing to your fellow workers is elementary too—those who stand by you, who hold up your arms as Aaron and Hur did for Moses; those whose prayers are lifted to the Father on your behalf; and those who give contributions of faithfulness, support, and loyalty, without which you'd be fighting the battle alone. Every servant is equally valuable in the Lord's work and passes to each other great advantage for ministry.

Putting teamwork first puts the goal of Christian ministry in noble perspective.

"You can easily enough see how this kind of thing works by looking no further than your own body . . . No matter how many parts you can name, you're still one body . . . A body isn't just a single part blown up into something huge. It's all the different—but similar—parts arranged and functioning together" (1 Corinthians 12:12-14, Third Millennium Bible).

People in ministry, those whose work affects life most deeply, are great team players. They know their coach and what He expects. They easily and quickly point to their teammates. They say thanks. They know that to qualify for true servant-hood, transformation is needed. And to that transformation, they say yes! It's a good rule. It's God's rule.

So we say thanks to Alta Washburn, pastor of All Tribes Assembly of God in Phoenix, Arizona. In 1956, she saw the need for a school to train workers to serve the Native American churches and began the foundation with the start of All Tribes Bible School to equip Native American leaders that would build up the churches in their communities. AIC's dean of Institutional Research, Jim Dempsey, says in *Readings in Native American Missions*, "Sister Washburn operated the school on faith, hope, love, and lots of beans."[1] When I went back to the canoe building instructions, it emphasized that a quality canoe starts with quality materials. I'd say the faith, hope, and love that was part of AIC's foundation will keep us afloat for a long time to come.

More builders added their skills to the endeavor. We point to people like Lonnie Thomas and Virgil Sampson, and we know that without them AIC would not be the great institution it is today.

We gratefully remember Don Ramsey, who became the second leader of the school, leading it under a new name, American Indian Bible Institute (AIBI), from 1965–1978. For thirteen years he applied his craftsmanship to the construction of facilities and the advancement of curriculum development. His excellence was marked by the endorsement of AIBI from the Assemblies of God Department of Education. This canoe was already in the water!

There are many others to express thanks to. Simon J. Peter, an Oklahoma Choctaw, became the school's President in 1978, and although his tenure was cut short by his heavenly homegoing, it marked the dedication of the school's central mission, which is to equip each generation to carry the gospel to every tribe and every nation.

Carl Collins took the helm in 1979 and led the school into an era of growing ministry, returning students to their communities equipped to serve in clinics and schools and businesses—with an unequivocal commitment to take Christ's light and truth with them.

We salute T. E. Gannon, former General Council Home Missions (now Assemblies of God U.S. Missions) director, who worked on the sidelines to gain recognition for the school by the Bureau of Indian Affairs. Many graduates can look back at that funding that opened the door for them to attend a Christian college.

Thanks to David J. Moore, the next leader who brought his considerable skill to the task of improving educational opportunities for the growing student body. Under President Moore's tenure the college received regional accreditation with the North Central Association of Colleges and Schools (now known as the Higher Learning Commission). This enormous undertaking began during the tenure of President Carl Collins.

David J. Moore was followed by Dr. W. Duane Collins, who served as President through May 1998 after having served for a number of years as a world missionary in Africa and Europe.

Perhaps one of the best measurements of a school's success is when students graduate and become the teachers and the leaders. We are thankful for Jim H. Lopez, a graduate of (then) AIBI, who became the next president and ably led us into the new millennium. During his years of service to AIC, both as dean of students and later as president, Jim was capably assisted by his wife, Belinda Flame Lopez, who served in both the Learning Resource and Elementary Education departments as both instructor and chair. Today, the legacy of the Lopez Family continues as their son Jameson, "J. D.", is a student majoring in elementary education and remains very active with both the college and activities related to the Native American Fellowship (NAF) of the Assemblies of God. Even though Jim and Belinda Lopez are no longer formally serving at the college, they continue to frequently visit the campus—always as honored guests who have left a lasting legacy to the Native people.

The current president, James V. Comer, has the distinct privilege of looking back on AIC's rich heritage and moving forward to a bright future, bringing transformation to every tribe and every nation it touches.

A report from the American Indian Higher Education Consortium (AIHEC) back in 2000 notes that the history of higher education for American Indians has been filled with challenges. The report's authors note that American Indians have had low educational attainment and conclude with a call to create role models for change.[2]

AIC is a leader in creating role models for change. Each graduate takes with him or her a spiritual as well as an intellectual standard. They return to their families and communities with the determination to live out their faith and carry it forward to future generations.

In the tribal traditions of both the Mohawk and the Lakota, the elders have always passed on wisdom to those in leadership positions and charged them with the responsibility to base their actions and decisions on the well-being of the next seven generations.

Connie Tsosie is an example of passing on a model of excellence to the next generation. Connie graduated from AIC in 1995 with a BA in education and is a teacher on a Navajo reservation in the community of Shonto, Arizona. Since leaving AIC she has also completed her master's degree in education and at present is en route to a doctorate. Her daughters, Crystal and Cheryl, both followed her example and graduated from AIC. Both became teachers, Crystal on the Salt River reservation near Phoenix and Cheryl in her home community of Shonto in northern Arizona on the Navajo reservation. Less than three years after graduating from AIC, Crystal has already completed her master's degree in education at Grand Canyon University in Phoenix, Arizona!

After five decades of serving the American Indian community, AIC is ready for the next generation! AIC is a role model for change. I'm proud to be a canoe builder, serving as a member of the Board of Regents of American Indian College.

NOTES

1 J. E. Dempsey, *Native American Leadership Training in the Assemblies of God in Readings in Native American Missions,* J.E. Dempsey, ed., (Phoenix, Arizona: 1992): 38.

2 See Alisa F. Cunningham and Kenneth E. Redd, *Creating Role Models for Change, A Survey of Tribal College Graduates,* May 2000. Prepared by the American Indian Higher Education Consortium (AIHEC). (ERIC Document Reproduction Service No. ED 456 947). Available at: http://eric.ed.gov/ERICDOCS/data/ericdocs2/content_storage_01/0000000b/80/0d/79/38.pdf (accessed 10/20/2006).

Vice President David DeGarmo and President Jim Comer with
AIC 2005 Alumna of the Year, Connie Tsosie, with daughters Crystal and Cheryl Grass

AIC Board Meeting, Fall 2005

Rodger and Esther Cree

left: William Fragua; right: Rodger Cree

Rodger Cree praying for Carolyn D. Baker at her ordination

1988 Seniors: Front to Back - Rosie Lee, Arlene Hinton, Linda Dempsey(Senior Advisor), Renada Gooday, Gloria (Pechuli) Smith, Donna Shendo, Warren Matson, Doreen (Smiley) Baki, Pete Cordova, Roy Stewart

RODGER A. CREE, SR.

(Mohawk) Pastor, Morgan Assembly of God, Gresham, Wisconsin

My wife, Esther, and I had been married only three years in the summer of 1958, and we were just starting our ministry in Kanewake, Quebec, Canada, when we were made aware of a World Pentecostal Conference to be held in Toronto, Ontario at the National Exhibition of Canada. Esther and I wanted to be a part of this great gathering composed of Pentecostal leaders from around the world. However, for us to attend this conference would be a financial struggle; nonetheless, we felt that it was so important—God was in it, and we would be blessed if we could make it there. It was an inspiring gathering of Pentecostal leaders from many nations around the world. However, we were struck by the total lack of any Native ministers at the conference except for us!

The marked absence of other Indian leaders at this gathering confirmed to us that indeed Native ministers were few and far between. Over six previous years of traveling and reaching many Native communities, I had sadly observed that this was indeed the case. In the crowd was a seemingly frail Anglo woman to whom we were providentially introduced. Her name was Alta Washburn, and she had started an Indian Bible school in Phoenix, Arizona, just a year earlier. Also, I should mention that her "frail" appearance failed to suppress an irrepressible call and indomitable spirit to serve the Lord as a missionary among the Indians of the southwestern United States. Looks *can* be deceiving.

In the conversation that followed with Sister Washburn, Esther and I both sensed that she was indeed a visionary pioneer in uncharted and even controversial territory—that of "raising up" indigenous Native pastors. It was so touching and yet hard to believe that anyone else cared about Native people like we did— but her call to Native ministry was clearly confirmed in our spirits. It was also clear to Esther and me that she saw great value in the people she was called to minister to. Her vision was not only to reach Native Americans with the gospel, but also to equip them to reach their own people—an integral component of the indigenous principle propagated throughout the apostolic era, especially by the great apostle Paul. (Little did I know at that meeting that our paths would cross again in just over a year's time.) This providential meeting left my wife and I amazed at the fact that God had not forgotten His people, but indeed was "raising up" others with the same burden for Indians that we had.

At the conclusion of this large convention we returned, greatly encouraged, to the church we served on the Mohawk Reserve to resume our pastoral ministry. During the summer of 1959 we scheduled a tent meeting with David Wilkerson—who would later distinguish himself as the author of the Christian best-seller *The Cross and the Switchblade* and also as founder of Teen Challenge, arguably the most successful substance abuse rehabilitation program in history— as our speaker. At that time he was pastoring a small church in Phillipsburg, Pennsylvania. The day before the camp meeting was to start I received a telegram from Brother Wilkerson, informing me that his doctor had ordered him to go away for a complete rest and that he would be unable to preach our services. I had no idea what to do and went to bed early that night very discouraged.

Shortly after I was in bed, Esther called me from downstairs and asked me to come down and speak with a minister who had unexpectedly come to the door, having come all the way from Arizona to hear Brother Wilkerson speak the next day. What is so amazing about his unexpected arrival was that he even found our home in this small Native community of three to four thousand Mohawks. There were no street signs; we had no telephone, no running water or bathroom. But God knew where we were and led him to us! When I came down the stairs to greet the preacher I was surprised to find a "Pima giant," who introduced himself as Leslie Sampson. He was one of the first preachers to be called and equipped under Sister Washburn's vision and ministry to the Pima Indians. I asked Brother Sampson if he would be willing to preach our tent meeting, and he readily agreed to do so. He had a beat-up old guitar, but he was able to play "sweet notes" that brought glory to God and ministered to the hearts of those gathered for the tent meeting services.

Brother Leslie Sampson was truly an answer to our prayers. Just before arriving in our village, Leslie had been traveling with Sister Washburn and a group of students around the northeastern United States raising money for the All Tribes Indian Bible School, and through the *Pentecostal Evangel* they had read about our meeting with David Wilkerson, and Brother Sampson alone had taken the bus to reach our town. People were saved in those meetings, and even though it was a predominantly Catholic community, people were touched by the full gospel messages. The Mohawks felt a kinship with this fellow Native from the Southwest.

Due to severe illness, less than a year later I was told that if I wished to preserve my health we must move to a warmer climate. My wife and I and our two small children packed up our few belongings and the scant savings we had accumulated and headed for Arizona, little knowing what we would face when we reached this "strange land." When we finally arrived in Phoenix, Arizona, we went immediately to the All Tribes Indian Bible School. Not until we arrived there did we truly become aware of the full magnitude of what this one woman and her willingness to serve had been able to accomplish. Sister Washburn had been instrumental in planting and starting churches throughout the greater Phoenix area, including local reservation communities located at San Tan, Casa Blanca, Salt River, Guadalupe, Laveen, as well as All Tribes Assembly of God in downtown Phoenix.

Sister Washburn graciously took us in, fed us, and gave us a place to stay until we were able to get established as pastors at a Papago church in Sells, Arizona. During this time we met the remainder of the Sampson family, including Leslie's brother Virgil, who was also a preacher. The church that we went to pastor had been through a very difficult period prior to our arrival, and these two dear men were instrumental in helping us to make this transition less painful.

It was at this point that we became convinced that the Papago people (now known as the Tohono O'odham Nation) needed to be involved in a meaningful way in evangelizing. We saw a number of young people from our church enroll at the All Tribes Indian Bible School for training. We then decided to set aside Thanksgiving as a time to invite the whole school to celebrate with our church for a huge feast! This meal included at least fifty pies that my wife would bake and no less than five turkeys—not to mention countless tortillas cooked by the ladies of the church for all to share. We also collected the most generous offering of the year to give to the school, since this was a very special time for the students. They all looked forward to this holiday celebration each year and would attend the celebration before going to their homes for the holiday. This yearly celebration resulted in people being saved, and even now there are those still serving the Lord from that wonderful era.

After that time in Sells, Arizona, and over the years of our ministry, we were privileged to remain connected with ATBS (including through its various name changes). One role I fulfilled was by serving on the school's board of directors (now board of regents). During this time I was blessed to serve with such brethren as Richard W. DuBose, T. Ray Rachels, Charles E. Lee (Navajo), William Lee (Navajo), and Robert A. Sites. These godly men impressed me by their dedication to expanding the gospel ministry with not only their time and prayer—but also their finances. When difficult problems arose in developing the college, they never failed to come up with practical ways to develop the campus and select needed faculty members. These important decisions were bathed in much prayer as the board worked to understand and bridge our individual Native cultural differences. As a result, I could clearly see each individual board member fitting into God's perfect plan for the college.

Over the years we continued to support the school financially and to send students to study there. I spoke at a commencement service, and even served as campus pastor for two years during the presidential tenure of David J. Moore, who when asked to serve as president of the school agreed on the condition that I would come to serve in that particular capacity. I served in that role from 1987–1989, while continuing to pastor on the Salt River Indian Reservation, serving concurrently as sectional presbyter of the Metro Indian Section. The college is so vitally important that I knew that my service there in tandem with my pastoral ministry would have eternal implications. At the Bible college we were so blessed to meet such faithful servants as Joe and Betty Hanna, Jim and Belinda Lopez, Nadine Waldrop, and Alma Thomas. We also met many precious Native students during this time. Several that I had the joy of mentoring at the beginnings of their ministry are Joel and Sharon Cornelius, Albert and Donna Nez, and Marvin and Delia Begay. I'm proud to say that they all remain active in the Lord's work to this very day.

One special memory that I fondly recall is when Marvin Begay (Navajo) was coming from New Mexico to serve as our youth pastor in Washington State—sometime after we had moved from Arizona. His Jimmy broke down in Moab, Utah, so he called his parents, and they drove up to Moab and towed it back home. In spite of this set back, Marvin determinedly boarded the bus and came all the way to our church in Taholah, Washington, which served the Quinault Indians, to become our youth pastor. I knew then that there was resoluteness about this young man—a product of AIC—that testified to his faith in God's plan for his future and that of Native ministry. Today, Pastor Marvin, along with his lovely wife, Delia, and their daughter, Autumn Skye, serves successfully as senior pastor at Canyon Day AG on the White Mountain Apache reservation. He is now an AIC board member, also serving as the national youth representative for the Native American Fellowship (NAF) of the Assemblies of God. In addition to serving as a school teacher and worship leader in their church, his wife, Delia, has served for the past few years on the steering committee for the National Native Women's Conference held at American Indian College under the direction of Belinda F. Lopez.

My prayer for the future of the college is that AIC will always have a Pentecostal environment that fosters faith and Spirit-empowered leadership towards Native people so that like Sister Alta Washburn, AIC will continue to develop Native American leadership who can realize their God-given purpose and potential to reach the lost and forgotten people of Native America.

Attendees at the dedication of the new campus

Charles W. H. Scott

The AIBI choir sang at the dedication at the site of the new campus.

Gannon Dormitory Dedication, 1983
Curtis Ringness, Robert A. Sites, Glen Miller, Joe Hanna, Fred Cottriel, Mrs. T. E. Gannon, Robert Pirtle, W.E. Cummings, Carl Collins, T. C. Cunningham

CURTIS W. RINGNESS

Honorary Board of Regents Member
Former National Secretary of Home Missions of the General Council of the Assemblies of God

For some forty years I have been associated with the American Indian College both as an active board member and in more recent years as an honorary member. My initial interest in Native American ministry occurred when Fred Vogler, then assistant general superintendent of the Assemblies of God, introduced Charles E. Lee, a Navajo Indian, to the brethren serving on the General Presbytery. Lee was a student at Central Bible Institute (now Central Bible College) in Springfield, Missouri in the late 1940s and early 1950s. Charlie Lee made quite an impression on the General Presbytery as he expressed to them his desire to minister to his people and to see them properly trained and equipped for ministry.

At that time I was serving as pastor of Bethel Temple in Tampa, Florida, while concurrently serving as assistant district superintendent, a position which included the portfolio of district home missions director. During the course of our friendship, Charlie Lee inspired me to consider the spiritual needs of the Seminole Indians living in and near the Everglades located in south Florida. A member of our church (with Seminole Indian blood lines) had moved to Florida from Oklahoma. She and her husband, a businessman, were ready to invest their time and resources to establish the first Assemblies of God mission to the Seminole Indians with backing of the AG church in Copeland, Florida, which was a small community in the Everglades.

Soon thereafter I was called upon to serve at our General Council headquarters in Springfield, Missouri. Along with a host of other responsibilities, I was appointed as the national secretary of the Home Missions Department, which included administrative oversight of the AG work among American Indians. Being involved with our missionaries, as well as Native American ministers and lay people, was a most exciting, heart-warming, and rewarding ministry. One of our primary areas of focus was the establishment of Bible institutes and colleges to serve the Native American constituency. Over the years, these institutions have proven invaluable in developing a core of indigenous leadership throughout our fellowship.

The American Indian College in Phoenix, Arizona, is now a nationally recognized institution holding regional accreditation. This has come about due to the vision and willingness to venture out by dedicated leaders, along with the sacrifices and the godly love and respect of our clergy and laity alike, towards Native Americans. Missionaries such as Alta M. Washburn, Don Ramsey, Carl Collins, and many others laid a foundation for future generations of Native leadership. Subsequently, outstanding Native leaders such as Simon Peter (Choctaw), Jim Lopez (Cocopah/Hispanic), and Charles E. Lee (Navajo) built upon that foundation, strengthening it greatly. I am also grateful that the Arizona district along with numbers of other sponsoring districts has provided gifted leadership and resources to assist the college over the years in its growth and development.

In retrospect, AIC has experienced many miracles of provision through God's providence. In fact, the acquisition of the north Phoenix property upon which the campus is presently located is one of the greatest miracles of provision that I have had the privilege of witnessing. I feel truly blessed by the Lord to have had a role in seeing that miracle come to pass.

In 1941 my wife and I conducted evangelistic services in Tulsa, Oklahoma, for Pastor Morrison (a man whose first name I can no longer recall). Many years later, for health reasons, Rev. Morrison relocated to Phoenix, Arizona, and at that time was involved in part-time ministry as well as his real estate business. It was at that time that we became reacquainted, and knowing of the school's interest in finding a property for the campus, he located a beautiful acreage on the north side of town owned by a widow. Parenthetically, I should mention that by the early 1970s the Bible school had outgrown the property on East Washington Street and needed to move to a location more conducive to serving the educational and spiritual needs of a growing student body. Rev. Morrison initiated negotiations with the property owner and presented a purchase proposal to (then) AIBI's board of directors. The board visited the property, were favorably impressed, and reconvened to consider the sales proposition. However, in my viewpoint—and one that was shared by others—the offer seemed too good to be true. At that time finances were a major concern for the Bible school. Also, the Arizona district seemed especially cautious about incurring any additional indebtedness that it felt AIBI couldn't handle.

Recognizing the enormous financial challenge before us, the Lord laid it upon my heart to say that the Home Missions Department and the Executive Presbytery would be asked to come up with 50% of the purchase price and that every effort would be made to raise the finances. Privately, I had resolved to the Lord to do everything I could to assume personal responsibility for raising that portion of the real estate price.

Not long afterwards, I was a speaker at a missions convention at the historic Glad Tidings Tabernacle in New York City. That night as I addressed the service, I prefaced my message by mentioning the possibility of American Indian Bible Institute acquiring this urgently needed piece of property. The very next morning I received a call at my hotel room from an elderly woman who had served the church's co-pastors Robert and Marie Brown as personal secretary for many years. She told me that she had inherited a sizeable sum of money just a few days prior and that the Lord had impressed upon her to make a donation towards the Indian school property. The amount that she gave came to 50% of the property's cost—exactly the amount I had committed myself to raise on behalf of the Home Missions Department and Executive Presbytery! Needless to say, I was overjoyed! Yes, this is just one example of many that has blessed our school. God is good!

In conclusion, the progress of the Bible college, both spiritually and academically, through the years, along with the process of gaining accreditation, which began during the tenure of President Carl Collins, has been invaluable. My prayer is that we will soon see an enrollment of 200 American Indian students each year at the college.

Left to right: Mark Chief, Adrienne Bowechop, Lenora (Shorty) Holgate, Genita Yazzie, Delia (Orduno) Begay

Marvin, Delia, and Autumn Skye Begay

Alma Thomas and Delia (Orduno) Begay

Marvin Begay washing the feet of Marco Burnette in a chapel service

1992-1993 ASB Officers:
Arcenio Charleston, Bobbie Hunter, & Marvin Begay

MARVIN B. BEGAY

(Navajo) Pastor, Canyon Day Assembly of God, Canyon Day, Arizona

My name is Marvin Bryant Begay, and I was born in a small community called Brother in Christ Mission, New Mexico, located about forty miles southeast of Farmington. I am a full-blooded Navajo and enrolled tribal member. I am also a 1994 graduate of American Indian College and now a board of regents member, who has the privilege of giving back to a school that I have loved for many years.

To give you some background on my life, I need to mention that I wasn't raised in church as a child—in fact I can only remember attending church about one time when we were living out in Los Angeles. In the mid-1970s, when I was about seven or eight years old, we moved back to New Mexico. My mom's side of the family are committed Christians—very dedicated to serving the Lord Jesus Christ. My Pentecostal grandparents strongly influenced my mom with their faith, and in time she gave her life to Jesus. I also have two older sisters. My middle sister received Christ, so when she and my mom started attending church, I started tagging along when I was thirteen years old. At about fifteen years of age I accepted the Lord and was baptized in the Holy Spirit shortly afterwards. Since then, the Lord has really changed my life, and I've always felt the call of God upon my life to preach the Word, and that's what led me to American Indian College.

It was an interesting series of events that brought me to AIC, beginning with the fact that the independent Pentecostal church I was attending at the time underwent some internal difficulties, and some people left our fellowship. Those of us who remained decided to affiliate with the Assemblies of God after we met with Rev. William Lee, a Navajo AG minister from Albuquerque, New Mexico, who counseled us on how to become part of a denominational structure that would serve our church's needs.

One Sunday a group from (then) AIBC under the direction of Rev. Charley Odell (who now serves the Arizona District Council of the Assemblies of God in coordinating Native church building projects) came out to our church in Carson, New Mexico, and ministered through song, testimony, and preaching. I was very impressed by young Native American men and women who had a passion for serving Christ, knew the Word of God, and were confident in their speaking. I was especially pleased to see the young men; as I was growing up in church I saw mostly women and girls but very few men serving God. As a result I was very impressed, and we made plans to go to the school for the college days in November 1988.

Before that time I had never visited Phoenix very much, but it was a good opportunity and we attended the college days. I can still remember sitting in the back of the chapel service—where there was close to 140 Native young people with their hands raised worshipping the Lord—and thinking, "God this is so amazing to see all these Native Americans worshipping you!" That's when I first thought that I would really like to come and be a part of this College. We sat through some classes and got involved in the whole weekend, had fun and fellowshipped, and saw the Lord do some incredible things. After that we returned home, where I prayed and was really excited about the possibility of coming here.

In February 1989, just a few short months later, I returned to the campus to attend the Convocation of Christian Indian Leaders and got another exposure to the school's culture and was very impressed with the quality of the Native American speakers, who demonstrated that it was possible for Native people to activate the gifts and callings within themselves to serve the Lord and reach their people for Christ. While I was at the convocation I also went down to the gymnasium, to the Native youth gathering that was going as part of the activities, and got to hear an anointed evangelist by the name of Alvin "Dobie" Weasel, an Assiniboine Indian who most recently has served as the pastor of a very large multicultural church in Omaha, Nebraska.

As Pastor Dobie was preaching to the gymnasium full of

Native youth, he challenged us by saying, "If you're a Christian, you ought to attend at least a year or so of Bible college before you go anywhere else to get a strong foundation in God's Word." He further challenged us to attend this college and to come down to the basketball court to publicly declare our willingness to do so. At that point I felt that God was really speaking to my heart to attend AIC.

Walking down from the bleachers, I was joined by about fifty other Native youth, and as I stood there on the court I looked down and saw the warrior emblem that is AIC's symbol, and I started to worry about whether or not I could really be a successful college student since I wasn't a very good student in high school. But I knew that this was what God had called me to do, and I was determined to make it!

As a young Christian man I really desired to have godly male role models to draw from. I have been blessed to have a wonderful father I love dearly, but additionally I longed for other spiritual role models who could show me what it meant to be godly Native American man and pour into me. Although I had godly female role models, including a woman pastor—for which I thank God—I really longed for a godly male role model because I had not really had one during my teen years.

When I first came to AIC I finally had my prayer answered when I met Rev. Jim Lopez, who was the dean of students, and later served as the college's president for over six years. I was amazed at his leadership ability, how he had lots of confidence in himself, and how he conducted himself and loved his wife and family. Brother Lopez didn't just say it, but he demonstrated it before the whole school—and outside the school as well. I had never really seen anyone exemplify his great love for his family in that way before, and I wanted that in my own life because one day I would be married and have a family as well.

One day I was undergoing some personal struggles, and I needed someone to talk to. By this time it was after six o'clock in the evening, and I saw Brother Lopez coming out of his office looking very tired after having worked a long day. Waving him over, I told him, "I've got to talk to somebody." Despite his evident fatigue, Brother Lopez replied, "Hey, let's go and talk." So we drove over to a nearby park and for about two hours I really just poured out my heart to him, and he prayed and really listened to me. I clearly remember this because Brother Lopez had worked a full day, was tired and ready to go home, but yet he took another two hours to pour into my life—that says a lot! With God's help, Brother Lopez went the extra mile for me, and I'll never forget that.

When I think back on other powerful experiences in my life I remember when we had Sunday night services and prayer times on campus. We had student preachers during those special times, and afterwards we'd hit those altars just weeping and praying. The one thing that I always looked forward to was the time of prayer, and after the services, I just wanted to get down to those altars and pray, lingering in the presence of God—sometimes for two hours afterwards, as the Holy Spirit ministered to us. Those times really changed and impacted my life.

In addition to the mentoring and special prayer times, the Lord provided a third real blessing to me—my lovely wife, Delia! I met Delia Orduno, a Yaqui Indian from Tucson, Arizona, here at the college, and one of the first things I noticed about her was she was kind of silly, but I also quickly realized that she loved the Lord with all of her heart and that she was the same person at all times: she never changed! Some people may be one way at church, one way outside church, and another way at home—but not Delia. She was always the same, and that really impressed me. She genuinely loved people; there was never any show. She didn't care if they were dirty or clean, rich or poor; she loved them completely. I'll never forget that she once told me, "The ground is level at the foot of the cross. We're all the same in the eyes of God." I'll never forget when she said that. She's always up front with people; if she sees something in your life that needs correction, she'll tell you—but in a loving way. You need people like her in your life to make you a better person.

I truly believe I am a better person today because of my wife, Delia, because she speaks straight to me in love, wanting me to be a better person and seeing the potential in others and me. Delia and I have now been married for ten years, and we've been blessed with a beautiful little girl, Autumn Skye, as well as privileged to pastor an awesome church at Canyon Day, Arizona, on the White Mountain Apache Reservation.

Over the years, I've really come to appreciate AIC and all it stands for—especially looking back to that time when I was standing on the basketball court and I wondered whether or not I could make the grade as a college student. Sometimes we may doubt ourselves, but the Lord sees the potential in us. When I came here I really needed the Lord to help me gain confidence in my calling to the ministry. It was great to be in a nurturing environment, where the faculty, staff, and administrators cared about you and loved Native people—an environment of great encouragement.

For me, AIC was like a greenhouse, where I received lots of love and encouragement so that I could grow and mature into my calling. Instead of people saying, "You can't do it! You can't do it!" I was blessed to hear instead, "You can do it! You can do it!" That's really changed my attitude and how I viewed myself, because I now realize that I am special to the Lord and that He can use me and mold me into what He wants me to be. Several years after graduating from AIC, I went on to Arizona State University and earned my post-baccalaureate certification in teacher education— something I would not have had the confidence to do if I hadn't come to AIC first.

Over the past thirteen years since graduating from AIC, I've studied the Bible, prayed, received my ministerial license and ordination with the Assemblies of God, and I've been changed through the power of the Holy Spirit. Moreover, God has taken me to different places and allowed me to flow in different areas of leadership that I probably wouldn't have thought that I was capable of doing.

Today I am a member of the board of regents here at the college, and I really enjoy it, because as one person once told me, "If you hang around with the giants, you will become a giant." So I sit here with some of these powerful and influential men and women of God who are leaders within our fellowship. I'm very encouraged to sit and listen to these folks because as a Native leader I want to see our own people arise and make a huge impact in Native communities. I also believe that the day is coming when we will see even greater leadership among our Native people.

I want to see Native churches that grow in attendance way beyond fifty people and to see some of our Native churches grow up into the hundreds in membership, that's one of the things that I desire as a pastor. My vision is to see our church, Canyon Day AG become one of the largest Native churches in the country. After all, there's nothing too difficult for God. But I believe that the key to successful growth and maturation in our churches comes out of leadership development. We're excited to be averaging around 140 people on Sunday mornings, which is well above average for a Native church, and we're also very pleased to have three of our youth from the church attending AIC—and we hope to send more! Although many of our young people could gain admission to a university, I still believe that many of them will benefit from going to AIC just as I benefited from being here.

AIC is a great resource to Native people, with talented faculty, staff, and administrators. One thing that I'd like to see is our Native churches begin to really send their students to our College. When I came to this College we had close to 130 students enrolled, but unfortunately there are not as many today. In the AG we have 190 Native churches[1] and if each one of them averaged sending one student to AIC every year we could have over 800 students here in just a short time. We need more pastors, youth pastors, and children's pastors to serve our Native churches— something I'm well aware of because of my work as both a pastor and as the National Native Youth Director for the Native American Fellowship of the AG. But we also need schoolteachers and business people to lay a foundation for strong lay leadership as well to strengthen our churches by helping them to become self-supporting. I'm very grateful that I'm financially supported by my church and don't have to work on the outside—I'm free to devote all of my energies to Canyon Day AG, and I wish this for all of our Native churches.

My prayer is that more and more strong Native leadership will continue to come out of this school in the years to come!

Front Row: Joseph J. Saggio, Betty Hanna, Alma Thomas Back Row: J.R. Boyd, Mia Boyd, Billie Fox,

Guys having fun: Front: Denis Billy, Troy Beedle, Daniel Fuller, Back: Gordon Bowechop and Philson Benally

Front to back: J.R. Boyd, Kristen (Billy) Williams, Marvin Begay, Aaron Williams

NOTES

1 This most recent figure provided by Rev. John E. Maracle (Mohawk, Wolf Clan), President of the Native American Fellowship of the AG and General Council Executive Presbytier for Ethnic Fellowships.

The first published account of the early history of American Indian Bible College, this account covers the early years from 1957-1984 and is written by Pauline Dunn, who along with her husband, Glen, were long-time missionaries, first to China, then later to the American Indians. Like Alta Washburn's autobiography, Pauline Dunn's work has been long out of print and very difficult to obtain. However, unlike *Trail to the Tribes* by Alta M. Washburn, *A Trail of Beauty: A Short History of American Indian Bible College* focuses exclusively on the history of the Bible college and does not provide extensive background on Rev. Washburn's early ministry prior to coming to Phoenix.

From an archival standpoint, this work is a valuable account that captures some of the early history of (then) American Indian Bible College, showing the tenacity of many early key actors, including its early presidents: Alta M. Washburn, Don Ramsey, Simon Peter, and Carl Collins. This second "book within a book" is preceded by a specially written introduction that provides some background on Glen and Pauline Dunn, who after a lifetime of service as missionaries in the Far East saw fit to continue in a new calling: equipping Native Americans for service as pastors, evangelists, and church leaders to their own people as well as wherever the Lord directed.

Just as in *Trail to the Tribes*, in order to preserve as much as possible the original content and flavor of this work, the editors have chosen to do minimal editing, once again realizing that the reader may notice that some terminology is dated and perhaps offensive by contemporary standards.

PART THREE ▲▲▲

A Trail of Beauty

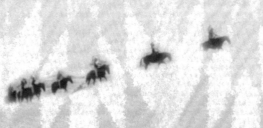

Introduction to A Trail of Beauty
Joseph J. Saggio

A Trail of Beauty:
A Short History of American Indian Bible College
Pauline Dunn

Marlene (Yazzie) Vallo

Irving Terry, with daughter, Denise, and wife, Carolyn

Tribalaires Summer Tour Group, 1976. Left to right: Becky (Peter) Good, Charlene (Kirk) Harris, Janice (Davis) Tsosie, Lloyd Lee, Adolf Cota, Patricia (Kirk) Stephens, Elizabeth (Maytubby) Lee, Sissie Stafford

Go Warriors!

JoeAnn Caudle and Joe Saggio praying for President Duane and Ruth Collins, 1998

Introduction to
A TRAIL of BEAUTY

Introduction by Joseph J. Saggio

Over the years, this school has been blessed by the talented services of dedicated and gifted personnel, not the least of which were veteran missionaries Glen and Pauline Dunn, who served at AIBC from 1978–1984 as faculty members, bringing to the Bible college their rich background of forty-three years of successful ministry on the foreign mission fields of the Philippines and China. During their service abroad they served as evangelists, founding and establishing two Bible schools. Pauline Dunn, who served as a tutor, instructor, and yearbook sponsor for AIBC, was the author of *A Trail of Beauty: A Short History of American Indian Bible College*, originally published in 1984 during the presidential tenure of Carl Collins. This was the first complete chronicle of the Bible college's history published by AIBC. Prior to their foreign missions work in the Far East, Pauline Dunn served as the North Texas district director for W.M.C.'s[1], Missionettes[2], and Sunday School. During their time as missionaries overseas she was a contributor to the *Pentecostal Evangel*, occasionally publishing reports of the victories and challenges they encountered in their missions work in the Far East.

Brother and Sister Dunn received their diplomas from (then) Southwestern AG Bible College in Waxahachie, Texas. Brother Dunn went on to earn a BS degree from Texas Christian University in education, as well as a master's degree from the University of Texas. He also completed additional studies at the South China

Language Institute and the University of California–Berkeley. Sister Dunn also pursued additional studies at Howard Payne College (Texas), Texas Christian University, and the University of California–Berkeley.

While serving as missionaries in China in the 1930s they preached regularly in Hong Kong, which required them to travel over one hundred miles by train or river boat to reach their destination from their home base.[3] At times missionary life was very challenging for the Dunns. During their sojourn in China they saw many hardships, including a great famine that struck the southern province of Kwangsi in 1946. Pauline Dunn reported:

> There was a terrible famine in this section last April and May. People had to sell their children as there was not enough to feed them. Even then, thousands in this and the adjoining country starved to death.[4]

Although they encountered many challenges in their overseas ministry—including Sister Dunn contracting malaria—they had many victories and successes. In 1947, soon after the famine account, Pauline reported:

> To get to Lei Clung for our next revival, we took a tiny two-wheeled cart drawn by a little horse for eight miles. We walked the next thirteen miles into the mountains: Mr. Dunn and Mr. Ngai rode their bicycles. They had to push and carry them over the steepest slope of 572 stone steps. The Lei Chung work is new. They have never had a preacher, and this was their first revival. Someone heard the gospel in Paat Po and went home to tell their family and friends. Soon the good news spread until now there are about thirty Christians who have been baptized in water. More than ten were saved while we were there.[5]

After spending a number of years in overseas ministry the Dunns found a new niche at AIBC. Although Brother Dunn had had extensive administrative experience running Bible schools in the past, he indicated that his desire was to spend time in the classroom, working directly with students as a Bible teacher. The Dunns served the college from 1978-1984. Bringing the richness of their overseas missionary experience, they were able to add a wider scope of understanding of missions work for the students at the Bible college. Longtime AIC faculty member Betty J. Hanna remembers Brother Dunn as "an excellent teacher—an intellectual with a great background in Bible schools."[6] Alma Thomas also fondly remembers that he was an avid chess player and had an ongoing chess game, which lasted through many lunch hours with then Vice President Don Keeter.[7]

As you read through the account that Sister Dunn carefully compiled about the school's history from 1957–1984, you will no doubt recognize that she had a great love and appreciation for AIBC, including its leadership, faculty, students, and, perhaps most importantly, its mission to train Native leadership in order to develop indigenous church leaders. Her carefully crafted historical account manages both to chronicle the Bible college's first twenty-seven years of history as well as inspire the reader, for she details many of the challenges, miracles, and victories during that portion of the school's history. Her optimistic vantage point—as well as her sense of humor—clearly comes through. The reader will find this a helpful follow-up to Alta Washburn's memoirs—even though it was actually written earlier—since it goes into detail about events after the Washburns had left the school to resume pastoral ministry. As a historical record of some of the early players in the school's history it is an invaluable work.

Although both Brother and Sister Dunn are now with the Lord, longtime members of the AIC community still fondly remember them. After they retired from a lifetime of active ministry they moved to their cabin on the Arizona district campgrounds in Prescott, where they spent their final years. Remembering Pauline's sunny disposition, Betty Hanna remarked, "She was an optimist. When she walked in, the room brightened up—she always had a smile. She was one of the sweetest and most caring individuals I have ever met."[8] Retired faculty member Alma Thomas remembers her as being loved by everybody.[9]

While they were only with AIBC for a few short years, the Dunns left a wonderful legacy that continues to this day. Although they were at retirement age when they came and could have rested from their fruitful labors as foreign missionaries, they chose to serve at AIBC as home missionaries because they knew that God still had more wonderful ministry challenges ahead for them in the desert Southwest. During their six years here they served joyfully and faithfully, bringing a dedication to excellence to the tasks they were called to. Moreover, it can truly be said that Glen and Pauline Dunn did their part in contributing to the college's legacy of "a trail of beauty."

NOTES

1 At that time W.M.C. stood for Women's Missionary Council, the original name chosen in 1925 by Etta Calhoun, the founder of what we now refer to as Women's Ministries. In 1975 the Assemblies of God officially changed that designation to the current Women's Ministries.

2 Since March 2007, Missionettes is now known as National Girls Ministries.

3 Pauline Dunn, "Brief Notes from Far and Away," *Pentecostal Evangel* No. 1196 (April 10, 1937): 9.

4 Pauline Dunn, "Chinese Grateful for Relief Clothing," *Pentecostal Evangel* No. 1722 (May 10, 1947): 9.

5 Pauline Dunn, "Revivals in China," *Pentecostal Evangel* No. 1736 (August 16, 1947): 9.

6 Betty J. Hanna, personal interview, April 12, 2007.

7 Alma F. Thomas, telephone interview, April 14, 2007.

8 Betty J. Hanna, ibid.

9 Alma F. Thomas, ibid.

A Trail of Beauty:

A Short History of American Indian Bible College

Pauline Dunn

"Let the beauty of the

Lord our God be upon us:

and . . . the work of our hands

establish thou it."

—Psalm 90:17, KJV

1966 Board of Directors. Front: T. C. Cunningham, Raymond Hudson, Charles Scott, J. K. Gressett Back: W. E. Cummings, O. W. Killingsworth, Carl Holleman, V. L. Hertweck, Vernon Shores (not pictured)

J.K. Gressett praying for 1968 graduates

PROLOGUE

When the founder started out on the trail of a Bible school for American Indians twenty-seven years ago, little did she and the early staff realize where the trail would lead. The trail's beauty? Not AIBC's modern facilities, but the fulfillment of the school's mission.

Along the trail one will find graduates in remote preaching points, modern churches, and various evangelical related ministries. The trail winds through barren deserts, red rock canyons, rugged terrain, and tall ponderosa forests—never ending, always extending to new horizons.

The trail will continue on and on until the day of the Great Gathering Feast, when all those along the trail will give honor to the Great Chief Jesus Christ.

Carl E. Collins, President
American Indian Bible College
1984

THE TRAIL BEGINS
Alta Washburn, Founder–President, 1957–1965

TRAIL TO THE APACHES

Drums! The eerie chant of a medicine man! The new missionaries awakened and peered from their trailer windows. Across the clearing a campfire blazed. Men with painted bodies and grotesque headdresses leaped and danced around a dying woman laid on a blanket beside the fire. Hour after hour. For three days and nights. Then suddenly the Apache "healing sing" stopped. Stillness settled over the pine-covered hills.

The woman was dead.

Alta and Clarence Washburn had just spent their first three nights as missionaries. They arrived at the San Carlos Apache Indian Reservation in October 1947.

As an unsaved young mother on her deathbed, Alta Washburn had been granted a vision of hell and of heaven. During the vision she received forgiveness of her sins, healing of her body, and a call to preach. Beginning immediately, she held evangelistic meetings in the North and East and pastored churches in Ohio.

In the 1930s, Ernest and Ethel Marshall pioneered the first Assemblies of God mission to the Indians of Arizona. They invited Alta to come and evangelize the Apache Indians.

The Washburn family—Alta and Clarence, son, Thomas, and wife, Vida, and 10-year-old son Floyd—moved to Arizona in the fall of 1947. The ceremonial Apache "sing" for the sick woman introduced them to Indian life.

As pastor of the thriving San Carlos Apache Assembly of God, Alta preached on "The Right and Wrong Trails to Heaven": "Some of you are on a trail like the Salt River Canyon Road. It's steep. It's dangerous. It leads to death. It's the wrong trail."

The slender, dark-haired missionary punched out her sermon like a prize fighter: every sentence like a physical blow.

"God's trail is straight. On it there's deliverance from your drunkenness. There's forgiveness for your sins. God's trail leads to heaven."

The big Apache cowboy interpreter began to weep. "I've been on the wrong trail all my life," he said. That day the Indian cowboy found Christ, the true Way. Today, members of his family to the fifth generation travel the heavenly trail.

TO ALL TRIBES

AIta Washburn remembers, "We found the whole state full of Indian people, waiting to hear the gospel that sets men free. God gave me a vision for all tribes."

From San Carlos, the Washburns moved to Phoenix. Besides the desert Indians on nearby reservations, thousands of Indians from many tribes were attracted to Phoenix by the Indian Hospital, Phoenix Indian High School, job training, and work opportunities.

Pastor Claude Wood and First Assembly of God encouraged the Washburns to bring new Indian friends to the church.

Easter Sunday afternoon 1948, a happy crowd met in First Assembly's education building. They celebrated the first public service of Phoenix All Tribes Assembly of God.

While Alta pastored the congregation, Clarence worked to support his family and helped with the ministry to the Indian people.

A young Pima girl accepted the Lord and was healed in the Indian Hospital. She and her mother led workers to their own Salt River Indian Reservation.

"Let's not knock on this door," said the girl to the worker with her.

"Why not?"

"Mrs. Sampson lives here. She's got a lot of big boys and they're always drunk. I'm afraid of them."

"We'll knock and see."

Mrs. Sampson opened the door and accepted some literature. Through VBS, Sunday afternoon services under a ramada on the reservation, and trips to All Tribes Assembly, Mrs. Sampson and her large family were won to the Lord.

Meanwhile, Supterintendent J. K. Gressett negotiated for an empty church building. "That building was dedicated to the Lord," he said to the owners.

"The lodge that's offering you twice as much as the Indian church can pay will use it for bingo and dances. You'd rather it were used for the Lord, wouldn't you?"

Soon All Tribes Assembly moved into its own building on East Washington, bought at half price. People from Salt River, Gila River, and Maricopa Indian Reservations crowded into the church. Indians came from Guadalupe, a Yaqui settlement.

Alta Washburn started training classes to help Indian youth spread the good news to their own tribes.

About this time, friends helped send two of the Sampson brothers to Southwestern Bible Institute in Waxahachie, Texas. But the food was different. The culture was different. The young Native Americans felt like foreigners in their own land.

One of the Sampson brothers stayed two years. The other persisted and graduated from Southwestern in 1957.

TO BUILD A BIBLE SCHOOL

Alta Washburn realized that the Indian youth needed their own Indian Bible school. She began raising money to build a school on the lot adjoining the church.

Clarence Washburn continued with his night job. He also directed construction and worked on the building. Indian men, preachers, and laymen from Arizona's non-Indian churches all worked in the searing desert heat.

Offerings for the building often came just in time. A missions convention in Texas gave $1,500 for building materials. A Southern California assembly sent $1,000 for the building, helped furnish the rooms, and later helped support a couple from their church on the staff.

At last the Washburns set an opening date. The new office secretary writes, "Sis. Washburn and I brought pots and pans from our own kitchens. We rushed from one surplus store to another to buy the few items we could afford."

All Tribes Bible School opened September 28, 1957, in the new building at 4123 East Washington Street, Phoenix. The thirty-two who enrolled included dormitory students and young people from Phoenix and nearby reservations who came in for night classes.

"I cannot pay you, but you may eat with the students. You will have to trust God for your own support," Alta Washburn told prospective faculty and staff members.

They came—a trained office worker with business experience, teachers, missionaries, a school nurse, drivers, cooks, maintenance men. Dedicated men and women still continue to come, with a sense that God has called them to help train Indian workers to reach their own people with the gospel.

A TABLE IN THE DESERT

"You must pray and believe God with me for your daily food," Alta Washburn announced to the first boarding students. Phoenix area pastors and laymen often brought pickup loads of oranges, grapefruit, and lemons, and boxes of canned goods from the WMs. The Washburn's son Thomas and his wife shared milk, butter, honey, and cheese from their South Mountain ranch.

Many times, Arizona District Women's Director Lois Gribling dashed to the school to preach in an evening chapel service. The next morning she baked a supply of bread, cakes, and cookies; preached in morning chapel; and hurried away to her next task.

Alta Washburn's eyes gleam with tears as she tells some of the unique ways the Lord supplied food. The first students—mostly Pimas and Papagos from the Arizona desert—seldom complained about the food. They enjoyed the steady diet of beans and fry bread (wheat flour tortillas).

However, when the Canadian Mohawk students came and were faced with pinto beans every day, they were not happy. "Please, Sister Washburn, we are not sorry we came to school," they said, "but this desert wind, it is so dry. This food—there is no fish to eat. And we are very, very homesick for our beautiful green Canada."

Alta Washburn bombarded heaven, "Lord, if I could just serve them one big mess of fish." The next day a man's voice on the phone asked, "Can you use a hundred pounds of frozen fish? My freezer is crowded."

After their feast of fish, the Canadian students settled down to live in the desert.

When Navajo students came to school, they longed for their mothers' mutton stew. Alta Washburn's eyes sparkle as she tells about the phone call she received: "Could you use two big fat lambs? They're too big for pets any more." The next day the whole school smelled like Navajo stew.

One fall, Plains Indians—used to venison, but not pinto beans—enrolled in the school.

"Brethren, please share your kill with the Bible school and we will pray for your successful hunting," Alta Washburn wrote Arizona ministers.

The school ate venison for weeks. Superintendent Gressett brought them half an elk.

Lois Gribling accidentally killed a deer on the highway near San Miguel. The game warden said, "I'll give you the deer for your school and help load it onto your car."

BLESSINGS AND TESTINGS

When automobile accidents killed two of the young men, their family gave a tithe of their insurance money to the school. These amounts met an urgent need.

In the February 1962 *Trail of the Tribes*, Alta Washburn's newsletter, she wrote, "Today, I find myself running at my work. After last year's serious illness, God has given me wonderful health again. I shall use it daily for His glory." She reported revival in the church and school and rejoiced over new personnel who had joined the faculty.

Again she reported, "A cold winter in Phoenix, most unusual. Students had a siege of mumps and flu. Hardest month ever to pay bills. Fewest contributions for the work. The washer broke down. The refrigerator. The car. The record player. Had a leak in the roof and I lost my Scofield Bible. We turned the sheets, patched the blankets, and added pinto beans for breakfast."

Another issue of *Trails* told of the new gospel tent packed with Indian people who heard the gospel for the first time when Bible school students preached to them in their own languages.

From September 1957 to June 1965, Alta Washburn operated the school as a ministry of All Tribes Assembly of God—with the cooperation and advice of Arizona District Council officials. Two principals served the school during that time: Lonnie Thomas, 1962–1964, and Virgil Sampson, 1964–1965.

In 1965, Alta Washburn resigned because of poor health. At that time Arizona district officials arranged for the school to be placed under a board. This opened the way for the school to come under the direction of the Division of Home Missions and to expand from a local church project to a regional school operated by the six southwestern districts of the Assemblies of God. The Washburns moved All Tribes Assembly to a new location.

The Bible school's first office secretary graphically wrote about the transfer of the school:

"As I look back, I see this infant in his cradleboard, struggling to hold onto life. He begins to crawl. Pulls to his feet. Gains strength to stand . . . May our little papoose grow to great stature and always be 'meet for the Master's use.' Good-by little American Indian Bible Institute; we wish you Godspeed."

THE TRAIL BROADENS
Donald R. Ramsey, President, 1965–1978

THROUGH THE NAVAJO RESERVATION.

"What is your name?" the new teacher asked his pre-first grade beginners class of Navajo boys and girls. Confused by the strange words, the little girls hid their faces in the crooks of their arms on their desktops. The little boys stared, straight-backed and stoic.

They had been brought from home only yesterday, but the little ones already hated the strange food, high fences, and locked dormitories of Greasewood Indian Boarding School. They longed for their families in their cozy hogans, with the smell of food coming from the pots on the open fires and warm sheepskins spread on the smooth earthen floors.

Instead, they faced this paleface teacher with his brown hair, blue eyes, and white skin! As the teacher talked, the bewildered little Indian students began to comprehend the terrible truth—this teacher didn't know a word of Navajo!

Then the truth also began to dawn on teacher Don Ramsey. His worst fears were realized—these little Navajos didn't know a word of English!

Virginia Ramsey tells, with a smile and a twinkle in her eyes, of her husband's frustration the day he faced his first class of Indian students.

When the Lord called Don and Virginia Ramsey as missionaries to the American Indian people, they began to prepare. They pastored two assemblies in their native Oklahoma. Don and Virginia earned BA degrees from Oklahoma East Central State College, and Don earned his MA. To gain the needed opening for missionary work on the vast Navajo Reservation, Don applied to teach in a Bureau of Indian Affairs (BIA) school.

In September 1948, the Ramseys set out for Arizona with their two small daughters. Sand gritted between Don's teeth and sweat ran down his face as they bumped across the reservation on the rough, rutted roads. Virginia kept wiping the little girls' faces with a damp washcloth.

Near Ganado, Arizona, they found the school with the uninspiring name of Greasewood. Don Ramsey fully expected to teach in the upper grades, but, of course, that was not what happened.

Two years later, the BIA transferred Don to the Navajo Indian Boarding School at Tuba City, Arizona. That school promoted him to assistant director of the guidance department for boys. While they lived at Tuba City, the Ramseys also began a church at Cameron, twenty-five miles away.

TRAIL OF REORGANIZATION

In 1965, the new Bible school board composed of Arizona and Southern California leaders invited Donald R. Ramsey to succeed Alta Washburn, who had resigned. The Ramsey family, which now included four children—Becky, Debbie, Stevie, and David—moved to Phoenix that summer.

Don Ramsey began at once to upgrade the faculty and curriculum.

The first two months, he received sixty dollars to run the school. The government commodity center stopped helping with food. Dormitory boys had always slept on the floor until the owner of an old hotel donated beds for them.

In 1966-1967 the southwestern districts—Arizona, New Mexico, West Texas, Rocky Mountain, Northern California-Nevada, and Southern California—formed a regional school board. With the National Home Missions Department, they incorporated the school as the American Indian Bible Institute. The board approved the new Assemblies of God Bible Institute curriculum for AIBI.

When Tom Cunningham, Southern California missions secretary, drafted a constitution for AIBI, Arizona Superintendant J. K. Gressett read it and remarked, "I'm afraid the britches are too big for the boy."

"Never mind. The boy will grow to the britches," answered Tom.

Today Tom Cunningham adds, "And he has!"

WITH A PICKUP AND A SECONDHAND BUS

Using the school's only vehicle—an ancient pickup—students gleaned carrots, onions, cabbage, grapefruit, and oranges from land where Metro Shopping Center now stands. As Don Ramsey says, "Vegetables for plenty of stews."

During the 1966–1967 school year, the whole school went on weekend preaching and choir tours in the "new" (i.e., reconditioned) Speed-the-Light bus. On a trip to Yuma, students visited house-to-house on the reservation. A Cocopah Indian student brought her sister to church.

Convicted of her need for salvation, the sister called on the Lord for forgiveness. Then she begged the faculty and students to pray for her alcoholic, drug-abusing husband. Today the Lord uses this couple to help young people involved in drugs and alcohol.

TO A RUGGED HILL

When AIBI outgrew its facilities in an industrial section, a friend took Don Ramsey to look at land in northwest Phoenix.

Entering at Seventeenth and Ironwood Avenue, they saw a nine-and-a-half-acre semidesert plot. Though level where they stood, a sharp, rocky ridge ran beside Fifteenth Avenue. On their left, a round volcanic hill rose in an ever-steeper incline. Its boulder-crowned peak loomed a hundred feet above them, in the northeast corner of the lot.

Like Caleb of old, Don Ramsey's heart cried, "Give me this mountain."

About the down payment on the new campus Don Ramsey writes, "First, the owner lowered the price considerably—a substantial gift—then a $5,500 loan completed it."

At the new campus dedication, February 20, 1968, Home Missions Department Director Charles W. H. Scott spoke of the task of putting up adequate buildings. "Faith walks on the waters of difficulty," he said.

The board discussed architects' plans. Don Ramsey had the land surveyed and began a master plan for a four-level campus.

THROUGH A BUILDING CAMPAIGN

Although the school still owed $20,000 on the land, friends started a building fund. Don Ramsey, faculty members, and student groups seized every opportunity to represent AIBI and its building project.

The Leonard Sampiers started the Pow Wow Club to enroll regular donors for AIBI. Delbert and Lois Gribling, the Harvey Dunns, Claude Maples, the Silas Rexroats, the Roswell Dillinghams, the Butterfields, and others traveled widely to promote the school's building fund. Many people caught the vision of training Indian youth to reach their own tribes.

"Where did you get that dilapidated old walk-in cold room, anyway?" asked Pastor Clyde Henson of Sacramento one day.

"Goodwill," replied Don Ramsey.

"I thought so! Well, give it back to them. My church will buy you a new walk-in for your new building."

That promise was made on Washington Street. Today a brass plaque on the door of AIBC's double cold room reads, "Donated by Bethel Temple Assembly of God [now Capital Christian Center] Sacramento, California, Clyde Henson, Pastor."

Eager to see the whole campus developed according to the master plan, Clyde Henson began a separate fund for AIBI's second building, to house library, classrooms, and a chapel. He planned a promotional film featuring the school.

Clyde Henson went to be with the Lord August 9, 1971. Six years later, when the chapel was begun, the board named it Henson Memorial Chapel.

Don Ramsey's life accelerated in the summer of 1970 with the dual responsibility of helping supervise construction and directing the school. He leaned heavily on his faculty and staff.

The board sold the Washington Street property in the spring of 1970 but were unable to find a temporary location. Don Ramsey feared they must delay school opening in the fall. Then Pastor Willis Hirschey and Faith Assembly invited AIBI to use their facilities for classrooms and chapel. The school rented a nearby residence for living quarters.

"We started the building with $45,000," says Don Ramsey. "Only one-fifth enough. The day we ran out of money we received an unexpected $10,000 check from a church in Minnesota.

"The school board didn't want us to go with just plaster and plywood and chicken wire. They wanted us to put up a building to last till Jesus comes."

The dense green stone the contractors encountered in the mountainside required five blasts of dynamite. A brother from First Assembly donated two weeks of work with his bulldozer. The hard stone wore out the blade.

When vandals poured sand into gas tanks and damaged other equipment, two faculty men brought a small trailer to the campus and lived there. A brother solved the problem when he donated cyclone fence for the campus.

The plan for the multipurpose building called for a long two story structure with 14,000 square feet of floor space. Set into the hillside about halfway up, it was built of reinforced cement block faced with sand-colored slump block. The center section of the building was designed for administration. The upstairs held the dining hall and kitchen. The wings, planned for dormitories, had to yield some downstairs space for a maintenance shop, a print-shop, and classrooms.

Arizona pastors, laymen, faculty, and male students helped erect the building, and expert builders came to help. A brother newly retired from the Air Force moved to Arizona so he and his wife could help. A couple came from Washington to install the electric wiring. Week after week people worked in the unrelenting Arizona sun. Gradually the building grew.

Everybody on the site ran to watch the day the great crane lifted ninety-seven prestressed concrete beams into place to support the upstairs floors. Precast in Oregon, the beams fit perfectly.

Workmen poured the upper floor in six big concrete slabs, brought them to the campus, and laid them in place—with cranes.

On October 1, 1971, three hundred friends gathered to dedicate the almost completed building. Rev. Charles W. H. Scott led the act of dedication:

We dedicate this building . . . as a school of the Bible.
We dedicate this building to the Indian tribes.
We dedicate this building . . . to endue the students with a
new dimension of consecration
through the sufficiency of the Holy Spirit.

After sixteen months of work, AIBI moved into the new building November 1. The yearbook editor writes, "After an unusually hot summer, rain fell in the fall and winter, as we finished roofs and cement walks." In some areas floors were awash. Faculty and students began another year of inconvenience and disorder. But students could say, "We're the first to live on the new campus. We're the pioneers." The seniors called themselves the Mobile Class: Freshmen on Washington, juniors at Faith Assembly, and seniors at 10020 North Fifteenth Avenue.

The yearbook editor writes, "Hundreds of people helped build the multipurpose building, and hundreds of WMs helped furnish it."

On April 30, AIBI held open house. A crowd of friends came to see the new school. Indian parents said to their small children, "This is your school. Someday you will study here."

At the 1972 graduation in the new dining hall–chapel the school bid farewell to Home Missions Director Charles W. H. Scott. That summer they welcomed the new Division of Home Missions Director T. E. Gannon. Bro. Gannon became the chairman of AIBI's board.

An AIBI faculty member, speaking for the school in another state, said to the man before him, "AIBI needs your printing expertise and background. Why don't you move to Phoenix where you can set up an AIBI press. You want to print literature for the Indians? Arizona has more Indian people than any other state."

When the brother and his wife retired from a large corporation and moved to Arizona in 1968, their home church gave him the printing equipment he had used there. In Phoenix, the printer ran a "suitcase operation" from his home for several years. At last, in April 1972, he moved his equipment into the new print shop in the AIBI building.

Friends donated more printing equipment in 1973: a larger press, a platemaker, a folding machine, and an IBM Selectric Typewriter. During the following years AIBI Press printed the school paper (*The Thunderer*), the yearbook, the school catalog, and thousands of other pieces of literature.

In 1973 a musical friend formed the Tribalaires, AIBI's select singing group. The Tribalaires traveled for the school much of that summer of 1973. A brother in Bethel Temple, Sacramento, saw that the men of the group needed clothing. He bought them more than $500 worth of clothing at the store where he worked.

A school revival in the fall of 1973 followed student reports of revival in their summer ministries. Afterwards, the following conversation was overheard:

"Why did your Yaqui student go home? He just received the baptism of the Holy Spirit and he was so happy."

"Sure, he's happy. He just ran home to tell his folks."

"You mean he is running all the way to Guadalupe Village?"

"Sure. Why not? He's an athlete, you know, and it's only 26 miles."

In 1973 Don Ramsey wrote, "Two-thirds of the faculty and staff support their ministry to the school with personal retirement income." AIBI's full time faculty members are appointed home missionaries. From time to time volunteers help the school.

When a businessman donated $10,000 for a maintenance shop, builders quickly put it up and the maintenance department moved. With thankful hearts AIBI family and friends dedicated the new shop: space for car repairs, workshop, and storage.

In the fall of 1974, classes met in the two classrooms vacated by the maintenance shop, and AIBI was not quite so crowded. But in the office area, the hubbub sometimes became almost unbearable. Beyond the two offices and the receptionist's desk, the area served as post office, student lounge, hallway, and a combination library–classroom. AIBI needed another building.

HENSON MEMORIAL CHAPEL

AIBI was still paying on the multipurpose building. Board members agreed to appeal to churches in their own districts.

"Let's make the chapel a beautiful place of worship," they said. "Let's build a substantial building, not the cheap barracks type."

The '76 yearbook showed the floor plan of the proposed building: chapel and classrooms on the upper level, library below. A photo shows WM Director Goldia Anderson and District Superintendent Joseph Gerhart presenting a check for $29,354.54 from the Penney fund project of Northern California WMs for the new building.

Alpha Henson set herself to raise funds for the chapel, designated as a memorial to her husband. The Sampiers, the Griblings, and others raised funds. Thousands of offerings came in for the chapel building. But the day-to-day financing of the school was still a heavy burden.

When AIBI celebrated its twentieth year in 1977, J. K. Gressett wrote, "I get a real thrill when I reflect on what has happened at AIBI through the years. To God be the glory!"

To reach people in the neighborhood with the gospel, AIBI rented a small church building a few blocks from the campus, calling it Hillside Chapel. Neighbors enjoyed the student and faculty-led services. Some attended regularly.

A busy staff member during these years was the school seamstress. Friends sent new sewing materials from as near as California and as far away as the textile country of South Carolina.

One year the seamstress sewed 180 new garments for students.

At the Henson Memorial Chapel groundbreaking, September 30, 1977, Rev. T. E. Gannon spoke. Pastor Leroy Cloud, building project supervisor, presented an $8,000 check from

Valley Christian Assembly. Construction of the chapel on the high ground toward Fifteenth Avenue and Mountain View Elementary School took the entire school year.

The walls rose. Inside the sanctuary, the great laminated wood beams were hoisted into place. Students and faculty thrilled to the sight of the arrowhead shaped building looming high against the blue sky.

At the May 1978 board meeting Don Ramsey resigned. As president, he had upgraded AIBI to receive endorsement from the Assemblies of God Department of Education. For thirteen years he had led the school with its day-to-day financial burdens, relocation problems, and two building campaigns. The board called an Indian brother, Simon Peter, to succeed him as president. AIBI had come a long way up the trail.

THROUGH HEIGHTS AND DEPTHS

President Simon J. Peter, July 1978–March 1979
Acting President C. Eugene Herd, March–June 1979

FROM THE CHOCTAW NATION

The young Oklahoma Choctaw Indian couple sat in church, a small son and daughter between them. After the long separation of overseas service in World War II, Simon Peter was glad to get back to his family and friends.

As a young man, he had attended Chilocco Indian School and Oklahoma Presbyterian College. He earned his BA degree at Oklahoma State University in Durant. Now a civilian, what would life hold for him?

"Jesus died for you," proclaimed the preacher. "He will forgive your sins and make a new man of you. God has a plan for your life."

As Simon Peter listened, the Lord spoke to his heart. That day, he began a new life in Christ.

"He began to preach immediately," says his wife, Sammy Peter. Soon, as pastor of Green's Chapel Community Church, he led the congregation to join the Assemblies of God. Through sacrifice and hard work the Peters built the church up to support a full-time pastor.

Ordained by the Oklahoma District Council in 1951, Simon Peter pastored Indian and non-Indian churches in Oklahoma, Arkansas, Texas, and Colorado. Mrs. Peter remembers a revival in Idabel, Oklahoma, when twenty-one Choctaw Indian people were converted. In the Rocky Mountain district, he served as sectional youth leader, Sunday School representative, and presbyter.

Of their six children—Bill, Lyda Ann, Jacqueline, Timothy, Rebecca, and Philip—five are in active ministry today. Three serve as home missionaires to the American Indians.

Mrs. Peter recalls one instance of Simon's patience.

"I'll never call on that woman again!" she had cried one day as she stormed into her husband's study. "Every time I invite her to church, she talks uglier than before."

"Now, Mother," insisted Simon Peter in his calm voice (Sammy Peter said she never heard her husband raise his voice in anger or impatience), "you will go back and invite her one more time, won't you?"

When Sammy Peter called again, the woman welcomed her and asked for prayer. Today that woman is a fine WM worker.

When their youngest daughter enrolled in AIBI, the Peters' interest in AIBI increased. At her graduation in 1976, Bro. Peter delivered the commencement message.

After Simon Peter miraculously recovered from a malignancy during his pastorate in Clifton, Colorado, the Lord led him into more and more ministry to the Indian people. He preached at Indian camp meetings, revivals, and rallies.

Following President Donald Ramsey's resignation in the spring of 1978, the board invited Simon Peter to become president of AIBI. The Peters moved to Phoenix from Colorado. Simon J. Peter assumed the office of president on July 1, 1978.

That summer, workers moved library books to the Dorothy Cummings Memorial Library on the lower floor of the new chapel building. Southern California WMs paid for library shelving, a teacher's lectern, a projector with screen, and partitions for five faculty offices.

The Etta Calhoun Fund of the national WM office paid for typewriters and for carrels for the library. Mrs. Alpha Henson donated the desk, chair, bookshelves, and library of her late husband, Clyde Henson.

Meanwhile, in the president's office, a tremendous weight settled on Simon Peter. He felt the spiritual burden of trusting God for funds for the day-to-day operation of a faith school, for monthly payments on the remaining debt of the multipurpose building, and for around $60,000 borrowed for the new chapel building.

TRAIL OF VISION

As he sought the Lord, Simon Peter received a burden for revival to sweep over the Indian people of America. He envisioned AIBI sending forth Indian youth who would carry revival fires to the tribes all across America.

When school opened, students' faces glowed with enthusiasm as they said to each other,

"We have an Indian president now!"

"He is one of us."

"Great things are ahead."

President Simon Peter preached the school-opening revival services in the dining hall. One of the teachers says, "Brother Peter had rapport with the students from the first. This quiet-spoken man seldom preached elaborate sermons. But he preached under such an anointing of the Holy Spirit that God was able to speak to our hearts in every sermon."

In a blaze of revival, faculty and students knelt together to dedicate their lives to reaching every Indian with the gospel.

Friends and board members gathered at AIBI on the evening of September 28, 1978, in the first of three gala events. They inaugurated Simon J. Peter as AIBI president, with Assistant General Superintendent G. Raymond Carlson and national Director of the Division of Home Missions T. E. Gannon officiating.

The next morning, several hundred Arizona women arrived for

their annual Harvest Rally—begun in 1959 by Lois Gribling and carried on by Kathleen Cummings—to help supply the AIBI kitchen. The women brought $4,200 in cash and staples to their 1978 rally.

As the women met in the new chapel, they rejoiced over their special project: red carpet and pews, altars, pulpit, and communion table. Southern California WMs had given a challenge offering to start them off, but the Arizona women worked sacrificially to buy these handsome, durable furnishings.

The Missionettes selected as their national project for 1978 a three-manual Thomas organ. They raised $6,420.61, but when prices escalated, the sum was insufficient. A California brother made up the difference. Hillside Chapel—mostly students and faculty—donated the piano. The South Texas District Council bought the furnishings for the three new classrooms.

An issue of the *Thunderer* reported, "Many friends and churches throughout the nation have sacrificially given to build and furnish this needed facility."

Simon Peter preached on the rally day theme "By Love Compelled." He stirred listeners to believe God for spiritual blessing on AIBI and for a revival that would sweep across the American Indian reservations.

That afternoon, brethren from the six districts of the Southwest Region and from the Division of Home Missions dedicated the new building to the Lord. Dr. T. E. Gannon preached the dedicatory message.

FELLOWSHIP OF SUFFERING

In October, a recurrence of the malignancy struck President Peter with disabling, almost unendurable pain. He told friends later, "All I could do that month was try to sit in my office day after day and claim victory through the blood of Jesus."

The whole school sought God desperately, believingly. Simon Peter seemed to completely recover—without pain and with great plans for the school.

During November and December he spoke often in chapel and took the choir and Tribalaires to churches. Wherever he preached, people were blessed.

The Southern California WM's Christmas party brightened the month of December. Each year WM Director Barbara Forrest and her husband, Gene, brought the WM-prepared gifts.

Each person, children of faculty and students included, was given a big plastic bag filled with clothing to fit, cosmetics, toilet articles, bed covers, and funny stuffed animals. At that time the WMs valued the gifts at "no less than one hundred dollars per person."

In January 1979, the Peters went to Oklahoma to be with a sister during her terminal illness. While they were there, another recurrence of malignancy attacked Simon Peter, and he entered a hospital. He never returned to AIBI.

Sammy Peter brought her husband to the Veteran's Hospital in Phoenix. Students and faculty rallied around their president with visits, prayers, and gifts. Then the doctors transferred him to Tucson.

Day after day, loving hearts upheld Simon Peter in prayer. Students and faculty encouraged each other in the Lord. They expected him to be delivered from his sickness and restored to them. But deliverance did not come in that way. In March, Simon Peter resigned from the school, and in May, Sammy Peter moved her husband to their home in Oklahoma.

In the May 1979 *Thunderer* we read, "Effectiveness in the kingdom of God cannot be measured in days, weeks or months . . . . Trusting in the sovereignty of God is the guiding force of Brother Peter's life."

Simon Peter went to be with the Lord November 5, 1979. A student wrote in the 1980 *Four Winds*, AIBI's yearbook, "For a small school like ours, where the president is close to every student and staff member, Brother Peter's long illness was a traumatic experience. But we continually prayed and drew nearer to God. From Brother and Sister Peter we have received a lasting enrichment of joy, courage and strength."

In March 1979, the board's executive committee asked Vice-President C. Eugene Herd to assume the responsibilities of acting president of AIBI.

VIA THE HOPI MESAS

As the missionary couple approached the top of the mesa, they saw a forlorn group of Christians staring at the rented residence they had used for worship services. Lightning had struck it.

"Lightning! Surely the Christians are evil or lightning would never strike the house where they meet."

The Lightning Clan of the Hopi Pueblo hurried to loot the place. Their right by Hopi custom, they took boxes of used clothing and a sewing machine from the back room. The pulpit and benches they merely dragged out into the rain and piled the songbooks and Bibles on top. Miraculously, the books remained dry.

When the missionaries arrived, the missionary was for quiet, his wife, for action. She traced the sewing machine—a borrowed one—to the house of the chief's sister.

"By Hopi custom it's mine," insisted the woman.

"I'm not an Indian. I'm not under Hopi custom," the missionary's wife insisted. "By my custom you stole it and I want it back. Besides, I only borrowed the machine."

Finally the Hopi woman spoke quietly, "You talk too fast. I can't listen anymore. Just take your machine and go."

The next day the Hopi Medicine Man and his council of twelve met with the missionary. "Different kinds of people are going up a mountain by different paths," he said. "We have our path. You have yours."

"No! Jesus is the pathway. The only one," the missionary replied.

Forbidden to hold services on the mesa, the missionary and converts devised a plan. After dark on service nights the men individually and secretly slipped down the steep 500 foot sides of the mesa and rode with the missionary to a Hopi church eight miles away.

Eugene Herd, a former Game Protector in Kansas, came to Arizona in 1958 with his wife, Marion, and their children: Roger, 11, Merletha, 9, and Ironda, 7. The lightning incident happened soon after the Herds began work as appointed home missionaries to the Hopi tribe near Polacca, Arizona.

Later, they pioneered the Indian Assembly at Holbrook. Eugene Herd came to AIBI in March 1973 as vice-president and business manager.

Even before he became acting president, the school year of 1978-79 was particularly burdensome to him. Because of the new president's incapacitating illness, Gene had to face many problems in addition to his own heavy responsibilities. The varied activities of the school must go on.

From the 1980 *Four Winds* dedicated to Eugene Herd, we read, "He's a cheerful giver of his time and self . . . . He's understanding and cares about others."

That spring at AIBI's first annual home and foreign missions convention, students were surprised to hear a visiting missionary say, "With your dark complexion and hair, you Indian young people would be very acceptable as missionaries to the people of East Asia."

Promoted by the Student Missions Fellowship, the February 1979 convention featured a film and special missionary speakers. Students arranged three foreign missions displays and six American Indian tribal exhibits in the chapel and foyer. They borrowed valuable blankets, baskets, pottery, turquoise and silver jewelry, distinctive tribal costumes, and other beautiful items. Each year, friends drop in to see the Indian exhibits during the school's missions convention.

The Spring 1979 *Thunderer* announced extension classes in Indian churches. Over a period of several semesters, some faculty members held extension classes for the Paiute Indian people in Nixon, Nevada; the Hopis in Polacca, Arizona; the Navajos in Albuquerque, New Mexico; and a combined class for the White Mountain and San Carlos Apache people of Arizona.

Twelve young people from the Navajo, Ute, Pima, and Hoh River Tribes graduated in the new chapel May 29, 1979. At the graduation ceremony, Carl E. Collins was presented as the next president of AIBI.

STILL UPWARD THE TRAIL

Carl E. Collins, President 1979 —

TO INDIAN CHILDREN

"With Jesus in the family,
happy, happy home."

The Apache children clapped their hands as they sang—straight, black hair flying, dark eyes dancing with mischief. The little girls' long, full dresses of bright cotton swayed to the rhythm of the song.

Professor Carl Collins and his wife, Alice, had driven from their home in South Carolina to lead children's services for the 1971 campmeeting on the White River Apache Indian Reservation and the camp at Kayenta, on the Navajo Reservation. In this, their first experience on a reservation, Carl and Alice and their children—Wesley, 11; Mark, 9; and Michelle, 6—learned to love the Indian people.

In the children's tabernacle, the boys and girls eagerly learned Bible verses and songs. Alice's puppet, Herman—a chimpanzee as large as a four-year-old child—fascinated the boys. During afternoon hikes, mountain climbs, and arrowhead hunts, the children constantly played pranks on Carl and Alice.

At Kayenta, where the temperature was almost 120 degrees, the Collinses waded through hot sand to a solitary old juniper. "This is your camping place. It's the coolest spot on the campground," said the director. Alice set up her campstove and picnic table under the tree's low-hanging branches.

Carl helped the brethren put up the ramada, an arbor of poles and branches, for the adult meetings. Under a smaller ramada the Collinses began children's services. Too timid to answer questions, the Navajo children easily learned by rote. Soon they could recite all the memory verses in unison.

Back at home, in Spartanburg, South Carolina, Carl and Alice sent offerings to the missionaries and Indian churches. After they came to Phoenix to work in child evangelism seminars in January of 1975 and 1977, President Don Ramsey urged them to join the staff of AIBI.

Carl Collins earned a BA degree in Bible from Bob Jones University and an MA in higher education administration from Appalachian State College. He pastored churches in Georgia and South Carolina for twenty-one years. He also taught in the University of South Carolina–Union campus; Clemson University; Spartanburg Technical College; and Cecil's Business College, where he served as business manager.

Alice operated the largest privately-owned day care center in South Carolina. She led children's crusades and kids' camps throughout the southeastern states.

TO INDIAN YOUNG PEOPLE

The Collins family moved to Phoenix in time for the fall semester 1977. Carl began as instructor and director of AIBI's student employment program.

"Sister Collins, remember me?" asked a Navajo freshman in 1983. "You taught me at Kayenta Campmeeting in 1971. Now I'm here at AIBC." Since then, other Navajo and Apache students from the Collins' campmeeting children's services have identified themselves.

The Lord gave Carl Collins two years to become acclimated to the Arizona desert, accustomed to teaching in AIBI, and acculturated to the Indian students' way of thinking. When Simon Peter resigned in the spring of 1979, the school board elected Carl Collins as president of AIBI, to take office June 1.

"How can we operate the school to better help Indian youth become what God has called them to be?" the new president asked alumni, missionaries to the Indian people, faculty members, and denominational leaders. "What do you consider are our weaknesses? Our strengths? What paths would you like to see AIBI take?"

Many Saturday nights, he sat till midnight in some pastor's home listening and talking. Often he preached in two Indian churches the next day, then drove home to Phoenix in the early morning hours.

Through Carl Collins' August appeal for the $38,000 outstanding on the new chapel, nearly enough came in. The school consolidated the rest with the multipurpose building debt.

Students liked the new dual curriculum begun in the fall of 1979 with majors in both religious education and Bible ministry.

God blessed the student-led weekend revivals in several Indian churches. The school sponsored recruitment dinners in Indian areas. In Denver, brethren held a "Let's Get Acquainted Banquet" honoring AIBI's president and Tribalaires.

Carl Collins was concerned about the students' attitudes and problems. "I hate white people!" a handsome young man told his fellow students. "They have always mistreated our people. Every treaty they ever made with us, they broke. How can I study under such teachers?" He stormed out of the dining hall.

A teacher spoke with this student privately. "Now, brother," she said, "I know many wrongs were done in the past, but you and I are living now. You are my brother and I am your sister in Christ.

"I don't hate the Indian people. With God's help you must forgive. God will take all the bitterness out of your heart." After prayer together, the student's attitude changed. He became a top student.

Indian students faced other problems. "One year while I was in AIBI, students enrolled from seventeen different tribes," says a former student. "I remember my friend saying, 'I don't like my roommate. She's always longing for the ocean and the green forests. She even eats fish! I don't think she really likes Navajos, either. Why doesn't she just go back to her North Country anyway?'

"But," I reminded my friend, "Bro. Collins said we must love all the tribes, especially the ones in our dormitory. They are Indians too."

"That year," continued the former student, "I learned to appreciate students from other tribes: Ute, Yakima, Pueblo, Apache, Choctaw, Otoe, Papago, Shoshone, Pima, Chippewa, Cree, Acoma, Cheyenne, Paiute, Oneida, Hoh River, and Alabama-Coushatta."

Besides the problems of adapting to the white man's frantic-seeming lifestyle—bells to get up by, bells to get to class by, always rushing about—students had other adjustments to make.

Some young people found it difficult to accept what Christ had done and was doing for them. They had been involved with drugs and alcohol or their parents were drunkards or they felt non-Indians looked down on them as "indigents looking for a handout."

Even today, many American Indians resent the effort to make them a part of the great American melting pot. Some students fear that AIBI will want them to give up their Indian ways. Instead, at AIBI they find love and respect as Indian persons. Students are encouraged to retain all of their tribal culture that is not anti-Christian.

The student editor of the 1980 yearbook wrote, "AIBI does not try to take away our beautiful Indian heritage, but to look at it from a new perspective, as we place our identity in Christ Jesus."

To help these Indian young people deal with their problems, President Collins appointed a dean of students and counselors. He urged all faculty members to close their books and take time to listen to students who dropped by their offices.

Specialists spoke to the faculty on cross-cultural communications, leadership concepts, interpersonal relationships, and self-acceptance. When they spoke to the students, many received a new feeling of self-worth.

Indian brethren came to explain certain facets of their culture. They showed why Indian people react as they do to some of the white man's customs.

TO A BETTER LIBRARY

Early in 1980, a Christian foundation donated $40,000 to the school library. The faculty library committee analyzed AIBI's existing library and faculty members happily requisitioned books to enrich their courses. With help and advice from Central Bible College and Southwestern Assemblies of God College libraries, the school began to buy books and audiovisual materials. A team of finish carpenters, painters, and an electrician came from a Colorado Assembly to put cupboards and shelves in the library and other buildings.

As of December 1983, the AIBC library houses almost 13,000 books and several hundred tapes. Special sections display books on the Holy Spirit, American Indian history, and anthropology.

In an August 1980 retreat, faculty and administration considered, among other things, a plan for alumni follow-up and relations with Indian and non-Indian churches. After analyzing the reasons for each dropout in recent years, they began a written retention plan. They left the cool mountain retreat site with spiritual refreshing, with greater appreciation for each other, and with a renewed sense of divine call.

That year Carl Collins appointed self-study committees. On each committee a student and an alumnus served with faculty and staff members. Begun in 1974, these ongoing in-depth evaluations of every phase of school life revealed the strengths and weaknesses of AIBI. Dr. Donald Bogue, who serves as an accrediting commissioner for the allied medical field, volunteered to critique the self-study reports.

"Brother Collins, right now our students need technical training more than accreditation," said a missionary in a reservation meeting to discuss accreditation for the school. "We need AIBI graduates qualified to hold jobs on the reservation. Our graduates need to support themselves while they pioneer churches."

An older alumnus said, "We AIBI graduates who preach and support ourselves with work for the tribal governments had to get more training before we could become office managers, counselors for drug and alcohol abuse victims, or school teachers. Let's train AIBI students to take their places on the reservations."

AIBI needed to offer technical subjects, but it also needed accreditation. Most tribes share scholarship funds only with their young people in accredited schools. That year, a consecrated Indian veteran transferred from AIBI to a secular college because he could not support his family at AIBI. The Veterans Administration assisted him at the accredited school. AIBI lost other young people with leadership capabilities to accredited Bible colleges. With inflation and economic depression, lack of accreditation was now defeating the purpose of the school—to train leaders.

In 1980 the board voted for AIBI to work toward becoming a four year Bible college. The school would grant BA degrees in ministerial studies and in Christian education but would retain the three-year diploma program. They planned to grant AA degrees in business management, secretarial science, and social work. With each technical degree, a number of hours in Bible and Bible-related courses would be required.

Revival overflowing from the summer 1980 Arizona Indian youth camp blessed the Indian churches and AIBI also with revival, and more students. However, deteriorating U.S. economic conditions left most male students without work. The few available weekend jobs in fast-food restaurants hindered the men's training in outreach ministry and choir. Friends who rallied to keep these young men in school received the first "Partners in Harvest" certificates. Carl Collins concluded his report to the board, "As one crisis eases, another arises. But I have peace in my heart because 'I know whom I have believed.'"

TWENTY-FIFTH YEAR ON THE TRAIL

In his fall 1981 letter to WM leaders, the president reported, "Enrollment—63 students.

"Four new technical programs to support Indian lay ministries.

"Our first-time recognition by the Bureau of Indian Affairs."

A new survey showed that tribal governments favored hiring AIBI graduates because they are dependable and non-drinking.

That semester, the board appointed Burl and Berneice Rogers to represent AIBI. In its twenty-fifth year, Arizona and Oklahoma youth gave the school a new Speed-the-Light Dodge van. God continued to bless AIBI.

"A happy buzz of conversation greeted us from the turquoise and silver decorated banquet room," wrote a teacher about the October 8, 1981, gathering of AIBI family and friends to celebrate the school's silver anniversary.

"To one side, alumni and former faculty members laughed over a collage of school photos dating back to 1957. Several board members were there. The beautiful Tribalaires sang during our meal.

"Programs in turquoise and silver displayed the Navajo-Christian theme "In Beauty We Walk." President Carl Collins presided over the gala event, during which he honored AIBI's founder Alta Washburn and her husband, Clarence. From Don Ramsey, AIBI president for 13 years, we heard tape-recorded greetings from Alaska. Sister Sammy Peter represented her late husband, President Simon Peter.

"Retiring Director of the Division of Home Missions T. E. Gannon and his wife, Flora, received a plaque, a Papago jar, a Navajo rug, and a Papago landscape.

"'A Trail of Beauty'—a slide presentation of AIBI's history—was followed by a living presentation of a missionary who won an Indian youth to the Lord. A chain reaction from this brought three students to AIBI. Former Home Missions Director Charles W. H. Scott led the closing devotional."

TRAIL TO ACCREDITATION

The AIBI board recommended that the school begin work for accreditation with the North Central Association of Colleges and Schools. Months of intense preparation preceded the visit of the NCA accreditation committee in April 1982. Committee members had never dealt with either a mission school or a school for a cultural minority.

They met with members of the AIBI board and with student leaders. Although the committee found areas where the school needed to improve, they also found "commendable strengths" in some areas. Among them:

"The students presently at AIBI voiced strong affirmation that the school has helped them develop their lives . . . consistent with their Christian mission.

"The board of directors is a supportive, enthusiastic, dedicated and valuable resource to the institution.

"There is an excellent relationship between the students, the faculty, and the administration."

In June 1982, the North Central Association officially approved AIBI as a candidate for accreditation, and during the 1982–1983 school year, the board changed the school's name to American Indian Bible College. Along with BA and AA degrees, the school is to continue to offer the three year diploma.

In 1982 AIBC set up a developmental studies program which enables students who are not yet high school graduates to work toward their high school graduate equivalency diploma. Seven students earned their diplomas in 1983.

That fall student interns, Tribalaires, and others who helped in their home churches returned from summer ministries with victorious reports of what they called a super summer.

TOWARD SPACE FOR MORE STUDENTS

The larger fall 1982 enrollment brought a greater number of serious students. Dormitories were overcrowded. The school also needed more classrooms. In October, the board approved the building of a new dormitory to eventually accommodate 72 students. Today part of the building is used for three classrooms.

In the winter *Thunderer*, President Collins, inspired by Charles Swindoll's *Hand Me Another Brick*, wrote, "Nehemiah rebuilt the walls of Jerusalem despite incredible odds: economic depression, unemployment, high taxes and corruption.

"God gave Nehemiah the vision, but he did not build alone. Others caught the vision and the burden, and the walls were built.

"A severe economic slump? Incredible odds? But AIBC has wonderful assets in its Partners in Harvest, who pray for and give to this school. Partners who are burdened to see this school continue to train more and more Indian young people to reach their own tribes with the gospel. Will you please, please, hand me another brick!"

In the '82–'83 school year an alumnus led AIBC students' coffee house ministry at Phoenix Indian High School. Forty high school students from many tribes responded to the gospel message, and nine of them were baptized by the All Tribes Assembly of God pastor.

President Carl Collins wrote about AIBC alumni, "This summer at the Apache camp I heard an alumnus challenge everyone with his messages on the family. Two alumni were camp speakers at the Central Arizona Camp. On the Navajo Reservation, where Alice and I were children's evangelists only a few years ago, I saw Navajo pastors, alumni, and AIBC students conducting the services.

"Last Sunday, 112 of the 132 living graduates were involved in some area of Christian ministry," continued President Collins. "Pastors, pastor's wives, evangelists, assistant pastors, Sunday school superintendents, and Sunday school teachers were reaching their people with the gospel."

AIBC's twenty-sixth graduation on May 5, 1983, set a precedent. In addition to six Bible institute diplomas, the school granted its first nine AA degrees: in social work, business management, and secretarial science.

Accreditation calls for higher faculty academic qualifications. In 1983 two faculty members received MA degrees from the Assemblies of God Graduate School. One has just begun his doctorate program. Another is completing his. Three are working on master's degrees.

AIBC started the fall '83 semester with a record-setting enrollment of seventy-nine, with eleven working on BA degrees. Students consistently tested higher than in past years.

Weekend outreach ministry began with enthusiasm and blessing. A rally on the Phoenix Indian High School campus attracted two hundred young people.

A new survey in October 1983 showed of AIBC graduates:
–112 active in local churches,
–36 in full-time ministry,
–116 employed full-time in social work, health, education,
    Christian service, etc.,
–115 employed in the Indian community.

In March 1983, Dr. T. E. Gannon, AIBC's board chairman, went to be with the Lord. He served as director of the Division of Home Missions and chairman of the board of AIBC from 1972 until he retired in January 1981. Then the AIBC board asked him to continue as their chairman an additional year.

Interested in the school from the first, T. E. Gannon was eager for AIBC to become accredited. He energetically pursued the minutest details of the tasks involved. Persistence and striving for excellence marked everything he did.

After his death, the AIBC board of directors voted to name the new dormitory the T. E. Gannon Memorial Building. Two Gannon sons participated in the ground-breaking service in June 1983.

"Brother Collins, you can get someone else to finish the excavation for this building. I've broken the teeth of my big backhoe on this hard stone," said the brother excavating the hillside for the building.

"But your insurance will replace it, won't it?"

"Yes. But I don't want anything more to do with this awful rock."

The comment above was only one of the many frustrations in getting the building started and built on schedule. However, in answer to the prayers of God's people and their sacrificial giving — along with a large gift from Evangelist Jimmy Swaggart—the school was able to move into the new Gannon Memorial Building on January 3, 1984, with a March 1984 Dedication.

As in times past, the Women's Ministries Departments of AIBC's regional districts and of other districts rallied to help build and furnish the new facility. Southern California, Northern California- Nevada, Arizona, Rocky Mountain, West Texas, and New Mexico WMs sent their offerings. Arkansas WMs furnished new carpets and drapes for the eleven-year-old multipurpose building. Recently, the national Women's Ministries Department gave the school a new ice maker and a memory IBM typewriter from the Etta Calhoun Fund.

EPILOGUE

"Walk in beauty," intones the Navajo father to his infant son. As he holds the child upright, feet touching the earth, he repeats this life-motto to him. The father often repeats the motto to the small child, that he may grow up in harmony with his surroundings.

This poem, "A Prayer," by Washington Matthews, a Navajo Indian, is the prayer of many Navajo Christians:

With beauty may I walk,
With beauty before me may I walk,
With beauty behind me may I walk,
With beauty above me may I walk,
With beauty below me may I walk,
With beauty all around me may I walk .
It is finished in beauty.

We have seen the beginnings of a Trail of Beauty—Alta Washburn's God-given vision of Indian youth trained to bring the beautiful gospel to their own people. Along the trail, we saw God's beautiful supply of the needs of the school these many years.

As the trail leads ever upward, we see the beauty of the Lord worked into the lives by the power of the Holy spirit—lives of faculty, students, alumni, and their beautiful Indian converts.

"Let the beauty of the Lord our God be upon us: and...the work of our hands establish thou it" (Psalm 90:17, KJV). May He continually lead AIBC along His Trail of Beauty until He comes.

AIBC FACULTY AND STAFF
(One Semester or More)

Alta Washburn	
Founder	
President	1958–65
Virginia Kridler	1958–61, 1965–70
Ruth Gardiner	1957–62, 1976–83
Lois Carruthers	1958–61
Rose Grant	1958
Rose Chase	1958–65
Dee Rickey	1958–65
Helen Rickey	1958–65
Marcia McCorkle	1958, 1959
Mable Holland	1958
Barbara Willoughby	1958, 1959, 1966
Jack Ireland	1958
Wallace Weatherford	1959
Ruby Weatherford	1959
Jan Stewart	1959
William Comstock	1960–62
Harold Hansen	1960, 1961, 1984
Eva McClintock	1960
Lucille (Farmer) Greathouse	1960, 1962, 1977
Virgil Sampson	1961–65
Principal	1965
Eunice Sampson	1961–65, 1983
Lonnie Thomas	1962–64
Principal	1963, 1964
Alma Thomas	1962–64, 1976–84
Academic Dean	1976–84
Joseph Leichty	1962–65
Mrs. Joseph Leichty	1962–65
T. L. Johnson	1962–65
Mrs. T. L. Johnson	1962–65
Illie Dingman	1963
Hilda (Cree) Garcia	1963–65
Joe Hanna	1964–68
Vice President	1966–68
Betty Hanna	1964–68, 1982–84
Joe Lack	1964
Donald R. Ramsey	1966–78, 1983–84
President	1966–78
Virginia Ramsey	1966–78
Belle Kennedy	1966–70
Del Bittner	1966
Roy Mikesell	1966
Thelma Cox	1966, 1967
David G. Geist	1966
Pauline Mastries	1966, 1967
Doris Carlson	1967–75
Anna Staley	1967–70
Raymond Wiseman	1967–69
Janice Wiseman	1967–69
Joseph Eddy	1967, 1968
Noreen Eddy	1967, 1968
W. E. Cummings	1968–71
Albert Campbell	1968–73
Business Manager	1968–73
Geraldine Campbell	1968–73
Julius Panda	1968–82
Bernard Bresson	1969–72
Vice President	1969–72
Paul Basler	1969–73
Audrey Basler	1969–71
George Garcia	1969–71
Patricia Garcia	1969–71
William Morley	1970–74
Judith Uselman	1969–72
Dolly Royse	1970, 1975, 1981–84
Noureen Heath	1970–73
Lavern Heath	1973
Maude Florida	1971
Dorothy Johnston	1971, 1973
Yvonne (Daly) Hunter	1971–74
Ernest Hosier	1971
Sarah Hosier	1971
Burton York	1972–74
Emily York	1972–75
Glenn Harris	1972
Pauline Harris	1972, 1982
Gloria Moore	1972
Angie Pablo	1972
Eugene Herd	1973–79
Vice Pres./Bus. Mgr.	1973–79
Acting President	Spring 1979
Marion Herd	1977–79
Jim Johnson	1973
Rhonda Johnson	1973
Mattie Patillo	1973
Edna Land	1973–75
Naomi Land	1973–74
Al Cranston	1973
Elizabeth Oakes	1973–78
Rowena Cranston	1973
John Chisnell	1974–78
Bernard Rossier	1974, 1975
Eileen Rossier	1974, 1975
Naomi Foster	1974–76
Roland Waller	1974–76, 1978, 1982–84
Pearl Waller	1975, 1976, 1978
Lila Haycook	1973–75
Henry Culbreth	1975
Samuel Mims	1975
Kenneth McIntyre	1975
Jeannie Stephens	1975, 1976
Eugene Hunter	1976–84
David Moore	1976–84
Bus. Administrator	1983, 1984
Cheri Moore	1976, 1977, 1983
Bene Shafer	1976
Norbert Nopah	1976
Patty Stephens	1976, 1977
James Green	1976
Adeline Green	1976
William McDaniel	1976
Alice McDaniel	1976
Alicia Nix	1976
Mrs. Jack Wallace	1976
Johnny Stephens	1976
Don Stanley	1977, 1979
Alvin Booher	1977–80
John Nohr	1977
Gladys Yuhas	1977
Ethel Metler	1978
Irene Westlund	1977, 1978
Carl Collins	1978–84
President	1980–84
Alice Collins	1981–84
Bonnie (Jacques) Lee	1978, 1979, 1983, 1984
William Collier	1978, 1979
Tommye Cox	1978, 1979, 1981
Thalia Livengood	1978
Ruth (Hay) Jolly	1978–80
William Murray	1978
George Parker	1978–80
Marjorie Parker	1978
Shelly Washalanta	1978–82
Simon Peter	
President	1979
Sammy Peter	1981, 1982
Glenn Dunn	1979–83

Pauline Dunn	1980–83
Janice Isherwood	1979–82
Velma Huckabee	1979
Donald Keeter	1979–84
Vice President	1979–82
Grace Willard	1979, 1980
Leslie Davis	1979, 1980, 1982
Rita Davis	1979, 1980, 1982
George Anderson	1980
Nadine Waldrop	1980–84
Business Manager	1980–82
Beth Evans	1980
Charley Odell	1980–82, 1984
Janice Odell	1980–82, 1984
Ralph Gomez	1980
J. D. Jolly	1980
Albert Hamilton	1980, 1981
Mavis Hamilton	1980, 1981
J. W. Collins	1980, 1983
Norman Wolff	1981–84
Florence Cottle	1980, 1983
Harry Cottle	1980
Nora Kruse	1982, 1983
Don Skipp	1982–84
Dorothy Skipp	1982–84
Viola Peabody	1982
Myrna Yellowhair	1982, 1983
Carol Knissel	1982
Lillian Ellingson	1982
Alretta Plues	1982–84
Ethel K. Anderson	1983
James Boulware	1983, 1984
Jean Howe	1983, 1984
Jim Lopez	1983, 1984
Belinda Lopez	1983, 1984
Joseph Marafino	1983
Emmalene Shields	1983
Wayne Soemo	1983
Robert Moore	1984
Mamie Beaver	1984
Joe Robinson	1984
Dolores Wren	1984
Brenda Hargis	1984
Ruby Pruitt	1984
Brian Martin	1984
Daniel Wilson	1984

AIBC ALUMNI

1961
Lillie Irving
Mary Wallen
Juanita (Miguel) Juan

1962
Elvira (Dennis) Ochoa
Jacob Escalante
Laverne Sampson
Nandla (Key) Irving

1963
Irma Cooya
Judy (Salem) Williams
Herman Hoffman
Mary Hoffman

1964
Joe Ellis

1965
George Garcia
Patricia Garcia
Helen (Morino) Miguel

1966
Wilson A. Nelson

1967
Agnes Rose Yazzie
Pauline Bitoni
Priscilla (Papel) Brown
Vickie (Cota) Valenzuela
Vera Buck

1968
Stephen Brown
Albert Buck
Betty Morgan
Jeannie Stephens
Linda (Cota) Willie
Roy Zehney
Lillie Zehney

1969
Rose Marie (Begay) Spencer
Delvin Smith
Fred Begay
Joe Wilson

1970
Ellen Danford
Citaria (Gibson) Pablo
Rose Ann Gordy
Vernon Brown
Evelyn Antonio

1971
Durango Palmer
Ingrid Palmer
Ernest Christman
Helen Christman
Margaret (Nelson) Dude
Mary Jane (Ethelbah) Tenijieth

1972
Vernon Poncho
Geraldine Poncho
Johnny Stephens

Teresa (Pablo) Williams
Angie (Pablo) Acunia
Vera Shirley

1973
Pauline (Sharkey) Allen
Susan (Bryant) Barley
Raymond Acunia
John Estrella
Ron Boni
Judy (Wolfblack) Liney

1974
Buster Beatty
Johnny Dixon
Anne Redfox
Patty (Kirk) Stephens
Ernie Lister
Jim Lopez
Willie John Willie
Alicia Nix

1975
Wayne Bill
Dana Howard
Charlene (Kirk) Pedro
Ramon Martinez
Anthony Ross

1976
David Cota
Benjamin Davis
Alberta (Justin) Yucupicio
Louisa Lee
Mayda (Maytubby) Martinez
Augustine Mecham
Daniel Pablo
Beckie (Peter) Good
Arlene Russell
Joe Semallie
Donna (Williams) Shendo
Marie Yucupicio

1977
Adolph Cota
Noreen (Enas) Davis
Ralph Gomez
Elizabeth (Maytubby) Lee
Sarra Semallie
Darlene Sharkey
Sissie Stafford
Janice (Davis) Tsosie

1978
Salim Deans
Geneva Villiman
Rebecca Hubbard
Rita Jim
Floyd Lee
Lloyd Lee
Eddie Lupe
Eric Manuel
Jennie Manuel
Jimmy Shendo

1979
Marion (Charles) Yazzie
Larry Cuthair
Maritta (Descheenie) Lynch
Delorah Lee
Eric Lee

Henry McKerry
Virginia Moses
Judy (Riebe) Cathers
Willardine Sampson
Jeanette Todachine
Marie Thompson
Ron Yazzie
Paula Toehe

1980
Ellen Attakai
Darlene Fuller
Jeremy Gulfan
Theron Johns
Susie Peshlakai
Chris Tenijieth
Marie (Riebe) Dreher
Elouise Toehe

1981
Helen Harry
Paul Lanuza
Ralph Morris
Faithe Sampson
Dana Nosaka
Arthur Wilson
Vandy Yazzie

1982
Stephanie Jordan
Julie Manuel
Juda Mendoza
Monty Tully
Lia (Sarabia) Lanuza

1983
Bible Institute
Valda Henry
Terry Noon
Denise Terry
Bennie Yazzie
Jimmy Yellowhair

AA Degree
Juda Mendoza
Julie Manuel
Helen Harry
Charleen Pino
Tina Hawthorne
Juanita Jim
Cynthia Johns
Barbara (Ramos) May
Carleen Myers

AIBC BOARD OF DIRECTORS
(Past and Present)

Gloria Anderson
Grant Auker
Doris Bernard
John Bowerstock
Paul Boyer
Stephen Brown
Herschel A. Brummett
Leroy Cloud
Fred Cottriel
Kathleen Cummings
W. E. Cummings
T. C. Cunningham
Ruby Davis
Jacob Escalante
Blake Farmer
Donald Farmer
J. W. Farmer
Raleigh Farrell
Barbara Forrest
Russell G. Fulford
T. E. Gannon
Elmer Geesey
Kenneth George
Joseph Gerhart
H. T. Goodwin
J. K. Gressett
Lois Gribling
Joe Hanna
Louis Hauff
Kenneth Haystead
Ron Hembree
Alpha Henson
Clyde Henson
V. I. Hertweck
Carl Holleman
Elva Hoover
Raymond Hudson
Ralph Hutchinson
Dwayne Johnson
Earl Johnson
O. W. Killingsworth
Clifton Kornmueller
Clarence Lambert
Charles Lee
William D. Lee
Gayle Lewis
Thomas Lofton
Paul Markstrom
John McPherson
Jack Mitchell
Ernest Moen
David Moore
Hal C. Noah
Robert W. Pirtle
Don R. Ramsey
Silas Rexroat
Curtis Ringness
Jerry Roberts
William Robertson
Gene Roe
Haskell Rogers
Leroy Sanders
Paul Savage
Charles W. H. Scott
Bill Sharp
V. E. Shores
Robert A. Sites
Robert G. Slaton

Bryan Smith
Everett Stenhouse
Melvin Steward
Shirley Tinsman
Earl Vanzant
William G. Vickery
Grant Wacker
Wilbur H. Wacker
Alta Washburn
M. D. Williams
Robert J. Willis
Virgil Ziegler

WOMEN'S MINISTRIES LEADERS
of AIBC's Regional Districts

Southern California:
Sis. Halverson
Juanita England
Sis. Campbell
Florence Beck
Barbara Forrest

Northern California:
Goldia Anderson
Shirley Tinsman
Alpha Henson
Mary Farington

West Texas:
Ruby Davis
Doris Bernard

Rocky Mountain:
Eloise Fulford
Norma Emerson
Francis Wagner
Clara Gustafsen
Joylene Belville

Arizona:
Lois Gribling
Kathleen Cummings

New Mexico:
Mrs. Earl Vanzant
Ruth Savage

PART FOUR ▲▲▲

Presidential Reflections

Don Ramsey

William E. Peters

Carl E. and Alice Collins

David J. Moore

Jim H. Lopez

James V. Comer

▲

Left, Donald R. Ramsey; right, Donald P. Keeter

Don Ramsey presenting diploma to Anthony Ross, 1975

1965–1966 School Year

TV Program circa 1970.

AMERICAN INDIAN COLLEGE: A Witness to the Tribes

DON RAMSEY

President 1965-1973

As I followed in the footsteps of Rev. Alta M. Washburn, founder of All Tribes Bible School in 1957, I marvel at how God has continued blessing this institution in subsequent years. In 1965, after eight years at the helm, illness forced Rev. Washburn to resign from her leadership at the school. Clearly, it had now become too much for her to bear the burden of pastoring All Tribes Assembly of God while simultaneously directing the daily administration of the Bible school. Stepping down from directing ATBS allowed her to focus exclusively on her pastoral ministry and the eventual relocation of the All Tribes Assembly of God church campus to a larger facility.

From the onset of founding the school in 1957 up until her resignation as director[1] in 1965, Sister Washburn's intended purpose for establishing ATBS was to equip Native people for ministry service among their respective tribal nations. Some of the field missionaries serving as pastors in Native churches had already caught the vision and began sending their most promising individuals to the school for discipleship and leadership training.

Before Virginia and I came to the school in the summer of 1965, the Branch of Education, a division within the Bureau of Indian Affairs (BIA), employed me from 1958–1965 as an educator. At first, I was hired to teach children residing on the Navajo Reservation how to speak English; subsequently I was promoted to serve as guidance director at the Greasewood and Tuba City Boarding Schools. Utilizing whatever off duty time I had from my school assignments, Virginia and I pioneered two Navajo churches in the Grand Canyon region of northern Arizona at Cameron and Sunrise Springs. During those seven years, I baptized at least a hundred new converts before we moved to Phoenix to assume our new responsibilities at ATBS.

In the summer of 1965, Rev. J. K. Gressett, superintendent of the Arizona District Council of the Assemblies of God, and Rev. Tom Cunningham, missions director for the Southern California District Council, teamed up to visit several Native missions in northern Arizona. This tour included the church at Cameron, near the Grand Canyon, where they observed the missionaries' desperate need for Native help in evangelizing the lost. Most missionaries knew little of the language or understood the cultural traditions of those they were attempting to reach. Reasoning that the indigenous principle had been utilized successfully on the foreign missions field overseas, they asked, "Why wouldn't it work for America's Native Americans as well?"

Following their tour, Brother Gressett asked me to consider moving down from the Navajo reservation to administer the ATBS program in Phoenix. He said that if I could not come, the school would be closed because no one else who had been contacted felt called to fill the vacancy created by Sister Washburn's resignation.

After much prayer—and also thoughtful consultation with my wife, Virginia—I resigned my employment with the BIA, and we both agreed that I should accept the position in Phoenix. However, Virginia and I felt it necessary to stipulate that the two districts interested in investing in the Bible school program pledge to financially support our family, for we had no dependable source of missions support. Accordingly, a stipend of $600 per month was agreed upon with each of the two districts contributing to our family's support. Later churches in other districts would be approached to provide offerings for both the school and our personal budget.

One of the first actions taken during our inaugural year at ATBS was that Brother Gressett establish the board of directors[2]. He invited a select group of leadership representing the two sponsoring districts, Native American missions, as well as some other interested individuals who had a deep desire to see Native Americans equipped for ministry. Later, officials from the

Division of Home Missions at our denominational headquarters in Springfield, Missouri, would chair the board. Other key players would be added in the years ahead. Soon a new name was chosen for ATBS. The school became incorporated as the American Indian Bible Institute (AIBI), and at that time my job title of "director" was changed to "president."

Sandwiched in between auto junkyards, taverns, an airport, and the main truck route, the original Bible school campus was located at 4123 East Washington Street in downtown Phoenix. The school's campus consisted of three simple buildings, one of which was occupied by All Tribes Assembly of God and a tight space for three small mobile homes. At times the nearly overwhelming "aroma" of slaughtered livestock from the nearby stockyard permeated the air we breathed! The Bible school desperately needed a new location—but that would have to wait. It would take several more years before the Lord would providentially provide AIBI with the beautiful, spacious campus location that AIC has today.

After my first year as president, the bookkeeper and office manager were both amazed when they discovered that our books miraculously balanced at the end of the first twelve months of operation. Trusting God to supply the needs of an unforeseen budget that would average $1,000 each month, the school was able to pay the last electric bill when the fiscal year ended. Every school year thereafter, for thirteen years, the school's operating budget ended in the black.

During the early years, St. Mary's Food Bank provided groceries for the school. That source, when combined with other foodstuffs brought in by Pastor Charles E. Lee and Tony Nez, from the Navajo reservation, helped feed both students and faculty. Another resource we tapped into was surplus produce donated by truck garden growers located around Phoenix. Students worked in the cabbage and carrot fields across town after classes each weekday, from which they were permitted to bring the vegetable gleanings to the campus. In the late 1960s we received our first Speed-the-Light (STL) grant from our headquarters in

Springfield, Missouri, to purchase a vehicle. From then on, STL has generously met the transportation needs of the school.

The original ATBS library comprised approximately two-dozen books; however, in time it grew to include many thousands of volumes: the national Department of Women's Ministries and retired ministers contributed to this need until a line-item budget for library holdings was later established. [Editors' note: Today the AIC library has well over 20,000 volumes, many of them purchased in the last three years through two generous $50,000 grants from the United Parcel Service.] The Dorothy Cummings Memorial Library was funded in memory of the beloved wife of Rev. Earl Cummings, Arizona district secretary–treasurer at that time.

By 1965, the Bible school had twelve alumni and an enrollment of five women and one man. After contacting missionaries and recruiting new prospective students, enrollment increased to twenty-two students that fall. In the spring of 1966, a three-year diploma was presented to Wilson Nelson of Bluewater, New Mexico. Wilson became an effective, anointed evangelist, winning hundreds of Native people to Christ in revival meetings following his graduation.

Missionary educators, such as Lonnie and Alma Thomas as well as Joe and Betty Hanna, were already serving under missionary appointment as administrators and faculty members. Alma and Betty would eventually come to work at the school longer than anyone else ever associated with it. Other faculty, such as Doris Carlson, who had recently returned from the world missions field overseas, joined the staff. Instructors such as Pauline Mastries and Eugene Hunter frequently encouraged students to seek the fullness of the baptism in the Holy Spirit in order to bring a seamless integration to the academic knowledge that they were acquiring in the classroom. Bill and Naomi Morley, along with other members of the faculty, helped to mentor promising ministers as they traveled to nearby reservations each Sunday morning for their internship experiences.

Supplementing the active missionaries, retirees including Paul and Audrey Basler, Joe and Noreen Eddy, Belle Kennedy, Thelma

Cox, Janice and Raymond Wiseman, Ann Staley (along with many others) were dedicated to making the school program fully functional. Since no salaries were available, faculty members had to depend upon regular missionary support from their home districts to provide the financial remuneration they needed to remain in service with us.

In 1968, Julius Panda, a Ford Company retiree from Michigan, established a campus print shop. The *Thunderer*, our school's newspaper, as well as a yearbook, was published for many years through his untiring efforts. Ruth Lyon, Home Missions editor for the *Pentecostal Evangel*, also regularly promoted AIBI through a series of published articles that publicized our school to the entire constituency.

During weekends, students assisted missionaries like Al and Vesta Cranston in Stanfield and Native pastors such as ATBS alumni George and Alberta Yucapicio in Casa Blanca. The school sponsored many evangelistic outreaches to Indian communities in states other than just Arizona. Staff members from the school would accompany The Tribalaires, a singing group of students, on long summer tours during which we promoted the school program throughout North America, including Canada and Mexico. Each trip saw many people receive Christ as their Lord and Savior and scores filled with the Holy Spirit!

To teach financial responsibility, we charged a dollar-a-day for student's room and board. Few of them brought public work experience with them so we helped them to find employment in restaurants, schools, dry cleaning establishments, and housekeeping positions. Everyone connected with its operation—board members, administrators, students, and faculty—contributed to help the budget balance and maintain an atmosphere of fiscal integrity. Over time the enrollment grew and the curriculum developed. Numerous donors from across the country joined in by prayerfully and financially supporting our vision. Later we were greatly encouraged when graduates began making such a positive impression on their employers that it resulted in various tribal education committees deciding to grant scholarships to new enrollees.

In 1968, a new ten-acre campus site in the Sunnyslope neighborhood of north Phoenix was purchased. In 1972, after sixteen months of construction, a beautiful, multipurpose building was completed, and we assumed occupancy. It was appropriately dedicated to the Washburns and is known today as the Washburn building. Today the Washburn building serves as one of the dormitories, as well as housing both floors of the library, moved from its previous location, and the MacPherson Education Center. The latter is a learning laboratory and resource center used for both Christian education learning and the elementary education program, named in honor of the late Rev. John MacPherson, noted Cherokee evangelist who served as the first National Indian Representative for the Assemblies of God. During my presidential tenure two other needed facilities, a maintenance shop and a combination chapel, library, and classroom building, were also completed prior to 1978.

Between the years of 1965–1978, I presented diplomas to ninety-five deserving graduates of our school. Finally, after thirteen years as president I resigned my position. Later, after serving briefly at Far North Bible School (now Far North Bible College) in Anchorage, Alaska, I was asked to rejoin the newly renamed AIBC. This time I served as a full-time faculty member for the next seven years. During three of those years, I chaired one of the committees that later helped the college to become regionally accredited in 1988 with the Higher Learning Commission of the North Central Association of Colleges and Schools. Today—to God's glory—the college has evolved into what is known today as the American Indian College of the Assemblies of God.

NOTES

1 During Alta Washburn's tenure as the founding director of the Bible school her title was "director," but when ATBS became a regional Bible institute of the Assemblies of God in 1965, it was renamed as American Indian Bible Institute (AIBI). At that time the title of the institute's director was changed to "president."

2 Today that group is now known as the board of regents.

Don Ramsey

Construction progresses

Don Ramsey at construction site

Don and Virginia Ramsey with their children: left to right: Debbie, Steve, David, and Becky (standing)

Simon and Sammy Peter

Presidential Reflections ▲▲▲

WILLIAM E. PETER on behalf of SIMON PETER

(Choctaw) President 1978

My father, Simon Peter, who served as president of (then) American Indian Bible Institute (AIBI) from 1978–1979, was a Native American who had a burden for his people to know Jesus Christ as their Lord and Savior. He was dedicated to spreading the good news. Born and raised in McCurtain County, Oklahoma, in 1918 my dad, a Choctaw Indian, saw firsthand the problems and despair his people faced.

After graduating from an Indian boarding school in Chilocco, Oklahoma, he went on to Oklahoma Presbyterian College. While there, he volunteered for ROTC. Then when World War II began, he was working in Arizona and returned to Oklahoma, being one of the first in his community's Native Americans to volunteer for combat duty. A patriot, Dad saw his duty to his country and boldly lived up to his commitment.

In time, Simon Peter was severely wounded in Europe by a bombing raid, spending a lengthy time in military hospitals. In 1945, the Army Air Corp escorted him home to Glover, Oklahoma, with the aftereffects of injuries that limited movement to crutches—with reports he would never walk again without them. In effect, this left him a military veteran with a 100% disability. However, a few months later my dad attended a revival being preached by a close friend and Choctaw Indian, Taft Gibbs, which was held under a brush arbor in Glover. There he was marvelously saved and filled with the Holy Spirit. Shortly afterwards, Simon Peter was healed, put down the crutches, and enthusiastically surrendered to the call to full-time ministry. Not long afterwards, Dad returned to college under the G.I. Bill, with a new zeal for learning. There he continued as a university student, worked at a local public school, and even found time to serve as pastor of a nearby church!

▲
▲

Mother and Dad met while they were both students at the Presbyterian's Co-ed Goodland Indian Boarding School, in rural Choctaw County in southern Oklahoma. Mother was from a different clan and area of the Choctaw tribe, but she quickly adapted to the new family she had married into. Somewhat like the Ruth and Naomi narrative in the Old Testament Book of Ruth, the "newly married into family" became her family, their ways became her ways, their home became her home.

When Dad volunteered for military service in World War II, Mother moved my sister and me along with some other family members from Oklahoma to Omaha, Nebraska, where she found employment in an airplane factory in a job traditionally held by men at that time. Because most of the men were off fighting the war, my mother rose to the occasion and proudly did her patriotic duty. Her task was operating a rivet gun to assemble B-29 bombers. I can still recall her telling the other women on the assembly line, "These planes must be made well—who knows, this may be the one our husbands will be riding in above Germany!" Due to her work in the airplane factory during WWII, Mother never cashed any of Dad's allotment checks, saving them so they could buy cattle, ranching equipment, and other items needed by our family upon his return from military service overseas. At every mealtime and also every night before bedtime, we prayed for Dad's safe return from Europe. After his return, Mother was not particularly overjoyed when Dad announced he sensed a call towards full-time ministry since at that time they were running a large herd of cattle on family ranch land. But in time, she gave up her home and moved with Dad as they together launched out into working for the Master. Early on in their joint ministry work, my mother, Sammy Peter, became Simon Peter's most ardent supporter, with a ready word of encouragement whenever she sensed it was needed. They worked together so completely in their joint vision that it became their life's mission. Her dedication continued even after Dad's homegoing: AIBI continued to be a part of her life. Eventually, she returned to the campus and worked there with the students for a few years before retiring.

Simon Peter ministered several years before he was ordained in 1951 with the Oklahoma District Council of the Assemblies of God. He served faithfully as a pastor in Oklahoma, Arkansas, Texas, and Colorado. At each pastorate, the church grew in a number of areas. High on his list of priorities was the spiritual growth and Bible knowledge of his congregants.

With a passionate burden for Native Americans, Simon Peter became a much sought-after speaker for camp meetings on Indian reservations and in Native American communities across the western United States. Many people responded to Christ's call and turned their lives around. In 1978, Dad left a successful pastorate in Colorado and became the first Native American to serve as president of the American Indian Bible Institute, now American Indian College, in Phoenix, Arizona. While still in the prime of his ministry, Brother Peter went home to be with the Lord in 1979 after a lengthy illness. During his short time at AIBI, he helped equip Native people for ministry, instilling the commitment to carry Christ's saving message to American Indians throughout North America.

Undoubtedly, Simon Peter left behind some big tracks to follow and a legacy of life-changing faith that serves as a model for those who aspire to Native American ministry. Dad always told his children that if a cause was worth an effort then it was worth their best effort! My dad's great love for the Native people and Native ministry led the Intercultural Ministries Department of the Division of Home Missions[2] to establish the Simon Peter Fund. This fund has helped Native Americans enter the ministry and plant churches.

Although Mother and Dad are now with the Lord, their dream of spreading the gospel and equipping people for ministry has not dissipated. As I see it, their vision and longing to reach Native people with the gospel continues to this day at American Indian College. I can't help but believe that many of the college's alumni have ministry that has been enhanced by their experiences on AIC's campus. As each of my siblings and I picked up the torch, we have come to realize that our parents opened so many doors for us. Moreover, we enjoy a wonderful life of serving Him in the clear path laid out by our parents, Simon and Sammy Peter. As children we were richly blessed by both the diversity and depth of ministry they came to be involved in. In addition to their service at AIBI in Arizona, Mother and Dad served a total of nineteen different congregations in various pastoral capacities in Oklahoma, Arkansas, Colorado, and Texas!

Incidentally, not long before her own heavenly homegoing, I remember Mother relating how she told her Sunday School class at First Assembly in Poteau, Oklahoma that they had lived in so many parsonages that she could come in at night after church and not even remember the location of a light switch! Well today, they are where He is the light, and I suspect that from time to time, with joined hands, Mom and Dad peep over a heavenly cloud, looking toward churches they have served, AIBI students they remember, and what the alumni are now out doing for the Master.

Indeed, only Jesus knows how many lives were touched by my parents' participation in seminars, rallies, convocations, camp meetings, and revivals. I would be remiss if I didn't also mention their presiding over weddings, funerals, baptisms, baby dedications, hospital calls, and crisis interventions as well! Their willingness to sacrificially serve each church God called them to greatly endeared them to their congregations. Dad served not only his local church and community, but his disctrict as well: his ministry extended to that of a sectional presbyter, as well as involvement in district programs and committees. My parents' ministry has left an indelible mark on my brothers and sisters and me—calling us to march to a higher call, with an ongoing dedication of ourselves so as to be found faithful and fruitful.

One of my sisters, Rebecca Good, is a 1976 graduate of AIBI. She served on reservations in South Texas, Arizona, New Mexico, and in other areas for many years before accepting a teaching job in our native Oklahoma. Today Rebecca is director of Remedial Reading and Early Childhood Development for the Haskell County Choctaw Head Start program in Stigler, Oklahoma. For many years she has conducted "Kids Camp" for Native American children at various summer camps. Rebecca continues to work at summer youth camps and is frequently sought after by various denominations when her schedule will allow. AIBI was greatly instrumental in preparing Rebecca for her life's joy of serving Christ.

Another sister, Ann Thompson, has also dedicated her life to Native American ministry. For many years, assisted by her husband, Mack, Ann served as a pastor on the White Mountain Apache Reservation in the little community of Cibecue, Arizona. Today she is now working on the Yakima Reservation, as pastor of All Tribes Worship Center in Wapata, Washington, approaching forty years in pastoral ministry. When I observe her minister I see the fulfillment of Mother and Dad's dream of ministry to Native Americans richly and vibrantly living on!

My third sister, Jacquie Stout, and her husband, John, have also been in ministry virtually all of their lives, starting when they were teenagers in a church in Texas where Dad served as pastor. They have pastored churches in Utah, Colorado, and have now been in Texas nearly thirty-five years. About thirty years ago, they planted a new church, Bethel Temple, in Denton, Texas, starting with less than ten people—including themselves. The Lord has marvelously directed and blessed their efforts with now literally hundreds attending weekly worship services!

Early on, my brothers Timothy, Phillip, and I committed ourselves to carry out the legacy of our parents. Each of us has served in pastoral ministry in different churches in a number of states. Today, our family now has a third generation of Native Americans from Mother Sammy and Dad Simon, serving the Lord in so many ways. One grandson, Jay Thompson, is a graduate of the University of Washington and a certified public accountant. Another of their grandchildren, Kathy Littlebull—also a graduate of the University of Washington—is now a registered nurse. A few are now in the ministry themselves—some having served churches where Mother and Dad used to be pastors over sixty years ago! For example, Dosha Good Furr and her husband, Gary, are graduates of the Osteen School of Ministry in Houston, Texas, and Carl

Albert State College. Today they are serving on the ministerial staff of OKC Victory Church. Jason and Aimee Peter are on staff at a church in California as the ministers of youth and worship. And there are many more! Unfortunately, the constraints of space won't allow me to list all of them. However, the one thing in which we take the most pride is that they all have a good relationship with the Lord.

Indeed, God continues to be so good to us!

NOTES

Some of the information for this essay was drawn from an earlier article by the author, Simon Peter's son William E. Peter. See William E. Peter, "Simon Peter was a Native American," *Pentecostal Evangel* No. 3980 (August 19, 1990): 17.

2   Today the Division of Home Missions is known as the Division of U.S. Missions.

Bernard Bresson with student praying before class begins, 1970s

Native Leaders, left to right: Charles E. Lee, William Lee, John E. Maracle

Completed Clyde Henson Chapel, 1978

President Carl Collins

Carl & Alice Collins

President Carl Collins praying for graduate Donna (Williams) Shendo

Don Keeter and Sophomore Class, 1983

Carl E. Collins teaching David Cota, Mayda (Maytubby) Martinez, Louisa Lee, and Alberta (Justin) Yucupicio

Presidential Reflections ▲▲▲

CARL E. & ALICE COLLINS

President 1979-1987

On numerous occasions, my beloved wife, Alice, has shared the story of how she as a twelve-year-old girl wrote a paper in school, announcing that some day she would be living and working among the American Indians. Growing up, she held steadfastly to that belief. Later, being married to a pastor did not dampen that calling— in fact, the calling only intensified! Knowing that ultimately we would work together as a team, the timing would be right at any age. In 1970, as a family we led the children's services at camp meetings on the Apache and Navajo reservations. For several years Alice came out to (then) AIBI to work on several occasions with the late Leonard Sampier, his wife, Frankie, and daughter, Martha, in puppet ministry and assisted them in putting on Christian Education workshops.

In 1976, then AIBI President Donald Ramsey recognized the great love that Alice had for the Native students at the school, challenging us to consider leaving everything behind in South Carolina and becoming part of the team at AIBI. After many weeks of rejecting the idea of leaving our home, our friends, the close-knit church that we pastored, and a good salary, we finally said yes. Initially we found that our biggest challenge was asking others to invest in our monthly missions support—this was a real step of faith for us to have to do that! Yet, the Lord revealed to us that it was not "begging," but rather it was giving others the opportunity to reach Native people across all of North America for Christ.

My wife and I will never forget that sweltering August day in 1977 when we stumbled up the steps leading to the entrance of the American Bible Institute with three sweaty kids in tow. Sister Alma Thomas, later to become my great mentor, was there to greet us. How well we remember the laughter at the sight of all of us! Thus, our journey had begun.

Regrettably, we had only one year to work with Brother Ramsey. The time had come for one of God's choice servants, who had a tremendous sense of integrity and love for Native Americans, to say farewell. The time had come for Don and Virginia to assume new responsibilities at Far North Bible Institute in Anchorage, Alaska, and they would be greatly missed here at AIBI.

Thirty years ago the arrangement of the campus was quite a bit different than it is today, in part because there are now several more buildings. However, back in the late 1970s the layout was such that as you entered the front lobby at the Bible school, the president's office was on the right. One of my greatest memories from that time was observing our new president, Rev. Simon Peter, with his Bible open and his head bowed. He was seeking God's guidance for the school. Brother Peter's greatest desire was to see a great revival among the student body that would spread across the reservations like wildfire. This spiritual giant exuded so much strength. Brother Peter faithfully fulfilled his tasks, ministering frequently in the chapel services, encouraging both faculty and students—yet he himself was facing a time of severe testing in a recurring illness. Everyone who knew him was praying for his complete healing. Sadly, by late winter Brother Peter was forced to resign his position as president because of the progression of his illness. Soon afterwards, this great Choctaw leader went home to be with the Lord.

Brother Peter's short tenure as president was traumatic for AIBI. The entire campus community had been so excited to have a Native American assume the presidency of our Indian Bible college. During faculty meeting and chapel services, we diligently sought the Lord to give our board of directors direction in the selection of the next president.

Unbeknownst to me, several faculty members had written a letter to Rev. Theodore Gannon, the board chairman, requesting that I be considered for the presidency. At the same time several board members had mentioned my name due to my background in education. (I had been an administrator and instructor at three different colleges in South Carolina. I also hold a master's degree in higher education, and my thesis was on college accreditation.)

Rev. Earl Cummings, superintendent of the Arizona district of the Assemblies of God and vice president of the board, approached me about taking the position. My response was that I felt that I was more of a "support person" than a "chief executive officer," but if it was the desire of the faculty and board, I would not decline the opportunity to serve as president. Alice and I were interviewed thoroughly at the board of directors meeting, where I was questioned as to my loyalty to the mission of the school and was asked what my vision would be. Although expressing some concern about our newness to this field of ministry, the board felt that it was in God's timing for me to assume the leadership of the school.

Brother Cummings met with me frequently during the first few months of my presidency, giving excellent suggestions for the new administration. Rev. Donald P. Keeter, who had served successfully as pastor of Phoenix All Tribes Assembly of God was invited to become the vice president. Rev. M. Nadine Waldrop, pastor of Co-Op Assembly of God on the nearby Gila River Indian Reservation, became the school's business administrator. Along with Rev. Alma Thomas, serving as the Academic Dean, the three administrators provided over forty years of combined experience from several reservations as well as urban ministry. These three leaders provided a great deal of substance to the work in the early part of my presidency. I listened closely to their suggestions to changes that would take place in the coming months and years.

Just a few days after I assumed office, Superintendent Cummings took me out for breakfast one morning. Eyeing me carefully he remarked, "Collins, you are the 'new man on the block.' You automatically have two strikes against you because you haven't yet fully earned the trust of the people. Do you know what the third one means?" Nodding, I responded, "Yes, I will be out!" Brother Cummings explained that God had given me three excellent administrators. He further emphasized that I should go out to be with the missionaries (at that time we had only four Native pastors in the Arizona district), sit at their tables, and drink coffee with them. Brother Cummings reminded me that I should carefully listen to and seriously consider everything that they had to say. So much learning during those first few months! However, this helped me to realize the urgency of the school's needing to make some drastic changes. With God's help, I gained the confidence and favor of most of the missionaries during those one-on-one times around the coffeepot.

The vision I offered in the early days of my presidency is summarized in *Indian Harvest: A History of American Indian Bible College*:

> *AIBI plays a vital role in the development of the Assemblies of God Indian community. If the Lord delays His coming, graduates will be involved not only in pastoral ministry, but the light of the gospel will shine forth within reservation medical clinics, tribal offices, and drug and alcohol rehabilitation centers. The graduates' stewardship of time and money will help make the local church self-sufficient.[1]*

In 1980, the administration, faculty, and staff conducted a self-study of the institution's future. The study included interviews of missionary pastors, Native pastors, graduates, students, and other stakeholders in the school's future. The culmination of this study was a report entitled *AIBI: How Can We Better Fulfill Our Objectives?* A pleasing outcome of the report's findings was that 87 percent of AIBI's graduates were active in some form of Christian ministry and that 98 percent of our alumni were gainfully employed![2]

The report generated a number of recommendations, including the offering of vocational education programs in order that our graduates could find better employment opportunities upon their return to the reservation. The report also recommended pursuing regional accreditation. As we considered applying for accreditation we continually asked ourselves, "What effect will accreditation have on the original purpose of the school?" The entire AIBI community, including the student body and the board of directors, conducted further study. Each representative group felt that expanding into vocational programs and offering bachelor's degrees in ministry and Christian education would not adversely affect the mission of AIBI.

David J. Moore became deeply interested in the school expanding its scope of ministry and spent countless hours developing surveys and compiling the report data. The board of directors requested that Brother Moore oversee the expansion of the new areas of ministry while yet maintaining the original purpose of the institution. As the expansion began, the school quickly discovered that it would need to establish a foundational studies program, providing remedial education to enable students to improve their skills in reading, writing, and basic mathematics.

Dr. Donald Bogue, who held the dual distinction of being both the former director of a national specialized accrediting agency in health care and an Assemblies of God minister, was invited to the campus. With his assistance, AIBI was able to receive recognition from the Bureau of Indian Affairs (BIA) with the understanding that the school would pursue regional accreditation. Dr. Bogue was instrumental in opening the door to that opportunity and in our eventually receiving regional accreditation.

We all were pleasantly surprised that the regional accrediting body that we were pursuing accreditation with looked upon our "little Indian Bible institute" so favorably. On one occasion after a church service where I had spoken, a retired professor from one of our other AG institutions approached me with: "Our large AG colleges have struggled to receive regional accreditation. How do you think a little known Indian school can do such!" God alone knows! Yet, His timing is always perfect.

Indeed, we sensed the Lord's hand throughout the entire process. In June 1982, AIBI was given "candidate status" for accreditation with the North Central Association of Colleges and Schools (now known as the Higher Learning Commission). Shortly thereafter the name of the school was changed to American Indian Bible College. Arkansas, South Texas, and Oklahoma became sponsoring districts of the college. During this time we adopted as our theme "Taking the Message Home." We emphasized that our graduates would become pastors, youth pastors, and assume other key positions within the Native American communities. We also believed our ministers would be better able to support themselves with a vocational degree. Others would become lay leaders assisting the local church in many areas of ministry. With more lucrative employment possibilities, these graduates would be better able to assist their churches financially. Our key emphasis was recognizing that the American Indian can more effectively minister to his (or her) own people than a nonnative can. We expanded our student recruitment program and initiated a student group, known as the Sounds of Praise, that traveled to churches, camp meetings, and schools, sharing their testimonies of the influence that AIBC had on their lives.

At that time our library consisted primarily of donated books. We recognized that we had an urgent need to upgrade in order to serve the introduction of our new programs. Through one of our board member's influence, a noted philanthropist developed an interest in AIBC and made a substantial donation of $40,000 toward library resources.

As a result of the Lord's favor upon our institution, we began to see increased enrollment. Additional housing and classrooms were needed, so plans were drawn for a two-story building that would house both classrooms and a women's dormitory. Since AIBC already had a heavy indebtedness at that time, we made the decision to build the $280,000 building debt free. We received sizable donations from the Arizona district Women's Ministries, the Northern California/Nevada Women's Ministries, the Ohio district Missionettes, and the Southern California District Council. Still, we needed an additional $100,000, so the board of directors decided to have its own telethon. A number of our board members stayed on after one of our board of directors meetings to make calls to churches within their own districts that were known to be major contributors to missions. By Friday afternoon we were still far short of our stated goal. Rev. T. C. Cunningham, who years earlier had encouraged the college to become a regional institution of the AG, called his close friend Evangelist Jimmy Swaggart. Just as the five o'clock closing time approached, Brother Cunningham received a return call stating that a gift of $150,000 would be on its way! Again, God's perfect timing.

Not only was the building to be erected debt free, but the extra money remaining was used on some urgently needed major repairs. The new building was dedicated as the Gannon Memorial Building in January 1984 in honor of Rev. T.E. Gannon, a great champion of the college who served as the national Director of Home Missions and also for many years as the chairman of the AIBC Board of Directors.

Two years later, the Holy Spirit spoke again to the heart of Rev. Swaggart, who had contributed so heavily to the need of the Gannon building, challenging his organization to provide monthly support to various Native ministries. His mission's director flew to the college and was given a three-day whirlwind tour of many of the local reservations, meeting with some of our graduates, including some who were pastoring churches. It was my hope that this ministry would help to fund some of the work of our graduates out in the field, many of them pastoring small struggling churches. While on our campus, the mission's director met with several of our missionary staff from the college and was very impressed with their high caliber and dedication. Upon his return to their headquarters, the evangelist's organization decided to assist with some of their monthly support, making a substantial monthly contribution that was a blessing to these missionaries.

In May 1983, AIBIC granted its first nine associate of arts degrees in social work, business management, and secretarial science. Two years later, the first bachelor's degrees were added in addition to six ministerial diplomas. Indeed, the college was progressing in a new direction; yet I was pleased to see that it remained true to its original moorings established by Sister

Washburn in 1957. I often felt that I was a coordinator of a plan that God had placed within the hearts of people from every area, including board members, administrators, faculty, staff, students, alumni, and pastors who believed in the ministry of this great institution.

During my final years as college president, God began placing a new vision upon the hearts of Alice and me. We both had come to realize that the primary focus of most denominations' outreaches to Native Americans centered on the reservations, while urban areas were rapidly gaining in Indian population. Secondly, many of our most dedicated graduates were expressing a desire to work alongside a more experienced minister before launching out into their own senior pastorate. Moreover, very few missionary pastors were willing to assist the college in this endeavor. Thus, this became a vital part of our vision to provide on-the-job training to some of these emerging Native leaders. When the pastorate at All Tribes Assembly of God became open, Alice and I discussed our vision with Rev. Robert Sites, the Arizona district superintendent, and also with Rev. Robert Pirtle, our national director of Home Missions.

After much prayer and consultation, we felt that God had given us a new field of ministry. Now, twenty years after transitioning from AIBC, we are still at All Tribes, continuing to facilitate Native ministry by developing Native leadership in the local church. Nevertheless, Alice and I will forever regard our years at AIC as a time of great personal blessing in our lives, and we will forever hold them with the highest esteem.

NOTES

1 See Carl E. Collins cited in Carolyn D. Baker, *Indian Harvest: A History of American Indian Bible College* (Phoenix, AZ, 1992), 23.

2 *AIBI: How Can We Better Fulfill Our Objectives?* Unpublished self-study report, American Indian Bible College, 1980.

Marcus & Tina (Hawthorne) James

Floyd Lee

Presentation to Kathleen Cummings, AZ District WM Director

Lia & Paul Lanuza with son, Jonathan

Stanley Tom

Cheri and David Moore with their children, Rachael, Royce, & Ryan

Charlie Lee and David J. Moo

David J. Moore speaking with student Vince Roubideaux at Cree Student Union construction site; other students: Michael Shorty, Gareth Abbey, Ronald Watchman

224

Presidential Reflections ▲▲▲

DAVID J. MOORE

President 1987-1994

Reflecting on my tenure at American Indian College, I have to say from the onset that it is nearly impossible for me to confine my thoughts to the eight year period I served as president—especially since I actually joined the staff twelve years previously, serving in several capacities (faculty member, student financial aid director, student employment coordinator, business administrator, and academic dean) as AIC developed in ministry scope, educational programs, and professional recognition.

While it was during my tenure as president that the college expanded its physical facilities by constructing the Rodger Cree Student Union, the Charles Scott Gymnasium, and the Charles Lee Academic Center (classroom building and faculty offices), I was simply in place as president when this physical expansion occurred. My predecessors laid the groundwork as AIC grew from a three-year institute with a fixed curriculum to a four-year Bible college with academic majors in ministerial studies, Christian education, business, and elementary education. My presidential predecessors Don Ramsey and Carl Collins deserve much of the credit for being the visionaries who led in this institutional development.

With programmatic and physical expansion came inevitable increase in enrollment. This required an emphasis on student recruitment that the college had not previously stressed with such emphasis. Again, I was simply filling the leadership chair at the right time when enrollment reached 126 students in 1993. This was a high-water mark for student enrollment and a sizeable increase from the 22 students who were enrolled when I joined the college staff in 1975! Our recruiters, Charley Odell and Pete

225

Cordova, traveled many miles, spoke on the telephone with countless potential students, and worked tirelessly to achieve this enrollment growth. Nadine Waldrop, our director of student financial aid, learned the government regulations for the various student financial aid programs and served a critical role during this time in helping students to find various revenue sources through which to pay their educational expenses.

Numerous individuals stand out as being an encouragement to me during my leadership. First and foremost is Jim H. Lopez, who served as dean of students, later as vice president, and eventually as president of the college from 1998–2004. Incidentally, today Jim serves as the director of Intercultural Ministries for the Arizona District Council of the Assemblies of God. He and his wife, Belinda, remain under national U.S. Missions appointment and are actively involved in promoting church planting efforts among diverse cultural groups throughout the state of Arizona—including the seventeen Indian tribes found throughout the state.

Nadine Waldrop was also a constant source of encouragement. Alma Thomas, though a generation older than I, consistently supported my leadership, believing with me that AIC could and should pursue regional accreditation when other voices outside the school said that it couldn't be done.

For a time, Jan Odell served loyally and with great distinction as my personal secretary, shouldering an enormous load at times. Later, Doris Knoles also served as my secretary, and she too was a gifted office manager, capable of multitasking and also very loyal to my leadership. There are so many names that deserve mention I fear I will omit someone, but let me add the following to the list of those with whom I served and whom I considered to be outstanding and loyal colleagues: Charlene Pino (business administrator), Paul and Lia Lanuza (various capacities), Dr. Judy Mattes (academic dean), Betty Hanna (faculty member)—who, like Alma Thomas, was ahead of her time in progressive thinking—Mr. and Mrs. Gene Martin (faithful volunteers), and Dorothy Runyan (another faithful volunteer, now with the Lord, who used to call me "next to none," whatever that meant!).

I would be remiss if I failed to mention great Native Christian leaders like Rodger A. Cree (who served briefly as campus pastor) and the late Charles E. Lee (who taught at the college and previously while pastoring in Shiprock, New Mexico, had sent some ninety students to AIC to receive their postsecondary education). His wife, Corilee, served faithfully for over six years as the secretary to the academic dean. Brother Cree and Brother Lee were true giants of the faith in Native American ministry. How fortunate I was to have them on staff while I served as president!

Still, my fondest memories of campus life were the works that God did in the lives of students around the altars in the Clyde Henson Chapel. We used to have early morning prayers, and I recall many times how grieving students came with broken hearts from situations back home on the reservation (over which they had no control). I enjoyed praying and counseling with many students who would later enter the ministry. This brought me the single greatest satisfaction during my time of ministry at the college.

I remember visiting some students one summer and I discovered that Rafael (not his real name) was living in a Sunday School room in a church on one of the reservations. When I asked him how this had happened, Rafael told me his mother had ordered him out of the home because of his faith in Christ and his decision to attend AIC to prepare for ministry. I left with a sick feeling in my stomach, wanting to take him home with me, yet knowing that there would be similar situations in other communities I would visit.

When the new school year opened the following fall I looked for Rafael, not sure if he would be returning. Then our eyes met and he greeted me with a big smile and proceeded to tell me how much my visit had encouraged him. He also told me he had led a man to the Lord later that summer. Perhaps most importantly, Rafael said the day before he left he noticed that the man he had just led to the Lord was now listed in the obituary column of the local paper. But Rafael also joyfully shared with me, "Now I know his name is also written in the Lamb's Book of Life!" Rafael's mother also eventually gave her heart to the Lord and attended his graduation.

Another story I vividly recall came several years after I left the college. A graduate who was now serving as a pastor related to me, "You know, what I remember most about you was seeing you walk across campus picking up trash." At first I was offended by this because I thought I might have left something of a more lasting impact—like a chapel sermon, or a word of advice, or some leadership decision I had made. But I quickly realized that this was the highest compliment I could have received! Someone noticed an example of the servant leadership approach I sought to preach and teach at every opportunity.

In addition to the miracles in the lives of the students, I need to mention that on a personal level I grew tremendously in my own leadership philosophy during those seven years I served as president. I found nothing more exciting than to see someone else succeed—a student, a fellow administrator, or a faculty member. I particularly sought out those who others might have considered under qualified—perhaps having what many might regard as rough edges. I tried to see value in everyone, though I was not so tolerant of those who came to me complaining about other people and who wanted me to do something about the other person's "problem."

In retrospect I remember that the college's board of directors always seemed to be supportive of my initiatives. That served as a great comfort to me, but I guess it was because I was always able to present them with a balanced budget. We were fortunate enough to finish every fiscal year in the black, and I owe this to all the colleagues with whom I served. They helped to raise funds, sometimes doing without during a tight budget year, and most importantly, they raised most of their own financial support through missionary deputation.

When it comes to fundraising, one story stands out as an absolute miracle. One morning I was driving to the college with my wife, Cheri. I turned to her and said, "Honey, today I'm going to call someone and they are going to give me $100,000 for the Charles Lee Academic Center," which I had been raising funds to construct. This need was critical because I had scheduled construction teams, and although the board was very supportive, they said I first needed to raise another $100,000 before they would approve our breaking ground on construction. Perhaps I should mention that I had already had the city approve of the plans, and excavation was scheduled the next day, so I was a bit under the gun! I didn't want to have to cancel the excavation or the construction teams who were scheduled, and we urgently needed the $100,000.

When I arrived at my office I looked at Doris Knoles, who was my secretary at the time, and said the same thing to her (except this time I left out the word "honey"). I said, "Get me the Rolodex (we used those back then!), and I'm going to look through the file and call someone who will give us $100,000." That's the second time that morning a woman looked at me as if I had lost my mind.

As I started thumbing through the Rolodex I became more and more disinterested in the process. Who was I to assume that I knew what capabilities various past donors would have? Also, who was I to be so presumptuous as to call one of them and say, "Can you give us $100,000?" Literally as I pushed the Rolodex away from me, my intercom sounded and Doris informed me that a gentleman was on the phone who wanted to talk to me about the building project. I assumed he was someone who was scheduled as part of a construction team so I tried to avoid the call, but he insisted on talking with me.

When I answered the phone the voice at the other end inquired, "I understand that you want to build a classroom facility. How much do you need?" Immediately I found myself saying, "Right now I need someone to give us $100,000." There was a brief, deafening silence on the other end. Then the man answered back, "Okay, I'll check with my wife and call you back." In less than a minute he called back and said the check would be in the mail that day!

To sum this up, the check arrived right on time, cleared the bank, and I did not have to so much as lift a finger to make a phone call to get the $100,000 I needed at that exact moment. I had never even heard of the man. His name was not in the Rolodex. I have no idea how he even heard about this project since he was from another state. When I hung up the phone I engaged in my first ever Jericho march, in my office (with the doors closed of course).

This faith-building incident taught me a valuable lesson. Be faithful to God and He will be faithful to you. When you have done all you can, and when you have run out of resources on your own initiative and imagination He will come through, perhaps in a most unusual way. I had told two women I was going to call someone and ask for $100,000. Instead someone called me and asked how much I needed. I've always wondered why I didn't say I needed $200,000. (Just kidding.) I asked for and received exactly what the college needed at that moment.

I just want to conclude by saying it was our great joy to be a part of the AIC family for nearly 20 years. Cheri and I had the privilege of having our three children born in Arizona and of knowing we did well in both serving the Lord at AIC and in raising our children. Today all of them are now grown and married and serving the Lord faithfully.

In terms of my presidential tenure at AIC, I simply blended my gifts with the gifts of many others. I've also come to see that no one person's gift is any greater than any other's—we're all an integral part of the body of Christ. By working together, we have had the privilege of creating some wonderful memories and achieving some notable spiritual experiences that will be with us for eternity. Nothing of significance that happened at AIC while I was president was because of any outstanding contribution that I made. It was a total team effort, and most of the credit goes to those who supported me and whose ideas I simply helped bring to implementation.

1988–89 School Year

Mia & J.R. Boyd

President David Moore congratulating a graduate

Pete Cordova, Admissions Director

Then General Supterintendent of the Assemblies of God
Thomas E. Trask with Jim Lopez

Jim & Belinda Lopez

Jim & Belinda Lopez with their children:
Camellia, Jameson, and Joylina

Jim Lopez praying with student

JIM H. LOPEZ

(Hispanic/Cocopah) President 1998-2004

I first came to know about AIC back in 1970 when I gave my heart to the Lord, while under the ministry of our pastor, Jacob Escalante (Tohono O'odham), who graduated from the college when it was called All Tribes Bible School. As an alumnus he actively promoted this institution. On a regular basis we had speakers and ministry teams come to visit our church on the Ft. Yuma/Quechan Reservation in Winterhaven, California. These speakers and teams would enthusiastically promote what the school stood for and what it offered prospective students.

As I mentioned, I (and incidentally my wife, Belinda) are from Winterhaven, California, which is surrounded by the Ft. Yuma/ Quechan Indian Reservation. I'm Mexican and part Cocopah, but I was raised there on the reservation by a single parent, my mother, who found herself responsible for raising six children by herself after a divorce when I was relatively young. Two siblings were sent to live with other relatives, so my mom was left with the primary responsibility for four of us. I was raised as a Roman Catholic right up until the time that I made a personal commitment to Jesus Christ in 1970. What really made me want to search and find a Pentecostal experience was the need of finding something in life—and I found it at the Assemblies of God church that I attended right there in my community.

Our family was in many ways dysfunctional because my mother had to do everything for us by working two jobs, and we children had additional responsibilities thrust upon us as well. It was certainly a time of learning and development in my life! All of my previous life experience helped to prepare me for the various roles that I played here at the college over the twenty-two years we spent here. Not only did Belinda and I go through some enormous challenges in our growing up years, we also came to work with students who came from similar backgrounds as well.

Adding to our "growing up" experiences was our five years as pastors at Whiteriver Assembly of God on the Ft. Apache Reservation in northern Arizona in the years after I graduated from AIBI. When I came back in 1982 as the newly appointed dean of students, I was able to relate to the needs of our students with a hand in glove relationship because in many cases I could say, "Been there, gone through that—and made it!" We were able to make it and go beyond, because by then I already had my diploma from AIBI, my bachelor's degree from Southwestern Assemblies of God University, and had just started my master's level studies through Fuller Theological Seminary in Pasadena, California. Therefore I was able to say to our students as the apostle Paul told the Philippians (4:13, NIV): "I can do everything through him who gives me strength." I also told our students that their background didn't have to be a hindrance, but could actually become a stepping-stone to success! Belinda and I also found that one's cultural background, including being bicultural, could be a tremendous asset to our students so that they function successfully not only in their Native community but in the Anglo one as well.

Of all my years spent at AIC, I found that the sixteen years as dean of students was a special growing time for me. I recall many times students saying, "Brother Lopez, thanks for sharing with me." After hearing that I would quietly reflect, "Thank you Lord for these students coming into my life, because I've been able to learn and grow from them, and if anything, they've made me a better person and challenged me to step outside my comfort zone." To me, the students were always a blessing in that setting. One I remember in particular is Vince Roubideaux, now serving as the dean of students here at the college. He gave his life to the Lord when he came over here from Nevada to visit his sister, who was a student at the time. At the same time, Vince was studying at the DeVry Institute here in Phoenix. After coming over to visit our school, he began interacting with the students and subsequently gave his heart to the Lord. After graduating from DeVry Institute, Vince enrolled here as a student. Over the years he developed in ministry, met his wife, Jennifer (Smith), here, completed his education, and served in various pastoral roles. Today he is back at the college serving as dean of students. It's always exciting to see that. It was also a blessing to see people like Fred Billie, who came from a military background, then studied here, and went out into pastoral ministry at Kayenta, way up in the northeast corner of the state, to serve among the Hopi and Navajo for a number of years.

I think also of Pete Cordova, who went into evangelistic work; of Jennifer Smith (now Roubideaux) and her involvement in ministry; Tonita (Yazzie) and her husband, Dennis Keith, accomplishing so much among their people, the Navajo. Tina (Yazzie) Abbey and her husband, Gareth ("Geo"), have remained involved in ministry and are leading people to Christ as laypeople in the local congregation. I remember ones like Sandy Ticeahkie, who now serves as the director of admissions—I look to see what God is accomplishing in her life. Sandra (Smith) Gonzales came here with the challenges of being a single parent, and God has taken her through to academic success, teaching in the public schools, and now here serving as the registrar of the college. I also remember how she met her husband, Ryan, here and how the Lord is now using them both together.

God has also used people like Pastor Marvin Begay and his wife, Delia (Orduno), as successful pastors up at Canyon Day on the Ft. Apache Reservation. Pat Merino, who now serves as the director of Plant Operations, came out here from his Native community in northern California and went on to minister up in Alaska. It's wonderful to see not only where our students come from—but where He takes them!

I was also gratified to see how much the faculty and staff had to be a part of the lives of the students as well, even if they weren't able to be out there with them as much as I was. They had a great part in their lives through classroom instruction, personal prayer, and all that was involved in preparing them for these various opportunities of ministry that they have. Even to this day I still hear some of our graduates talk about the influence that the faculty and staff at AIC have had on their lives, preparing them for what they are doing today. That was (and is) part of the team spirit that we always strived to cultivate at AIC.

When I served as president of the college, I was able to draw heavily from the presidents that preceded me: Don Ramsey, Carl Collins, David Moore, and Dr. Duane Collins. All of these leaders set a foundation for me to build upon, so I thank them for their accomplishments. One thing that really spoke to my heart (perhaps a year or so after I came into the presidency) was when a Hispanic man who was a self-employed landscape artist was doing some work at my home, and he asked me what my occupation was. I told him that I was working at American Indian College. He asked me (in Spanish) if I "oversaw maintenance." I paused for a moment, realizing that he was probably viewing me as the stereotypical Mexican who might oversee maintenance or manual labor on the campus. I told him that yes, I oversaw maintenance. Of course, that wasn't the full scope of my duties—but it certainly was part of what I did. As we talked further, I shared additional details about my role, and when he asked me to explain exactly what I did, I told him (still in Spanish) that I was the president (el presidenté) of the college. He put down the shovel, looked me in the eyes, and without saying anything gave me the thumbs-up sign. His non-verbal language told me that one of us had arrived! I realized then that I was in a role that God had called me to and that I needed to consider not only acknowledging the title but fulfilling the role that was expected of me.

That gentleman's response clearly underscored in my mind that not too many people of color have been able to hold this level of leadership within the higher educational community. Therefore, I've always looked at my position as one of service—not only to the students, staff, and faculty of the college, but to the broader constituency of the Native people within both the Assemblies of God and elsewhere.

After becoming president I believed that we needed to meet the needs of not only our students but our college as well. I wanted to make sure the college's academic needs were met. When

I first became the president, we had no doctoral holders on our faculty, so we began by adjusting teaching and administrative roles to achieve such academic advancement. Dr. Joe Saggio was the first one under my presidential administration to complete his post-graduate work, obtaining his doctorate at Arizona State University, and then he encouraged others to do so as well. During my time at AIC we saw a number of others also launch into their post-graduate studies, like Dr. Boyd Tolbert, Dr. David DeGarmo, Dr. Everett Peralta, and Dr. Glen Gray. Their academic attainment helped to increase our academic viability and credibility. By the time Belinda and I left in 2004, there were four residential faculty and administrators with doctorates, and at least one or two additional adjunct professors as well. It excites Belinda and me that we had a part in that and that each professor encouraged the next one towards completion.

I am also proud that AIC is a Pentecostal college that emphasizes the role of the Holy Spirit not only within the chapel services but also in the classroom. It was not unusual for the faculty to see a need among the students, stop the class session, and then go to prayer on behalf of that need, whether it was healing, salvation of a loved one, or finances. I found the same to be true of our staff: they would also stop whatever they were doing and immediately go to prayer on behalf of student needs. That was something I remember from my days as a student in the early 1970s up to the present time of my son who just graduated from the college with a degree in elementary education. I can truly say that when it comes to Pentecost, AIC is a Pentecostal college. However, there's also a balance so that all things are done "decently and in order," so that students can gain a real genuine experience with the Holy Spirit.

One time when Belinda and I were having a conversation with our son, J. D., we all came to the same conclusion: every generation has a responsibility to take it to the next level. My parents never had the opportunity to complete middle school, but my sister and I went on to earn our master's degrees, and the same is true of Belinda. We now see our children pursuing their own goals. Our son, J. D., has set his sights on completing a PhD in the future. And now we are seeing our graduates take it to the next level as well. We look to see each generation of AIC students do the same in ways only dreamed about by previous generations of students.

Because of Jacob Escalante's example as both a pastor and alumnus from the school, it made me just want to accomplish more, not to be content with where I was at. Many of our graduates have left here knowing that God has more for them, so they've furthered themselves in both ministry and educational attainment. There was always a sense that God had great things in store for our students and that we could indeed do "all things through Christ who strengthens us" (see Philippians 4:13). AIC emphasized that, and I see that still to this day. AIC has always emphasized that what God has given you, you are to use to reach out to others and to be a part of their life so that they can have a better life and take it to the next level!

Jim Lopez teaching

Front: Belinda Lopez, Joy Sarabia, Lia Lanuza
Back: Jim Lopez, Danny Sarabia, Paul Lanuza

Ralph Morris and Jim Lopez

John Rose and Jim Lopez

STL Van Dedication: Tommy Carpenter, Duane Collins, Jim Lopez, Joe Saggio, Jack Caudle

These signs shall fo[llow th]em that believe.

Jim Lopez speaking at a California camp meeting

AIC Administration. Front: David DeGarmo, Jim Comer
Back: Vince Roubideaux, Jim Dempsey, Joe Saggio, David Cleaveland

Jim & Sue Comer

Kee & Marie Smith with Jim Comer praying
for Sandra (Smith) Gonzales at her graduation

2005 Resident Staff.
Front: Cheryl Grass, Miracle (VanZant) Johnso
Back: Paul Lent, Austin Jones, Ron Burnette

President Jim Comer presenting communion with
Sylvia Rivera, David Cleaveland, Sandra Gonzales and Sandy Ticeahkie assisting

Presidential Reflections ▲▲▲

JAMES V. COMER

President 2005-

I want to begin by stating that I am firmly persuaded that each and every day of our lives is a gift from the Lord. I say this because as a child I was not expected to live—I was born with a hole in my heart. When I was about four years old, my parents took me to Children's Hospital in Kansas City, Missouri. The only option the doctors gave me for survival was closed-heart surgery, a procedure that yielded me only a 10 percent chance of survival! By the time I was seven, medical advances created an opportunity for me to have an experimental surgery through the combined generous underwriting of the Crippled Children's Fund, Red Cross, and Blue Shield. So, at Stanford University in Palo Alto, California, I became the second person in the United States to ever undergo open-heart surgery—and it must have been a success because nearly fifty years later I'm still here!

I came from a Christian family with five children. My parents were always involved in church life, with my father serving as deacon. Unfortunately, when I was twelve years of age, some things happened in the church my family was attending, and I rebelled by turning my back on the Lord. I had written the Lord a note and told Him that if I was ever going to have a relationship with him, I wanted it to be real; I did not want any kind of hypocrisy in it. I put that note in my billfold and carried it with me for the next four years. Shortly thereafter, my dad went into the ministry. That summer, at age sixteen, I almost drowned, swimming in the Salmon River in central Idaho near our home. I called out to God, and He was faithful to save my life. I told Him at that time that if He would save me, I would do my best to serve Him. Since that time, I've done my best to serve the

Lord Jesus Christ with all of my heart. Shortly after my near-death experience, I found that note and realized that my relationship with God was real. However, I had a lot of things to overcome as far as being able to enjoy the emotional freedom of serving God.

Later on, I married my wife, Sue, and we entered Trinity Bible College in Jamestown[1], North Dakota. While there, I received a call to missions. I had hoped to serve the Lord in Alaska, and I prayed that the Lord would send me there. Sue, however, was called to Africa, and we married with the understanding that though I did not sense a personal call to go to Africa, if God called me I would be willing.

During my junior year at Trinity, we had been involved in special missions prayer services that featured a visiting missionary from Africa. Following one of those services, Sue asked me, "What would you do if God called you to be a missionary to Africa?" I told her God would not do that to me! I went to my next class, and the instructor opened the class by saying, "I sense there is someone here who has told God no." I immediately knew who he was talking about. So I told the Lord that if He wanted me to go to Africa, I'd go—but I would rather not.

When Sue and I were attending Trinity, we were assisting a pastor in a church thirty-five miles south of Jamestown, throughout the duration of our studies. (By the way, I believe that every Christian needs to be actively involved in ministry.) On the first night that we were trying to get a youth group started, I arrived early to pray. While I was pacing the floor, seeking God, my eye fell upon a world missions map at the back of the church. At that moment, in a vision experience, the part of the map representing the Congo[2] enlarged until it consumed the whole world, and God miraculously placed a desire and a passion to serve Him in that part of His harvest. Something very special was imparted to me at that time through the Holy Spirit and has grown into a stronger conviction over the years: God's will is not what we desire, but it is submitting to God, who has a plan for our good.

Sue and I answered that call, and we went to Africa as Assemblies of God missionaries, working first with the

International Correspondence Institute (ICI) (which now operates under the auspices of Global University based out of our denominational headquarters in Springfield, Missouri.) Later I became director of Bethel Bible College located in the interior of the Congo.

The greatest thing I learned in Africa was our schedules and plans are less important than people, and our job as the Church is to love and support one another ("For God so loved the world..."). That pivotal life lesson has followed us from Africa, and later to Europe, and now here to American Indian College in Phoenix, Arizona.

We thought we would be in Africa for the duration of our ministry, but in 1991, Sue and I had to leave there because of health concerns. Returning to the United States was a difficult time, because we both left a piece of our heart in Africa. However, the Lord opened the doors for us to go to Belgium and serve at Continental Theological Seminary, just outside of Brussels. While we were there, besides teaching, I worked with student ministries and enjoyed working with over thirty different cultures—as we had when we were in Africa.

To a large degree I believe those experiences prepared me for coming to AIC, because our students come from such varied cultures, with each tribe having its own cultural distinctives that must be recognized and appreciated. I think that grasping that truth has proven to be one of my strengths, as here at AIC we are working with many different peoples and cultures. So accordingly, we must treat each ethnicity within its own cultural context.

Over the years I've become convinced that God gives divine assignments. In 1996, during our first year at AIC, while the students were arriving, I saw a young woman get out of a car, and I really believe that the Lord spoke to my heart that she was someone who would be special in my life and ministry. I "adopted" her as a spiritual daughter. She was in some of my classes, and I asked her to serve on a committee for student ministries, and later on the Campus Missions Fellowship leadership team. This young woman had come from a very difficult home situation and was very angry—yet she really loved God and wanted to serve Him. I was able to work with her over the course of five years, counseling and praying with her, and see God bring out the beauty in her nature and develop the relationship with the man who became her husband. In fact, it was my privilege to marry them, and Sue and I continue to enjoy watching their family grow, for they have both moved into this new stage of their lives. I know that it must be a delight to God's heart to see how they are serving Him together—I know it's been a delight to my heart! This sort of "divine assignment" has happened regularly at AIC. The relationships begun with students and continued through the years is something I hold very dear to my heart.

I have been greatly impressed with the tremendous leadership that God has given the Christian Native American community through such Native leaders as Rodger A. Cree (Mohawk) and Irving Terry (Pima). Both are sterling examples of godly integrity and great spiritual stature. I have tremendous memories of watching them in their quiet way of worship influence the atmosphere of a service. I'm also grateful for the relationship that I have with my presidential predecessor, Jim H. Lopez. I had the privilege of serving alongside him as a faculty member, and then later, as business administrator and vice president. I grew to respect the way that he led. You were aware of his quiet presence and spiritual strength. Just by watching him, you were also aware of his love for God.

Some of the students who've graduated from this college have had a profound effect on my wife and me: Pastor Joel Cornelius, who along with his wife, Sharon, graduated just a few years before we got here, served as our pastor out on the Salt River Indian Reservation for five years. Joel is a young man in love with God and very sensitive to the Holy Spirit. I've also been blessed as a president to have other Native alumni like Vince Roubideaux, who now serves as dean of students, Sandy Ticeahkie, our director of admissions, and Sandra Gonzales, serving as registrar. All of these returning alumni have such an incredible love for God, which they cultivate in our students, thereby impacting the next generation.

As I've watched them, I've been able to see the stamp of both God and this college on their lives and watch them grow and mature.

I would be remiss if I didn't mention some of the other warriors of the faith who have served this college, helping in the educational and spiritual formation of our students during my tenure here. People like Joe Hanna and Donald Keeter, who are both now with the Lord, faithfully served this college and our students for years. Their spouses, Betty Hanna and Gayle Keeter, continue in their chosen callings here as shining examples as well (Betty as a beloved faculty member and Gay as our account manager). Nadine Waldrop, our director of student financial aid, and John Rose, our librarian: each has given exceptional service to the college for more than twenty years. Rev. Eugene Hunter also continues to serve as a shining example to our students. Although now given the honor of professor emeritus for his full-time teaching from 1975–1991, he continues to teach part-time. Also, Alma Thomas, another professor emerita, continues as a prayer intercessor for AIC. Her late husband, Lonnie, served many years earlier as one of the college's vice presidents. What a legacy of faithful service for our students!

The staff and faculty at American Indian College serve tirelessly with great sacrifice. At AIC we all come together with a common purpose and calling—to see God's plan and purposes fulfilled in the students of American Indian College, thus impacting Native America and elsewhere for eternity.

A great big thank-you goes to the board of regents of American Indian College; they continue to give wisdom and guidance for the direction of AIC. The support of the board and many churches and individuals who have caught the vision of God's work in this place make it possible for God's plan to be accomplished.

I would also like to mention that through the years countless volunteers have made a huge impact on American Indian College. Churches have come with groups to do renovations and building; RVer's have come to help with renovations, general maintenance, and the like. Churches have donated time to preparing our mailings. The list goes on and on.

Only eternity will tell the effect of each person's gift of time, talent, and finances on the spiritual well-being of our students and on the people they in turn influence for God.

As I evaluate American Indian College, I realize its unswerving commitment to Christ's Great Commission (Matthew 28:18-20) is undoubtedly the strongest evidence of its claim to be a Pentecostal college. Our students have a tremendous desire to reach those who are lost on the reservations; however, they are not limited to a vision only for the unsaved among their own people. They have also developed a global vision, which has propelled them to Mexico, Honduras, Belize, Canada, the Philippines, and Mongolia, as well as to the homeless in the inner city. I've watched our students over the years sacrifice their summer vacations, spring breaks, and long weekends, putting in long hours to go out to the reservations, travel abroad, or minister in their local church setting.

What would I like the legacy of AIC to be? I would have to respond: young men and women sold out to God, full of the Holy Spirit, determined to minister no matter what profession God has called them to; young men and women filled with a love for Christ that is evident in every aspect of their lives, who are determined to make a difference for the kingdom of God that is undeniable; young men and women whose values are not placed upon position or title but rather on the work of the Kingdom—the total focus and desire of their hearts!

NOTES

1 Today Trinity Bible College's campus is located in Ellendale, North Dakota.

2 The nation known in colonial times as the Belgian Congo was subsequently named the Democratic Republic of the Congo when it gained independence in 1964. Its name was changed to Zaire in 1971 by then President Mobutu, but subsequently the country was renamed the Democratic Republic of the Congo during the 1997 revolution that ousted him from power.

Tammy Tunney speaking to children at a Birthday Party for Jesus

Dolores Wren, Director of Food Services

Glen Gray, Chair of Christian Ministry Department

Fall 2003 Student Body

Michael Johnson with Vice President David DeGarmo

EDITORS' NOTE:

This third (and final) "book within a book" was written in 1992 by Carolyn D. Baker, who at that time served as a faculty member of American Indian Bible College. This work, while covering some of the same history that *Trail to the Tribes* and *A Trail of Beauty: A Short History of American Indian Bible College*, served to update as well as set the tone for (then) AIBC's role in the 1990's Decade of the Harvest. Dr. Baker was also assisted by Joe and Betty Hanna, as well as Betty Jeter Jernigan, in her compilation of this work. A formal introduction to this work provides additional background information on this work and its contributors.

Once again, as in *Trail to the Tribes* and *A Trail of Beauty: A Short History of American Indian Bible College*, the Editors have chosen—in order to preserve as much as possible the original content and flavor of this work—to do minimal editing except where necessary.

PART FIVE ▲▲▲

Indian Harvest

Introduction to Indian Harvest:
A History of American Indian Bible College

Joseph J. Saggio

Indian Harvest: A History of American Indian Bible College

Carolyn D. Baker

249

Dorothy Plake with student group - Circa 1997

Connie Pereida, Dorothy Plake, Brigette Fominyam, Nathan Wright, Demetria (Wimbish) Bryant, Millicent (Thompson) Canales, Dorie (Brume) Simpson and two unidentified girls

Far right: Art teacher Louisa Lee, with students: Charles Tuckfield with his daughter, Josie, and (seated) Tawnee Sykes

Coach Tim Grant with students. Front: Craig Bidtah, Nathan Wright, Tara Smith, Tiffany Grant. Middle: Tonya (Zospah) Bidtah Ursala Watchman, Pearlene Benally, unknown. Back: Tim Grant, unknown, Jarrett Grant

AZ Women's Ministries Director Betty Owens, with Debbie Rice, at AIC Harvest Festival

Tribalaires, 1982

Front (left to right): Juanita Jim, Julie Mendoza, Lia Lanuza, Back: Stanley Brooks, Denise Terry, Modesta Scott, Arthur Volares, Carlene Myers, Juda Mendoza

Introduction to
INDIAN HARVEST:
A History of American Indian Bible College

Introduction by Joseph J. Saggio

Originally published in 1992, *Indian Harvest: A History of American Indian Bible College* was written by Carolyn Denise Baker with able assistance from Joe and Betty Hanna as well as Betty Jeter Jernigan. Originally conceived as a book to commemorate Heritage Week in 1992, *Indian Harvest: A History of American Indian Bible College* served to update two previous accounts about the Bible college[1] and to provide momentum for AIC's involvement in the General Council's theme for the 1990s: Decade of Harvest.

An ordained AG minister and former nationally appointed home missionary, Dr. Baker served as an instructor at AIC from 1987–1998. During that time she taught Christian education, theology, biblical studies, Hebrew and Greek. She also found time to serve as assistant librarian during part of that period. In 1995, Dr. Baker completed her D.Min. degree at Western Conservative Baptist Seminary in Portland, Oregon, and was a participant in January 1998 at the En Gedi excavation cosponsored by the Hebrew University of Jerusalem and the University of Hartford in Hartford, Connecticut. As a professor, Dr. Baker has come to be known for her creative approach to teaching, which integrates strong academics with practical application. She is often remembered for her caring approach to students and belief that learning can be fun—even when it's hard work!

Subsequent to teaching at AIC, Dr. Baker served as professor of Biblical studies, Hebrew, and Greek at Trinity Bible College in Ellendale, North Dakota, from 1998–2002. Always the learner, Dr. Baker completed a master of arts in English (literary analysis with a linguistics cognate) at the University of North Dakota (Grand Forks), culminating that experience with an award-winning thesis: "The Haiku Poetry of Internee Itaru Ina at Fort Lincoln, Bismarck ND."

Presently, Dr. Baker serves as assistant professor of English at Mayville State University in North Dakota, advising Campus Crusade for Christ and chairing the diversity committee. In 2005–2006 the student senate nominated her for the Teacher of the Year award. In addition to her duties as a university professor, Dr. Baker remains active in pulpit ministry, speaking in both Assemblies of God and Evangelical Lutheran Church of America (ELCA) churches, also teaching English as a Second Language (ESL) to Sudanese refugees at All Nations Assembly of God (West Fargo). She serves as a mentor for master of arts students at Global University and has lectured as a visiting professor at universities and seminaries in South Africa, China, and Singapore. Dr. Baker remains a frequent contributor to publications in the areas of theology and English.

Rev. Joe Hanna and Rev. Betty Hanna have served for over forty-five years in various capacities as nationally appointed missionaries to Native Americans. With pastorates in Bloomfield, New Mexico, and San Tan and Casa Grande, Arizona, the Hannas have served with distinction for many years. Before his death in 2001, Brother Hanna, in addition to his pastoral responsibilities and services as the sectional Indian representative, taught extension Berean School of the Bible classes for fourteen years to a number of Native ministers. During that time he traveled tirelessly throughout the region, mentoring aspiring Native pastors. A number of those he mentored are now in full-time ministry, including Rev. Irving, Carolyn Terry, Rev. Lorenzo Coops, Rev. George Yucapicio, as well as a host of others. A graduate of Southwestern Assemblies of

God Bible College, Brother Hanna also served as vice president of ATBS as well as a Bible and ministry instructor from 1963–1968.

Those who remember Brother Hanna remember his great love for Native people and how he loved fellowshipping at various church, sectional, and district activities. Even in his seventies, Brother Hanna served as a camp counselor at the Arizona district Native youth camps, staying in the boys' dorms and ministering to the youth during the altar services. Only eternity will tell the influence that this giant of the faith had on the Native people that he so joyfully and faithfully served!

Rev. Betty Hanna continues to serve American Indian College as an instructor in the Christian Ministry and Elementary Education Departments. Like her late husband, Sister Hanna was first licensed as a minister through the Illinois district in 1950, subsequently being ordained in 1982. After graduating from Southwestern Assemblies of God Bible College, Sister Hanna went on to earn her teaching degree from Grand Canyon College and subsequent graduate studies at both Arizona State University and University of Arizona. For sixteen consecutive years she has overseen the Birthday Party for Jesus, which each year has grown to attract some 400 plus visitors to the AIC campus from the community adjacent to the campus! Over the years, this event has resulted in literally hundreds of decisions for Christ by children and adults alike. Sister Hanna is especially proud of the fact that the students actually conduct this event themselves.

At a time when many would be contemplating retirement, Sister Hanna remains active as one of AIC's most popular and respected instructors. Sister Hanna has taught at the Bible college for more than twenty-five years—not including time taken out to teach in the public school system and work with her husband as they pastored.

Betty Jeter Jernigan also assisted with the editing of *Indian Harvest: A History of American Bible College* during the time that she and her husband, Robby, were associated with American Indian Bible College (1985–1990). During their time at AIBC, Robby served as the college's business manager. Betty is a graduate of

Southwestern Assemblies of God University in Waxahachie, Texas, and later received her master's degree in intercultural ministry from the Assemblies of God Theological Seminary (AGTS) in Springfield, Missouri. During her graduate studies she met Robby there, also an AGTS graduate.

Marrying in 1982, the Jernigans began their missionary work with home missions in 1984, joining American Indian Bible College in 1985. During Betty's tenure at the college she taught in the area of foundational studies and Bible. The Jernigans have three children and currently reside in Marshfield, Missouri where Robby is an Assemblies of God crisis and fire department chaplain.

NOTES

1 *A Trail of Beauty: A Short History of American Indian Bible College* by Pauline Dunn, originally published in 1984, and *Trail to the Tribes* by Alta M. Washburn, originally published in 1990.

Indian Harvest

A HISTORY OF AMERICAN INDIAN COLLEGE

Carolyn D. Baker

We trust that the story of AIBC presented in this book will be used of God to encourage Christian laborers for the harvest among Native Americans. May these brief accounts of dedication and sacrifice inspire us to new vision. May we rejoice as we review the stories of God's faithfulness. And may we renew our commitment to the task that lies before us, with the strong confidence that "He who began a good work...will carry it on to completion until the day of Christ Jesus" (Philippians 1:6, NIV).

PREFACE

The heritage of an institution is a blending of the stories of many people over the years. Their vision, their labors, their defeats and victories—all are part of the story that is told when people gather and reminisce. Our heritage is our collective memory. We remember not only the notable occasions, but also those personal stories that somehow capture the essence of who we are.

It seems appropriate that a book recording this type of story would be the combined effort of many individuals. Carolyn Baker conceived the design for how the story would be told. She also did most of the research, sifting through numerous interviews and publications. Joe and Betty Hanna reviewed the original manuscript, checking the accuracy of the information. Others were consulted as well. Many of their helpful suggestions were incorporated. Betty Jernigan put the final touches on the document, editing it and enhancing style and structure.

This book has been prepared for presentation during Heritage Week at American Indian Bible College. Our hope is that students, faculty, staff, board members, contributors, and prayer partners will all benefit from reading an updated history of the school.

We believe that reviewing our history from time to time is not only appropriate but necessary. By this means we may gain a proper appreciation of the ministry God has entrusted to us and maintain a correct perspective for future endeavors.

This book is lovingly dedicated to Sister Alta Washburn. Though many have contributed to AIBC's story through the years, she holds a unique place in our hearts. Her vision for All Tribes Bible School and the dedication and sacrifice with which she pursued that vision were the seed from which our present institution has grown. Sister Washburn, we thank God for you and for your labor in this great harvest.

A MAN SCATTERS SEED UPON THE GROUND
▼▼▼

In considering the work of the harvest it is always difficult to point out when the effort began. Who can say what watering occurred to soften the ground before the sower scattered the seed? Only God knows how many individuals submitted to intercessory prayer on behalf of America's Native population before the first missionaries came into the Southwest bearing the gospel seed. We do know that "in the fullness of time" (Gal. 4:4; see also Eph, 1:10) God sent out laborers to a field that He had been preparing and would continue to cultivate for harvest.

Our story goes back to 1931, when the Ernest Marshall and Dewey Beadle families left Salineville, Ohio, on their long trek to San Carlos, Arizona. America was experiencing a time of great economic depression. But financial concerns were not uppermost in the minds of these godly families. Their concern was for the unevangelized Apache tribe. They wanted to fulfill the call of God on their lives, taking this Indian tribe the message of hope in Christ.

As they began the new work in San Carlos, the new missionaries regularly reported back to their home church and requested that their friends uphold them in prayer. This sharing of their burden for Indian ministry began to have an effect they could not have anticipated. In 1946, Alta Washburn, the pastor of the church in Salineville, resigned from that work to move to San Carlos. She and her husband, Clarence, were led by God to assist in the ministry among the Apaches. Upon the Washburns' arrival, the results of the Marshall's and Beadle's labors were already evident. One hundred Apache converts were there to greet them—a thriving full-gospel church!

The missionaries in San Carlos began training the Indian converts to share the gospel with their own people. When Dick Boni, a Native preacher, began taking God's Word to neighboring communities, it was a great step forward in Indian ministry. The vision began to spread, and soon more missionaries and Native

▲
▼

Americans were responding to the challenge of presenting the message of Christ to southwestern Indians. They spread the precious seed, the Word of God, throughout the area. Though in some places the ground was hard and the Word was not freely received, some seed was finding fertile ground in seeking hearts.

In 1947, the Washburns faced the distressing reality that they would be unable to stay in San Carlos due to lack of funds. They had been using their own money they had saved before leaving Ohio, and it had run out. Since Clarence Washburn could not be employed on the reservation, he went to look for work in Phoenix. There he not only found a job to support their missions effort, he also discovered that Phoenix had a substantial Indian population.

So the couple moved to Phoenix, and Sister Washburn began All Tribes Indian Assembly. Her sorrow at having to leave San Carlos was replaced with rejoicing. What a wonderful open door for ministry lay before her!

Much like a storm pounding its rain against young crops in the field, adversity comes from time to time in the work of God. The young Indian churches faced a new phenomenon in the 1950s. Eager young Indian believers began responding to various evangelists who would gather crowds around themselves and their ministries in great tent campaigns. Many of the converts won through the sincere labors of godly pastors and teachers were extremely susceptible to the appeal of these campaigns—for they were not always able to discern error when it presented itself.

Some Indian believers were driving long distances to attend the campaigns. They gave sacrificial offerings to evangelists who offered no credentials but their own promotional materials. Many sincere seekers left the campaigns not only with empty pockets, but with hearts full of turmoil and confusion.

In the wake of many of these meetings, Sister Washburn began to see an influx of Indian Christians coming to her church for help. These believers needed sound biblical teaching. A vision began to form in Sister Washburn's heart: "You must build a Bible school and train these Indian people in sound doctrine, so that they will not be led astray—so that they can carry the true gospel to their people."

Though the enemy had brought about a potentially destructive situation for the young Indian church, God used it for their good. Adversity resulted in new strength. The Harvest Master planted a seed in Sister Washburn's heart that would yield a greater harvest than she could have imagined.

From that point her objective was sure, and she did not waver from it. She had the answer to her heart's cry. She dedicated herself to the work of establishing a training center for Indian converts—All Tribes Bible School.

THE SEED SPROUTS AND GROWS

▼▼▼

First, the stalk

As Sister Washburn surveyed the need for training Indian converts for ministry she saw more and more indications that confirmed this was the time for such a work to begin. New Christians and aspiring ministers needed a Bible-centered, Spirit-empowered, and culturally relevant education. Other institutions existed which provided Bible training, but the cultural factor became an increasing concern.

Pauline Dunn comments in *A Trail of Beauty*: "About this time, friends helped send two of the Sampson brothers to Southwestern Bible Institute in Waxahachie, Texas. But the food was different. The culture was different. The young Native Americans felt like foreigners in their own land. One of the Sampson brothers stayed two years. The other persisted and graduated from Southwestern in 1957."[1]

The Sampsons' experience reinforced the idea that there were Indian Christians who felt their need for a Bible school education. It also pointed out the fact that many cultural barriers had to be dealt with when Indian students attended non-Indian schools for the first time. Certainly there would be many Indian students who would appreciate a Bible school geared to their culture.

Convinced that the time was right for establishing a training center for Indian students, Sister Washburn began to wonder where the school should be located. Should it be started in Phoenix? There was a significant Indian population in Phoenix already. Many attended Phoenix Indian High School, a boarding high school serving tribes from across the western states. Others came to Phoenix from the reservations to receive medical and dental care at the Indian Hospital. Still others were drawn to the "Valley of the Sun" by employment opportunities.

Sister Washburn decided to start the new work in conjunction with the existing All Tribes Indian Assembly in Phoenix. But how would funds be provided? Facilities would have to be expanded.

Who would support her in this venture? One day her telephone rang. On the line was Arizona District Superintendent J.K. Gressett: "Sister Washburn, there is a church in Baytown, Texas, that desires to contribute to an Indian project in Arizona."

Awestruck, Sister Washburn responded: "Brother Gressett, this is the first open door. God is answering our prayer for the needs to be met. Soon Sister Washburn and some Indian youth from All Tribes Indian Assembly were traveling to Baytown to present the need that was on their hearts. They returned rejoicing, with an offering from the Baytown church to pay for a foundation, blocks, flooring, walls, and plumbing!

More and more people joined in the vision. An additional $1,000 was collected for building materials. Then furniture was donated. Two more workers volunteered, a man and his wife from Southern California. They were on hand to serve the new students when school began.

On September 28, 1957, All Tribes Bible School opened its doors. What a day of victory! A new building at 4123 East Washington Street awaited the arrival of thirty-two students. What a flurry of last-minute preparations! Sister Washburn and others brought pans from their own kitchens. They rushed from one surplus store to another to buy the few items they could afford to be able to serve the students.

When school began, daily provisions came in unusual ways. Some remember that for breakfast, lunch, and supper they had pinto beans. They had them hot and cold. They had them with tortillas. They had them with fry bread. They had them with store-bought bread. They had them with everything imaginable! Then they began to pray, "Lord, help us!" There had to be some other provision. Soon a man appeared at the door to deliver a truckload of fish. After that it was fish for breakfast, lunch, and supper!

Once Lois Gribling, the Arizona district Women's Ministries director, hit a deer when she was driving near San Manuel. She donated it to the school, and the menu was changed to venison for breakfast, lunch, and supper! Those were exciting days. The school never knew how God's provision would come or exactly what it would be.

Those who would come to join in the work—missionaries and maintenance men, office workers and faculty—would hear the words: "I cannot pay you, but you may eat with the students. You will have to trust God for your own support." A faith work had begun.

Convinced of ATBS's strategic role, these servants of God labored "in faith, not having received the promises, but having seen them afar off, and were persuaded of them, and embraced them" (Hebrews 11:13, KJV).

NOTES
1 Pauline Dunn, A Trail of Beauty: A Short History of American Indian Bible College. (Phoenix, AZ: 1984), 4.

THE SEED SPROUTS AND GROWS

▼▼▼

Then, the blade

The 1960s were years of expansion for ATBS. After eight years of nurture by Sister Washburn and the early volunteer workers, the school had become well established. It was in July of 1965 that Sister Washburn turned over her administrative responsibilities at the school to a new president, Rev. Donald Ramsey.

Brother Ramsey came to the school as a veteran missionary under appointment with the Assemblies of God. He had a background in public education, having received his masters degree from East Central State University in Oklahoma. His most recent assignment had been on the Navajo reservation. He had been pastor of the church in Cameron while teaching at the BIA boarding school in Tuba City.

The growth the school had experienced was bringing about changes. No longer operating solely as a department of All Tribes Assembly, ATBS's influence was reaching well beyond the Arizona district's borders into the Rocky Mountain, New Mexico, West Texas, Southern California, and Northern California/Nevada districts. It had taken on the characteristics of a regional school. The Assemblies of God Division of Home Missions noticed that development and granted its endorsement. All Tribes Bible School became incorporated as American Indian Bible Institute. The school then became regionally governed by six districts and overseen by the Division of Home Missions.

Even with its expanding influence, AIBI retained the characteristics of a "faith mission." But it was not faith alone that kept the school going. Perhaps the most memorable feature of those days was how hard everyone had to work! Instructors and administrators not only performed their academic tasks but would cook, scrub floors, gather food, drive students to work, and monitor study halls. Each willingly worked ten to twelve hours a day.

Though resources were quite limited, God always supplied.

For eight years the students and staff had enjoyed meals prepared from government commodities. But suddenly that source was cut off. Not only was further provision denied, but all the remaining government-supplied canned goods were removed. The school's cupboards were left bare!

Questions flooded President Ramsey's mind: "What will we eat? We've depended on those commodities, and now there isn't anything left. Everything has been taken. School is about to start. What are we going to do?" The monthly donations the school received were meager, at best. They were not adequate to provide food for the students and staff; and besides, that money had to be applied to other pressing bills. In faith, the decision was made to begin the school year as scheduled.

God's provision followed that step of faith. It came from many sources. Staple goods were donated by St. Mary's Food Bank in Phoenix. A downtown Phoenix mission gave bread and even ice cream to the school. Trucks and vans from near and far, filled with food, pulled on to the school property and unloaded their goods onto the empty shelves. What a wonderful sight!

The Arizona District Council Women's Ministries had begun a project in 1961 that they named the "Harvest Rally." Soon after school would begin in the fall, an appeal would go out to women's groups throughout the state. On the appointed day, the women would bring groceries they had been collecting and give them to AIBI in a great rally on the school campus. Never had the Harvest Rally been more welcome than during this food crisis. What a blessing to be able to depend on the women to minister in such a practical way! The worst part of the crisis was over. The shelves were no longer empty. No one had to go hungry. God had supplied and would continue to supply.

God provided an ongoing source of supply through a unique opportunity given to the students. They were allowed to work some nearby fields and then were granted the privilege of gleaning after the work was done. On the site of the present-day Metro Center Mall were abundant crops. Each day after class the students were bussed to the fields, where they joined other Indians—migrant workers. Together they worked and then gleaned for carrots, onions, broccoli, and cabbage. Time spent in the fields became not only a source of supply for the food needs of the school, but an open-air classroom in evangelism. Many migrant workers received the gospel witness of their new Christian friends.

The students' personal needs were also met in unusual ways. One student secured a job as housekeeper for Dr. Loyal Davis, stepfather of former First Lady Nancy Reagan. Living with the Davis family year-round, she was furnished with room, board, and even a Cadillac to use for transportation to and from school!

As years passed, the material needs of the school continued to present opportunities for God to demonstrate His faithfulness. One fall the school faced a critical need for furniture. The Bible school was using beds borrowed from the Arizona district campground, and they would have to be returned soon. President Ramsey was considering the problem as the school year approached. There were no beds for the young men to sleep on. Then one day the phone rang. The call was from Laveen, Arizona. "I have several box springs and mattresses. Would you have any use for them?"

It was not long before an old cattle truck delivered the promised supply of beds. Once more God had met the need just in time. He did it in His own way, through the obedience of one of His servants.

As the school progressed, it faced more dilemmas concerning facilities. AIBI outgrew its Washington Street building. Not only had the number of students increased, but the original teaching staff of 3 in 1958 increased to 9 by 1971. The addition of maintenance personnel, secretaries, cooks, and dormitory supervisors strained the already cramped quarters.

Though a move seemed inevitable, it would not be easy. So much had to be considered. Finances were a big hurdle. Property, buildings, the move itself—all presented problems. It was time to seek God for answers.

One day President Ramsey returned from north central Phoenix and announced to his fellow workers, "We have bought a mountain!" Located on North Fifteenth Avenue, the newly-purchased ten-acre plot was easily identified because of the small mountain on its north boundary. The owner had substantially lowered the required down payment for the land, and when a sizeable gift came in, followed by a $5,000 loan, AIBI's offer was accepted. On February 28, 1968, AIBI dedicated its new property.

The construction of a multipurpose building set into the mountain was the next challenge. Construction was begun with only one-fifth of the funds needed for the large 14,000 square-foot facility. But the very day the building fund was exhausted, $10,000 arrived from the Minnesota district. As always, God's provision was both sufficient and timely.

The construction of the new building was a labor of love, with retired military couples, pastors, students, faculty, and administrators all participating in the work. On October 1, 1971, the nearly completed building was dedicated. On that day, Rev. Charles W. H. Scott, national director of the Division of Home Missions, articulated the vision shared by all present.

He dedicated the new campus "as a school of the Bible...and to the Indian tribes...to endue students with a new dimension of consecration through the sufficiency of the Holy Spirit."

Though the purchase of the new campus did not immediately solve all the problems of the growing school, it certainly opened many doors for improvement and expansion. A retired businessman from Sun City visited the campus one day and remarked to President Ramsey: "Brother Ramsey, the school needs a maintenance shop." The maintenance shop was at that time housed in the multipurpose building, occupying space that could otherwise be used for a much-needed additional classroom.

With the businessman's $10,000 gift and a $2,000 offering from the Georgia district's Christ's Ambassadors, a separate maintenance garage was built on the campus's southwest corner. Little by little the new campus became more functional.

Another area of need at the time was the school's library. Dusty and worn sets of Pulpit Commentaries, Sunday School teachers' training manuals, and public school textbooks all lined the uncatalogued shelves and sat stacked in boxes.

From unexpected and sometimes sacrificial donations, the library's resources began to expand. An administrator gave 300 of his own theology books, practically his whole library, so that students might have more complete references. A grant of $2,000 dollars was used to initiate a Native American collection, which became widely esteemed. Occasional cash offerings for books helped to supplement the holdings. In 1968, AIBI had only 1,000 volumes, but by the summer of 1978, the library holdings had increased to 6,500. (The library's growth has been constant, its present inventory standing at 14,000 volumes.)

Though the move to the multipurpose building on the new campus did remove the library from the threat of the Washington Street building's leaky roof, facilities for storage and the atmosphere for study were still lacking. The Dorothy Cummings Memorial Fund, established as a memorial to the wife of Arizona District Secretary/Treasurer W. E. Cummings, provided the resources for shelving units, study tables, comfortable chairs, and even a typewriter. The timing of the donation was crucial. The school could not have provided for a genuine library atmosphere and comfortable furniture for study through its own budget. Once again, God found a way through the generosity of His servants.

As the development of the new campus proceeded, it became evident that God was doing something beyond the limits of the school grounds. He was raising up a number of ministers and laymen to help with promotion and fund-raising for the school. He placed a burden on their hearts to see AIBI become all it could be to the glory of God. And they spread the vision to those they met.

One such friend of the school was Rev. Clyde Henson, pastor of Capital Assembly of God in Sacramento, California. Brother Henson had visited the old campus on Washington Street and had been moved by the needs he saw. As a member of AIBI's board of directors, he stayed in close contact with the school. When the move to the new campus was made, he committed himself and his resources to seeing adequate facilities built. Not only was his church heavily involved in supporting the school, but he became an outspoken promoter of AIBI wherever he went. His wife, Alpha, also a strong supporter of the school, became a great blessing through her work as president of the Women's Ministries of the Northern California/Nevada District Council.

In 1976, the Hensons and many others saw a pressing campus need and began to work toward its solution. Students needed more classroom and library space, as well as a place for worship. The Northern California/Nevada Women's Ministries presented AIBI with nearly $30,000 from their Penny Fund Project for a proposed building to house chapel, classrooms, and library. The Arizona district Women's Ministries raised nearly $9,000 for the project, and the Southern California Women's Ministries donated over $5,000 for the new facility's equipment. A generous Georgia district layman sent the school $10,000. A Windsor, Virginia, church gave $5,000. The list of donors went on and on. Individuals and groups with a heart for missions responded sacrificially to see the new building erected. On September 29, 1978, the Clyde Henson Memorial Chapel was dedicated. With Brother Henson's untimely death, the school had lost a great friend. Dedicating the chapel to his memory was a fitting tribute. As a place for worship, for evangelism, and for the training of Indian students the chapel would become a landmark. Students for generations to come would point back to times in that chapel, around those altars, where their lives were changed by the power of God.

THE SEED SPROUTS AND GROWS
▼▼▼

Then, the head

During the years of Brother Ramsey's presidency, AIBI experienced many changes. An advanced curriculum had been adopted, a new ten-acre campus had been purchased and developed, the Institute had been incorporated, and American Indian Bible Institute received the Assemblies of God Education Department's endorsement. The institution was making great strides forward.

Another era was beginning. On July 1, 1978, the school's next president, Reverend Simon Peter, was installed. President Peter, a Choctaw Indian from Oklahoma, had a rich ministerial background and a personal interest in AIBI. His daughter had attended the school, and he was committed to its goals. Moving to Arizona from a pastorate in Colorado, he brought inspiration to students and faculty alike. The reality of Indian leadership for the Indian school was an exciting new dimension in the school's development.

But President Peter's administration, though rich in quality and inspiration, was severely limited in its duration. The recurrence of a former illness produced a time of great testing. As early as August, the gravity of his condition became evident, and students and faculty began to intercede for their beloved brother and for the school's future. As President Peter preached for the opening school revival, the student body, faculty, and staff were encouraged, revived, and renewed in the Lord. In November and December he preached chapel services and traveled with the Tribalaires in spite of his illness.

The steadfastness of his faith became a standard for others to emulate. Yet in January 1979, President Peter had to be hospitalized at the Veterans Hospital in Phoenix. He was later transferred to Tucson. In March, Simon Peter resigned his position at AIBI. The faculty, staff, and students continued to pray for Brother Peter and to receive inspiration from his faith and courage in this time of trial.

On November 5, 1979, the Lord called Brother Peter home, and he entered into rest.

Though Brother Peter was granted only nine months to serve at AIBI, effectiveness in the kingdom of God cannot be measured in days, weeks, or months. His example left an indelible mark on the lives of those he touched. Trust in God was the guiding force in Simon Peter's life. The legacy of faith and courage that Brother Peter imparted to AIBI wove its way into the very fabric of the institution and became a part of its strength.

Brother Peter's death had been a blow to the school, but faithful men stood in the gap, and God continued to work out His purposes. During President Peter's illness, Vice President Eugene Herd had carried a heavy load of responsibility. He assumed administrative responsibilities upon Simon Peter's resignation in March, 1979, and guided the school until the time when the board could install a new president.

AIBI's next president was Rev. Carl Collins. He held a master's degree in higher education from Appalachian State University and had been effective in children's evangelism on the reservations. An appointed home missionary, Brother Collins began serving at AIBI in 1977 as a teacher and director of employment for the students. He was installed as president of AIBI on May 29, 1979. His vision and direction for the school ushered in the next phase of AIBI's growth and development.

President Collins summarized his vision for the school with these words: "AIBI plays a vital role in the development of the Assemblies of God Indian community. If the Lord delays His coming, graduates will be involved not only in pastoral ministry, but the light of the gospel will shine forth within reservation medical clinics, tribal offices, and drug and alcohol rehabilitation centers. The graduates' stewardship of time and money will help make the local church self-sufficient."

President Collins kept attuned to comments from friends of the school. He heard them saying, "Right now our students need technical training. We need AIBI graduates qualified to hold jobs on the reservation. Our graduates need to support themselves while they pioneer churches."

Economic woes on the reservations in the 1980s were undeniable. President Collins embarked on a course of action that would address the practical implications of taking the message home to the reservations and other Indian communities.

In 1980, AIBI began granting associate of arts degrees in newly-instituted occupational programs. Ministerial programs were upgraded to offer bachelor of arts degrees in ministerial studies and Christian education as well as the three-year diploma already being offered. Students were being trained both to minister and to support themselves in the types of jobs that would be available on the reservations.

In order to serve the newly-expanded programs, the library once again had to be upgraded. A member of AIBI's board communicated with the school that he knew of someone who might be interested in helping. Through this board member's influence, a noted California philanthropist became interested in AIBI. When he became convinced that donating books and equipment to the school library would be a lasting contribution to benefit Native Americans, he donated $40,000 for library holdings.

The improvements and changes in the school were welcomed, but not without some concern. Was this new growth in line with the school's purposes? Or would the changes AIBI was experiencing bring about a change of ideals and goals? In 1980, the faculty, staff, and administration began to take a closer look at the school's direction for the future. They conducted a thorough self-evaluation and produced the document "AIBI: How Can We Better Fulfill Our Objectives?" Though at that point the school had not begun to seek accreditation, AIBI's willingness to seriously evaluate its strengths and concerns was a significant step. What would it take to receive accreditation? They would have to provide data to prove that the school was faithfully carrying out its objectives. The process was one of measuring the school against its stated goals to determine its effectiveness. AIBI was ready for that process. In practical terms, they had already started it! The decision to apply for accreditation was made, and the official process began in 1981. It was the beginning of many hundreds of hours of hard work.

In deciding to pursue accreditation, the faculty, and administration had to address several concerns. Among them was the question of whether accreditation would change the traditional open door policy for prospective students. What about those students who due to limitations in their secondary education still struggled with their basic academic skills? Would they be denied access to AIBI's expanding programs? There had to be a way of meeting the needs of these students and still attaining the standards needed to receive accreditation.

The answer to this dilemma came in 1982 when AIBI instituted the Foundational Studies Department. The Foundational Studies program was designed to enable students to improve their foundational skills in the areas of reading, writing, and basic mathematics.

One student who took advantage of the program had more of an impact on the school's progress than she could have known. Though she was lacking many of the necessary college skills, she came to AIBI and enrolled in Foundational Studies. With much determination on her part and encouragement on the part of her tutors, she tried and tried again to pass her GED (general equivalency diploma) test.

One day, on her fourth try, she passed the GED test administered at Glendale Community College. She and the Foundational Studies director arrived back at the AIBI campus, where they immediately met with the academic dean. As the excited student shared her joy with those who had helped her achieve this milestone, it created quite a commotion.

The three had been oblivious to the accreditation committee standing nearby. Observing the student rejoicing with her instructor and the academic dean over this success, the committee witnessed a striking illustration of the Foundational Studies program at work.

Visits from members of the North Central Accrediting Association to interview students, faculty, and administrators were a significant part of the evaluation process. But much of the research required was to be presented to the accrediting board by the school. It was a valuable learning process for AIBI.

The board of directors, administration, faculty, and students were given the opportunity to examine the institution, review the past, and plan for the challenges of the future. Faculty and students were involved in developing questionnaires for surveys. Board members reviewed documents and added their comments. Personnel on every level became involved in the process.

When the accreditation committee evaluated the information they had gathered and gave their report, they voiced both areas of concern and commendable strengths. The Foundational Studies program was an area that received commendation from the committee for the "significant progress in student achievement." Another thing that impressed the accrediting committee was the school's ability to develop student lives "consistent with its Christian mission." They noted the report that 87.2 percent of the school's graduates were "active in some form of Christian ministry," and 98 percent were "gainfully employed." Yet another commendation was given for the "excellent relationship" among staff, faculty, and administrators.

On June 25, 1982, the long-awaited day came when AIBI became approved as a candidate for regional accreditation. The comprehensive study took seven years to reach the final phase. But already at this early stage in the process, all indications were that a positive outcome could be expected.

The student population numbered 59 in 1982, and the outlook for a continued increase in enrollment was promising. A new student recruitment program was initiated, and three new districts became sponsors of the school—Arkansas, South Texas, and Oklahoma.

Once again another building was needed, this time for both dormitory and classroom space. Plans were drawn for a two-story building to be built adjacent to the existing multipurpose structure. An ambitious goal was set: to complete the $280,000 building debt free. Once again it was a time to couple faith with hard work in order to see the goal fulfilled.

Many significant donations came in from across the country. Among the major contributors were a large evangelistic association, the Arizona district Women's Ministries, the Southern California District Council, the Northern California/Nevada district Women's Ministries, and the Ohio district Missionettes.

But the financial challenges were not the only obstacles to be overcome. The mountainside of solid granite had to be conquered. In trying to excavate the site, the hydraulics on the backhoe being used broke several times. It was estimated that about fifty picks were broken on the hard rock. But eventually the ground was prepared, and the building began to take shape. After much hard work, the project was completed. Built debt free, as projected, the new facility originally comprised both dormitory and classroom space. Later it housed up to 56 students.

In January 1984, the new building was dedicated on the rocky mountainside. It was named the T. E. Gannon Memorial Building, in honor of the former director of the national Division of Home Missions and chairman of the board of AIBI. It was to become a memorial to a man with a heart for Native American ministry. General Superintendent Thomas Zimmerman sent his greetings and penned a prayer for the dedication ceremony: "We pray that the presence of God will grace this occasion, and it will be the beginning of a new era of growth. We believe this institution is destined to play a most strategic role in preparing a host of qualified workers to become meaningfully involved in the whitened harvest field, reaching multiplied thousands in the days that remain ere Christ returns."

In June of 1984, the name "American Indian Bible Institute" was changed to American Indian Bible College to reflect the changing academic status of the school. Enrollment continued to climb. In 1986, enrollment passed the 100-student mark. The vision of the college's strategic role in preparing Indian ministers for the harvest was being fulfilled.

Then the full kernel in the head

President Collins had guided the school during a time of unprecedented numerical growth. Now it was time for another change of leadership. Collinses' resignation became effective January 1987. W. E. Cummings served as interim president until the board of directors could meet and elect his successor. AIBC's new president, appointed in March 1987, was Rev. David Moore. Originally from Ohio, Brother Moore had been associated with the school for many years. His involvement went back to the summer of 1969, when he had worked at the school as a student intern from Evangel College. He had helped dig postholes for the electricity on the new campus that year. Later, the Lord led him to receive a Division of Home Missions appointment. He returned to AIBC as an appointed missionary in 1975 and served in various positions at the college. He received a master's degree in intercultural ministries from the Assemblies of God Theological Seminary and became a doctoral candidate in higher education at the University of Arizona. Most recently, he had served as academic dean at AIBC and had a leading role in the pursuit of accreditation. He was able to maintain continuity in the accreditation process as president.

Accreditation was awarded to AIBC on August 22, 1988. American Indian Bible College became the only accredited Indian Bible college in the United States.

At that time, 85 percent of AIBC's former students were living in American Indian communities, 94 percent of the graduates were employed, and 77 percent were involved in some form of Christian service. The effectiveness of the school's ministry could not be questioned. The institution was flourishing.

President Moore stated his vision for the college: "I want to be sure AIBC continues on its present path and is committed to its purpose of preparing Indian men and women for ministry to their own people."

The potential for the college was greater than ever. But greater potential also meant greater needs. Once again it was time to consider a new building. Though the students had dormitories, cafeteria, library, chapel, and classrooms, they had no place to gather for fellowship and recreation. The board of directors noted the need and revised the master plan for the campus to include a student center.

Appeals were launched to solicit funds for the new facility. At first, response was slow. But in His time, God sent help from various sources. MAPS workers, "Recreational Vehicle Ministry," came to the campus to help build the student center. Skilled construction workers and others volunteered their services under this program, saving thousands of dollars in labor costs. When funds to purchase supplies would run low, God would meet the need, and the work continued. The Northern California/Nevada District Council Women's Ministries contributed $29,000. The Arizona District Council Women's Ministries contributed $15,000. And many more individuals and groups had a part in funding this project.

God had another miracle of financial provision in store for the growing school. Through a pastor in Pomona, California, President Moore was invited to make a presentation at a very important board meeting. An elderly sister in the Pomona church had made the church board trustees of her estate. Upon her death, the board would be entrusted with decisions concerning the disbursement of her estate according to her desire to be a blessing to American Indian ministry. For many years she had a love and burden for American Indian missions. She longed to see the full gospel message put into the hands of Native American men and women committed to serving God. The board was very impressed by what it heard of AIBC and its ministry. Later, President Moore was invited back to the church to speak at its missions convention.

When the time came for the funds from the estate to be disbursed, the trustees decided to give $225,000 to American Indian Bible College. The board of directors of the college designated the grant to (1) fund an endowment for student scholarships, (2)

complete the Scott Student Center, and (3) assist in much needed campus renovations. Once again, a dear servant of God was used to bring a lasting blessing to His work.

The Scott Student Center, named for former national director of the Division of Home Missions, Charles W. H. Scott, was completed in 1988. It was dedicated, debt free, on September 13, 1988, for the glory of God, at a cost of $285,000.

With the new student center available, a sports program in men's and women's volleyball and basketball was initiated. It was greeted with enthusiasm by students and faculty alike. But the sports program did not just provide a recreational outlet. From the beginning, these activities became a tool of evangelism. Athletic contests were scheduled on or near reservations, from California to Louisiana. Young people from the reservations would attend. They would hear testimonies from the players at halftime. They were encouraged to remain after the games for evangelistic rallies. The new outreach proved very effective.

Providing opportunities for outreach had always been a goal of the college. In 1988, another ministry began. That summer, selected students ministered to the Ketchi and Mayan Indians of Belize, Central America. It was the first overseas missions trip by AIBC students. They found both a personal acceptance and a receptivity to the gospel among these Central American Indians. When the student group returned to campus, they shared about their missions experiences, injecting a new enthusiasm into the school's missions prayer groups and activities.

The possibilities for American Indian Bible College and its ministry seem limitless. Perhaps God will choose to send an Indian graduate of AIBC into foreign ministry one day as a result of new outreaches. Perhaps God will raise up more Indian leaders to fill key positions at the college. But whatever the future holds, we know that God will use AIBC to prepare laborers for His harvest field.

American Indian Bible College has grown and flourished under the hand of God. The seed planted in Alta Washburn's heart has produced a mature plant. We see the present maturity and abundance at AIBC as the fruit of many servants' labors and a tribute to God's grace and power. He has brought about "the full kernel" (Mark 4:28, NIV).

Today the AIBC campus consists of six buildings and is valued at over $1.5 million. The college family, including students, faculty, staff, and administrators, has grown to about 150. Each year, between 20 and 25 graduates receive their diplomas or degrees. With the addition of the North Texas District Council in 1987, AIBC now has 10 supporting districts on its regional board. We rejoice in God's goodness that has brought us to this hour.

But we must not forget another harvest that is still to be reaped—the harvest that is our very reason for being. It is the harvest of Indian souls that will be gathered for the Master by AIBC's students. It is a vast harvest, sometimes difficult to reach, and in many cases already ripe. The Scriptures tell us that we "must work...while it is day: the night cometh, when no man can work" (John 9:4, KJV). AIBC's students and graduates are being sent out, even as darkness is falling, to participate in that great and final harvest. May the Harvest Master give us all an ever increasing faith and determination for the task that is yet to be accomplished.

EPILOGUE

The Decade of Harvest is upon us: the 1990s. What a long way we have come from those early beginnings on Washington Street! But the same vision is before us that the early pioneers of this ministry saw—the great harvest of Indian souls that must be reaped for the Master.

American Indian Bible College has set these goals for the Decade of Harvest:

- To win 12,000 souls to Christ
- To train 200 ministers
- To plant 25 new Indian churches

The most exciting part of AIBC's story is still ahead of us. We believe these Decade of Harvest goals will be met, should the Lord tarry. It will require vision and sacrifice among our students and all the support personnel involved in their training. It will take the same anointed, prayerful ministry that has characterized AIBC's existence from the very beginning. May we live up to the wonderful heritage we have received and complete the task that is set before us. Any sacrifice will be amply repaid when we hear the Harvest Master say, "Well done, thou good and faithful servant" (Matt. 25:21, KJV)."

PART SIX ▲▲▲

Faculty Reflections

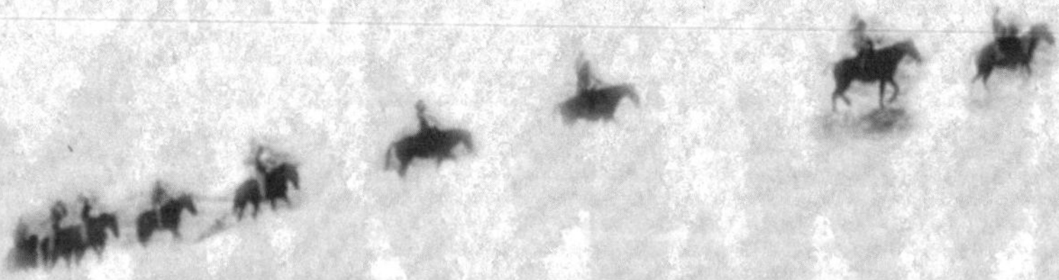

Alma F. Thomas

Eugene Hunter

Betty J. Hanna

Belinda F. Lopez

Nancy J. Saggio

Everett F. Peralta

Alma & Lonnie Thomas

Alma Thomas teaching

Tribalaires, 1977

Alma Thomas and Eric Lee, 1979

AMERICAN INDIAN COLLEGE: A Witness to the Tribes

ALMA F. THOMAS

Professor Emerita (Elementary Education, General Education, and Ministry)

When I returned to the Bible college in 1975, my husband, Lonnie, and I had been away for over a decade, pastoring two different Indian churches, the most recent one being on the Navajo reservation in Tuba City, Arizona. During this time I also taught public school, so it was quite a change for me to go from eighth graders back to working with adults. But I was delighted when we were invited to come back! All the time I was teaching public school in Tuba City I used to sit at my desk when the students were quietly working, and I'd think to myself, "Oh God, I wish this were a Bible school where I could teach Bible to these eighth graders instead of just English." That was a hunger that I had always had as a public school teacher with a Bible in front of me—but I knew that I could never fulfill that dream serving in secular education. You see, I have a call on my life as a teacher, and I felt so fulfilled when I returned to the college in 1975 (after that ten year hiatus) because I could then share the Word and see the young Native students grow in the knowledge of God's Word.

In my forty plus years being associated with American Indian College (under all of its various name changes) I've enjoyed some profound experiences, dating all the way back to the early 1960s when Lonnie and I first joined the teaching staff. I've seen God move in the lives of countless students, but I'd like to tell you about three students in particular from the early 1960s who impacted my teaching career immeasurably.

When we first arrived in 1961, ATBS was a small school, and we never had more than about eighteen students during those early years. Conditions were cramped as far as dormitory space for the men and the women. We had just one little building; yet in spite of such "close fellowship," everybody got along.

We had a young man enrolled by the name of George Garcia. He was from Sells, Arizona, and was a member of the Papago tribe (now known as the Tohono O'Odham Nation). George could not read, but any time that he would open his Bible he could read every word without faltering the least bit! He was amazing to all of us, because he had to have somebody read his other textbooks to him—but when it came to his Bible, he was able to read every word without any hesitation. As I recall, George was very crippled and also played the guitar. Although he wasn't the most academically-inclined student, nonetheless his miraculous ability to read the Bible was such a blessing to behold right in front of our own eyes!

A second student that also made a measurable impact on my life was another Papago student. Jacob Escalante was also from Sells, and he and his wife had care of eight children—some of whom were his own, others were relatives who had been abandoned and needed their loving attention. Jacob worked all day on a construction job to support his large family, and then in the evening he would come over and take evening classes at ATBS. He was a man of great integrity and dependability. Though he was not well-educated in the broadest sense of the word, he had a great deal of wisdom. I remember two things about Jacob in particular: first, he loved the Lord with all of his heart and second, he had not yet received the baptism in the Holy Spirit by the time he graduated after four years of night courses. When Jacob completed his studies, we were all thrilled for him because he had shown so much tenacity, allowing nothing to deter him from his goal of completing his Bible school education. He accomplished all this despite the challenges of toiling all day at manual labor and then having to stay awake and focus on nighttime studies.

Jacob struggled in his learning, but he did learn and was able to master the material. When he graduated, we rejoiced, thinking, "He'll be quitting his job and going back to the reservation—or to wherever the Lord opens a door for him." But to our surprise, Jacob told us that he wasn't going to leave yet! He wanted to stay at the school and attend the church, because as he put it, "I have not received the baptism of the Holy Spirit, and I know that I cannot go and minister anywhere without the power of the Spirit in my life." So he stayed! In every service we had in the little chapel, which served both the church and the Bible school, Jacob was on his knees up on the little black platform way in the back, seeking the Lord and praying to be filled with the Holy Spirit with the evidence of speaking in other tongues.

A number of services passed, but Jacob faithfully and diligently sought the Baptism. Finally, one Sunday night as he was praying, he did receive the Holy Spirit. Needless to say, we all rejoiced and praised the Lord, because Jacob's prayers had been answered and what he had been seeking for so long had now come to pass, and he was truly overjoyed. Sure enough, the next day when Jacob went to work at his construction job, he resigned. Jacob boldly told his boss the truth: "Now that I have received the baptism of the Holy Spirit I know I'm equipped to go back to my reservation—or wherever the Lord wishes to send me." Jacob returned to his home reservation and served as a pastor there, later serving as a leader in tribal government. Afterwards, he returned to pastoring, settling on the Ft. Yuma Reservation near Winterhaven, California, and reached out to the Cocopah and Quechan Indians. Lonnie and I always felt that Jacob had a tremendous potential and ability to succeed in ministry—and he did!

Before I tell you about the third student, I'm reminded that AIC has always had a strong Pentecostal influence throughout its history, and demonstrations of the Spirit have always been important here. One special miracle that I will always treasure took place at a White Mountain Apache camp meeting where many of our students were involved in various leadership capacities. In fact, part of the reason that we were attending this camp meeting was to recruit more students to attend our school. During the service, one of the Apache men present gave a message in tongues, followed by an interpretation in the Apache language. Shortly after the interpretation was given in Apache, one of the visiting missionaries (who did not speak Apache) gave the same interpretation in English! I was greatly blessed by this because clearly God wanted everyone present there at that meeting to be able to hear and respond to His

Word—regardless of whether they spoke English or Apache. Truly God is no respecter of persons!

Since the early 1960s I remember seeing many demonstrations and manifestations of the Spirit at the Bible college. There has never been any doubt that this is a Pentecostal school! We saw many physical and spiritual healings, as well as broken lives restored. It was spiritually invigorating to be a part of this school because of the freedom that we had in the Holy Spirit moving among us, never feeling any constrictions at all.

The third student that I remember was a woman we met during our very first year at the Bible school in 1961. It was a hot summer evening in the beginning of that first year soon after arriving that we took our group of students down to the river to have a barbeque and to just meet together and get acquainted.

As we were enjoying ourselves towards nightfall around the fire, all of a sudden we heard a coyote howling across the river. We had a woman student present there with us whose name I cannot remember. At the sound of the coyote howling her face froze in an expression of absolute terror. Lonnie and I had absolutely no idea what was going on, and for the rest of the evening she didn't say anything to any of us—she just sat there without moving or responding in any way to anyone around her. When we returned to the campus that night, I asked her, "What was wrong?" Fearfully she recounted to me, "Well, I remember when I came to school (she was from California) the medicine man from our tribe put a curse on me and told me that when I heard the coyote howl, that would remind me that I was going to die on January the first." Visibly shaken, she explained to me, "The curses are real! They really do happen!"

I could clearly see that she had come under bondage to this old feeling of her tribal religion. I told her, "We're going to pray for you. I would advise you to go to your room and stay until you get deliverance from this." I could see that she was clearly shaken by this event, so I told her, "Go, get your Bible, drink some fluids, and fast—don't eat any big meals right now. Stay on your knees and pray—and we'll be praying with you—because you've allowed yourself to come under the bondages of your old ways."

So she went into her room, and we didn't see her for three days. Then on the third day she came out of her room and had this big smile on her face—she just looked so free! You could tell that she had been with Jesus! I went up to her, I called her by name, and I asked her what happened. She said, "As I was praying and reading the Word I came to Galatians 5:1, which reads: 'Stand fast therefore in the liberty wherewith Christ hath made us free, and be not entangled again with the yoke of bondage' (KJV). All of a sudden everything left me! I had such a wonderful peace that came back into my heart!"

She was now totally free from the bondage of fear placed in her heart by the medicine man. It was such a blessing to see God's power to deliver these students from the bondage and control of their tribal religions. I will never forget this as long as I live!

In retrospect, I've seen so many changes over the past forty-five years. Of course the school is larger today than it was in the beginning. One thing I've been pleased to see is that the power of the Holy Spirit continues to be allowed to move in the lives of the students. It's also been wonderful to see all of the improvements in the college, including the new buildings, increases to the size of the faculty and staff, as well as the upgrading of its academic credentials.

AIC passed another major milestone when it received regional accreditation in 1988 from the North Central Association of Colleges and Schools (now the Higher Learning Commission). Pursuit of accreditation has allowed us to be able to upgrade the curriculum and add additional degree programs. I'm also pleased that we have such a beautiful campus today—especially when I remember how our old site looked down on East Washington Street. The improvements in the appearance of the campus over the years have been a tangible demonstration of God's blessing upon this place—and I'm grateful for that. But most importantly I'm delighted by the outpouring of God's favor in the lives of our students—that's where the real blessings have been!

Eugene Hunter, far right, with students in the 1970s

Alma Thomas and Eugene Hunter working together

Eugene Hunter with student in 1983

Isabel Espinoza, left, and Nick Zamorano, right, in class

EUGENE HUNTER

Professor Emeritus (Bible and Ministry)

In 1974 I drove a Speed-the-Light van for one of the Arizona missionaries from Springfield, Missouri, where we were living at the time, to (then) American Indian Bible Institute (AIBI) to look it over. My wife, Emily, and I had been encouraged to do so by her boss, Rev. T. E. Gannon, who was then the national director of the Division of Home Missions for the Assemblies of God.

It was not long afterwards before my teaching career began at AIBI in August 1975, continuing full-time until the fall semester of 1991.

One of my ongoing privileges as a missionary educator has been seeing how many of my students by God's grace have undergone dramatic life changes to become what they are today. Back in the mid-1980s I remember asking the students in a psychology course to write down some of their early life experiences and how these incidents subsequently affected them. Based on what some of them wrote, many mental health professionals might have predicted these students would be emotionally scarred for life and incapable of ever functioning successfully in society. Yet, because of the transformation in their lives by being born-again and filled with the Holy Spirit, many of them became successful pastors or ministry spouses, attaining God's best in their lives and marriages! Many of our students grew up in alcoholic homes and were themselves enslaved by substance abuse. Others suffered abuse in boarding schools, separated from their family, friends, and even their own tribal culture.

Over the years I also discovered that many of our female students had been sexually abused at an early age by family members and close family acquaintances while they were growing up. Here are some edited examples compiled from their own written recollections:

> "I was molested by a close relative from ages five until nine years of age. It scarred my emotions. We were abused physically and emotionally. I told my father I didn't care for him as a father anymore. I cried out for love and understanding, that through this he would stop hurting me and the others. All I had for Dad was HATE. I felt hurt and not loved. I left and went to Grandpa's house—no family communication."

> "My parents believe in a medicine man—they paid him much money. My family is very traditional. My aunt put a curse on another person and amnesia was the result."

> "[Because we are superstitious] we sleep with a feather under our pillow."

> "My mother died when I was three or four years old. I lived with an aunt."

> "Aunt [Name] is a wonderful aunt and I love her very much—I think of her as a mother, but she is a medicine lady. She prays for people [by traditional means]. She is presented with blanket material, jewelry, clothes, and money. She is into tradition—participating in the Sunrise Dance."

These examples display God's marvelous grace and divine love, showing how He can take ruined lives and so completely change them that they become powerful trophies of His grace—despite what facts and statistics say they should have become. I remember once telling our missions supporters in southern Missouri that Jesus would not be coming in the immediate future because He said in Matthew 24:14, "And this gospel of the kingdom will be preached in the whole world as a testimony to all nations, and then the end will come" (NIV). At that time there were some remote areas of the Navajo reservation where the gospel message had not yet been preached. However, only a few short years later I was able to tell these same supporters that now they have heard because Christ's gospel had been preached to the furthest reaches of that great reservation—no doubt in part because of the faithfulness of some of our own students!

In my early years at AIBI we had a few Navajo students who spoke very little English and had to be taught the English language. At the end of the year they didn't want to return home because they feared that over the summer they would only hear Navajo back home and would forget all the English they had learned.

On one occasion a student came to our campus that had some dealings with the occult; as a result her roommate refused to stay in the room because of the oppression of demonic spirits. Some of the faculty and staff went to that dorm room and prayed—commanding the evil spirits to depart in Jesus' name. As a result, the roommate was able to return to study and sleep in peace.

Over the years I have indeed discovered that God has a sense of humor. On one particular occasion we were ministering house-to-house on the Navajo reservation; at one home we came to a teenage girl who was home alone. She would not open the door to us so one of our young men from the Bible school coaxed her into opening a bedroom window, allowing us to witness to her that way. Through our "window evangelism" she was won to the Lord that day!

Subsequently, I recall an instance when we were ministering inside a hogan (traditional Navajo dwelling) where a man and his wife lived. We walked across the dirt floor where they would put down their sheepskins to sleep at night, and we sat on the shelves where they had to move things aside for us to sit down. Their tiny wood-burning stove sat in the center of the room. They sure seemed glad to visit and pray with us even though we could tell they were not used to entertaining strangers. In fact we found that some Native people will not allow you to enter their home no matter how long they have known you—even if they were former students of ours. Instead, their custom was to meet and visit with you outside or in another building. As missionaries, we wanted to show respect to the people we were trying to reach, so we always learned to respect specific local tribal customs wherever the Lord opened doors for us.

Around 1977, Eugene Herd, who served as the vice president and business manager of the school, and I attended a camp meeting together at Cove, Arizona, on the Navajo reservation. This was historic for AIBI: two former students who had graduated in 1974, Ernie Lister and Willie John Willie, were the local church pastor and evangelist respectively. It was exciting to see these two men serving together. Never have I seen a people so anxious for Jesus to come! They would break out in testimony, and there were physical healings taking place as well. During the services the children were often asleep on the floors or amused themselves by catching grasshoppers. When everyone stood to sing and clap, the floor and rafters would shake! I fully expected the building to collapse at any time, but fortunately it never did. During the camp meeting, the partitions had been removed from a house to open it up so that it could be used as a church.

Another example of God's sense of humor occurred when a fly flew into the mouth of our evangelist while he was preaching. Without missing a beat the evangelist declared, "A fly has entered the ministry!" Both the evangelist (and the fly) continued without further interruption that evening!

During that camp meeting there was no water available nearby, so we had to have it hauled in from fifteen or twenty miles away. A coffeepot was kept brewing on the fire at all times, and it sure was strong! I drank some, and surprisingly that strong brew did not (thankfully) hinder my sleep that night. The sheep that we cooked to feed everyone was cooked over that same fire. On one occasion I enjoyed two bowls of mutton stew, and it was quite good. I thought the third bowl would "bless" me equally, but I didn't realize at the time that the entire sheep was used when preparing the mutton stew, and whatever I got in that third bowl left a horrible aftertaste. I tried washing my mouth out with soap to get rid of it—the worst I had ever experienced!

In 1978 we were privileged to have our first Native president of the school, Rev. Simon Peter, a Choctaw Indian from Oklahoma. President Peter followed President Don Ramsey, who served as the school's president from 1965-1978. Unfortunately, Brother Peter's cancer returned very soon after he accepted the presidency of AIBI. My wife, Emily Hunter, was his secretary and office manager. During his lengthy illness she wrote most of his correspondence and even had his permission to sign his signature when he was physically unable to do so. The rapid progression of the cancer forced his untimely resignation in March 1979. Emily and I were able to visit him in the hospital back in Oklahoma just before he went home to be with the Lord. His passing was a tremendous loss to the kingdom of God, but we rejoiced that Brother Peter's suffering had ended. As a further enhancement to his legacy, Brother Peter's daughter Becky graduated from our school in 1976; she served as our pianist during the chapel services.

Many other defining moments in my life and ministry took place while I was serving at the college. My beloved wife, Emily, who served both as secretary and instructor, collapsed one day while conducting one of her classes and was rushed to the hospital, where doctors found a cancerous brain tumor the size of a golf ball. After the school engaged intercessory prayer partners around the country, the tumor miraculously shrank to the size of a pea. For a period of time afterwards, Emily served as a travel agent, making overseas visits to Russia, South America, Hawaii, and other exotic locations. Just prior to her passing she was preparing for a trip to the Philippines, having already purchased her ticket. Just before her homegoing, Emily had a heavenly vision of the hereafter, which greatly encouraged her. Recounting the vision, she told me that she had a conversation with Jesus in which he twice asked her why she was afraid of dying, explaining to her that it was just a transition from one life to the next. Emily also told me that she saw beautiful flowers that had magnificent, unusual colors and hues unlike anything she had ever seen before. When I questioned her about the flowers, she explained to me, "There is nothing on earth to compare with what I've seen." Emily passed away in the City of Faith Hospital in Tulsa, Oklahoma, on April 24, 1985. A scholarship in her honor was established at the college, which provided for female students for nearly fifteen years.

In the following years I married again, this time to Pauline Harris Hunter, who also shared my love and calling for serving Native Americans. We had fourteen wonderful years together until she too went to be with the Lord on November 17, 2000.

By the time I was accorded the status of professor emeritus in 1995, I thought that my teaching days were through, but to my delight in 2000, shortly after the passing of my wife Pauline, President Jim Lopez asked me to return to the college and teach on a part-time basis. This was exactly what I needed at this time and afforded me the privilege of teaching the sons and daughters of former students. I am so thrilled that through God's faithfulness I am accorded the honor of teaching at 84 years of age!

Joe Hanna teaching, 1965–1966

J. R. Boyd honoring Betty and Joe Hanna at the 1997 Native American Fellowship, Convocation of Native Christian Leaders

Betty Hanna tutoring Joy (Kaneswah) Wyatt

BETTY J. HANNA

Elementary Education and Christian Education

My husband, Joe, and I always knew that God had called us to missions. We were pastoring a small church in northern New Mexico when a lady came and asked for prayer. Her mother was dying from cancer, and she wanted prayer for her mother and family. We went down to the pueblo and prayed with her mother. We talked to her about Jesus and how much He loved her. She immediately accepted the Lord. She assured us that she was now ready to meet the Lord! She died a few days later and her daughter and family continued coming to church.

We continued to pray about our calling to missions. Rev. Raymond Hudson, the district superintendent of New Mexico, and later, general treasurer of the Assemblies of God, was talking to us about taking another church as we began to share about our burden for Native Americans. He encouraged us to make application for appointment as national home missionaries. We did—and to our surprise, six weeks later we received word that we were appointed as missionaries!

Brother Hudson asked us then to go to Bloomfield, New Mexico, and establish a church there, a task that we gladly took on. Nevertheless, Joe and I both knew that our calling was to a teaching ministry. Two years later, the door opened for us to come to All Tribes Bible School (ATBS), which had just recently opened in Phoenix, Arizona. This created many opportunities for us, including the chance for me to go back to school and earn a bachelor of arts degree in elementary education. Joe served as the first vice president of ATBS. He loved teaching but he missed pastoring. After five years, we took the church at San Tan, south of Chandler, on the Gila River Indian Reservation. The attendance was down to three women and five or six children. I was also hired as a teacher at Florence Elementary School in the nearby community of Florence.

While pastoring, Joe started teaching Berean School of the Bible classes in some of the Indian churches in Eloy, Casa Grande, and Sacaton. During that time he also served as the sectional representative for Native American ministry. Those were good years for us. The church grew, he loved teaching, and his ministry as the sectional representative helped prepare the way for the creation of the Phoenix Metro Indian Section, the first Native section in the Arizona district. Joe also served as a board member of American Indian College for twenty-two years. (In 2001, my husband, Joe, went home to be with the Lord, but during his lifetime he always had a soft spot in his heart for the work that we were involved with at the Bible college, and even after his retirement from full-time ministry due to health reasons, Joe remained involved as a board member and in fund-raising efforts on behalf of our students.)

In 1981, five years after Joe and I had left to pastor, I received a call from President Carl Collins asking me to return to the college (now renamed American Indian Bible College [AIBC]). He asked me if I would consider coming back to provide tutoring for students who were struggling with reading and writing. At that time, AIBC was applying for regional accreditation and one of the college's main concerns was that many of the students were not academically prepared to do collegiate level work. By then I had been teaching for ten years in Florence, but I felt it was time for a change. I met with President Collins and agreed to start a tutoring program that fall at AIBC. Initially we offered only unstructured tutoring, since we did not yet have a formalized remedial educational program— that would come later. Prior to that time, AIBC accepted students who did not have a GED or a high school diploma. But when federal financial aid became available, the students needed a high school diploma or a GED to qualify. During the summer of 1982, I consulted with nearby Glendale Community College and received advice concerning classes, books, etc. Through my consultation with them I discovered that in order for students to receive financial aid, a student had to take at least nine credit hours in addition to the five classes for the GED.

While overseeing the Foundational Studies Program (later renamed the Learning Resource Department), I taught reading, writing, and social studies, ably supported by Belinda Lopez, who taught mathematics and science. Dorothy Runyan, a pastor's widow, came to us from Minnesota, working under the auspices of Mission America Placement Service (MAPS), which provides volunteer help to various Assemblies of God ministries, educational institutions, and churches. Dorothy was a tremendous help to us in tutoring since she was a former teacher. In fact, Dorothy was so valuable to us that she ended up spending seventeen years working at the college as a MAPS volunteer after her "retirement"!

At that time the format that we utilized involved conducting all the instructional and tutoring activities on AIBC's campus, and then once each semester we would take the students over to Glendale Community College to take the GED test. Several of the students would pass on the first try, but others would need to take further classes and receive additional tutoring before they could retake the test and obtain a passing score.

Over the years there were many students I had the pleasure of working with and whom I will always remember. Mary (not her real name), a Navajo student, is one person that I most certainly will never forget. She was a hard worker and always came for tutoring, in part because her earlier schooling had been difficult; as a result, she had dropped out of school. When she came to AIBC in 1984, Mary signed up to take her GED. Three times she took the GED test, but each time she would fail to get a passing score. She became very discouraged. But determined to pass, Mary signed up for the fourth time! She and I knew that if she didn't make it this time, she would probably not return to school.

Mary continued every day to work very hard. I knew she had made progress, but I did not know if she could transfer that learning when the time came to take the test. In 1985, when the day came for her to take the examination, she was very nervous. We prayed—but I too was nervous! When Mary finished the test, she was tired. I asked her how she felt about the test. She said she felt that she had answered correctly on many of the questions, but she wasn't sure. A few days later, I received a call from the director of the General Education Services at Glendale Community College, asking if Mary and I would come over right away. He did not say why, and we had no idea what to expect.

When we walked in, the director had a big smile on his face and told us that he had just talked to the state department of education and had been informed that Mary had passed her GED! As the director started to congratulate us, Mary and I both began to cry—and even the director started crying! We both were saying "Thank you!" to him as he put his arms around us both. The director told us, "I know that you have both worked hard, and I wanted to tell you in person." We told him how we had prayed! He nodded his head in agreement. I will never forget how kind the director and others were to us. The people at Glendale Community College did everything possible to help our students receive their GED's. For that we will remain forever grateful.

We drove back to the Bible college (still crying and praising the Lord). We went immediately to the academic dean's office because we were so excited that we had to tell someone the wonderful news. Upon arrival we told the academic dean, Rev. Alma Thomas, the good news. Sister Thomas also hugged us, and once again we rejoiced in God's favor. While this was all going on, I had forgotten that the visiting accreditation team from the North Central Association of Colleges and Schools (now known as the Higher Learning Commission) was visiting the school. At that time AIBC had applied for "candidate status" with this regional accrediting body, and the team members were visiting the campus, interviewing both faculty and students. At that point in the college's history, all faculty offices were located in the Washburn Building, which was the first building erected on our present campus site. Back then each office was just an open cubicle, which offered little or no privacy. We didn't realize that the visiting team could hear every word we were saying!

After we left the academic dean's office, the team members came over to her office and asked questions about what they had just overheard. Dean Thomas explained that Mary had taken the GED three times previously and on her fourth try had received a passing score on the test. She also told them that when Mary first came to AIBC, she was reading at a sixth grade level but was now reading at a tenth grade level!

The accreditation team said later that they saw the value of American Indian Bible College when they witnessed the excitement that accompanied Mary's tremendous accomplishment. We only offered the GED program for a total of four years, but during that time twenty-three students received their GED certificate. By then many high schools began offering preparation for the GED test, and it was no longer necessary for us to offer that service. Students who already had their GED could receive tribal funding and other educational benefits.

Offering the GED program presented many challenges, but we received excellent cooperation from a number of people, including President Carl Collins, Academic Dean Alma Thomas, and David Moore, who served first as academic dean and subsequently as president. These individuals trusted me to set up a program that would meet the needs not only of GED students, but of those who had a high school diploma but needed additional remedial help. Belinda Lopez (wife of Rev. Jim Lopez, who later served as president) faithfully taught and worked in the department. Belinda has not only been a fellow laborer in the Learning Resource Department, but a true friend as well. Finally, we would not have been able to handle all of the people in the Learning Resource Department if we had not had the help of Dorothy Runyan, who ably assisted us by tutoring every subject. I miss Dorothy tremendously, but she gave seventeen years of service to the college under the MAPS program and only just recently went home to be with the Lord.

The success that we had belongs to many of the people I have named, but I also want to mention the students who faithfully came for tutoring and faithfully attended class sessions. I think of them often and remember them with love and affection, including my dear friend Mary, who will always hold a special place in my heart.

Left to right: Jeremiah Declay, Genita Yazzie, Belinda Lopez, Bobbie (Hunter) Morego , and Michelle (Antonio) Mix

Front: Corilee Lee, Carolyn Baker, Belinda Lopez
Back: Alma Thomas, Judith Mattes, Betty Hanna

J. D. Lopez student teaching

Jim & Belinda ready for the banquet

Belinda Lopez receiving 2004 Distinquished Service Award. Don Keeter and Joe Saggio looking on.

BELINDA F. LOPEZ

(Quechan) Learning Resource, Elementary Education, and General Education

My first experience with American Indian College (at that time ATBS) was through Pastor Jacob Escalante, at Winterhaven Assembly of God church in Winterhaven, California. I'm a Quechan Indian from the Ft. Yuma/Quechan Reservation in Winterhaven, California. Both of my parents were alcoholics, and growing up in poverty, I had eight brothers and sisters. There were actually only three of us siblings raised within the home; the rest were raised by aunts and uncles. Of the other five, two of them died prematurely. My brother Ramsey was killed in a car crash at seventeen soon after being released from a juvenile lockup facility in San Diego. My youngest sister, Aretha, who was about three years younger than me, died before her first birthday after drinking kerosene. Needless to say, those early years were very difficult for me, but the Lord graciously saw me through my sometimes heartbreaking childhood.

In 1967, when I was twelve years of age, I had just recently gotten saved, and I heard that students from the Bible school were to be at our church for a service. As I recall, there were many students who would come throughout the year to have services at our church. Pastor Escalante would always welcome them and give them a chance to minister while they traveled throughout our Native community, holding weekend revivals and passing out tracts.

I was so excited because they were the first Native American young people I had seen serving the Lord. I could hardly wait until they finished ministering in song and preaching! As soon as they finished, I remember making my way down to the altar and just crying out to the Lord for the infilling of the Holy Spirit with the evidence of speaking in tongues. I will never forget the feeling that I had at that moment! The experience of receiving the indwelling of the Holy Spirit reminded me of a warm bucket of water flowing from the top of my head down. It was just an exciting feeling of freshness and newness. It was wonderful as I began to speak in tongues not only through the rest of that service but throughout the rest of that evening. When I got home that evening my family was wondering what had happened to me. They heard me, but I don't think they knew what was happening because I was still speaking in tongues when I got home. Thankfully, that experience prepared me for a life dedicated to Christ, because there would be many obstacles, challenges, and struggles that I would have to face in the next few years. So it was very helpful for God to fill me with His Holy Spirit so that I might not only witness, but also stand firm on His Word through the trials.

When it came time for me to go away to college I knew that I had always wanted to become a teacher. But I was also aware that there were not any degree programs for school teachers offered at AIC at the time. Betty Ayers, one of the Assemblies of God missionaries working in the area, and whom I stayed with for about six months, directed me to go to Southwestern Assemblies of God College in Texas and complete my degree. Later, after I was married to Jim and he became the dean of students (and later president), I came back to American Indian College to teach. When we returned to the college in 1982, Betty Hanna, a member of our faculty, really inspired me to come and teach at AIC. At first I planned to work in the public school system, but Betty told me they needed someone to teach in the Foundational Studies (now Learning Resource Department [LRD]). She also mentioned that it would be wonderful if I could be the one to fill that role, so I accepted the position, not thinking that I was going to be here for twenty-two years! I thought I would probably only be here for two years until they found someone else to do it long-term. But what a tremendous blessing to see a number of students come through that department and brush up on their basic skills and become successful pastors, teachers, ministry spouses, etc. Some of the students had been out of school for a period of time, others spoke English as their second language, and others just needed the benefits of remedial education, so we worked hard to upgrade their skills to a collegiate level.

During the twenty-two years that I taught at AIC (1982-2004), we were very fortunate to have the services of talented people like Dr. Judy Mattes, who had a doctorate in adult education from Indiana University. During her time at the college as an administrator and faculty member, she helped Betty Hanna and me to further develop the LRD program. As a result we were able to significantly improve our testing, assessment, and curriculum because of their input and desire to help make the program successful.

Perhaps one of the reasons that the Lord placed me working with LRD was that I came from a dysfunctional home, where I received no encouragement to further my education. Therefore, when I accepted the Lord as my Savior, He instilled in me this truth: "I can do everything through him who gives me strength" (Phil. 4:13, NIV). The support of the church family that I came from—and seeing the Bible college students who came to our church—made me want to further my education, so that when I went to college and faced difficulties in some of my classes, I didn't give up. I remember that in some classes it took me a little longer to fulfill the course requirements. But that helped me when I was a teacher because I was able to be more patient and compassionate by explaining the more difficult concepts in the textbooks to our students. I just tried to encourage them that they could do it through Christ's help and by putting more effort into their studies.

Moreover, many students were shy and afraid to express themselves, but I was able to see many of them develop confidence and succeed. Since we were a small college, our faculty was able to give them a lot of one-on-one attention, providing them with small classroom settings where they would not get lost in the crowd. Here at AIC, our students were able to get a lot more help than they might in other collegiate settings. Jim and I were thrilled to be able to see people who came from backgrounds like ours still make it as pastors, business professionals, and educators. In fact, because we had a measure of success in mentoring students, some of them mistakenly assumed that Jim and I both came from strong

Christian homes—with lots of money! They were quite surprised to find out that we had come from living situations very much like theirs. When they would hear my testimony, they would tell me afterwards, "Wow, if you can do it, with the Lord's help I can do it too!"

I think that one of the ways that AIC has established its identity as a Pentecostal college is through the chapel services. We invited different Native Christian leaders, including some of our own graduates, who shared a Pentecostal message during those chapel services. Students frequently come up to be prayed for during those times and were sometimes filled with the Holy Spirit. In fact, demonstrations of the Spirit were not limited to just the chapel services. Over the years we've heard reports of people being filled with the Holy Spirit even in the classrooms. Students took time to pray with one another to be filled in chapel, in classes (such as the late Don Keeter's Book of Acts class), and even back in the dormitories. This has contributed towards our Pentecostal distinctive of being a college where the Spirit is welcome in our midst.

It's also been important that our students have been able to go out to local Native AG churches located at Salt River, San Tan, Sacaton, Laveen, Estrella Mountain, Casa Blanca, Stanfield, etc. Our students not only are immersed in a spiritual environment here at the college, but they are exposed to our Pentecostal heritage at these (and many other) Native churches. We have been pleased to see our students not only attend, but also become actively involved in many of these churches.

One of the visions birthed in my heart about ten years ago was to host a national Native women's conference here at the college because of our facilities, resources, and accessibility of being located in the heart of the southwestern United States. For the past five years we've enjoyed hosting this conference on AIC's campus. We've had women come from throughout the United States and Canada, many of them burdened with tremendous hurts and emotional needs. Since I came from such a background myself, I understood the intense load that many of these women were bearing. I continue to be excited to have committee members like Rev. Valerie Boyd (Sioux), Delia Begay (Yaqui), and Cheryl Grass (Navajo), all graduates of the college, along with Rita Kallappa, who with her husband, Rev. George Kallappa (Makah), has served among the Native people for many years in various capacities. These ladies all have the same love and desire to see Native women empowered to reach their full potential in Christ. Our committee has sat together praying and brainstorming to see what God wants to do in the lives of Native women. It's been truly awesome to see both young and old overcome obstacles like spousal abuse, alcoholism, suicides within their families, etc. These women come to our conference and see others living for Christ, and they are inspired and empowered to succeed and live a victorious life in Christ.

I think that AIC's lasting legacy will be that it provides an exceptional Pentecostal education through its programs by building character and integrity in the students. Jim and I have looked at our own past and seen where our own pastor, Jacob Escalante, and his generation came from and how they've learned to "rightly divid[e] the word of truth" (2 Tim. 2:15, KJV). That first generation of AIC students instilled within us the importance of following Christ and reaching our Native peoples in order to give them a hope and a future through the gospel message. I feel like in our generation that we've picked up that legacy, the baton that they've given to us, and carried it to another level, with some of us going on to earn master's degrees—something unheard of for Native students just a few years earlier. As a result of that, we're now starting to see students going on to attain their doctorates— Native students from the reservations who in the past would never have conceived of such a thing being possible for them!

AIC has been part of not only my life and Jim's, but of our children's as well: we had the distinct privilege of raising our three children within this campus community. Joylina, our oldest daughter, was five years old when we came here, and then we added two more while we were here: "Cammie" (Camelia) and then "J. D." (Jameson). All three of them were so thrilled to be a part of the AIC family. Our children have also seen the legacy of those students who were here learning and promoting education, so their own personal educational goals were also stretched. Our youngest son, J. D., could hardly wait to attend AIC; as a boy he was always hanging around the gymnasium playing basketball or playing elsewhere on the school's grounds.

Now he's just completed his degree in elementary education and is getting ready to launch himself out into either teaching or further graduate studies, after he finishes an additional semester of language studies in Costa Rica. It's been especially exciting for us to see J.D. involved for the past couple of years in a leadership capacity with the National Native Youth Conference, working with both AIC and the Native American Fellowship (NAF) on that. Imagine our joy to know that he (and other AIC students) were integral in ministering to over 800 students at this past year's conference, where over 300 decisions were made for Christ and a number of young people were also baptized in the Holy Spirit! Also, this past year for the first time, two AIC students, Maurice "Mo" Ubaldo and our son, J. D., presented workshops at the annual NAF Convocation hosted here at AIC. We're now seeing the next generation of AIC students take it to the next level.

All of these things give a legacy not only to the present generation, but also to future generations. It's been an awesome, wonderful privilege to be a part of AIC and where it's heading. Jim and I can't wait to see what God's going to do next!

Some of the 2001 Graduates. Front to back: Marcia Lyman, Sam Juarez, Craig Bidtah, Matilda Yazzie, & Arlene Lang

NANCY J. SAGGIO

Psychology and Sociology

If I were to give this essay another title other than the one it was assigned, it would probably be "AIC, More Than a Decade of Impact." If you were to see that as the title, you might anticipate that I would be writing about the impact I have had on AIC over the past thirteen plus years. However, what I am really contemplating is the impact that the people composing the AIC family over the years have had on me—and on each other. AIC, not unlike the Church, is much more than a place. It is a gathering of people, over seasons of life, that come together for a purpose, for a focus, and during that season, they have an amazing influence on each other that ripples out to the world.

For my husband, Joe, and me, the season of life that includes AIC began back in 1992, when he was feeling a stirring in his heart to move towards the next stage of his ministry. At that time we were pastoring a small church in the San Bernardino mountain resort area of Crestline, California, which is near the upscale resort town of Lake Arrowhead. After nearly seven years in that community, Joe sensed that he was to be involved in Christian higher education. At that time, I was a person who dreaded and resisted change, but I went along and investigated various schools to see where we would be a good fit. It was during that period that we had our first visit to the (then) American Indian Bible College campus while on a trip to visit family living in nearby Chandler, Arizona.

It was on a blazing hot Labor Day Weekend that we decided we wanted to see the AIBC campus, since we were somewhat familiar with the reputation of the school. Jim Dempsey gave us the "grand tour," taking over an hour to give us the history of the school as well as show us various campus highlights. With his characteristic East Texas humor he told us not to worry about the large tumble weeds that might be blowing through the middle of campus on that hot summer day—they in no way indicated a lack of spiritual vitality on the campus! He assured us that indeed God was at work among the student body and was accomplishing great things through them. On that first visit we also met (then) President David Moore, Dean of Students (and later, president) Jim Lopez, (then) Academic Dean Dr. Judy Mattes, and Pete Cordova, who was the director of admissions at that time.

After our visit to the campus we immediately "regrouped" at the Dairy Queen (which used to be at the intersection of nearby 19th and Peoria Avenues) and reflected on our visit to the campus. Yes, we were impressed with the call of God on those who served at the Bible college. Although there were no students around on that visit because it was a three-day weekend, we got an indirect look at them through the highly dedicated faculty and staff that we met. We were impressed with their evident call, dedication to the students, and high qualifications, which would easily have placed them in a more lucrative setting if they had so chosen. Nonetheless, we concluded after our first visit that God would never call *us* to a school where we had to raise our support to be there! Clearly, that was unacceptable.

Since that time we've learned that God has a remarkable sense of humor and does not easily take no for an answer, since just about three months after our visit Joe received a telephone call at the church office inviting us to apply for missions appointment and become part of the college's faculty. This time, we decided we had better pray before deciding—and pray we did! After praying, talking, and weighing our options, we decided to answer the call and go where we were needed. By June of 1994 we had raised most of our needed support through itineration, so we moved to Phoenix with our two daughters, Rachelle and Leah (who were then six and four respectively), while we finished off the last two months of deputation.

John C. Maxwell, in *The 17 Indisputable Laws of Teamwork*, tells us: "One is too small a number to achieve greatness....The truth is that no lone individual has done anything of value."[1] We all build on the foundation of those who have gone before us, and hopefully provide a launching ground for those who come after us. When I stand in a classroom, I am standing on the ground that comes from the dreams and hard work of many others who were there before me, and I send out students who will impact people wherever God leads them, to family first and then to those they touch in their ministries and professions.

I have now had the privilege to teach general psychology and marriage and family for over twelve years at American Indian College. I remember in my very first class, one of the students, Rev. J. R. Boyd (Sioux), had a real impact on my formation as a missionary educator. Today, J. R., along with his wife, Mia, is a successful pastor and recognized Native Christian leader in Montana, serving among the Crow Indians. J. R. gave me my first real glimpse of the collective nature of his Native American culture. To paraphrase, he said something like this, "We all have each other's back. I will help take care of you, you will help take care of me, and we all watch out for each other." That was the beginning of revisions in my approach to teaching psychology in the context of mostly collective cultures, in contrast to my own very individualistic culture. I am so grateful for the effect of that perspective on life. It has helped me grow in a significant way in my profession, also, increasing in me what counselors call "cross-cultural competence." I strive to have the attitude of a learner in my interactions with people, including my students. As a result I have learned a lot from them. In fact, I think it's safe to say that my students teach me at least as much as I teach them!

I remember, in the first years of teaching at AIC, that I would teach in the evening so that I could balance being a mom with my teaching. I would bring our daughters, Rachelle and Leah, to the school and drop them off at my husband's office on campus, and I would go teach. Upon arrival, they immediately went to the school cafeteria to eat dinner with "Daddy"—often loudly insisting on having Lucky Charms for dinner, to the delight of the AIC students, who enjoyed seeing the "Mean Dean" adamantly protest and then helplessly concede to their menu choices. (I'm glad the students got to see Joe let go of his "academic demeanor" when he was with the girls—I'm sure it made him seem somehow more "authentic.") We are both convinced that our daughters' interaction with students, faculty, and staff has had a tremendous influence on them over the years. The college credits that Rachelle now has are all from American Indian College, and it is like a second home to her. When we travel or when former students return to AIC for a visit, we share memories of them teaching our girls at convocation or eating a meal together and marvel at how everyone has grown. We share memories, and we have had an effect on each other.

One of the highlights of the general psychology class is when the students present orally the results of their research in a particular area. I particularly enjoy when the students include their own testimony of God's grace and intervention. In one instance, a White Mountain Apache student named Ron gave a presentation on the topic of alcoholism, which included giving his own testimony in addition to the research. Both his passion as well as his compassion for his own people was evident in his presentation. At the end of his presentation, the whole class was moved to gather around him and pray not only for his continued sobriety, but also for the people he would touch with his life and ministry. The presence of the Word and of the Holy Spirit is of prime importance in every aspect of college life at AIC.

Often, "it is the little things that count" (to paraphrase one of our Navajo students who wrote me a nice card), that have significance. I see people using several different approaches in life when it comes to greeting one another. Some go for the hug, some go for the handshake, and others go for the wave from a distance, some stand and chat, others are purpose-driven in their travel across campus, headed to a scheduled activity. All of those things are ways that we connect, if even for a moment, with each other. And years of that seem to form a bond that goes beyond words.

Then there are the weddings, baby showers, and funerals that we have attended over the years together. American Indian "Bridal" College, as some affectionately call it, is indeed a great place to meet a mate. Research in the area of marriage and family even confirms it. A person can meet a future spouse who shares interests and values, a relationship with Christ, proximity in age, and a similar education and background. Of course, there is also a significant amount of diversity, even at a college specifically for Native American students, and that keeps the mix even more interesting! I have loved being able to hug the necks of present and former students at their weddings, then see their family grow as they have biological children as well as spiritual children in their various ministries. Some, like Pastor Marvin and Delia Begay, who serve at Canyon Day AG on the Ft. Apache Reservation in Arizona, are now even mentoring and sending students to AIC—people whom they have influenced—people they want to see trained in the caring, nurturing environment of American Indian College.

The testimonies of friends and strangers at the funerals of various ones who have gone to be with the Lord in the past thirteen years are a memorial to lives that have had a meaningful effect on many. I think of the memorial services for Rev. Don Keeter, long-time beloved professor, and Rev. Joe Hanna (former vice president of the college and long-time pastor) as examples of that kind of impact. Lives that were lived faithfully, lovingly growing fruit as they stayed connected to the Vine and to the people they loved and served. These two stalwart warriors of Christ received perhaps the greatest tribute that any missionary could receive: the funerals of both had in attendance large numbers of the Native people they so faithfully served.

When I reflect on AIC's future, I pray that we will always help each other, "have each other's back," and live in such a way as to have the impact that Christ wants us to have on each other and on the world. American Indian College wonderfully facilitates that. May it continue for generations!

NOTES
1 J. C. Maxwell, *The 17 Indisputable Laws of Teamwork* (Nashville,TN: Thomas Nelson Inc., 2001), 1–2.

Everett Peralta and Jim Comer

Everett Peralta and Boyd Tolbert

Everett Peralta hooding Marco Burnette, Glen Gray looking on

Celebrating with Everett Peralta as he receives his doctorate in 2005

Front (left to right): Joe Saggio, Boyd Tolbert, Dora de Peralta, Everett Peralta, Dora F. Peralta, Marcia Lyman
Back (left to right): Diane Webb, Sue & Jim Comer, Ray Garcia, Ruth & Dave DeGarmo, Pat Merino

Faculty Reflections ▲▲▲

EVERETT F. PERALTA

Chair, Education Department

Dear Jesus,

I want to thank you by providing this open letter of thanksgiving for this special place, AIC. This is both a letter of thanks to you and a slice of my life's journey, which led me to be a part of this unique and wonderful community of faith.

For the past twelve years it has been a blessing to me both in my educational formation and now as I'm privileged to give back as an educator. The wonderful thing is that here we prepare students not just for a profession but for life: and not only for this life but, more importantly, for the life to come!

AIC is nestled into a small mountainside, surrounded by a city searching for God. From my first moments on this campus, as I walked among the peace and beauty of its tree-lined sidewalks, I sensed its spirituality. This place called me! I'm convinced you placed me here to find sanctuary and refuge while you prepared me for the latest stage in my life's work and mission. Twelve years ago when I first saw the campus as a student preparing to become a teacher, I would never have dreamt the long-term impact that this special place would have on me.

As a young boy, my family came to this country from Hermosillo, Sonora, in northern Mexico. My parents, Everardo and Dora Peralta, were hardworking farmers and ranchers; they taught my two younger brothers, my younger sister, and me the value of hard work. Nothing was ever "given" to us—we were taught to earn our way in life. In the public schools in Willcox, Arizona, I began my education. In America, I had to learn English, so I can definitely identify with some of our students here at AIC who learned English as their second language in school. I know how hard that is. That's why I work so hard to help our students here succeed.

Because I had to work so hard and because of the example my parents showed all of us, I was able to excel academically, gaining a

▲
▲
▲

313

chance to attend college straight out of junior high school. Through hard work I was able to graduate from college very young and get a head start on a career that eventually led to the corporate world of investment banking. In hindsight, I can see the Lord's hand in moving me away from that. After a few years I got tired of the rat race, even though I had earned a very comfortable living and owned a home in an affluent Connecticut community, a suburb of New York City. I had all of the trappings of financial success but was left unfulfilled. I knew there had to be more to life than this. At a relatively young age I had a heart attack from all of my work-related stress and decided to return home to be closer to my family.

After returning briefly to Willcox, I settled in the Phoenix area and decided that I wanted to become an educator. Since I already had a college degree, I needed to find a place where I could pick up the elementary education hours I needed to become certified as a teacher in the state of Arizona. At that time I met Karen Bramble and Dr. Boyd Tolbert, who were both teaching in the elementary education program at AIC. They encouraged me to enroll at the college and gain my certification. Being the ambitious—or perhaps crazy—person that I am, I knocked off forty-five credit hours in one year with a 4.0 GPA, on top of teaching full-time under emergency certification. (If you are considering doing the same thing, I have one word of recommendation for you—Don't! Thank you, Lord, for getting me through that extraordinarily challenging time!)

After completing my certification at AIC, I worked as both a teacher and administrator for the Papago School in Phoenix and also completed my master's degree at the University of Phoenix. While attending the doctoral graduation party for Dr. Boyd Tolbert, who in many ways has been more than a friend and mentor to me, I met up with Dr. Joe Saggio, who was then serving as the academic dean. Dr. Saggio asked me to consider coming back to teach at AIC on a part-time basis, and I accepted the challenge to return to this special place. Soon after returning as a part-time professor, I decided to follow Boyd's advice and also pursue my doctorate, so I enrolled in the Delta II cohort of the EdD program in Educational Administration at Arizona State University.

When I had to give up my house in the middle of my graduate studies, this special place rallied to my needs. Through the generosity of then President Jim Lopez, I was provided with a room to live in, a chapel to pray in, and an office to work in—Lord, you helped me complete my doctorate. Frankly, it was humbling, and I could not have done it by myself. No doubt it was a miracle. I know, Lord, that you have angels because they surrounded me here! These angels ministered to me and touched my spirit with their gifts, love, and encouragement. I have been truly blessed by each member of this campus community, and I give to you, God, all the glory.

At a time when I faced incredible discouragement and needed an opportunity to serve, AIC accepted my volunteer services. With pleasure and pride, I cleaned restrooms, painted hallways, washed walls, collected trash, watered plants, moved furniture, mopped floors, tutored students, instructed classes, provided campus security, and helped others. The honor of the work kept me faithful and thankful, not to mention grounded in reality. I become a tireless worker in the vineyard of my Lord. As I was trained and educated at American Indian College and throughout my graduate education, I found work that draws me nearer to you, enhances my human dignity, and makes my life a real service to my fellowman.

I also found others to help carry my burdens. I remember how you sent Dr. Larry Kelly, who served briefly as interim president, and a couple of other "anonymous benefactors," who helped me with my eleventh hour financial need, allowing me to stay in school when it looked like I might have to drop out even though I was about to finish my doctoral studies. As always, Lord, you were right on time in meeting my need.

As I've already mentioned, one source of great strength has come through the encouragement and example of brothers and sisters in Christ here at AIC. I think of how my former instructor (and now colleague) Betty Hanna has always been a source of such encouragement to me. Even though we work together now, I still find myself drawing from the deep store of wisdom that she has. Because of her, and others, the fellowship in this special place has given me a mind and spirit that strives to be quiet, humble, peaceful, patient, and charitable.

AIC has continued to serve as your instrument while I chafed under the trials of unemployment, development, and rededication. Here under the watchful shadow of the mountain, I prayed to deepen my commitment to you as my personal Savior. From this special place, you answered my request to become a teacher and an administrator as I advanced in both training and degree attainment. I reached for the stars, and your hand pulled me up! Whenever I needed your help, you came to my assistance in this special place. Because of that, all that I am and possess is really yours. Here I have learned to surrender to your will. I have learned to answer your call, Lord, just as Isaiah did with a "Here am I. Send me!" (Isaiah 6:8, NIV).

Perhaps the most profound biblical truth that I know is that you died on the cross for me. Like the prophet Jeremiah declared: "'For I know the plans I have for you', declares the Lord, 'plans to prosper you and not to harm you, plans to give you hope and a future'" (Jeremiah 29:11, NIV). In fact, you have special plans for all of us here and that's why you've poured out your Holy Spirit in abundant measure. That's why our students prophesy, see visions, and dream dreams. They know that you have great plans for them to succeed as well. Many of them are determined to accomplish all that you have for them and to be all that they can be to your honor and glory, Lord.

I've often found that one of the great benefits of being here is seeing the students passionately worship you, Lord, in chapel four days each week. That's where many of their dreams and visions are borne into reality, as they encounter you, Lord Jesus, in a fresh way. Their zeal and fire has challenged me more than they will ever know!

By the way, it's a good thing that you have poured out your Spirit in such a way on this campus because here you prepare us for your work in a world of temptation, weakness, difficulties, and trials. I've watched how many of our students come here having experienced deep sorrows, failure, discouragement, and even the death of loved ones. But you've been there for us, Lord, and because of our education and faith, we will be able to carry the good news to the ends of the earth.

As I've observed, over the past ten plus years, the faculty, staff and leadership of American Indian College have earned a well-deserved reputation of going out of their way for those they serve and in so doing bring honor to your Name. We have found that when students show us effort, then we are in a position to help them to become all that You have called them to be. As students walk in the reality of that precious truth, they learn to "trust in the Lord with all [their] heart and lean not to [their] own understanding" (Proverbs 3:5,6, NIV). As our students grow and mature in the process, they begin to assume the role of teacher and servant while overcoming each obstacle barring them from fulfilling their roles and mission of furthering God's kingdom. I have also learned that as Christians we must ardently seek the "fruit of the Spirit"—thereby proving that we belong to God, crucifying our sinful nature with its passions and desires—and seek to keep in step with your Holy Spirit. We are not led by works or the Law but by the Spirit of God and for His love. Each student learns to wake up, dress up, stand up, look up, reach up, lift up, grow up, and live up to all that is good in Christ!

Because I have such a great love for this school, when I look at it through the eyes of faith, I long to see AIC with 5,000 students governed by a faculty and staff of 600 on a 150-acre campus that will serve as the educational and spiritual dove of the desert, equipping Native Americans and others to serve as leaders, mentors, and role models for both this nation and the world at large. I envision this to be a community where students and teachers proclaim the excellence of learning and the importance of service under the banner of our Christian faith.

Yes indeed this is a special place, where God's people can wonder in God and where God's people are given life. It is special because tomorrows always begin in you, Jesus Christ, and are blessed forever. It is also special because the Holy Spirit meets us in a personal way, and we are transformed. I know it is a special place because here My Heavenly Father has given me my place!

Thank you, my God, for this special place!

PART SEVEN ▲▲▲

Staff Reflections

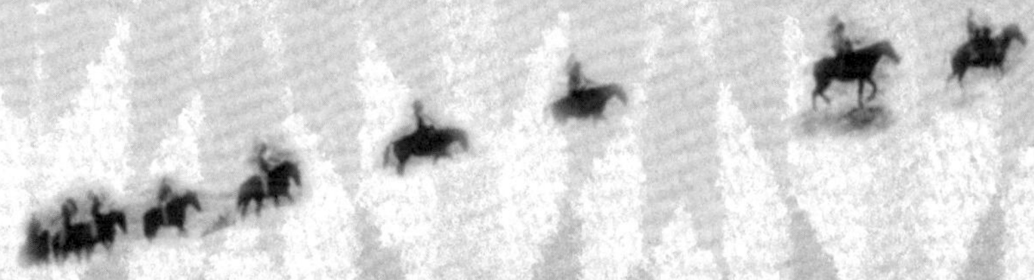

M. Nadine Waldrop

Sandra K. Ticeahkie

Sandra M. Gonzales

Donald P. Merino

▲

Nadine Waldrop

Nadine & Stephanie (Jordan) Coleman

Saul Cardenas, Genita Yazzie & Nadine
on missions trip to Poza Rica, Vera Cruz, M

Front to back: Nadine Waldrop, Gloria (Pechuli) Smith, Rosie (Lee) Jackson, Marlene (Yazzie) Vallo, Virgil Nez

M. NADINE WALDROP
Director of Student Financial Aid

It was the late 1950s and I was a teenager, attending First Assembly of God in Glendale, Arizona. Also attending at that time was a young brother and sister evangelistic team. The pastor allowed us to have a special revival for the Missionettes[1] group under the direction of the female evangelist. (In fact, this was just after Missionettes had been established as an organization within the Assemblies of God.) During the second week of the revival services, the Lord gave me a vision of ministering to "dark-skinned people": the Indian people. Having been raised here in the Phoenix area I was used to seeing Native Americans, but I had never felt a specific call towards them until the revival services. Soon afterwards, I contacted Rev. and Mrs. Leo Gilman, missionary pastors on Arizona's Fort Apache Reservation at Canyon Day Assembly of God and started working with them, traveling back and forth between the Ft. Apache Reservation and Phoenix. During that time I also did hospital chaplaincy at the old Phoenix Indian Medical Center. When there was a medical emergency, the head nurse would call me in to pray and minister to those in need. I also remember doing home Bible studies at the John Jacob Farms (where the large Metro Center shopping center is now located). By that time I had learned to read Navajo and Apache (related languages) and was able to both read the Bible and sing gospel songs in Navajo to some of the farm workers there.

All of this took place around 1957, when the Bible school was established and after I had just graduated from high school. Thus, I was actually aware of the school from its very inception. The Gilmans had several of their young people enrolled in the school, so I had quite a bit of connection there and would go and visit the students who had come down from Canyon Day because I had that relationship with them. That continued for a number of years until the time I was pastoring at Co-op Assembly of God on the Gila River Indian Reservation, from 1972–1979. During the 1970s I was connected to the school because I used the students as interns, and they would have their Sunday ministry at the church there at Co-op (which started as Gila Crossing Assembly of God and then was later changed to Co-op AG). The students were very helpful with leading songs, teaching Sunday School, testifying, preaching, even helping with work days.

Several students and graduates joined me as assistant pastors, including (later dean of students and eventually president) Jim Lopez and his wife, Belinda, the first year that they were married. The Lopezs remained with me for about a year, then after they left, Joe and Sarah Semallie, a Navajo couple from Cameron, Arizona, worked with me. After Joe graduated, they stayed an additional year as assistant pastors while Sarah finished her schooling. During the time that I served the church at Co-Op I would also come to the school and occasionally speak in chapel services.

In June 1979 I accepted an invitation to join the administrative team at the school. In retrospect, some of my early and fondest memories are of the chapel services. (Today, because of my responsibilities in the Financial Aid Office, I don't have nearly as many opportunities to be in chapel, so I treasure those early memories.) Even before I became a part of the staff, I used to visit some of the chapel services that were held in the old cafeteria, which is now the upstairs to our library. (At that time the dining hall and chapel were combined.) Those were special times because often the Holy Spirit began to move among us, bringing conviction and/or blessing—sometimes causing classes to be cancelled because of God's genuine presence and moving among us.

Not only were the spiritual times special, but I still fondly recall the more informal times in the old dining hall when we would get together with the students and play table games like Uno and Skip-Bo. These various activities with the students helped us all to develop pretty close relationships. At that time

I was the senior class sponsor, and we did a couple of trips as a class. I believe that I was the first one to have the privilege of taking a group of students on an overseas missions trip, to the Philippines where we spent an entire month. Those missions outreaches, both locally and abroad, were especially memorable for me.

The trip to the Philippines in 1989 really stands out because it was the first overseas trip made by our school. Dana Odell (now Gonzalez), Tonita Yazzie (now Keith), Paul Lanuza, and a number of others were a part of that trip. I especially remember almost being kidnapped and held for ransom there because some locals thought I was a "rich white lady" from America. (Boy, were they mistaken!) Thankfully, the Lord protected me from that experience. On that trip, we got to go to some of the outstation churches; I was also privileged to speak to one of the women's groups there. We traveled by all different modes of transportation, including motorized tricycles and jeepneys, which was interesting to say the least! Working with the children daily on an informal basis was also a special part of that trip.

In the summer of 1990 I was able to go to Honduras with Pam Mosely (now Cooper), Carlos Baki, a Mayan graduate of the college who now pastors on the Navajo reservation in Crownpoint, New Mexico, with his wife, Doreen (Smiley), and a number of others. We did puppet ministry on that trip and did thirteen services in eight days! While we were there we also got to visit some of the Latin American Childcare schools as well.[2] One thing I remember especially about the trip to Honduras was that while we were in Central America it got up to 122 degrees in Phoenix—an all time record and we missed it! (However, it was so hot and humid in Honduras I'm not sure we were any better off!)

When I first started at the college in June 1979, it was President Carl Collins's first year as president, and we had a whole new administration that year. Originally I came to be the school's bookkeeper, but with the departure of Eugene Herd as business manager I was asked to assume those duties. In addition to President Collins, Don Keeter was the vice president, Alma

Thomas was the academic dean, and I was the business manager, and we were all new in our positions! Needless to say, that was interesting and we all learned a lot. Although new in their roles, the others had already been at the school for a while, so I was really the new kid on the block. At that time we had thirty to thirty-five students and no computers, so we (or should I say "I") did all the bookkeeping the old-fashioned way—by hand! Thankfully, the son of one of our senior missionaries was the comptroller of a large company here in Phoenix, and he would come in the evenings and help us get the bookkeeping system on track the way it needed to be. Together, he and I worked till about nine o'clock each evening to be able to get a proper financial report ready to present to the board of directors for their October meeting. President Carl Collins also helped me a great deal in learning accounting since he had had his own accounting firm prior to coming to AIBI and was familiar with the fund accounting system that we are now using.

One funny thing I will always remember is that when I first came to AIBI it was summer, and Brother Collins said to me, "Nadine, next summer things will get easier because summers get easier." Now, I should mention that I've been with AIC through twenty-eight summers, and I'm still waiting for one of those "easy" summers! Perhaps they have never gotten easier because the learning curve in higher education is such that we always have to learn new federal regulations, new accounting software, etc. I don't know if I'll ever see an "easy" summer!

When we started working on the process that eventually led to our gaining regional accreditation in 1988, I remember there were a lot of hoops to jump through. Still, it was an exciting time, even with all the work that we had to go through. For me, that meant that once we received accreditation we were able to start receiving federal financial aid under the Department of Education's Title IV program, which assisted our students with paying for their education. Even before we received approval by the US Department of Education, we had already received approval by the Bureau of Indian Affairs (BIA), so some of the tribes began financially assisting our students even before we received our accreditation. Subsequently, we received regional accreditation, and we were truly blessed when that finally came into fruition. With that new status, we had to divide several administrative roles, so I transitioned out of the business manager role and assumed the responsibility of becoming the director of Student Financial Aid for the college. In fact, I should probably mention that due to the shifting of roles that has occurred over the years at the school, coupled with the accompanying name changes as we have transitioned from a Bible institute to a Bible college, I have been the business manager (or business administrator) at least three times as well as the role I currently have, director of Student Financial Aid. Yes, it's been a wild ride at times, but I've truly enjoyed it, even if the summers haven't been that easy!

Over the years many people have "poured into" my life and been positive influences. Alma Thomas, whom I've known since she first came to Arizona in the early 1960s, quickly comes to mind. The longevity of our relationship has created a very special bond between us, especially when we've been able to work together. She's always been a person I've looked up to as a role model for all aspects of my life: personal, professional, and, most of all, spiritual.

I appreciate President Carl Collins because he helped me greatly in understanding the business part of what I was doing, and so I appreciate his willingness to teach me those things. President Dave Moore always encouraged me. Even today he'll call on occasion just to touch base and see how I am doing (and that's greatly appreciated). I'll never forget how we were at his parents' home when he got word that his son had died, so I have no doubt that a special bond was formed there as well. Of course, President Jim Lopez, now serving as director of Intercultural Ministries for the Arizona District Council, was (and is) a tremendous blessing to me. I sometimes said that I used to tell him what to do (as his pastor), and now he tells me what to do (as the president).

There have also been some alumni that have really stood out as well. I always think about Paul Lanuza (now the pastor of Phoenix Full gospel Church for over ten years here in the Metro Indian Section of the Arizona district and a part-time AIC business professor) and his wife, Lia (Sarabia), and how they met here, dated, and then a number of us traveled up to the wedding reception in Stockton, California. That period of time was very relaxed even though we worked very hard, but it seemed like perhaps we had more time to spend with the students back then.

One student I formed a very special bond with is Modesta Scott. While she was a student here she participated in the Tribalaires (one of our traveling musical groups we used to have), and I remember how we went round and round a couple of times on one of those trips because she got offended at something I had asked her to do that she didn't want to do. Still, in spite of that altercation, when she started dating a young man back home whom she later married, I was the first one she called at the college to hear the "good news!" Modesta told me how she appreciated how I had dealt with her at that time, and even though I was worried that she'd never speak to me again, it meant a great deal that I was the first one that she called to share that information with.

Finally, I need to also mention that there's also a very special lady, Stephanie (Jordan) Coleman, who came as a student during my first year and to this day she calls me "mom." I performed Stephanie's wedding ceremony, and I'm "grandma" to her children. Not only am I close to many of our students, but I've also become quite attached to many of their children as well. In fact, many of them come back as students as well, so I've seen second and third generation AIC students as well. To me that is so exciting!

Every institution of higher education will have some sort of legacy, and I believe that AIC's lasting legacy will be the chapel services and the biblical classroom teaching. Our students have received both, as faculty were led by the Holy Spirit. In fact, our challenge and legacy need to be for our students not only to learn for themselves, but to go out and pass on to others what they've learned. I remember how President Moore used to say, "Each one teach one." We also want to see our students continue to reach out to their families and then to pass the torch to their children. Seeing the generations of students coming backs that up. Perhaps my greatest desire is to see AIC continue with the blessing of God upon it and its students and to know that the legacy will continue until our Lord's return.

Undoubtedly the Lord has had a hand in my ministry development since he combined the two loves of my life: ministry to the Native people and the business world. The years I spent working at Valley National Bank here in Phoenix while supporting my calling early on gave me the type of business experience that would later serve me well as pastor, business administrator, and now as student financial aid director. I am so grateful that He has allowed me to use my gifts to serve the Native people and so fulfill the vision that He placed within my heart over fifty years ago!

NOTES

1 As of March 2007, Missionettes is now known as National Girls Ministries.

2 Latin America Childcare (LACC), an integral part of AG World Missions, was originally established by L. John and Lois Bueno in 1963 when they were missionaries serving in El Salvador. LACC schools provide a Christ-centered education along with a daily meal for students who would otherwise be excluded by poverty from receiving an education. The LACC program has been successfully exported throughout Latin America, and there are now (as of 2007),over 300 LACC schools that have impacted over 100,000 children in twenty-one countries throughout Latin America. L. John Bueno, founder of LACC, has served as the executive director of World Missions for the Assemblies of God since 1997.

Sandra Ticeahkie

Left to right: Coleen Whitewolf, Michelle Upshaw, Stephanie Marsden, Kent Burnette Jr. Dean Doney, Samuel Ware, Charles Nestel, Thomas Blackstar, Sandra Ticeahkie

Don & Gayle Keeter

Sandy Ticeahkie (right) with unidentified student at Fall Harvest Festival sponsored by Arizona District Council Women's Ministries.

SANDRA K. TICEAHKIE

(Kiowa/Comanche) Director of Admissions

I first became acquainted with AIC through the influence of my pastors, Donald and Gay Keeter, of Indian Revival Center (IRC) in Los Angeles, California, where my family and I attended. Pastor Keeter had recommended the college to me when I was attending California State University–Long Beach. At the time I didn't think AIC would meet the academic threshold that I had set as a communications major, and I knew that my major wasn't available at the college. Yet one desire became prevalent, my desire to grow closer to God and to be surrounded by a Christian community. This was especially important to me since I had not had the opportunity of growing up in a church setting. My parents had only recently accepted Christ themselves and previously had been active in a militant organization known as the American Indian Movement (AIM), perhaps best remembered in recent years for their unauthorized occupation of both Alcatraz Island in the San Francisco Bay (1969-1971) and at Wounded Knee, South Dakota (1973).

I remember one day registering for the upcoming semester at Cal State–Long Beach after having dismissed the idea of ever attending AIC, yet sensing the Holy Spirit speaking to my heart, "If you don't go you'll never know." A few days later, the basketball team from the college came out to IRC. I heard the testimonies of the team members and felt a little more comfortable about enrolling at the college. I was especially impressed to see young Native adults serving the Lord. That was something that was definitely drawing me to attend the school. As a result I made the decision to go to AIC. I went not only as a brand new Christian but also as never having been on a reservation. I was really more of an "urban Indian." Growing up in Los Angeles, I was much more familiar with gangs and urban life than I was with anything having to do with Native Americans on the reservation.

One of my fondest memories was my first ministry outreach. Pete Cordova, our director of admissions at the time, signed me up—without telling me! Before I knew it, I was in a school van bound for Cameron, Arizona, a remote part of the Navajo reservation in the region near the Grand Canyon, about an hour north of Flagstaff. Pastor Gary and Gloria Smith (AIBI graduates) were serving as pastors there at that time. One of the student leaders on that trip was Jackie Holgate, a Navajo, who today is serving as the pastor of Mountaintop AG in Flagstaff, Arizona. Back then, Jackie took me under his wing and was determined to transform me into a real "soldier for Christ"!

Upon arrival, the team was told to go and pass out tracts to some of the trailers up on one of the plateaus near the church. There I was out handing out literature in a long church dress with all of this dust and sand blowing around me! The other team members had already been dispatched to other locations, but I was left to fend for myself—handing out flyers to three or four trailer homes. I was really afraid because having lived in urban Los Angeles, I wasn't used to being dropped off in a strange area. I had climbed out of the van having no idea what I was supposed to be doing, and before I knew it I was surrounded by five or six growling "rez" dogs! (And I thought L. A. was dangerous!) What do I do now?! This wasn't in the book or mentioned in our outreach training. As the others were being driven off, abandoning me to my fate, the van kicked up dust and Jackie hollered out, "Pick up a rock!" I didn't know what that meant, and the van didn't stop—it just kept on moving. I just knew that this was a life-and-death situation. So I picked up the biggest rock I could find, and suddenly the dogs turned around and just wandered away! That was my first welcome to *real* Native ministry.

Later on that same trip, while witnessing, I needed a Navajo interpreter, so I had Jackie interpret for me. I remember witnessing to this big, mean-looking man who had lots of tattoos. As I began sharing the gospel with him (through Jackie), he and Jackie began to converse, so I stopped talking. The two of them kept chatting away, and suddenly I noticed they were both looking at me. I could tell that there was something personal being shared between them about me, so I asked Jackie, "What is he asking?" Jackie replied, "He wants to know what tribe you are. In the Navajo language we don't really have a name for your tribe, the Comanche tribe, so I had to improvise a little and I called you 'the enemy.'" I must admit it was kind of funny at the time, although I don't know if being called the enemy is the best opener when you are trying to witness to someone. However, the lessons of some of those early outreaches have served me well in the years since then. Now I know how to deal with rez dogs and enemies.

During the first time I served as the director of admissions, I remember how President Jim Lopez had just returned from the Native American Fellowship's Convocation when it was held in Anadarko, Oklahoma. He was all excited and told me, "Girl, we've got to go to Oklahoma because there is a Bureau of Indian Affairs (BIA) boarding school whose students attend Victory Assembly of God in Anadarko." So over the course of that year, we put together a ministry team, raised money, prayed together—planning how best to reach the youth. While in Okalahoma we went to the Riverside Boarding School and asked if we could have an outreach for them. Being a government school, they went ahead and allowed us to have two assemblies: one for junior high and one for high school. We were able to minister to the students as well as provide each of them with a Bible and a "goody bag." We invited them all to the church, not knowing how many of them would show, but that night we were packed out. We had a church full of youth, and the AIC students led the praise and worship, human videos, and games. So we began to develop that ministry, starting with Kent Burnette, Richard Coker, Samuel Ware, and Alferda (Malone) Walking-Eagle.

The students on that outreach were well prepared (in part) because for three months prior we had met regularly, planned, and prayed for successful results. I'm proud to say that I didn't have to do all of the work, but the students stepped up and volunteered for the various tasks—including fund-raising. Because they took ownership, we were ready to work together like a well-oiled machine. A couple years later, when I stepped away from my position here at AIC for the first time, I felt called to go back to Oklahoma. The impact of that outreach (which we did for four consecutive years) was still affecting the church, and as a result we had anywhere from sixty to eighty Native youth attending every Wednesday night because of the seed that was planted when AIC ministered to the youth at the Riverside School. Years later, one young man still had a Frisbee that he had received as a boarding school student in the third grade from one of our early outreaches! He still remembered when our group came, and continued to inquire, "When are you guys going to do that again?" To me that young man was representative of seeds that we have not yet begun to water or harvest.

Looking back as both a student and staff member, I remember a number of influential people in my spiritual formation, including Coach Tim Grant, who coached our volleyball team. One thing that I remain appreciative of about "Coach" (as we always called him) was that he was really down-to-earth, and he made you feel a part of the family. There were times when, as a student, I had to stop out for a semester or more to catch up on my finances, but Coach would keep in contact and let me know that he was praying and looking for different scholarships to help me—which was more than any other sports trainer had ever done for me. Playing volleyball and traveling with my teammates was something that I'll always thank God for. The last year I played, our volleyball team won the regional competition for small Christian colleges.

Jim Lopez was another person who tremendously influenced my life. I worked closely with him when he was dean of students and I was the ASB vice president and also a resident advisor. He worked to train us by helping us learn how to handle difficult situations. As a student you often don't relish having to deal with conflict or difficulties, but Brother Lopez would meet with us weekly, helping us to plan and prepare. After I made the transition from student to staff member and Jim Lopez became the president, our professional relationship matured as he developed more confidence in my abilities. President Lopez allowed me to be innovative and make changes in how we did the college days events and promote the school to prospective students.

Coming back a second time as director of admissions, after having been out in Okalahoma for several years, I am now spending more time developing the talents of our students, especially the two talented student workers I have working in my office: Jameson "J. D." Lopez, and Maurice "Mo" Ubaldo. I let these two young men know that I value their opinions and ideas immensely and that I've really come to depend on their youthful perspective on many issues. In many ways I see myself as a mentor to them. Out of this working relationship has come AIC's involvement in co-hosting the National Native Youth Convention, which was started by one of our alumni, Pastor Marvin Begay, in his role as National Native Youth Representative for the Native American Fellowship of the Assemblies of God (NAF). Both J. D. and Mo have truly invested themselves in this event the past two years—including long hours spent (often until after midnight), along with other personal sacrifices—to make this a successful event. The first year we held the conference we had over 500 Native youth attend; the second year we had over 800, from all over North America!

In my spiritual walk, I have been truly blessed by my association with AIC over the years. In fact, when I think of AIC, the first thing that comes to mind is that we are a Pentecostal college. That is in part because during our chapels we prioritize the presence of God. However, it isn't just in chapels that we experience God's presence. Even in the dorms during devotions I can remember seeing visible demonstrations of God's presence. I recall that once during a five-week period we had people laid out on the ground because they had been profoundly touched by the Lord's hand—it was like a bomb had gone off! What was really special is that this experience wasn't forced or artificial; it was a genuine, unplanned move of God. I can still remember having prayer times at 3:00 AM in the dormitories while people cried out in intercessory prayer.

Another spiritual milestone that I will never forget was how one of our basketball players, Troy Beadle, was filled with the Holy Spirit right there on the basketball court during practice. He had been seeking to be filled for a long time. As they were practicing drills, Troy stopped and told the other players, "I feel like I need to pray." So the others stopped, prayed, and he was filled with the Holy Spirit right there on the basketball court! I will forever cherish the memory of him running up the hill on our campus, shouting and screaming with excitement at being filled with God's Holy Spirit.

I believe that AIC's legacy will be that of service to our constituency. I still recall (then) President Jim Lopez telling those of us who worked with the college that we are servants first and foremost. When people think of AIC, they're going to remember our faculty and staff going on outreaches and being willing to do whatever needed to be done.

One fond memory that I have was an all-school workday, and the faculty, staff, and administration worked right alongside us students. Alma Thomas, one of our instructors (now retired), was out there working in her long dress and tennis shoes. At that time I believe she was already over seventy years of age—and she was digging with a shovel! We were all trying to take the shovel from her and give her something lighter, but she wouldn't hear of it. In fact, Sister Thomas almost started to swing that shovel to get the rest of us to back off and let her do her share. That was something to see! Out there in the heat of the day putting forth her effort, she was setting an amazing example that told us that it doesn't matter how long you've been in the ministry or how much education you've attained—the important thing is that we all work together and pray together to reach and develop Native people into pastors, teachers, and business leaders. By the way, Sister Thomas was later awarded the prestigious Delta Alpha Award (Distinguished Educator) by the General Council of the Assemblies of God at the 1997 General Council—one of only two awarded that year!

In closing, my Kiowa grandfather used to tell me, "If you're in a place and you know of a fellow Kiowa tribal member that is there, part of our tradition and sense of honor requires us to make sure that this person has everything they need: food, shelter, and a warm welcome. You always recognize them, talk to them, and let them know that you care." That same core value was instilled in me, that wherever I am, if I meet someone associated with AIC (whether or not I know them), there's a connection. That's one of the unique things that we have to offer—that there's a genuine love and connection. I believe that will be AIC's lasting legacy.

Left to right: Rewa (Charles) Blackstar, Lucinda Zospah, Alvin Owens, Alferda (Malone) Walking Eagle

Maurice "Mo" Ubaldo, Marshall Plummage, J. D. Lopez, Glendon Frank

Front to back: Tammy Tunney, Isaac Tartsah, William Littlecalf

Staff Reflections

Sandra (Smith) & Ryan Gonzales in ministry outreach

Sandra (Smith) Gonzales praying for student

Sandra & Ryan Gonzales with their children: Marc, Alyssa, & Christian

336   AMERICAN INDIAN COLLEGE: A Witness to the Tribes

SANDRA M. GONZALES

(Navajo) Registrar

I first came to visit AIC when my sister began attending the college in spring 1986, when I was in the fourth grade. I had always known that AIC was a very special place, even at that early age. I had an interest in the college through high school, and I sent my ACT college placement scores there. As I was making plans for where I would be attending school, I decided to start college a year after I completed high school. You could say that I just knew that this was the place that I was supposed to be—where God had called me to go.

When I was young, I kind of remember the campus; it was a lot different than it is now or even at the time I attended. I just remember that every time I would come on campus the people were very, very inviting. The faculty and staff were all very friendly and welcoming to the campus. I was also struck by how they related to each other and how well everyone worked together. I also liked the campus itself because it wasn't overwhelming in size. I've been on university campuses that were extremely large. My brother, Keith, did his pre-law studies at a large university in Colorado, and I remember that there were sometimes over 300 students in each of his individual classes! So I liked the size of the campus: it was perfect for what I was looking for and what I needed.

I would say that my fondest memories of the college as a student were class time. I loved the opening of every class with prayer; I thought that was cool because we did not have this opportunity in public schools, and I believe that this is an awesome way to start out class time. I also have wonderful friends that I made here and still remain in contact with, such as Andrea Avalos. She has just been an incredible friend through the time when I got here, especially after the second or third semester when we really got to know each other, pray together, and encourage one another. She's remained really close in the years since I've been married to Ryan and had children. It's been really neat to see each other grow after finishing school, and through ministry involvement. She's been a great friend! She's probably been the closest one to me of all the students I met at AIC.

The friendships I've had with faculty and staff have also been very special. I especially appreciate how (now President) Jim Comer and his wife, Sue, really invested in my spiritual growth and formation. I remember years ago when I took Brother Comer for a class, Introduction to Bible, during my first semester. I had been really serving the Lord for only about a year, and I was learning so much. The classes that I took were helping me to grow spiritually.

You see, I had just come out of a situation where I had made some poor decisions and was living with those consequences. There was something that Brother Comer taught as we were discussing the topic of redemption and how God was our "Redeemer." When he brought that word across, it really struck me in the heart—trying to fully grasp what it meant to receive the redemption of God and who Christ is as our Redeemer. I will never forget it—in fact, it changed my life! I knew that I was saved, but I struggled with forgiving myself for my past. Knowing that I didn't have to live with guilt made me realize how special it was to be redeemed! I still remember walking out of that class—free in what God had done for my life, realizing He gave me more strength to continue on. When I came to AIC, I was a single parent with a child, not knowing exactly how things would turn out. I'd meet people who promised me that they were going to stay by my side and see me through as a student. They were committed to all of us students here, seeing us through to the goals and the dreams that God placed in our lives. So faculty and staff like Jim and Sue Comer, Betty Hanna, Nadine Waldrop, Gay Keeter, Joe Saggio—everyone here just impacted my life in so many ways.

Looking back, it was like a new beginning, a new start, in my life. I was excited about being here: the privilege and honor of this opportunity—because society seems to tell single parents, "You're never going to do anything, so accept your life—that's all it's ever going to be!" I didn't understand until later, when I was doing some research about life circumstances and different things in our society and realized where I could have easily ended up. I think less than 1 percent of Native American single mothers are able to persist in getting a college degree. I just thank God for the blessings that came through the college and through each class.

Often it's very lonely being a single parent, so while I was here I just wanted to be able to attend basketball games and various on-campus events because those types of community events meant a lot to me, helping me to remain grounded. I am also grateful for the chapel services, the challenging words that we received from our speakers as they urged us to move forward in our spiritual walks. There were many times when a student or staff member came beside me, bringing words of encouragement. I remember how Blair Schlepp, who served as our director of Student Services (and later as dean of students) at the college, would meet with me every week for counseling, encouragement, and prayer. Former President Jim Lopez and his wife, Belinda, were also there for me. They've known my family since I was in fourth grade, so being able to talk with them was great as well.

Of course I can't forget to mention that one of the greatest highlights of my time as a student was when I met my husband Ryan here. We met in Old Testament Survey. I had prayed for years that God would bring me the right person into my life. I had told the Lord that I wasn't going to date or pursue anybody because I have a son and I don't want to bring people in and out of his life who weren't going to stick. I remember thinking, "Lord, you have a plan for my life and that's all I want. I know you'll bring me that person in your time." So God brought Ryan into my life in January 1998. He pursued me first as a friend, and that's how I felt it should be since that's what I really needed. We began to date, and even though others would sometimes ask me out, I had a strong inner assurance from the Lord that Ryan was the one for me, and so I couldn't even consider any of the others. Ryan and I often marvel between ourselves how the Lord brought us together to be married in 1999 and has given us three beautiful children: Christian, Marc, and Alyssa. Ryan and I are truly blessed!

American Indian College has many special qualities to offer Native American students. For one thing, the college has shown me as a Native woman what is possible for a Native American—or anyone else—to accomplish with the Lord's help. Many times I believe Native people have even used their ethnicity as an excuse for not succeeding. I've always refused to buy into that kind of thinking. Now that I have been blessed with being able to complete two degrees at this college, I am enabled to work with other Natives and take the opportunity to encourage students to take hold of all AIC has to offer them.

Recently I have been receiving phone calls from people, including relatives, who are asking, "How did you do it? How were you able to get through school with all of the challenges you had?" Now they want to contact AIC and say, "It must be the school." They say this because not only did my sister Jennifer graduate but I graduated as well, and they understand my background and what my life was like before. Some of them even called me in the past week and let me know that they want information from the college. I'm pleased to promote the school because I believe in what's happening here. I think it's awesome because we can also go and affect our families in this way. It's exciting and encouraging now to see that my cousins and different ones are calling and wanting to attend here. What an incredible opportunity for our students and alumni to go out and influence our reservations, communities, homes, and schools for Christ! Because of all of this I want people to know that I consider it a privilege and honor—as well as a responsibility— to be a Native American. Therefore, I can't live with excuses. I need to have goals and succeed by not living in the past, but by moving forward

As I mentioned earlier, before settling on attending AIC I had visited other universities. During those visits I noticed that the atmosphere was so different, and I felt that many people were out for themselves and to have a good time. I didn't see a lot of concern for others; I saw a concern and commitment to self. But AIC has encouraged members of this community to have relationships with, as well as a concern for, one another. There are also some established boundaries that help us with living a life that will glorify Christ. In other words, it's not just a free-for-all here; there are things that we are required to live by. We are encouraged to faithfully attend chapel services as well as services at our local church and to be involved in ministry. I remember starting with nursery ministry, moving to being a children's pastor, and then becoming a youth pastor. All of these experiences have been a rich blessing because we were always encouraged to take what we were learning in class and apply them to our life and ministry. Looking back, I marvel at how God has used each stage in my life and shown me different things. All these areas that I became involved in were in part because AIC encouraged us to develop our callings to bless the body of Christ.

All of this was facilitated by the Pentecostal atmosphere of this campus. I remember times when the instructors would put aside the class agenda and allow the Holy Spirit to minister to the immediate needs of the students. Not surprisingly, when instructors took the time to allow the ministry of the Spirit, we would always be able to return to the course content and still be able to accomplish the course objectives. I especially love how the Spirit can speak to us both individually and corporately here in the campus community!

I trust that AIC's greatest legacy will be the impact that this institution has had on the Native people and how our students have affected their communities in a positive way. For example, my sister Jennifer can still point to people who went through the college at the same time that she did and are still serving the Lord actively—not the least of whom is her husband, Vince Roubideaux, now an ordained minister and serving as our dean of students. In other words, I believe the greatest legacy will be the fruit of the college: those who have gone out and are successfully serving the Lord in their corner of the vineyard. I'd like to continue to see our graduates launch forth and touch their communities, schools, businesses, and churches. I'd like to see AIC be known as a place where a great move of God can and will take place, producing fruit for the Lord's harvest. I believe it is happening, and I look forward to the years ahead as more students come through the college, graduate, and move on to fulfill their chosen destiny. I'm excited to see what they're going to do and the effect they will have where God has called them to be!

Don Keeter presenting Bible to Pat Merino

James Buckel

Pat Merino, Zarah Goes Ahead, Tammy Tunney, Natashia Atcitty, Marco Burnette, Ronald Burnette, Felix Benally, Jim Comer

Outreach Team to Northern California

DONALD P. MERINO

(Maidu/Wintun) Director of Plant Operations

Family has always been very important to me. I was the ninth of sixteen children. (I guess that makes me a "middle child"!) My dad was a great man, a veteran of the Second World War. He fought under General Patton's command overseas. My dad was but a boy when his father died, which is why his grandmother raised him. Later on, Dad took care of his own mother and his siblings (a sister and two brothers). He truly was the man of the house and took those responsibilities seriously.

I also had a great relationship with my mother. In fact, I had the opportunity of leading her to faith in Jesus Christ when she lay in the hospital on a sickbed. Mom was not well, and the family was all there to see her. After they left, I came in and asked her, "Mom, do you know Jesus?" She answered by telling me, "No." I asked her if she would like to know Jesus. She looked up and smiled, "Sure I would—yes." So I prayed the sinner's prayer right there with her in the hospital. I thank God that Mom made that commitment. From that day forward she dedicated her life to Christ and began to go to church. She followed the pattern of her parents, who were already faithful Christians, and she served the Lord as well.

Speaking of my mom's parents, Grandma lived to be 106 years of age, a great Christian woman. In fact, I was asked to perform her funeral—the very first funeral I ever preached. My grandfather was ninety-four years of age when he passed away, a number of years before my grandmother. Grandpa was also a veteran of the First World War, having served his country as a young soldier.

Thinking back to how I came to be a part of the (then) American Indian Bible Institute, it began with my admiration for the school's founders, Brother Clarence and Sister Alta Washburn—they were really super people with a great vision for reaching Native America for Christ. I respected the commitment and dedication that the Washburn's had for Native Americans, having known them for two years before I started attending the All Tribes church. I was still working for the Salt River Indian Community, just outside of Scottsdale, to the east of Phoenix, where I also came to know Sister Eunice Sampson, another godly woman in my life. Sister Eunice was a prayer warrior and recognized leader in the Salt River Indian AG, where she continued to faithfully serve the Lord even after her husband, Virgil, a Pima evangelist, passed away.

The Sampsons would come to me often and encourage me to come to AIBI. On one occasion, Sister Eunice came to me and insisted, "Pat, you need to go to Bible school!" I laughed and replied, "Sister Eunice, I can't do that right now." Never one to give up, Eunice came up to me one day with great determination, grabbing me by the arms, "Pat, you need to come to my house and we're going to fill out this form and we're going to send you to Bible school."

Of course I laughed, and with resignation I told her, "All right, Sister Eunice—you win!" Still, two more years passed Finally, one day I went to her home and we sat down and she laid the form out, explaining to me, "I need you to fill this out—now!" I provided all the needed information, and Eunice promptly mailed it in. A week later a letter arrived informing me that I had been accepted to American Indian Bible Institute (AIBI).

So I went with an old suitcase and a couple of bucks. After arriving, I got ready to move into the west side of (what is now) the Washburn Dormitory. Greeting me upon my arrival in the lower parking lot, Brother Norm Wolf (then resident director) grabbed my suitcase, carried it up the hill, and with a grand, sweeping gesture, showed me my room, declaring, "This will be your home for the next nine months." So I made my entrance, and there was my first roommate: Joey Travella, who was a couple of years ahead of me. Joey was not only my roommate but ultimately a close friend as well. Soon after I arrived, the staff provided us with all the rules and regulations of the college, letting us know what we could and could not do as students. And by the way, back then we had room inspections every day.

Thinking back to the 1980s, I would have to say that there were a number of instructors who had a positive influence on my life. In particular I remember Brother Eugene Hunter (now a professor emeritus, still teaching part-time), who was one of my first professors. Brother Hunter was a great encourager. President Dave Moore was also one of my instructors before he became president, as well as President Carl Collins. Sister Alma Thomas (now also an emerita professor) was also one of my instructors back then. I certainly appreciated her commitment and dedication to the college and its students. In fact, I'm convinced that all of these instructors loved the students far more than they loved themselves. That's how committed they were at that time.

Back when I was a student here the first time, working on my diploma, every student had a counselor, or advisor, they chose from among the faculty or staff—someone they could go to when they needed help. The faculty and staff members were there to be mentors to walk by our sides, to pray us through the hard times—I'll never forget that!

I also remember when Rev. Rodger A. Cree (Mohawk) came to serve as the Campus Pastor, helping to "fill the gap" since the spiritual needs of the students could be quite time consuming. It was a blessing to have a man of Brother Cree's stature, wisdom, and keen sense of humor to work with students. A Mohawk Indian from Quebec Province in Canada, Brother Cree moved to Arizona for health reasons and for a while, he and his wife Esther pastored at Sells (on the Tohono O'odham Reservation) and later at the Salt River Indian Assembly of God, outside of Scottsdale. Brother Cree brought a rich background of experience, knowledge, and a passion for God borne from years of pastoring, to his role as campus pastor here at the college. In 1997, in recognition of his longstanding national leadership, Brother Cree was one of the three original Native ministers to be elected to the General Presbytery of the Assemblies of God, representing Native leadership before the General Council.[1]

President Jim and Belinda Lopez also were very formative in my experience, and I enjoyed them greatly as well. I've always liked teasing Brother Lopez about being a "southerner" since he was from the Ft. Yuma Reservation in California (home to the Quechan and Cocopah tribes), at the juncture of Mexico, Arizona, and Southern California. Of course I considered myself a "northerner" since I was from northern California. I used to remind Brother Lopez (just in fun of course), "You 'southerners' stay to your side, and us 'northerners' will stay to our side. We just need to stay our distance!"

When I graduated from AIBC in 1986, I had the privilege of taking a trip to the Hawaiian Islands as a graduation gift. We spent about two weeks there, one on Oahu and the other on the big island of Hawaii. I traveled with Norm Wolf (who had given me such a grand introduction to the campus four years earlier) as well as Paul and Lia Lanuza, alumni who now serve as the pastors of Phoenix Full Gospel Church (which meets here on AIC's campus). Now their children, Jonathan and Leilani, are students at AIC.

For a while after my return I was active at All Tribes Assembly of God, which by then had moved further north in Phoenix, up to Camelback Avenue, from its earlier location downtown. There I served as security detail, staying on site in a trailer to provide protection for the church campus. While I was there, we had a couple, Dale and Martha Langmade (Inupiat Eskimos), who invited me to become involved in ministry up in Alaska among their people.

So in 1994, I left my position at All Tribes and traveled from Phoenix, Arizona, to Pt. Barrow, Alaska—literally at the top of North America—what a contrast! Now I really was a northerner! I stayed up there for about a year and worked with Pastor Dwayne McKenzie, who at the time of this writing is still the pastor up there at Inupiat Assembly of God in Barrow, Alaska. While I was there I was involved in radio broadcasting, helping with programming that reached all over Alaska and Canada's northern tundra. KJNP, King Jesus North Pole, was the name of the Christian broadcasting network based out of Pt. Barrow, where we launched our two-hour radio broadcast every Sunday and Monday evenings. The broadcast was bi-lingual (English and Inupiat) and included singing, testifying, and preaching. Both the church and the radio ministry were a source of great spiritual refuge for our community because the village was ravaged by drug, alcohol, domestic violence, and child abuse. Because of this I was connected with a local coalition to assist people with overcoming these life-threatening issues. The community took action to ban alcohol and drugs by a local initiative; they also began to deal with the domestic and family violence issues. The turnaround was quite dramatic and, as far as I know, continues to this day. Looking back, I thoroughly enjoyed my time among the Eskimo people; they treated me so well, and I grew to love them dearly.

In 1995 I returned to the Lower 48 and became immersed in working among the homeless population in Minneapolis, Minnesota. Once again I saw Native people living in dire situations. In fact, I was profoundly affected by the large number of Indians living on the streets in Minneapolis–St. Paul. I clearly saw the need to bring people to Christ, actually living among the homeless so that I could serve as a personal witness of the love of Jesus Christ. That same year, I felt the call back to my home community in Greenville, California, where I stayed for several more years, remaining active in the church—especially in construction renovation projects.

In 2000, fourteen years after completing a diploma in ministry, I returned to (now) American Indian College to work as a staff member and also to complete a bachelor's degree in Christian ministry (graduating in 2002). When I returned in 2000, I saw a lot of improvements. AIC was now regionally accredited and offered four-year degrees. The Lee Academic Center and the Ramsey Cafeteria were just two of the beautiful additions to the campus completed between my two times here as a student at the college.

I have many fond memories over the years of students crying out to God in prayer, with the sounds of their intercession ringing through the corridors of the school. I have seen a number of graduates launch into ministry, people like Carolyn Norris (now Terry), married to Rev. Irving Terry (Pima), who served for a number of years as pastor at San Tan on the nearby Gila River Indian Reservation. Sammy Begay, Eric Lee, Marvin Paul, Gloria Gilson, Patricia Garcia, and others, who are now successful pastors, also made a great impact on my life. Today the range of their ministries stretches from the Gila River Indian Community here in central Arizona to the Navajo Reservation in northwest New Mexico and upwards to Alaska!

Today I now serve as the director of Plant Operations, and over the last twenty-five years I've seen a lot of changes. One thing that I am very thankful for now is seeing the number of faculty who have furthered their education by earning doctoral degrees. As a result, they have brought a higher level of educational attainment here to the college, which in turn is stretching our students to reach higher themselves. AIC has come a long way in a short time, and by faculty furthering themselves, it has raised the academic caliber of our students. I would strongly recommend to any student who would want to come to AIC to do so; there are some committed men and women who will pray with them, cry with them, and believe for God's best. I firmly believe that the great vision that God has given to the school's leadership, beginning in 1957, is what has carried ATBS to where it is in 2007—reaching and equipping Native Americans with the gospel.

In closing I'd like to recount the amazing story of James Buckel, a seventy-two year old traditional Navajo Medicine man, a shaman, who lived just down the street from our school in a trailer park. John Chee, one of our Navajo students answered the call to take the message of Christ's love to this elderly gentleman, who accepted Christ as his Lord and Savior. After that, he enrolled at our school as a student for two years! During that time he grew in his newly found faith. Two years later, Brother James Buckel went home to be with the Lord. A number of us had the privilege of attending his funeral at a military veteran's cemetery up in the northwest part of the state. First, a soldier for his country; at the end, a warrior in the King's army! You know, I'm convinced that if somebody at that age—and a traditional medicine man no less—can be reached by one of our students, then it's never too late to receive the gospel. Whether you are seven or seventy, Jesus can still teach you something! I've said it many times before, but I'll say it once again: "AIC is the place to be!"

Pat Merino and Gene Martin

Pat Merino, Jim Comer, and Steve Jester with work team from Butterfield Assembly of God, Russelville, Arkansas

NOTES

1 The other two were John E. Maracle (Mohawk) and C. Blair Schlepp (Lakota).

PART EIGHT ▲▲▲

Alumni Reflections

Lillie Ward Neal

Jimmy Yellowhair

Vince Roubideaux

James J. Bollinger

Marco J. Burnette

Jameson D. Lopez

▲

351

1961 Graduating Class: Lillie Ward Neal, Juanita (Miquel) Juan, Mary Wallen

1959 Student Body

352

LILLIE WARD NEAL

(Yavapai Apache)

My name is Lillie (Ward) Neal, I am a Yavapai Apache from the San Carlos Apache Reservation, and I had the privilege of attending All Tribes Bible School (ATBS) (now known as American Indian College) from 1957–1961 and being in the very first graduating class, the class of 1961. Nearly fifty years later I am still joyfully serving the Lord and the proud mother of four daughters, three sons, over thirty grandchildren, and three great-grandchildren! Here's my story.

When I first got married, we lived in Guadalupe, a Yaqui community just south of Tempe, Arizona. One day Sister Washburn came by looking for people to take to church. At that time, my mother said to me, "You know how to speak English. I think she's a missionary. Could you talk with her?" So I did. Soon afterwards I accepted Jesus Christ as my Savior, and I started attending on a daily basis the little church where they were meeting down on 46th Street. Then I moved to Phoenix, and I enrolled in the Bible school, where we used to have daily prayer. Some students attended classes during the day, and others of us attended at night because of our schedules—but all of us got together for a couple of hours at noon for prayer with Sister Washburn. Because of my work schedule I had to attend at night, as did also my daughter-in-law, Nan Irving, because of her children. I remember we also had students from the Salt River Indian Reservation near Scottsdale—there were a bunch of us! All of us were praying for another location for our Bible school because the place was very small and we had outgrown the facilities.

Back then we had to pray daily for our food because we had some students who came from the reservation and they were totally dependent on the Lord meeting their needs on a daily basis. In

353

addition to my job and studies, I was also a Sunday School teacher working with about six young boys. One of the boys in my class was Paul Carruthers, whose mother, Lois Carruthers, was one of our first Bible instructors. Knowing how little boys can sometimes be, she used to tell me, "Lillie, I know Paul is a 'bad boy'—you just tell me if he doesn't behave himself in your class." Of course, she knew Paul wasn't really bad; he was just energetic, like most little boys his age. By the way, Paul turned out all right. For many years he and his wife, Terri, served faithfully as both missionary– pastors and chaplains for the nursing home on the Gila River Indian Reservation. Today, Paul is a chaplain for the John C. Lincoln Hospital in Phoenix and also does visitation at the Phoenix Indian Hospital. Like his mother, he has a strong love and calling to Native people. Sister Carruthers, now with the Lord, would be so proud!

Remembering the original ATBS school, I recall that it was housed in a small adobe building with no air conditioning, only a swamp cooler. The Washburns had a small trailer that they lived in behind the school. From the Bible school we would launch out to do outreach ministry on the local reservations, including the Salt River Indian Reservation and the White Mountain Apache Reservation in northern Arizona. We also ministered locally among the Yaqui, Tohono O'odham (back then known as the Papago), and the Maricopa. I still recall the outdoor services under the ramadas that we had out at Salt River. I'll never forget the lamps hanging underneath and how the mosquitoes would bite us. But that never stopped us from praying for the folks who gathered there, and we ministered to ever-increasing crowds of spiritually hungry people. As a result of those outreaches, we saw a great harvest of souls come into the Kingdom, and many were also baptized in the Holy Spirit.

One day after our prayer time at the Bible school, Sister Washburn came over to me and declared, "Sister Lillie, the Lord spoke to me. We're not going to be here down on Washington Street very long. We're going to go on somewhere 'up the hill.' I don't know where, whether it will be on Camelback Avenue or somewhere else, but I believe the Lord is going to give us a larger place somewhere north of here." That's what she told me—and do you know what—that's just what happened! Today, AIC does sit up on a hill, just over ten miles north of the original location. God is faithful in keeping His promises.

When I think of Sister Alta Washburn, I remember that she was just like a mother to everyone she met. She was always ready to share her faith and love for the Lord Jesus Christ. I don't ever recall seeing her get mad. She was always there to help others—always praying, always encouraging each one of us. She wasn't afraid to help wherever needed in the Bible school. Even though she was the principal and had lots of administrative and teaching duties, she would come into the kitchen and help make tortillas if that was what was needed. She also believed in her calling to train Native people to become pastors and church leaders, even when people opposed her. There were some who did not agree that it was possible to train Indians to reach their own people with the gospel; in fact, some of her most vocal opponents to that vision were Indians themselves. Sister Washburn once told me, "Lillie, as long as God keeps me going, I'm going to go and continue to bring Native students here. I don't care if someone doesn't like that—I'm still going!"

Thankfully, in spite of the doubts and opposition of some, the church and school began to grow, and we experienced a great move of God through His Holy Spirit; people began to get healed and it was a different world. Sister Washburn was truly one of a kind. I've never known anyone who had such strength and ability; she could do anything she set her mind to! She was always there for us: whenever we were down, she was there to pray for us and encourage us. If it wasn't for her, I don't know where I'd be. All of us just wanted to follow in her footsteps.

Brother Clarence Washburn was also an important part of ATBS. Although he worked more behind the scenes (since he was not himself a minister), he was still very involved, especially helping to keep the two buses running that we used for outreaches to the various churches and reservation communities. It seemed like those buses were always in need of repair. But Brother Washburn's skill as a mechanic kept them in good running order.

When I am asked what my favorite time was at the Bible school, I would just have to say that every time we prayed was my favorite time. The joy of the Lord was there all the time—it was just wonderful! I hated to have to leave and come home sometimes because it was such a blessing to be there. Another thing that was so very special was that we were all like one big family of brothers and sisters. At ATBS it didn't matter what tribe you belonged to—Pima, Papago, Hopi, or Navajo—we were all united as one. I don't recall ever seeing anyone make fun of anyone else or ridicule their tribal background; we had a unity among us that couldn't be broken.

At the school we received many visitors, including those who came out for revival services—sometimes as far away as Oklahoma. Also, Sister Washburn's sister, Imogene Johnson, who along with her husband, Ted, served as missionaries among the Apaches up on the Ft. Apache Reservation in northern Arizona—they would come down and visit, bringing some of their congregation down as well.

Because of the wonderful spiritual environment, we saw many miracles in our midst. For example, I remember one couple in particular: the wife was crippled for a long time and had been routinely hospitalized. Sister Washburn announced to us that we needed to go to prayer on behalf of this woman, so we did. Just a few short weeks later, the woman who had been crippled walked right into our midst and announced joyfully, "I'm healed. I'm all right!" We just started rejoicing with her that the same God who healed in "Bible days," just like in the early days of Pentecost, was still healing today and continuing to work miracles.

Growing up on the San Carlos Apache Indian Reservation I went to church. But I did not have a personal relationship with Christ. My mother told me as a child that I needed to confess my sins to the priest, but I never felt forgiven even though I did so every Sunday. After I got saved while attending All Tribes Assembly—where I've now been attending since 1950—my whole life changed! Every summer, a number of the women from the church and Bible school would go up to Prescott for several days for special services. We'd gather with women from many different tribal backgrounds and just have a special time. How the Spirit of God would move! We had such an incredible time together, and even though it was many years ago, those memories are still very fresh to me.

I have definitely been impacted by my years at ATBS. I am just so thankful. Even today, my grown children still tell me, "Mom, you're the best mom—if it wasn't for you we wouldn't be here." My oldest daughter, now sixty-three years of age, told me that recently, adding, "Watching you do things and telling us what to do, it makes me feel good that I can sleep soundly at night knowing that I have a mother that will always be by my side." The Lord has been good to me, and my experiences years ago at All Tribes Bible school are a special part of the blessings that I have experienced in my life. It was the happiest moment in my life when I went to Bible School! Today, because of the effect those years had on me, I'm still working at a hospital and people look at me sometimes and tell me, "You don't seem to have any problems." I just tell them I don't have problems—I'm just so happy because I know the Lord!

Even today, I still pray for the Bible school. I remember how Sister Washburn would envision the building that we would someday have up on the hill. She used to tell us, "Rejoice, for that is the promise that He has given us so that we can have young people go into the church and go forth into their own land and to their own people to bring more students." Today, fifty years later, when my son drives me by the campus, I point to it and say, "This is what Sister Washburn was praying about—and there stands the building on a hill that she believed God for."

My advice to young Native men and women who have a call of God on their life would be to remember that we're not walking on a plain, flat road. We have hills and valleys and we're going "up and down, up and down," as Sister Washburn used to say. In other words, young people need to keep going and never give up. The trail will be hard sometimes, but it is going to get straighter and you're going to know when you're up there! Back when I was a student, I didn't know what Sis. Washburn meant, even as she tried to draw this illustration on the chalkboard to show us that the Christian walk wouldn't always be easy; but if we believed that we were going to be somebody and accomplish something, than we could work harder and face our problems—then it would all fade away. After fifty years and a lifetime of experience, I think I more fully understand what she was saying. So that's the counsel I would pass on to the young people at AIC today—to never give up, and stay on that road that the Lord has placed you on.

Jimmy & Myrna Yellowhair

Myrna & David Yellowhair

Jimmy Yellowhair

JIMMY YELLOWHAIR
(Navajo)

My name is Jimmy Yellowhair. I'm a Navajo and a 1983 graduate of AIBC. During the Spring of 2000, our son, David, graduated from Sinagua High School in Flagstaff, Arizona. At that time I was unsure of what his future plans were. So one day as I had occasion to take care of some business down in Phoenix, I invited David to come along. We spent our morning traveling and taking care of our obligations in downtown Phoenix. At noon, we returned to the AIC campus to have lunch. During the noon hour we socialized with some of the college's faculty and staff who were also there. I was particularly excited to get to visit with Rev. Donald P. Keeter (now with the Lord), who was one of my instructors when I was a student here. It was great for us to be able to reminisce about the "good old days."

As we relaxed and enjoyed our meal, I noticed Rev. Jim Dempsey, who was at that time the dean of students, at one of the other tables. I motioned to David, telling him, "The faculty members here sincerely care for their students. They love not just with their words but with their deeds. When you go to school here, you will make many good friends that will really stand by you." As I was telling a story to David about Jim Dempsey, memories about my experience as a student at AIBC flooded back to me.

Before I go any further, let me first take you back to how I got saved. As members of the Navajo tribe, my parents led all of us children to follow in the traditional Navajo religious ways. We participated in Navajo ceremonial rituals in the 1950s and 1960s. But in the 1970s, we joined a syncretistic religious expression, which mixed traditional Native beliefs with Christianity, known as the Native American Church or the "Peyote Way." It was during the late 1970s that I moved down from the Navajo reservation to

Phoenix, where I was isolated from my parents while I was going to a technical college that specialized in computer programming and technology. While studying and working in the city, I had some problems for which I could not resort to traditional spiritual help from the Navajo reservation. I found that I had to seek help from the "White Man's Religion."

During the summer of 1979, I was drawn to the Lord through a Sunday radio broadcast by Dr. Charles F. Stanley, the well-known pastor of a mega-church in Atlanta, Georgia, and one-time president of the Southern Baptist Convention. He ministered to me greatly through his weekly broadcast program. I also found myself enjoying the Christian gospel music that accompanied his program; so after a few Sundays, I said, "I will give myself to Jesus—and there is no turning back!"

So after I committed myself to faith in Jesus Christ and got saved, I became hungry for the Word of God. I went down to a nearby bookstore to get some literature to learn more about the Bible. As I searched through the used books section, I found one that had many Scripture verses. Not only did it quote verses from the Bible, but it followed them with explanations and pictures. I bought the book and started reading it. But the more I read, the more confused I got. The book seemed to be about God, but a "still small voice" inside me did not agree with it. After a few days of reading and studying, I came to realize it was released through the publishing house for a large religious cult based in Brooklyn, New York. Even then I realized that this book contained a great deal of false teachings.

After that experience, I decided to seriously study the Scriptures and church history thoroughly at a Bible school. Since Jesus Christ established His Church over 2,000 years ago, a number of false religions have been founded that confuse many people into thinking that they are an authentic expression of Christianity, when in fact they are counterfeit churches. During that time I checked out three or four Bible schools around the Valley of the Sun and finally settled on AIBC, enrolling during the spring semester of 1980. Rev. Alma Thomas became my spiritual mentor at school when I was just a new Christian. At that time I held many odd, unbiblical worldviews. Back then I didn't know much about the Lord and held many incorrect ideas and concepts about Him. But by getting good biblical teaching from the instructors and reading the Bible privately and worshipping almost daily in the chapel, I was able to gain a biblical perspective of God the Father, His Son Jesus Christ, and the Holy Spirit.

I was especially blessed by the chapel services. In fact, I gained a very important insight during one of those special times where the whole campus gathered for worship and preaching. One morning the chapel speaker taught on the importance of loving everybody. As we filed out of the chapel service afterwards, I kept recalling what the minister had said. The more I thought about it, the more impractical it seemed to me. Finally, I said to the Lord that such a thing as loving everybody might be possible for You, but it seems impossible for a "mere mortal," such as myself. When the speaker said "everybody," that included people like Hitler, Stalin, or, closer to home, the Hopi, our opponents in the Navajo-Hopi land-dispute, or a drunk friend who smashes a new car he borrowed from you! Praying to God, I requested that He open my spiritual insight for a better understanding of this.

After several days had passed, I was working at some task, when all of a sudden understanding popped into my mind. Suddenly it all made sense! I was able to grasp what it means to love everybody. This is what I understood: You have to divide each individual into two parts. One part is what a person is. The other part is what he does (his deeds). You have to love each person unconditionally—just like God. But what a person does, you can love or hate it, depending on if the deed is love or sin. God hates sin, and we should too. What a person is could be a Hopi, Apache, Pima, Russian, German, Japanese, or Chinese. They could be black, brown, red, yellow, or white. Nevertheless, we must love them all (all six billion individuals who are on the face of the Earth today).

Such was the wealth of knowledge and wisdom that I obtained at AIBC during my time as a student. Many times I gleaned insight from the faculty, sometimes by just reading the Bible, and at other times from trials and testing. There were even times when I gleaned insights directly from the Lord's still small voice during the chapel services. It was during those times that the following verse of Scripture came alive to me in special ways: "Thus says the Lord... 'Call to Me, and I will answer you, and show you great and mighty things, which you do not know'" (Jeremiah 33:2,3, NKJV).

I made many good and loyal friends at AIC. In fact, I first met my beautiful future wife, Myrna, there. (You never know what wonderful things you will find in Bible college!) About a year and half later (August 1, 1981), we got married in Eloy, Arizona. Our son David was born a year after that. Our other two children are Sarah and Jonathan.

Before I digress further, let me return to the main story I was trying to tell to my son about Jim Dempsey. On that special day— Mother's Day—things started off innocently enough. The days were getting warmer; the temperatures started to be consistently over the hundred-degree mark. I thought it sure would be nice to get out of this hot city. The past year had been a difficult one for my mother. She was sick and miserable most of the time, so I tried to see her as often as possible, usually taking a gift of a puzzle or some other item that I thought she might like.

My wife and I had two vehicles. Our newer truck was being repaired because of an oil problem, so I filled up our older car with gas and headed toward Kayenta, Arizona, about 300 miles away. I passed Camp Verde and climbed up the long hill toward Flagstaff. About that time the engine started getting very hot. Soon it started smoking and then it caught on fire! Obviously I could not stay in the car any longer, so I grabbed a few items and moved quickly away from the scene, fearing the car might explode at any minute. A number of travelers drove by, gawking at my burning car as they passed—but to my disappointment no one got out to help me. (Perhaps no one had a fire extinguisher or perhaps like me they were fearful of an explosion.)

After nearly an hour had passed, the fire truck arrived and put out the fire. By this time the car was a total loss. As the officer at the scene was taking down vital information for his report, he asked me, "How much gas did you have in the gas tank?" I told him, "I filled it up as I was leaving Phoenix." He responded, "It was a good thing. If a car still has a lot of liquid fuel in the tank, it will not explode."

Later, some kind person gave me a ride back to Camp Verde. From there I was able to call my wife, Myrna. A couple hours later, she drove up from Phoenix to pick me up. As I was waiting, I had time to ponder how I would get to work now. At the time, I was working for the Department of Public Safety (DPS), and Myrna was doing some part-time work at the Bible college. I was employed by DPS from 1978 through 1991. In the summer of 1991, I was offered a new job at Northern Arizona University (NAU) in Flagstaff, working with the campus's computer systems.

In the midst of this crisis, Jim Dempsey offered some help. What a blessing this help was! He gave us the key to one of his vehicles to use while we resolved our transportation problem. We used the Dempseys' Subaru for several months, until we were able to get our truck back from being repaired. What a timely help it was to us! Myrna and I are forever grateful for Jim's kindness.

I do not know if the story about Jim Dempsey had any influence on my son that day at lunch, but that fall David did enroll at AIC. It is very important for a young person just starting out in life to have a right perspective about his place in this big universe. At that time David's priorities were set in the right order. God came first, and everything else was second to that.

Most recently David served as the youth minister at the Whiteriver Assembly of God on the Fort Apache Reservation. Our daughter, Sarah, graduated last year from Southwestern AG University in Waxahachie, Texas. Our youngest son, Jonathan, graduated from Sinagua High School here in Flagstaff and is now serving his country in the armed forces. My wife served as the pastor at Mountaintop AG here in Flagstaff until a couple of years ago. I retired from NAU after working there for about twelve years. Recently, however, I have "un-retired" and am now back working for NAU. In my "spare time" I've taken some graduate courses towards a master's degree at the Assemblies of God Theological Seminary (AGTS) branch campus at AIC and also found time to recently complete a book called *Sinless*, a compilation of more than twenty years of my Christian education teachings specifically geared for a Native American audience.

In closing, I would have to say that many of the wonderful blessings in my family's life are connected to our relationship to American Indian College. The faculty members there not only teach spiritual truths to the students, but they demonstrate true love and concern for them. An effective teacher always puts action to the lessons that are taught. Our Lord Jesus Christ was a very good teacher. As He taught His disciples, He not only instructed them in words, but He actually lived out those teachings in front of them.

Looking back, I'm glad to have been part of AIC and was very happy to see my son, David, go to school there as well. I trust that many other parents will have the privilege of sending their children to this Bible college, where they can gain a strong spiritual walk through good biblical teaching and real life examples from instructors who truly care about their students.

Vince & Jennifer (Smith) Roubideaux with their children: Alicia, Erica, Amber & Joshua

Front to back: Vince Roubideaux, John Maracle, and Ed Bradford

VINCE ROUBIDEAUX

(Shoshone/Paiute-Rosebud Sioux) Dean of Students

Many writers find it a challenge to know just where to begin their story—and I can certainly identify with that! But I feel compelled to share how God first prepared my family to know that there is a Holy and Living God whose Son died for me and gave His all so that I might enter into a lasting relationship with Him. Even today, I marvel at how God took a tragedy in our family to eventually bring me to this college, a place where I would come to know Him and grow to serve Him with all my heart.

Back in the 1980s, I was enjoying life in Reno, Nevada, working several different construction jobs, playing in Native basketball tournaments, and not really taking my life or any type of relationships very seriously. Basically, you could say that I didn't have a strong sense of purpose or destiny at that time, which is a very familiar pattern of many young Native American men who grow up on reservations or in an urban Native lifestyle.

Part of my family's problem was that we did not have a father at home who could give us any type of positive guidance. Without a dad to provide that, I missed out on having a strong spiritual male role model in my home—something I urgently needed. My mother worked a full-time job for the state of Nevada in Reno, where we lived, and thankfully she was able to provide for many of basic necessities. My grandmother also helped to raise us—even after our grandfather passed away in the early 1970s. Looking back on that time, I believe that as a family we faced a great deal of insecurity that caused us to just passively accept the pattern that we believed was laid out for us. Little did we know that but that was going to change in a very real way!

At that same time, my sister, Rhonda Williams, was still attending school back on the reservation in Owyhee, Nevada (also known as the Duck Valley Indian Reservation). One evening she chose to go riding with friends, and just as they were speeding down a road right off the state highway, they turned to enter back on it and rolled the Jeep CJ they were riding in. This caused the Jeep to eject all the passengers because no one was wearing seatbelts. I believe that there were at least six young people in the Jeep, and two were seriously injured. One was a young man who received severe head injuries, and the other was my sister, Rhonda, who had the Jeep roll over on top of her.

My sister and the other injured passenger were quickly evacuated to a hospital in Boise, Idaho. When I first saw Rhonda, she had a metal halo drilled into her skull and weights hanging off it to keep her spine straight. She could not move her hands or her feet. I was devastated. Rhonda, a vibrant and energetic young lady who loved to play sports, was now lying confined to a bed, unable to move. It seemed to be a great tragedy—but we were about to find out that God was coming on the scene in a big way!

After several months in the hospital, Rhonda was taken to a local rehabilitation center where a lay volunteer from a local Assemblies of God church was conducting hospital visitations. My sister was not able to cope with her new condition and was in a deep depression over the sudden and tragic chain of events that led to her lying paralyzed in a hospital bed. Yet, when Rhonda heard that Jesus Christ died for her sins and could give her new life and help her to move forward in victory despite her circumstances—she then was receptive to everything the volunteer chaplain had to say. In fact, Rhonda received Christ as her personal Savior that very night and was given a vision that she would lead her family into a relationship with Him as well! The next day she was no longer depressed and was instantly delivered from that spirit of depression that had gained such a hold on her. Those who needed to be there for her now surrounded Rhonda. What was even more incredible is that she was able to go back to her high school and graduate with her class. A little later Rhonda heard of a Bible school in Phoenix, Arizona, for Native Christians. The school at the time was known as American Indian Bible College.

It was while Rhonda was attending the Bible college that God started to deal with my own heart. She consistently requested prayer for me in the chapel services and devotions. Like incense, the prayers of the students, faculty, staff, and administration reached the heavens, and the Holy Spirit began convicting me by creating a sense of uneasiness in me. The more the AIBC community prayed, the more miserable my life became! My sins started to haunt me day and night, and I knew that there needed to be a change. I started to make a plan to go back to school. My choice was to attend the DeVry Institute (now DeVry College) in Phoenix, where I would study to be an electronic technician. DeVry happened to be just a few miles from the Bible college, and conveniently, my apartment was just down the street from AIBC.

After a number of invitations, I finally came to a school chapel service where one of the instructors was preaching. Every word he spoke seemed to pierce my heart, and when the invitation to pray came, everyone responded except me. As all were on their knees praying I felt a gentle tugging at my heart, so I knelt down to pray as well. I had never prayed like this before, and the words that came out of my mouth were these: "God I give up!" I did not know what the "sinner's prayer" was at the time—but that was what came out of my mouth, and a load just lifted off of me that I had been carrying for years. Tears streamed down my face as God started to speak into my heart, and the "peace...that passeth all understanding" (Philippians 4:7, KJV) caused a comfort to well up inside of me.

I quickly discovered that the more time I spent at AIBC, the more everyone encouraged me. My life started to change dramatically. Three months after my life-changing experience of accepting Christ I was filled with the Holy Spirit; the next semester I started to take some classes from AIBC while still attending DeVry. I had not only a hunger to learn more about God but also an awareness that I needed to know Him more. That same semester a beautiful young Navajo lady, Jennifer Smith, from Cortez, Colorado, came to the college, and we started to show an interest in each other. This caused some concern in some of the staff—in part because I was such a new believer—and immediately they started to counsel us in our newfound relationship. You see, I had never dated as a Christian before, and now I needed someone to demonstrate to me how to have a Christ-centered relationship with Jennifer. Rev. Jim Lopez, who several years later served as the president, was dean of students at the time, and he took a great deal of time and patient care to mentor me. I don't know if he has any idea how much he influenced me as I watched him as a Christian husband and father. I was clearly impressed with how he treated his wife, Belinda, and their three children. Without even knowing it, Jim Lopez was my example of what a Christian man should be, and he has made a tremendous impact on my life, for which I will be forever grateful.

After Jennifer graduated with her associate of arts in business, we were married, and we started to work with Pastor Carl Collins (former president of AIBC) at All Tribes Assembly of God here in Phoenix. Serving as the associate pastor at All Tribes, I gained additional training and experience conducting hospital and home visitations, working with Royal Rangers, youth ministry, and filling the pulpit, where I was able to develop my preaching ministry. While Jennifer and I were there, we experienced the birth of our first daughter, Erica (who is now an AIC student). We stayed for five and one-half years with All Tribes and had three daughters by the time we moved to the Salt River Reservation (just adjacent to Scottsdale) to work among the Pima Indians. During our time at the Salt River AG working under Pastor Joel Cornelius, we were able to start a youth band because of the talented youth we had in the church. We stayed for two and one-half years, and then I felt the call to be a senior pastor at Carson Living Waters AG on the checkerboard area of the eastern portion of the Navajo Reservation in New Mexico.

By the time that we were headed to New Mexico, I realized that when I came to the Valley of the Sun in Phoenix several years earlier, I had only a suitcase full of belongings and the clothes I had on. But when I was leaving for New Mexico I now had a wife, children, a car, and some furniture. More importantly, I had godly friends who have forever impacted my life.

Yes, there can be no doubt that the promise that was given to my sister several years earlier was being fulfilled in an incredible way. Even today I recall the chain of events following her accident in which first she and then I came to the Lord. Next, when our mom came to visit us here in Arizona, she then gave her heart to the Lord as well. In fact, a real miracle took place when my mom was saved because she was instantly delivered from cigarette smoking after smoking for close to thirty years! (She told us she hated the taste of cigarettes after she came to Christ.) Later my brother also came to the Lord—which was a surprise to me because he was addicted to marijuana, smoking, gambling, and drinking. Just this past Easter my brother was sharing about what God did for him in the church that he attends. Before, my brother never liked to read, but he started to enjoy doing that when he started reading the Bible and his heart was opened up to the marvelous truths contained in God's Word.

Yes, I can say with complete confidence that God never lies! When he spoke those words to my sister about how her family would come to know Christ, it came to pass, and she saw it with her own eyes. Even though my sister is still in her wheelchair, she still loves the Lord and remains faithful to Him. Today, Jennifer and I have been ministers serving God for eighteen years, and yet He still surprises us with what He can do.

Now I am ministering exactly in the same place where I gave my heart to the Lord. I work at AIC as the dean of students. I am doing exactly the same job as one of my mentors, Jim Lopez, did on the campus. I even got to work with his son, J. D., who just recently graduated from here. Now it's my privilege to be an example to young people about what a godly man should be, and I intend to be true to that calling. You could say I've come full circle. God is good!

James Bollinger amidst "Christmas in October," provided by the West Texas Women's Ministries

Left to Right: Michael Johnson and James Bollinger waiting between classes

Paul Lanuza instructing in computer lab:
Left Front: James Bollinger, Right Back: Michael Johnson,
Right Front: Elizabeth Shonnie

Nancy Saggio interacting in class

Dobie Weasel preaching at Native American Fellowship Convocation.

JAMES J. BOLLINGER

(Omaha) Pastor of Glad Tidings Native AG in Omaha, Nebraska

From the guttermost to the uttermost! Yes, that's the theme of my life story! I am living proof that God can take a mixed-up young Native man and turn him into a trophy of His grace. Not only that, but American Indian College has played a major part in my character growth and spiritual maturity. Let me tell you my story.

My journey of faith begins back in 1994 when at age eighteen I was first incarcerated as an adult offender after being sent to the Douglas County Jail in Omaha, Nebraska, and placed inside of the Life Learning Dorm, a ministry with the Good News Jail and Prison Ministry. At that time I was racking up a string of incarcerations. Chaplain Morris Jackson was in charge of the ministry at the county facility when I came there, and that's where I first came to know and have a personal relationship with Jesus Christ. Unfortunately, since I was a new believer who hadn't yet been thoroughly rooted in God's Word, throughout the 1990s I continued to get sent back to jail. In fact, it wasn't until 1999, about five years later, when I was serving a year sentence there that Pastor Alvin "Dobie" Weasel came to visit me. Chaplain Jackson attends Glad Tidings AG and was sharing with me how a Native pastor, an Assiniboine Indian, had been elected as the senior pastor of this large multi-cultural congregation. He invited Pastor Dobie up to meet me and that's where I first met the man who would become my pastor and mentor—right there in the county jail! Pastor Dobie took time out of his busy schedule and came over to where I was being detained and met with me. That's how I came into acquaintance with Glad Tidings Church. Later, on March 4, 2001, during a church service, I rededicated my life to the Lord Jesus Christ at

Glad Tidings, and I knew that was the church that God would have me go to.

After rededicating my life to the Lord and actively attending church for about seven or eight months, I felt a call to ministry upon my life through the Scripture passage of Psalm 1:1–3 (actually the first memory verse that we learned in the Good News Jail and Prison Ministry). That specific passage challenges the believer to avoid walking in the wicked ways of the world and to delight oneself in God's Law. Accordingly, "whatsoever he doeth shall prosper" (Psalm 1:3, KJV).

With that portion of Scripture, God kept laying upon my heart His divine call. Excited, I approached Pastor Dobie and shared my heart with him: that I felt a call towards pastoral ministry upon my life and needed to go to Bible college. He wisely suggested the American Indian College in Phoenix, Arizona, and so it was through his reference that I first learned about AIC.

When I first saw the Bible College, my initial impression was pretty much what I expected. I saw a number of Native students there. Since many were from the southwestern tribes (particularly Navajo, Apache, and Pima), I knew that would bring some new people into my life, being a Plains Indian from the Midwest. The fact that the school enrolled many different tribes of American Indians made a really good impression on me and confirmed that God had called me there to spend four years of my life to finish a measure of the formative process He had already begun in me.

From my first contact with the school I felt very welcome, especially from my initial conversation with the admissions director, Sandy Ticeahkie, a Kiowa–Comanche. She was the person who handled my enrollment; she really helped put me at ease. In fact, she was like a sister to me, and we talked like we had been acquainted our entire lives. Because of that positive first impression, I felt comfortable and welcome coming to the college even before my family and I arrived. There were warm faces and smiles, a sense of openness from everyone I met, and, most of all, an overwhelming peace that this was where God wanted me to be.

Like many college students I was concerned from time to time about finances. As a married student with a growing family, I needed to see God undertake for our family financially—and He always did. We experienced many financial miracles, but one in particular had to do with my wife and me feeling challenged to give God our tithe even though we needed it for grocery money! As I recall, the tithe was from one of my wife's checks, and we sat there holding the money in one hand while we sensed God calling us to give it out of obedience and that He would take care of our needs. That very next Monday my wife got a $200 raise at the doctor's office she worked at! There were just so many times like that, including when we depended on the Lord to stretch our modest income to help us support our family of three children (now four). We have been able to live far beyond our actual income, and though we may have been poor on paper, we were rich in Jesus! I remember the Lord speaking to my heart this passage from Isaiah:

> Remember ye not the former things, neither consider the things of old. Behold, I will do a new thing; now it shall spring forth; shall ye not know it? I will even make a way in the wilderness, and rivers in the desert (Isaiah 43:18,19, KJV).

During my time at AIC I had the opportunity to see many "streams" brought up out of "the desert," and it was only by God's grace and love that our financial needs were met. We may not have been rich nor had a lot of extras, but God gave us what we needed. We lived within our means and we honor God in that way because He blessed us throughout the four years we were there. In fact, we were even able to take two vacations as a family— including one to Disneyland!

Even people from the college stepped alongside to bless us. I received expert financial aid advice from Nadine Waldrop, the director of student financial aid, and her assistant, Doris Preston. Both were able to locate scholarships that I qualified for. I also worked with my hands and was able to bless the college through maintenance and mechanical skills, applying the apostle Paul's teaching in 1 Thessalonians 4:11 calling on us to "work with [our] hands." Through God's grace (and the work of my hands) I was able to leave Bible college completely debt free. I am so blessed to be able to say that!

At this point I have to say that I could never have made it without the encouragement of my spiritual father, Pastor Dobie. Just knowing that I could call on him at any time and he would return my call—including when we were in a bind financially—meant so much to my family and me. Thankfully, I had to call on him only once, and I thank God for that because I didn't want to lean totally on my pastor or the church back home. Of course he answered that call and helped to meet our financial need.

When I think of the people at the college who influenced my life, there was Dr. Joe Saggio, Dr. David DeGarmo, and (now) President Jim Comer. In particular, Dr. DeGarmo taught me about what it meant to be a pastor and was available for me to call upon for wisdom and spiritual advice. From a very practical standpoint I still appreciate Brother Comer holding me accountable and modeling how to be a Christian man and treat my wife like a lady. He taught me that even if we didn't have any money, we could still have a regular date—even if it meant just going out for a walk. That sort of mentoring on being a godly leader in my home has even carried over into my graduate studies in business administration and finance. I'm seeing the value of using my degree.

Former President Jim Lopez, who served as an outstanding Native role model, was also a major influencer in my life. I will always appreciate these men, including Professor Don Keeter (who's now with the Lord). I continue to value all of what Brother Keeter poured into those of us who were his students. All in all, these men who mentored me all gave a little bit of Jesus out of their personal lives.

As a Native American who received his GED in jail eight years ago, I marvel at how far the Lord has taken me to where I'm at today. How could I ever forget that when I first came, like many students, I needed someone like Brother Jim Dempsey to show me how to write my first college term paper. He was so great in that class and even helped me to get excited about writing that paper!

When I look back, I'm so grateful that AIC is a Pentecostal

college. The doctrines that we hold to, the preaching during the services, the constant reminder in class to put into operation the gifts of the Holy Spirit, underscored all the Pentecostal heritage of AIC. I felt like we were encouraged to exercise the gifts of tongues and the interpretation when we were in chapel; after all, AIC was intended to be a training ground for ministry for men and women with a call of God on their lives. During special convocations and College Days we often had great speakers who would come in and preach and emphasize Pentecost, insisting that the Holy Spirit would come upon us in power just like He promised. After all, as Joel 2:28,29 says:

And it shall come to pass afterward, that I will pour out my spirit upon all flesh; and your sons and your daughters shall prophesy, your old men shall dream dreams, your young men shall see visions: And also upon the servants and upon the handmaids in those days will I pour out my spirit (KJV).

I still remember the class on Acts that I took with Dr. DeGarmo: we looked at the Church then but also looked at it now. In other words, the Book of Acts continues to this day, and I'm so thankful that Pentecost was emphasized here at AIC.

During our time in Phoenix I sure gained a lot of fond memories, including the banquets that we've had, the outreaches that we took part in, such as the Mexico Invasion, and just the fellowship that I've experienced through outreaches and going out with teams and having special times with my brothers and sisters in the Lord. There were also basketball games, homecoming games, and many other activities as well.

But I'd have to say my fondest memory was of course graduation—a high point of fulfilling four years there. I even had the privilege of being one of the graduation speakers. Who would have ever thought that someone who just a few years back had to get his GED in jail would be graduating magna cum laude and as the ASB President would be giving the response on behalf of all the graduates at commencement! It's just like I said at the beginning of this essay: Jesus brought me from the guttermost to the uttermost. Just looking back over these past several years,

God has taken me so far—and yes, I still have a long ways to go in Him!

Today I proudly serve as the pastor of a church plant launched from Glad Tidings AG that is called Glad Tidings Native AG. This church was originally planted by another AIC alumnus, Pastor Jackie Holgate (Navajo), now pastoring in Flagstaff, Arizona. This church plant was part of the vision of Pastor Dobie, who visited me in jail while he was the pastor of Glad Tidings AG, believed in me, mentored me, and saw my potential. My wife and I are now thrilled to be able to give back to the church that invested so richly in us. We will be forever grateful for the impact that Pastor Dobie and Glad Tidings AG has had on our lives.

Because of all I have seen and experienced, I think one of the keys to AIC's lasting legacy will be the ongoing training of Native Americans and building leaders, whether in the classroom, through student government, or through missions outreaches, etc. AIC is blessed to have many great professors who have poured out their lives to equip Native men and women for their calling. Truly, AIC is a place where Native leadership is trained and the consistency of the vision that was given from the beginning continues fifty years later. That was always the vision and dream, and AIC has stuck to that vision and dream—continuing to equip a new generation of quality Native leaders.

Marco Burnette giving commencement address - 2007

Marco Burnette with his parents: Kent Burnette Sr. & Marilyn Burnette

MARCO J. BURNETTE

(White Mountain Apache) AIC Graduation Address, 2007

(Editors' Note: This is the salutatorian address given by Marco J. Burnette from Ft. Apache, Arizona, on May 4, 2007 at the AIC Commencement. Marco graduated with a BA in elementary education, magna cum laude, and received the Sigma Chi Pi Award given to distinguished graduates of AG educational institutions by the Alliance of Christian Higher Education. He also attended a special summer program through the Bloomberg School of Public Health at Johns Hopkins University in Baltimore, Maryland, on full scholarship the summer following his graduation. Marco has returned to the White Mountain Apache Reservation, where he serves as the senior instructor/unit director for the Boys and Girls Club of the White Mountain Apache tribe. His long-range plans include returning to Johns Hopkins University and completing the Master of Public Health (MPH) degree so that he can do public health education on issues related to Native American health and wellness.)

"Welcome families, friends, faculty, staff, and fellow graduates to the 2007 American Indian College commencement ceremony. My name is Marco J. Burnette, and I am a member of the White Mountain Apache tribe. I am very honored to accept this prestigious award—the honor of being named salutatorian of the 2007 AIC graduating class. However, I must admit that the honor is not mine. The honor belongs to the Lord. To Him be all glory, honor, and praise!

I would like to begin by asking you a question. What is success? Some of you may say that success is handed to you. Others may say that success is earned. I believe that success is an option, and it is up to us to choose to be successful. Success does not know color, tribe, or gender. Success is chosen by individuals who decide to do something better for themselves. And success is an investment.

Some of you may be asking yourselves, "What does he know about success?" Let me share with you what success is by using my experiences in life. My parents raised me knowing I was going to be different. During birth, physicians reported to my parents that I was going to be mentally retarded, deaf, and mute. Obviously the reports were negative. However, it took me many years to escape the mentality that I was intellectually slow, deaf, and even stupid. Many people told me that I was neither smart enough nor able to succeed in life. Every year on my birthday my parents would remind me that I was special, unique, and a miracle. (My parents named me Marco because the semantics and phonology in the name is similar to Miracle.) Every time I heard those words, my mentality of unsuccessfulness was wiped away. It was at those times that I chose to be successful regardless of all the ridicule I've endured.

The well-known American author Henry David Thoreau once said: "What lies before us and what lies behind us are all small matters compared to what lies within us. And when we bring what is within out into the world, miracles happen."[1] Are you willing to unleash what is within out into the world so miracles can happen?

I chose to be successful because my first teachers—who are my parents—reminded me that I could overcome all obstacles in life and that those obstacles were only there to shape me. I would like to thank my parents for willingly accepting the challenge of raising and teaching me the Christian way of life. Thanks, Mom and Dad! There are other key individuals who also had tremendous impact on my life. Some of those individuals are my brother, Kent; my sisters, Dana and Lillian; my grandmother Ruth P. Goklish; my aunt, Dr. Rea Goklish; my friends here at American Indian College, Nick Zamarano, Felix Benally, Leticia Albert, Ernestina Yazzie; and all my professors. Thank you all for allowing me to realize that I, too, can be successful.

In conclusion, I would like to leave you with one question: Are you willing to choose success regardless of all the obstacles you will face? Thank you and God bless each and every one of you.

NOTES

1 This quote has also been attributed to Ralph Waldo Emerson and Oliver Wendell Holmes. Its actual origin is difficult to determine.

JAMESON D. LOPEZ

(Quechan/Cocopah)

I stood there at the top of the hill, looking at what seemed to be an endless ocean of green grass. I started to move towards the grass to stretch out across it and position my body in the straightest line possible. I lay there for a while not really thinking much about how itchy I might get later, how dizzy I might be, or who was watching—I just wanted to roll down that green grass hill as fast as I could! I rolled down that hill watching my world turn upside down. It was a long ride down for a six-year-old boy! All I could do was smile and think about how much fun I was having. When I had finally reached the bottom I stood up, staggering a little bit, and looked at where I had come from. What a wild ride I had just had! Believe it or not, this is one of my earliest and greatest memories that I have of AIC.

Please allow me to introduce myself. My name is Jameson David Lopez. Most people know me as J. D. I have grown up around AIC for more than twenty years—since I was born. My parents are Rev. Jim and Belinda Lopez. They served at the college for twenty-two years. During that time my father wore a number of hats, from instructor to dean of students to vice president—then finally he served as president for the last six years of his service there, until 2004. My mother served as an instructor and as the departmental chairs of both the Elementary Education and Learning Resource Departments. Together, their devoted service to AIC gave my two older sisters and me a unique childhood.

Looking back, there are many times I can recall God moving throughout the campus when I was a young child. My earliest memories of the school would probably start about age five. I was still a little too young for kindergarten, so my mother would bring me to the college whenever there was no babysitter available. I loved going to the school! Many times I would just lie around her little cubical office, which used to be located in what is now part of the library, and draw. I would lie there in my own little world, drawing everything that I found intriguing to my imagination. I still go into the library from time to time and reminisce about those times when that part of the building was filled with cubical offices.

Thinking back, I can recall only a handful of chapel services as a child, but I can still remember those times as a young kid walking into the chapel. I remembered looking inside and seeing all those college students raising their hands and crying out to the Lord. When you are five and six, you do not always know what is going on. Nonetheless, I would watch these students intercede for others as they would enter into praise and worship. How powerful it was to see that at a young age! I always knew that AIC was a praying school.

There were times when I remember watching my dad come home from the office. Being president is not always easy. I would watch him cry out for the school and see his commitment to AIC. He believed in the school with everything that he had. I always remembered that commitment he had during his service at AIC. He believed that the college would produce great spiritual leaders and that AIC would help equip them to reach people for Christ. My parents were always dedicated to work that God had called them to. Over the years there is something that I have come to believe in, and it is simply this: that God did not call just my parents to the school—He called us as a family to AIC.

As most ministers' kids know, you go to the same places that your parents go to when you are smaller—there is really no choice in the matter! Many times my dad's position here at AIC would require him to travel on behalf of the college. As a result, my parents would take us to reservations and cities across the United States during this time period. Wherever we traveled to, it never failed that my Dad would promote the college at churches and call upon our family to come up and testify or sing a song. My sisters and I would almost dread getting up there when we were smaller. But after awhile, testifying and singing became a normal part of our lives. Eventually

I started going on AIC outreaches with the students. There is one particular experience that I fondly recall.

In October 2000 I went with an outreach team to Riverside, California, to a boarding school operated by the Bureau of Indian Affairs (BIA) called Sherman Indian High School. At that time I was only fifteen years old, not yet an AIC student. That was one of the first teams I had been on apart from my family. Upon arrival, we started setting up our worship band's equipment on a sidewalk next to the grass area. I stood there with my guitar not knowing how these high school students were going to respond. Then we started to play a few metal songs. Then I watched as students started to come around to look and see what was going on. After awhile the Sherman High School students started to get into it! When we had finished playing, one of the team members gave a short sermon, along with a call for salvation. I watched as students came from that grass area over to the sidewalk. I was overwhelmed at that moment, watching as these Native high school students came to make a commitment to Jesus. I was so excited! And it made me think. I realized that these students' lives would change from that moment on! What would have happened if we had never come out? Would they have ever heard of Jesus, or would they have given their hearts to Him? There are moments in your life that make you realize that you can make a difference; for me this was one of them.

Since I had already been promoting the college, it was only natural that I would enroll as a student here. In 2003 I finally enrolled at AIC during my senior year of high school: concurrently a senior in high school and a freshman in college. Boy, was that a busy year! By the way, I still have not stopped promoting AIC. I have traveled the last two summers on the W.I.N.G.S (Warriors in God's Service) outreach team. On that team I played my guitar, helped in skits, and preached, along with other students. AIC has given me plenty of chances to develop relationships with several students through various activities.

One way that I've been able to develop relationships has been through music. Music in particular has always been for me one of those activities that create unique opportunities to develop relationships. One of the groups that I have been able to play guitar with is called The Three Amigos. Our group consisted of a percussionist and two or three guitarists (depending on how many "amigos" we had playing that day). That is, besides me, the other two guitar-playing friends (or should I say "amigos") were Pat Matt and Michael Johnson. By the way, Pat Matt, who graduated in 2006, is now working for his tribe (Salish Kootenai) in Montana in a professional staff role. He is also on the worship team at his church. Michael Johnson is now married to Miracle. Michael and Miracle, both of whom are licensed ministers, are now graduate students at the Assemblies of God Theological Seminary in Springfield, Missouri, after working for a couple of years as youth pastors in Wright City, Oklahoma, at Chihowa i Chuka Assembly of God Church (Choctaw). There they served as youth pastors for Rev. Lloyd Lee and his wife, Elizabeth, who like Michael and Miracle, are also alumni of the college.

Our percussionist has been either David Lanuza or Maurice "Mo" Ubaldo, who are both students at AIC getting ready to graduate. We have played at different venues, such as spring concerts, graduation banquets, graduation, the Native Pentecost in the New Millenium Conference held at AIC in 2004, the Native American Fellowship (NAF) Convocation of Christian Indian Leaders, as well as Native churches throughout the United States—and anywhere else people would ask us to minister!

Another very special relationship that means a lot to me is the one I have with my life-long friend Jonathan Lanuza. In fact, we are so close that Jonathan is much more like a brother to me than a friend. We grew up together on this campus since our parents worked together. Jonathan's dad, Rev. Paul Lanuza, was chair of the Business Department for many years before he became a full-time pastor of Phoenix Full gospel Church. Although he has a very full plate, Pastor Paul still finds time to teach part-time for the college in the Business Department, where he's a very popular instructor. Jonathan's mom, Lia, is also part of the AIC family, having worked in our college's dining hall for several years. She really loves the students, and they sure love her too. So you might say our two families are pretty connected! Jonathan and I have wonderful memories of rolling down that hill, watching the basketball games, working in the college's Maintenance Department, and even getting into trouble together! Now we both have just finished our degrees here at AIC.

So as I reminisce about where I was and where I am now, it definitely reminds me of that time when I was six years old rolling down that hill watching the world turn upside down, then getting up and looking back at where I had come from. There have been many ups and downs, but I am not at that same place that I was; instead, I am continuing to go forward. In closing, I've got to say what an opportunity the college has given me to develop! There could not have been a better place I could think of to grow up than this school. In fact, AIC has always been more than just a college for me—it's a home!

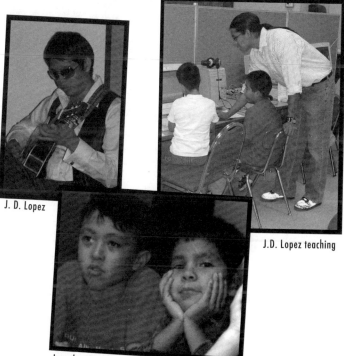

J. D. Lopez

J.D. Lopez teaching

Jonathan Lanuza (left) & J.D. Lopez (right) as boys

Jim and Linda Dempsey with Carolyn Baker

Ernie Scott and Jim Dempsey

Jim and Linda Dempsey, with their son, John

Linda Dempsey, John Rose, and Peggy Gray

After Fifty Years ▲▲▲
NOW WHAT?

▲▲▲

Jim Dempsey

To ask what's next is a legitimate question. Nothing in the kingdom of God stands still, except His Word. Everything else changes, including wonderful institutions like AIC. Is there even a purpose in our future? Some have asked that very question, and will continue to wonder until we have clearly answered the question ourselves.

So allow me to follow up on Dr. Saggio's opening chapter, and remake the case for an Indian Bible college. He has come from the vantage point of Pentecostal higher education—with a historical perspective drawn heavily from the academic discipline of higher education, a field in which he holds a doctorate from a leading research university. Dr. Saggio now fulfills his calling at AIC as a missionary educator; he has written well about how we got here and why we should be here.

My specific background is in missiology, the history and practice of missions. I am writing about why we must stay here. After twenty years of work in this field, these are some of my convictions, which I will explain in more detail after I state them.

▶ First and most importantly, in spite of over five centuries of shared history with Christians, the percentage of Native American people who know Jesus as Savior is only about 5 percent.[1]

▶ The primary obstacle to the salvation of Native people and to the evangelization of "Indian Country" is "vaccination."

▶ The only answer to this "vaccination" is the Indian church.

▶ A healthy Indian church will require leadership.

▶ Leadership must be cultivated with deliberation and diligence.

▶ American Indian College is crucial to the development of the next generation of Native leadership.

▶ It is not where students come from that makes AIC necessary for the future—it is where they are going that must be our focus. Now to explain!

First and most importantly, in spite of over five centuries of shared history with Christians, the percentage of Native American people who know Jesus as Savior is only about 5 percent.[2] Very few of the Europeans who came to this continent five centuries ago manifested a strong concern for the eternal destiny of the indigenous people they encountered. Genocide, colonialism, bad faith, and poor missiological practice were prevalent throughout much of this historical period, with bright spots being few and far between. Even many who came specifically in Christ's name were extremely ineffective and experienced very little long-term success.

When Christians have decided to become truly concerned about Native people, our efforts towards outreach have often been clumsy and ineffective. In the past, a low view of Native culture coupled with a "too-cozy" relationship with the U.S. Government has often crippled our evangelistic effectiveness. In recent generations, we have often found it hard to shake off the bands of paternalism and our tendencies toward autocratic control.[3]

However, we cannot overlook the fact that there are those who are distinguished for their heart of service to Native people. Among the first aliens to disembark in the "New World" was a sixteenth century Spanish Roman Catholic priest (and later the first Bishop of Chiapas), Bartolomé de las Casas, who passionately advocated on both sides of the Atlantic for the rights of the Arawak Indians in Cuba. He later attempted to establish a Utopian society for Native people in what is now Venezuela. Sadly, his heroic efforts ultimately failed, but Father de las Casas is fondly remembered for his attempts to promote the humanitarian treatment of indigenous people in the New World.

In New England during the seventeenth century, John Eliot, widely regarded as "the Apostle to the Indians," spent nearly sixty years of his life church planting among the indigenous peoples of Massachusetts. During his long and distinguished career as a missionary, Eliot translated the Bible into the Massachusetts dialect of the Algonquin Indians, established fourteen "praying towns" and two Native-led churches, developed a system for teaching catechism, and trained indigenous Native leaders for ministry. He is reported to have reached over 20 percent of the Indian population of the Massachusetts colony—leading thousands to faith in Christ. How tragic that many of the Massachusetts Indians that Eliot had successfully reached and had settled into the "praying towns" were ruthlessly slaughtered by the colonists.[4]

Subsequently, David Brainerd, who was greatly influenced by Eliot, planted himself in "Indian soil" and became another outstanding missionary, although it could be argued that his writing made a more lasting impact than his field ministry since he died quite young. Moreover, we could list many additional names of those who have given their lives to reach the First Nations, but unfortunately, with few exceptions, Indian missions is better known historically for great sacrifices rather than great lasting results.

Not long after the outbreak of the Pentecostal movement at the beginning of the twentieth century, a number of missionaries, such as Charles and Florence Personeus, Clyde Thompson, and J. D. Wells, began to evangelize the American Indians and Alaska Natives.[5] In the Assemblies of God, momentum built until a wave of missionaries went out, surging from the 1940s into the 1970s. These were the growth years in AG Native ministry.[6] The accounts given throughout this book tell a part of the story of one of the most successful attempts to reach Native Americans in the five-hundred-year shared history of our peoples. Yet, by the decade of the 1980s the wave had crested, and most of "Indian Country" remains without Christ to this day.

That any Native American has come to Christ for salvation is a wonder. That so few have, after all this time and effort, remains a challenge. Now is the time to see the miracle that centuries of believers have sought. However, we are way past the time when a great missionary force will be called to go to the Native Nations and reap an "Indian Harvest."

The primary obstacle to the salvation of Native people and to the evangelization of Indian Country is vaccination. By "vaccination," I mean that exposure to a weakened or dead form of a germ will cause the body to develop a resistance, keeping us from getting the real thing. Allegorically, this is what has happened to Native people spiritually. In 500 plus years of "missionizing," Native Americans have frequently been exposed to expressions of Christianity ranging from ineffective to blatantly evil. Contact with inauthentic and ineffective religious witness has resulted in today's Natives being sometimes disinterested in—at other times, overtly hostile toward—the Christian faith, even when it is genuine.

This is why I believe that the efforts of missionaries will never reach the First Nations. That train has left the station, and far too few Indians bought a ticket! This is not to say that efforts of missionaries are useless or that the witness of non-Natives cannot win individual Native Americans to Christ. Rather, the way we have been doing it for centuries is not going to get it done today. While it is true that no people ever first heard the gospel unless an outsider first brought the gospel to them (starting with Jesus' incarnation), it is also true that no nation has ever been successfully reached with the gospel until it has taken true ownership of its churches. Historically, missionaries such as Roland Allen and Melvin Hodges have articulated a compelling case for indigenous church strategies by recognizing that the apostle Paul's missiological approach was to develop local leadership who could contexualize the gospel most effectively by responding socially, culturally, and linguistically.[7]

The only answer to this vaccination is the Indian church. The

Native church is the answer. It must be authentically biblical and authentically Indian. This means that it must be connected to the rest of the body of Christ in America but must also be a truly Native incarnation of the gospel. Unreached Native people in North America must see a living answer to the question, "What would Jesus look like if he were in 'Ind'in' skin?'"

The only way to provide an answer to that question is for churches filled with Native Christian disciples to live the life as spiritually healthy Christians in the Native world. But disciples don't grow without cultivation by leadership. And leadership does not just happen! Leadership must be cultivated; it takes deliberate development.

A healthy Indian church will require leadership. Leadership comes when the church intentionally decides to prepare leaders. This is where the Holy Spirit was leading Alta Washburn fifty years ago, although at the time many missionaries were just trying to keep "their Indians" saved and out of the clutches of unscrupulous evangelists. From the beginning the students at All Tribes Bible School were inevitably going to flow into discipleship formation, and to the degree that the missionary leadership allowed this to happen, there was success.

American Indian College is crucial to the development of the next generation of Native leadership. As more leaders were prepared at AIBI, the Indian Pentecostal church was blessed and strengthened. If this leadership was squelched by missionary paternalism, the whole Church was made poorer as a result. If the leaders wandered off into moral or ethical deserts, the Native churches were robbed of their anointed and essential ministry.

Indigenous ministry is not a method to be tried; it is the biblical model that must be followed. There must be an Indian church, or Indians for whom Christ died will go to hell, and the rest of us will face judgment for it! For that church to succeed, it must have strong indigenous leadership, and the rest of us must do what the Spirit asks in order to help prepare them. AIC has done a historically remarkable job in contributing to the formation of this leadership, and it should be recognized that this has happened.

Please recognize that we at the college are not looking for a big pat on the back. That is not what I mean by "recognize." The recognition I am calling for is the commitment of the rest of the church, particularly the Native Pentecostal church, to our continued existence. We are accomplishing what God has placed us here to do. Consider the following AIC statistics from 2006:

▶ Students of American Indian College led over 1,000 people to make decisions to accept Jesus Christ as their Lord and Savior through evangelistic and outreach endeavors![8]

▶ 93 percent of our Christian ministry graduates in the previous five years are currently active in church work or full-time ministry[9]

▶ 90 percent of our elementary education graduates and alumni (since 1995) are professionally employed as educators, and 28 percent of them have attained a master's degree or higher![10]

It is not where students come from that makes AIC necessary for the future—it is where they are going that must be our focus. Sister Washburn quotes "one of the Sampson boys," articulating the need for the school before its beginning:

> *"Sister Washburn," he questioned, "why can't we Indians have our own Bible school? We can preach in our language but we need a place where we can study the Word together, a place where we have more in common than in a school where most of the students are Anglos.*[11]

He had just returned from another AG Bible college. He knew the struggles of leaving his world for studies in a "far country." Virgil Sampson exemplified the need for a culturally accommodating school in the late 1950s. In fifty years, some of the reasons for Indians to "have our own Bible school" have changed. Some have not.

What is different is today's AIC student. We cannot allow too much overgeneralization, but some observations are valid. Today's Native students are generally better educated and have had a broader exposure to educational technology and resources than students of the 1950s, 1960s, and 1970s. These young people are less likely to be from the "rez" than were students of our early decades. Among Native students, there is a growing likelihood that they will be from a mainstream (non-Native) church. Family income has also increased, although it is still comparatively low, by recent estimates, 27.7 percent below the median income of Anglo households.[12] Overall, Native youth in general (not just at AIC) have undergone some profound transformations in the last few decades.

In short, today's Native college students need "our own Bible school" less than the previous generation did. What does this mean for AIC? There are more Native people than ever going to college, but they are going everywhere. For example, from 1980 to 2003, there was a 30 percent increase in the representation of American Indians within the broader higher education landscape—and this trend continues to this day.[13] In 1994, an article in *Indian Country Today* reported on (then) AIBC under the headline, "AIBC is a little reservation in the city."[14] The headline was a direct quote from the admissions director, and at the time many regarded this as a positive statement about the college's institutional culture.

However, such a description is no longer seen as a completely positive reflection. Many Christian Native students may not be attracted by our cultural distinctive. They are trying to get "off the rez;" therefore, why would they choose a "rez-type" environment for college?

If the future purpose of AIC is to continue to provide an Indian-friendly insulating environment—because our students are presumed to need that for success—enrollment may dwindle. Fewer and fewer Native students require that. What, then? Have we reached the end of our time of usefulness to the Kingdom?

Not at all! Native students may not require us, academically or culturally, but the Indian churches—and lost Native people across North America—urgently need our continued existence. One of the best things that could happen is for Indian Country to have a college that specializes in Native Christian leadership, for the church and community. I am convinced that if we closed AIC today, someone else would be trying to create another Indian Bible college within five to ten years. Indian students may not need "our own Bible college," but the Indian church does.

The Indian church needs an institution that openly and devotedly specializes in Native American higher education, evangelism, and church growth. Not for the sake of exclusion, but for the sake of focus. This is the future of American Indian College of the Assemblies of God. This is what we are, and we must become more so. We must continue and increase our commitment to the Indian church.

Essential knowledge about Native Christianity should be collected, understood, and taught here. The Indian nations are still largely unreached for Christ, and the preparation of those whom the Lord of the Harvest has called is our reason for being. The American church still owes a debt to the Native people of this continent—a debt which can be discharged only by providing the gospel of reconciliation to God and by living in reconciliation to each other.

As we continue this commitment, the view of Native students will change regarding AIC. Most of those—Native or not—who feel a calling to serve Native people will recognize us as the place to prepare, not because of an inward comfort level, but because of an outward focus. As a greenhouse, we will be empty. As a warehouse, where hungry minds can find what they seek, and as a lighthouse, shining Christ's light into the dark places, we can be busy for the next fifty years!

We are not perfect. We never have been. People lead us, and we work with students who are people. The continued presence of humanity here will prevent perfection. But we are worthy of consideration by any young person who is thinking about how best to prepare for God's calling to leadership, especially if that calling includes a desire to serve the First Nations.

And we are worthy of support—in prayer, in finances, in encouragement of potential students—by those who now stand in positions of leadership in the Native church, both missionary and Indian. AIC is something that God has created, and we are convinced that He will continue to nurture us as long as there are Native people who need to hear and understand the gospel and as long as we remain faithful to that calling.

The world of Indian Country has changed in the last fifty years. Native people, particularly college students, remain in transition. The Indian churches have changed. The need, however, has not changed. AIC was borne out of a desire to prepare leadership for the church. That mission has not changed. The way we go about fulfilling our mission has changed. Our commitment to serve God and the Native church as "a witness to the tribes" will not.

Rodale Cooley and Cheryl Grass at 2006 graduation

NOTES

1 John E. Maracle (Mohawk, Wolf Clan), who currently serves as the president of the Native American Fellowship of the Assemblies of God (NAF) and as a General Council executive presbyter, reports that best estimates are that 5 percent or less of Native Americans are "born again" Christians.

2 Ibid.

3 See, for example, Vine Deloria Jr., *Custer Died for Your Sins* (Norman, OK: University of Oklahoma Press, 1969, 1988). Deloria's caustic yet insightful perspective on White America's cultural genocide of traditional Native American cultural values (including atrocities perpetrated by well-meaning missionaries) is a "must read" for anyone wanting to understand why so many Native Americans have rejected Christianity and Western culture.

4 John E. Maracle (Mohawk, Wolf Clan), "John Eliot's Vision for New England" (unpublished paper, 1991). See also, John Eliot, *A Brief Narrative of the Progress of the Gospel Amongst the Indians in New England in the Year 1670* (Ann Arbor: Xerox University Microfilms, Authorized Facsimile, 1976. Originally published in London in 1671).

5 Jim Dempsey, "Part I: Assemblies of God Ministry to Native Americans." *Assemblies of God Heritage* 22 (Summer 2002): 4–11.

6 For further information I recommend the following: Jim Dempsey, "Part I: Assemblies of God Ministry to Native Americans" and Jim Dempsey, "Concluding Part: Assemblies of God Ministry to Native Americans." *Assemblies of God Heritage* 22 (Fall 2002): 18-21. Joseph J. Saggio, "Towards an Indigenous Model of Native American Ministry in the Assemblies of God," in *Memories of the Azusa Street Revival: Interrogations and Interpretations.* 35th Annual Meeting of the Society for Pentecostal Studies held at Fuller Theological Seminary (March 23-25, 2006). Parallel Session Papers: 336-343.

7 See, for example, Roland Allen, *Missionary Methods: St. Paul's or Ours?*, 2nd ed. (Grand Rapids: W.B. Eerdman's Publishing Co., 1962). See also Melvin Hodges, *The Indigenous Church* (Springfield, MO: Gospel Publishing House, 1953) and Melvin Hodges, *Growing Young Churches* (Chicago: Moody Press, 1970).

8 Information provided by the Office of Student Ministry, American Indian College, 2007.

9 Information provided by the Office of Institutional Assessment, American Indian College, 2007.

10 Ibid.

11 Alta M. Washburn, *Trail to the Tribes* (Prescott, AZ: 1990), 48.

12 National Center for Education Statistics. "Status and Trends in the Education of American Indians and Alaska Natives." Available at http://nces.ed.gov/pubs2005/2005108.pdf (accessed November 26, 2006), 122.

13 Ibid., 2, 96. See also National Center for Educational Statistics. U.S. Department of Education Office of Educational Research and Improvement. Washington DC: U.S. Government Printing Office, 1998. For a better understanding of the importance of institutional culture's impact on Christian Native Americans see Joseph J. Saggio and Jim Dempsey, "Providing Positive Institutional Climates for American Indian/Alaska Native Students" in *A Collection of Papers on Self-Study and Institutional Improvement*, vol. 2, *Organizational Effectiveness and Future Directions*, ed. Susan Van Kollenburg (Chicago: The Higher Learning Commission, 2003), 117–122.

14 Amanda R. Just, "AIBC is a Little Reservation in the City," *Indian Country Today*, Monday August 29, 1994, B6.

CONTRIBUTORS

[Editors' Note: We have listed here those who wrote new essays and introductions for this book. We have not included here the original authors of *Trail to the Tribes, A Trail of Beauty: A Short History of American Indian Bible College*, or *Indian Harvest: A History of American Indian Bible College.* The introductions to those works include their respective biographical information.]

Marvin B. Begay is an enrolled member of the Navajo nation, born in Brother in Christ Mission (BIC), near Farmington, New Mexico. He is a 1994 graduate of American Indian College with an AA in business and a BA in ministerial studies. He is an ordained minister with the Assemblies and God and presently serves as pastor of Canyon Day AG on the White Mountain Apache Reservation, where he also serves as the assistant presbyter for the east section of the Arizona District Council. Pastor Begay is very active with the Native American Fellowship of the AG (NAF), serving as the National Native Youth Representative. In that capacity he was instrumental in starting the first National Native Youth Convention that has been held for the past two years on the campus of American Indian College, each time hosting in excess of 500 attendees. Pastor Begay is active as a board of regents member for American Indian College and also as an executive committee member for the Arizona AG Department of Youth Ministries. His wife, Delia, a Yaqui Indian, is a 1996 graduate of AIC with a BA in elementary education. Delia serves on the steering committee for the National Native Women's Conference and is a second grade teacher at Seven Mile Elementary School on the White Mountain Apache Reservation. Pastor Marvin and Delia are the proud parents of a daughter, Autumn Skye.

James J. Bollinger is an enrolled member of the Omaha tribe, born and raised in Omaha, Nebraska. He is a 2006 magna cum laude graduate of American Indian College with a bachelor of arts degree in Christian ministry. A licensed minister with the Assemblies of God, he serves as the pastor at Glad Tidings Native AG, a new church plant of Glad Tidings AG, a large multi-cultural congregation in Omaha, Nebraska. Pastor Bollinger and his wife, Monica, are blessed with four beautiful children. They have three daughters, Erica, Adrianna, and Mia, and a son, James Jr. In addition to his work in ministry, Rev. Bollinger is working towards his MBA in finance at Bellvue University in Bellvue, Nebraska.

Marco J. Burnette is an enrolled member of the White Mountain Apache tribe and was born and raised in Whiteriver, Arizona. He is a 2007 magna cum laude graduate of American Indian College in elementary education and was also the salutatorian and Sigma Chi Pi Award recipient. In the summer of 2007, he studied at the Bloomberg School of Public Health at Johns Hopkins University in Baltimore, Maryland. He hopes to return and complete his master of public health (MPH) degree. Marco is presently serving as the senior instructor/unit director for the Boys and Girls Club of the White Mountain Apache tribe. He has one brother and two sisters and presently attends the Cedar Creek Assembly of God.

Alice Collins was born in Greer, South Carolina. She has a bachelor's degree in ministerial studies and Christian education from American Indian College. While she and her husband, Carl, were residing in South Carolina, Alice was the owner of the largest day care center in the state. She was a well-known child evangelist and district children's camp speaker during their ministry in the south. Alice remains active by teaching Berean Bible courses at All Tribes Assembly of God in Phoenix, Arizona, as well as conducting Christian Education seminars on various Indian reservations. God has blessed Carl and Alice with three children, a foster daughter who is a Navajo Indian, seven grandchildren, and three foster granddaughters.

Carl E. Collins was born in Hollywood, Florida, the son of Assemblies of God ministers. Rev. Collins is a graduate of Bob Jones University with a double major in Bible and accounting. He also holds a master's degree in higher education from Appalachian State University. Rev. Collins pastored churches in Georgia and South Carolina before coming to serve at (then) American Indian Bible College. While serving as a pastor he also taught part-time at Clemson University and the University of South Carolina–Union campus.

Carl and Alice Collins came to the college in 1977 where he became the Student Employment director and faculty member. In 1979, Rev. Collins became the college's president. For the past twenty years, the Collinses have served as the pastors of All Tribes Assembly of God in Phoenix, Arizona.

James V. Comer has served as president of the American Indian College since 2004. President Comer and his wife, Sue, have served together in ministry for over thirty-five years, serving as assistant pastors at Alfred AG in Alfred, North Dakota, and First AG in Benton Harbor, Michigan. President Comer also served as the senior pastor of two congregations concurrently: Herreid AG and Herreid Congregational Church in Herreid, South Dakota, during which time he also served as presbyter for the German district of the AG for the Dakotas. From 1977–1995 they served as nationally appointed AG foreign missionaries in Zaire, Africa, and later at Continental Theological Seminary in Belgium. The Comers have served at American Indian College since 1996; James has served in various capacities, including as a faculty member teaching Bible, theology, and Christian ministry. He also served as dean of students, business administrator, and vice president before becoming the college's president in 2004. President Comer holds a certificate in pastoral studies from Trinity Bible College, then located in Jamestown, North Dakota (now Ellendale), a certificate in French language acquisition from the Centre de Formation Missionaire in Albertville, France, and an MA in Biblical studies from the Assemblies of God Theological Seminary.

Having a call into missions since the age of 13, Sue has actively pursued ministry wherever she and James have served. She administered Bethel Women's School in Zaire, where Bible courses, hygiene, literacy, sewing, and cooking were taught; then during their time in Brussels she served as registrar at Continental Theological Seminary. Since coming to AIC she has served as a graphic artist for the college, creating all the promotional literature, displays, and other materials, as well as graphic work for numerous Native ministries. Her gifts were also used in the layout of this book.

Together the Comers have two children. Their son, Jason, is in the army serving as a medic in Iraq. Jason and his wife, Stephanie, have four daughters. The Comer's daughter, Jami, lives in Show Low, Arizona, and is a stay-at-home mom, raising Marley and Maxwell; her husband, Chris, is a middle school music teacher and professional musician.

Rodger Austin Cree, Sr., an enrolled member of the Mohawk Nation was born in Kanesatake Mohawk Territory, Quebec, Canada, on November 21, 1931, to Morris and Susan Cree. He had four sisters and five brothers and was brought up in a Pentecostal home. He attended Institute Biblique de Berée in Montreal, Quebec, and graduated in 1952. In 1955, the Pentecostal Assemblies of Canada in Toronto, Ontario, ordained Rev. Cree. He married his God-given life mate, Esther Ritchey, on August 6, 1955. They have four children.

A successful church planter, builder, preacher, teacher, and pastor, Pastor Cree built churches in Pagwa River, Ontario; Ft. Severn, Ontario; Kanawake, Quebec; Sells, Arizona; Salt River, Arizona; Taholah, Washington; and was president of Eastern Indian Bible Institute in Shannon, North Carolina.

He has served as sectional presbyter in the Arizona District Council of the Assemblies of God, superintendent of the American Indian Fellowship of the Northwest district, served four years as an Assemblies of God general presbyter for the Native American Fellowship, and was on the Home Missions board for the Northwest district for quite a number of years. Rev. Cree also serves on the translation team for the Mohawk Bible project.

Pastor Cree is known for his integrity, love of prayer, and sense of humor.

Jim Dempsey is currently dean of institutional research at American Indian College. Prior to coming to AIC in 1986, he served on staff at churches in Humble and Alvin, Texas, and was pastor of Pearsall (Texas) Assembly of God from 1982–1986. Since coming to the college he has filled numerous faculty, staff, and administration roles.

Jim and his wife of twenty-nine years, Linda, live in Peoria, Arizona, with their son, John, born in 1989. They are under appointment with the U.S. Missions Division of the Assemblies of God. More information about their writing and music ministries is available at their website, www.phs2.com.

Sandra M. Gonzales is an alumna of American Indian College and currently serves as the registrar of the college. A Navajo Indian born in Cortez, Colorado, Sandra received both her AA in business and her BA in elementary education from AIC. Sandra was an elementary school teacher for three years before returning to work at AIC. She has a real family connection to the college in that her sister, Jennifer, is a graduate and married to Rev. Vince Roubideaux, who is the dean of students (and also a graduate of AIC). Her brother, Keith Smith, Esq., is an attorney and a law professor at the University of Colorado–Boulder and also a member of AIC's board of regents. She and her husband, Ryan (who is a staff member and part-time student at AIC), have three children: Christian, Marc, and Alyssa. They are involved in discipleship ministry at Phoenix First Assembly of God.

Betty J. Hanna is a longtime Assemblies of God missionary educator serving at the American Indian College in Phoenix, Arizona. She has taught in the areas of elementary education, general education, learning resource, and Christian ministry during her time at the college. She is a graduate of Southwestern Assemblies of God College and Grand Canyon College. Sister Hanna did additional graduate work at Arizona State University and the University of Arizona. For the past fifteen years at Christmas time, Sister Hanna oversees a large community outreach by AIC students, which has attracted over 400 local neighborhood people to hear the gospel on AIC's campus and is known as the "Birthday Party for Jesus."

During her time serving at American Indian College, Sister Hanna has served in a number of roles, including the establishment and direction of the Foundational Studies Program, which later became known as the Learning Resource Department. She also served as registrar for eight years. Having now returned to the classroom in the past few years, Betty has been extremely involved in founding and directing the John McPherson Resource Center, which provides Christian education materials and curriculum to assist in Christian education and outreach to children. She has tirelessly worked to organize, catalog, and generate resources for the McPherson Resource Center, which is named in honor of the late Rev. John McPherson, Cherokee pastor, evangelist, and the first National Indian Representative to the Assemblies of God. Along with her husband, the late Rev. Joe Hanna, Rev. Betty Hanna has given a lifetime of distinguished service in her ministry calling.

Eugene Hunter is professor emeritus of Bible and ministry at American Indian College. He was born to devout Christian parents on October 13, 1923, in Garden City, Kansas. His grandmother was one-half Cherokee, and he came to know Jesus Christ as his Lord and Savior at the age of nine. In the fall of 1942 he journeyed to Anderson, Indiana by train with only five dollars to his name. There Brother Hunter attended Anderson College and Seminary— as well as over the years a number of other institutions, ending up at Central Bible College in Springfield, Missouri, where he graduated in 1974 with a degree in Bible. Brother Hunter also did further graduate studies at Fuller Theological Seminary in Pasadena, California. He served at the college from 1975 to 1991, and once again since 2001 on a part-time basis.

Brother Hunter married Emily O. Mullins (now with the Lord) on February 3, 1944. On December 21, 1985, he married Pauline Harris (now also with the Lord). On March 13, 2002, he married Lois Schack, whose parents were Assemblies of God ministers in Illinois. Brother Hunter is also extremely proud of his four children and eight stepchildren.

Greatly loved by the AIC and Native American Christian community because of his great warmth, tremendous knowledge of the Bible, generosity, sense of godly integrity, and enthusiasm, Brother Hunter has achieved a stature that few educators ever attain: that of one who has led by example.

Belinda F. Lopez is an enrolled member of the Quechan tribe on the Ft. Yuma/Quechan Reservation near Winterhaven, California. For twenty-two years Belinda served as a faculty member in both the Learning Resource Department and the Elementary Education Department. During part of that time she also chaired both departments. Belinda received her BS in elementary education from Grand Canyon University in Phoenix, Arizona, and her MA in education from the University of Phoenix.

In addition to teaching at AIC, Belinda has also served as a schoolteacher in the public sector and in pastoral ministry with her husband, Rev. Jim H. Lopez, on the White Mountain Apache Reservation at Whiteriver, Arizona. Along with her husband, Belinda is a nationally known resource speaker on topics related to Native Americans, and she and Jim have presented in a variety of venues throughout North America. Belinda is also the founder of the annual Native Women's Conference held annually for the past several years on the campus of AIC. This growing annual conference reaches out to Native women throughout the United States and Canada. Belinda and Jim are the proud parents of Joylina, Camellia, and Jameson. They have also been blessed with five beautiful grandchildren.

Jameson David "J. D." Lopez is an enrolled member of the Quechan tribe, born and raised in Phoenix, Arizona. He is twenty-two years old and a 2008 graduate of American Indian College, with a BA in elementary education. Jameson's long-term educational goals include an MA in leadership and a PhD in administration.

Jameson's zeal to follow God has allowed him to minister to many tribes and reservations across the U.S., Canada, and Mexico. In addition, he has led several outreach teams, including trips to both the inner city and various Indian reservations. Currently he is a co-coordinator for the National Native Youth Convention under the Native American Fellowship of the Assemblies of God (NAF); he also serves as a recruiter under the Admissions Department at American Indian College.

A talented musician, one of Jameson's notable abilities includes a tremendous aptitude to play the guitar. In 2004, he competed in the National Fine Arts Festival in Austin, Texas, sponsored by the national Department of Youth Ministry of the Assemblies of God. He competed in the guitar solo category, receiving an Advanced rating, ranking among the top three in the nation. Jameson was one of the few Native American youth to compete in this festival.

Above all else, Jameson Lopez has a heart for Native People. His desire is to see Native Americans aspire for greater levels of leadership, serving God with all their heart.

Jim H. Lopez is a Hispanic/Cocopah Indian from the Ft. Yuma/Quechan Reservation near Winterhaven, California. Before being appointed director of intercultural ministries for the Arizona District Council of the Assemblies of God in 2004, Rev. Lopez served the American Indian College in a variety of roles for over twenty-two years, including faculty member, dean of students, vice president, and as president for the last six years of his time at AIC. Prior to his service at American Indian College, Rev. Lopez served for over five years as the pastor of Whiteriver Assembly of God on the Fort Apache Reservation in northern Arizona.

He received his diploma from American Indian College (then American Indian Bible Institute), and also holds a BA from Southwestern Assemblies of God University in Waxahachie, Texas, and a master's degree in theology from Fuller Theological Seminary in Pasadena, California. He is a much sought-after speaker and preacher in churches, conferences, camp meetings, etc., and has ministered throughout the United States and Canada. Jim Lopez also serves as the secretary/treasurer for the Native American Fellowship of the Assemblies of God.

Donald Patrick "Pat" Merino is an enrolled member of the Maidu tribe in northern California, and was born in Greenville, California, the ninth of sixteen children. Prior to attending (then) AIBC, Pat was employed by the Salt River Indian Community (Pima/Maricopa) as a heavy equipment operator. He received his diploma in ministerial studies in 1986. Pat later returned to AIC in 2000 and completed his BA in Christian ministry in 2002. During that time and since then, Pat has worked in plant operations; he now serves as the director of Plant Operations for AIC. He is actively involved with the Salt River Indian AG on the Salt River Indian Reservation, adjacent to Scottsdale, Arizona.

David J. Moore is currently IDA program coordinator for Convoy of Hope, an AG humanitarian aid organization. This program provides a combination of faith-based federal grant money and private donations to help individuals purchase homes, start up businesses, or pay postsecondary education costs. Moore has been with Convoy of Hope since 2001.

From 1994 to 2001 Moore served as director of Intercultural Ministries and department administrator for U. S. Missions at the Assemblies of God headquarters. Here he was responsible for the appointment process and supervision of some 400 missionaries ministering to over 40 different cultural groups across the U.S. He has also served on several ministry boards and continues to do so on a selective basis.

From 1975 to 1994 Moore served on the staff at American Indian College, from 1987 to 1994 as president. He holds a B.S. from Evangel University in Springfield, Missouri, in archaeology/anthropology and church history and an MA in cross-cultural studies from the Assemblies of God Theological Seminary, also located in Springfield. Moore pursued PhD studies in higher education administration at the University of Arizona in Tucson, Arizona. He is a member of several honor societies and professional associations and has served as an adjunct professor for both Evangel University and the Assemblies of God Theological Seminary (AGTS). Over the years his counsel has been frequently sought out because of his considerable expertise in higher education, leadership, and multicultural issues in church ministry.

Moore has been married for 34 years. He and his wife, Cheri, now reside in Clever, Missouri. They have three grown children. Rachael and her husband, Darin Lenz, serve on the faculty at Northwest University in Kirkland, Washington. Ryan and his wife, Alyson, are youth pastors at a church in Ocala, Florida. Royce and wife, Melanie, reside in Columbia, Missouri, where Royce is attending medical school and Melanie is an elementary school teacher.

Lillie Ward Neal is a Yavapai Apache born on the San Carlos Apache Reservation in Arizona. Sister Lillie attended (then) All Tribes Bible School from 1957 to 1961 and was one of the three original graduates of ATBS. She has been attending All Tribes Assembly of God in Phoenix, Arizona, since 1950 and is the proud mother of seven children, thirty grandchildren, and three great-grandchildren.

Everett Figueroa Peralta was born in Hermosillo, Mexico, and is a citizen of the United States. At age thirteen, Everett was accepted to the university after testing in the upper 10 percent of USA in science and math. He has earned a BS in social sciences at the University of the State of New York, an MA in educational administration and supervision at the University of Phoenix, and a doctorate in educational administration at Arizona State University. His educational career has included work as a teacher and administrator in K-12 education as well as service as a college professor and administrator. Everett is also a proud alumnus of American Indian College, having completed his postbaccalaureate teacher education here. He was selected for Phi Kappa Phi, Omicron Delta Kappa, Phi Delta Kappa, *Who's Who in America*, *Who's Who Among America's Teachers*, *National Scholars Honors Society*, *Oxford Round Table*, and *Who's Who in the West*. In Summer 2007 he was selected to be a Tribal College Fellow in order to attend the Management Development Program (MDP) at Harvard's Graduate School of Education in Cambridge, Massachusetts. Everett has served on the board of directors on the state committees for child abuse prevention, state board of family social services, county literacy council, and the state board for economic planning.

His aspirations are to be a college leader, a public education advocate, a teacher training scholar as well as expert on national education government policy. Dr. Everett F. Peralta currently serves as a professor and chairman of the Department of Education at American Indian College as well as an adjunct professor in both the undergraduate and graduate programs in education, social sciences, and public administration at both Ottawa University and Western International University.

William E. Peters, a Choctaw Indian and ordained Assemblies of God minister, has served with his father, the late Simon Peter, former president of the American Indian Bible Institute in Phoenix, Arizona, in evangelistic work in New Mexico, Texas, Oklahoma, and Arkansas. Brother Peters is a graduate of Draughons College of Business, having received a degree in accounting and commercial law. He has served as guest speaker at Native American camp meetings for a number of different denominations, including United Methodist, Presbyterian, General Baptist, Southern Baptist, as well as the Assemblies of God. Brother Peters has served as both a youth pastor and senior pastor at a number of churches in both Arkansas and Oklahoma. As a pastor he was active in radio broadcasting and hosted a morning program, "Devotion with the Parson." An accomplished writer he has had a number of sermons published, as well as an article on the life of his father in the *Pentecostal Evangel*. In addition to his ministry, Brother Peters has worked for many years in the public and tribal sector as a technical advisor and financial analyst and served on the boards of a number of organizations. Presently, William Peters serves in the legal department for the UKB Cherokees and also continues in ministry as a speaker in various church venues. (Note: William E. Peters spells his last name "Peters" because of a clerical error years ago whereby he is now legally known by that name.)

T. Ray Rachels currently serves as the chairman of the board of regents for American Indian College of the Assemblies of God. He was born and raised in Columbus, Georgia. He received his undergraduate education at Southeastern Bible College, Lakeland, Florida, and Troy State University, Troy, Alabama, with graduate studies at United Theological Seminary, Dayton, Ohio; Wright State University, Dayton, Ohio; and Santa Clara University, Santa Clara, California; and an MA from Vanguard University, Costa Mesa, California.

His extensive ministry experience includes associate pastor, Bethel Temple, Dayton, Ohio; director of youth and Christian education for the Ohio district; pastor, Neighborhood Church, Santa Clara, California; director of youth ministries, Northern California/Nevada district; pastor, Christian Life Church, Long

Beach, California; assistant superintendent and currently he serves as the superintendent of the Southern California District Council of the Assemblies of God. In addition to chairing the roard of regents of American Indian College, Rev. Rachels is also Chairman, Board of Directors, Vanguard University of Southern California and Chairman, Board of Directors, Church Extension Plan.

T. Ray Rachels and his wife, Judy, have three children: Scott, Lance, and Heather; two daughters-in-law, Julie and Brenda; one son-in-law, Caleb; three granddaughters; and two grandsons.

Don Ramsey, president of American Indian Bible Institute from 1965 to 1973, graduated from East Central College in Oklahoma with a bachelor of arts in education in 1955. Moving to the Navajo Reservation in Northern Arizona in 1958, Brother Ramsey taught English to Indian children and served in key supervisory positions in Bureau of Indian Affairs (BIA) schools. During this time he and his wife, Virginia, established two missions. In 1959 he received a master of arts degree in education from East Central State College. In 1973, Brother Ramsey resigned as president of AIBI and accepted the position of academic dean and business administrator at the Far North Bible College in Anchorage, Alaska. Soon afterwards he was invited to return once again to serve at AIBI as a faculty member, continuing there until 1985; thereafter he began pastoring on the Gila River Reservation, completing several years as a missionary pastor to the Pima and Maricopa Indians. While pastoring, Brother Ramsey also worked as an English teacher at the Maryvale High School in Phoenix. In 1999, the Ramseys retired to Oklahoma, where Brother Ramsey remains active by serving frequently at the local community college and in local church ministry.

Curtis W. Ringness has had a long and varied ministerial career. Ordained in 1938 by the Peninsular Florida District Council of the Assemblies of God, he attended North Central University and later Bethany University, from which he graduated. He also attended Trinity College and received his doctor of missiology (DMiss) degree from California Graduate School of Theology in Glendale, California. Dr. Ringness is most pleased that he has had the privilege of seeing forty-three of the young people that he mentored as pastor go into full-time ministry.

In addition to multiple pastorates in Florida and California,

Brother Ringness has served as secretary/treasurer, executive presbyter, assistant superintendent, and general presbyter for the Peninsular Florida district. He later served as assistant general secretary, the national secretary of benevolences, national secretary of Home Missions and secretary of the Assemblies of God Stewardship Division.

A prolific writer, he has edited two publications and wrote lessons for the *Adult Teacher* for the Church School Literature Department of the Assemblies of God for ten years. Also, his column "Viewpoint" regularly appeared in the *Pentecostal Evangel* for several years. After his retirement, Dr. Ringness directed the Senior Ministries Department of the Southern California District Council for nine years and continues as a contributor to several publications.

Vincent Robert Roubideaux is a Shoshone/Paiute/Rosebud Sioux born on the Duck Valley Indian Reservation in Owyhee, Nevada, and has served as the dean of students for American Indian College since fall 2006. A 1980 graduate of Owyhee High School, Vince also received an electronic technician diploma from the DeVry Institute of Technology in Phoenix, Arizona, an associate of arts in social work and a bachelor of arts in ministerial studies from American Indian College.

An ordained Assemblies of God minister, Rev. Roubideaux has served previously as an associate and youth pastor at All Tribes AG in Phoenix, Arizona, as well as at the Salt River Indian AG on the Salt River Indian Reservation adjacent to Scottsdale, Arizona. He has also served as a senior pastor at Carson Living Waters AG in Carson, New Mexico; Mohawk Assembly of God in St. Regis, New York, and Owyhee Presbyterian Church in Owyhee, Nevada. Vince is also frequently featured as a popular guest speaker in churches, missions conventions, Native convocations, and the like throughout the United States.

Vince has been married to his lovely wife, Jennifer (Navajo), (who is also a graduate of AIC with an AA in social work) for nineteen years. They have four children: Erica, Alicia, Amber, and Joshua.

Joseph J. Saggio serves as dean of institutional assessment and chair of general education for AIC, and as the Phoenix branch campus director for the Assemblies of God Theological Seminary

(AGTS). Previously, he served as the academic dean of AIC from 1994 to 2005 and continues as a faculty member in general education, elementary education, and Christian ministry. An ordained AG minister and nationally appointed U.S. missionary to Native Americans, Joe also serves as an adjunct professor for AGTS in Springfield, Missouri. A graduate of California State University–Fresno, Joe received his BA in speech communication. He also holds two masters degrees in religion from both Azusa Pacific University and Vanguard University. Dr. Saggio earned an EdD from Arizona State University in higher and adult education and also completed the management development program (postdoctoral studies) at Harvard's Graduate School of Education in Cambridge, Massachusetts. He is listed in *America's Registry of Outstanding Professionals*, *Strathmore's Who's Who*, *Marquis Who's Who in America*, and *Marquis Who's Who in Education*. Joe holds memberships in the Association for the Study of Higher Education (ASHE) and the Society for Pentecostal Studies (SPS) as well as the Native American Fellowship of the Assemblies of God (NAF).

In his roles as both a missionary educator and missionary historian, Dr. Saggio is a regular contributor to theological, educational, and business publications and has spoken at conferences, workshops, colleges, universities, and in over 300 churches throughout the United States as well as in Brazil, Honduras, and India.

He and his wife, Nancy, who also serves as a part-time member of the AIC faculty, have two daughters: Rachelle Lynn and Leah Nicole.

Effective June 2008, Dr. Saggio assumes the role of associate dean for graduate studies in the College of Ministry at Northwest University in Kirkland, Washington.

Nancy J. Saggio is a licensed professional counselor (LPC) in the state of Arizona and also holds national certification as an approved clinical supervisor (ACS). Nancy is an adjunct instructor teaching in the areas of psychology and marriage and family. Along with her husband, Dr. Joseph J. Saggio, Nancy is also a nationally appointed U.S. missionary to Native Americans, having served at American Indian College since the fall of 1994. She received her BS in social work from Northern Arizona University in Flagstaff, Arizona, and her MA, as well as pursued doctoral studies in clinical and counseling psychology, from Western Conservative Baptist Seminary in Portland, Oregon. In addition to her work at American Indian College, Nancy is the clinical director of Phoenix Christian Counseling Associates and a behavioral health consultant for Springbrook Homes. In her spare time (such as it is) she also teaches part-time for the Assemblies of God Theological Seminary and Southwestern College in Phoenix, Arizona.

Alma F. Thomas is professor emerita of general education, elementary education, and ministry at American Indian College, having had a long time association with the school, since its inception as All Tribes Bible School. Alma Thomas and her late husband, Lonnie, began their service at the college in 1961, serving intermittently until 2001 as an instructor, with time also spent pastoring along with her husband in Tuba City, Arizona, and on the Salt River Indian Reservation near Scottsdale, Arizona. She also taught junior high school while co-pastoring the Tuba City church. Sister Thomas received her diploma from Central Bible College, her AA from Lee Junior College, her BS from Grand Canyon University, and her MA from Arizona State University. She was instrumental in assisting Alta M. Washburn write and publish her memoirs, *Trail to the Tribes.*

A greatly beloved educator, Alma Thomas received the prestigious Delta Alpha Award (Distinguished Educator) in 1997 from the General Council of the Assemblies of God for her outstanding contributions to AG Christian higher education. She also received a lifetime achievement award and was recognized in an honoring ceremony at the Convocation of Christian Indian Leaders held at Hungry Horse, Montana, in 1996 and at the same time was adopted into the Dakota tribe as an honorary tribal member. Sister Thomas remains active in ministry by serving as chair of the missions committee at her home church, Bell Road Assembly of God in Phoenix, Arizona, where she remains active in a preaching and teaching ministry.

Sandra K. Ticeahkie is a Kiowa/Comanche, serving as the director of admissions for AIC. She is a 1997 graduate with a BA degree in elementary education and served as a kindergarten teacher for the Christian school at Phoenix First Assembly of God. Since then, Sandy was involved with the pioneering of the Comanche Nation Tribal College in Lawton, Oklahoma, working in their admissions office. During that time she was also actively involved at Victory

Assembly of God in Anadarko, Oklahoma, serving as a youth pastor and interim pastor. In 2005, Sandy returned to AIC as the director of admissions and is also actively involved for the past couple of years in helping to coordinate the National Native Youth Convention, jointly sponsored by the Native American Fellowship (NAF) of the Assemblies of God and AIC. Sandra K. Ticeahkie was named AIC's alumna of the year in 2007 for her outstanding leadership and service to the college. She enjoys working with AIC students, being known for her people skills and sense of humor; she's also an avid sports lover, especially volleyball.

M. Nadine Waldrop was born in Terrell, Texas, and moved with her family to Phoenix, Arizona, where she attended elementary school and high school. In 1958 she received her call into Native American ministry during a Missionettes revival in Glendale, Arizona. Over the years "Sister Nadine" (as she is affectionately referred to) has served the Native American population in a number of capacities, including (but not limited to) hospital visitation at the Phoenix Indian Hospital, as a missionary assistant at Canyon Day Assembly of God on the Ft. Apache Reservation, and as co-pastor, and later pastor, of Co-op Assembly of God on the Gila River Indian Reservation.

An ordained Assemblies of God minister and nationally appointed Assemblies of God U.S. Mission missionary to Native Americans, Sister Nadine has served at the American Indian College in various capacities since 1979, including admissions coordinator, instructor, business administrator, and most recently as director of student financial aid. She also received her AA degree in 1993 in business from AIC. She is also a member of the Arizona Association for Student Financial Aid Administrators (AASFAA).

In 2005, Sister Nadine was honored by the Native American Fellowship of the Assemblies of God (NAF) at their annual Convocation of Christian Indian Leaders for forty years of exemplary service to the Native American people, an honor given to only a handful of missionaries. She remains faithful to her calling and is still waiting for an "easy summer"!

Jimmy Yellowhair is an enrolled member of the Navajo Nation and a 1983 graduate of American Indian Bible College. He also graduated from Northern Arizona University in Flagstaff, Arizona, with a BSBA degree in computer information systems. He and his wife

Myrna—an ordained Assemblies of God minister, were married in 1981. They have three children: David, Sarah, and Jonathan. Sarah is a graduate of Southwestern AG University in Waxahachie, Texas. David served recently as a youth minister at Whiteriver AG in Whiteriver, Arizona, and Jonathan graduated from Sinagua High School in Flagstaff in 2007 and is now proudly serving in the armed forces.

Both Jimmy and Myrna have been active in ministry, with Myrna serving as the pastor of Mountaintop AG in Flagstaff, Arizona, from 1992 to 2006. Jimmy has remained active as a Sunday School teacher for over twenty years and has recently completed a self-published book called *Sinless*, a collection of his Sunday School teachings compiled over the last two decades.

APPENDICES

Appendix A
Historical Timeline for ATBS/AIBI/AIBC/AIC

1957–2007[1]

This timeline chronicles some of the major formative events that have taken place in the history of ATBS/AIBI/AIBC/AIC between the years of 1957 and 2007. The chronology displayed here is only an outline of major seminal and historical events; no attempt has been made to create an exhaustive list—that would prove wholly impractical.

1957

▶ All Tribes Indian Bible School (ATBS) officially opens its doors at 4123 E. Washington Street in Phoenix, Arizona, as a ministry extension of All Tribes Indian Assembly of God on September 23, 1957.

1961

▶ ATBS graduates its first three diploma recipients: Lillie Irving, Mary Wallen, and Juanita (Miguel) Juan.

1965

▶ Alta M. Washburn resigns as the first principal of ATBS. Don Ramsey is appointed the second principal (later president) of ATBS.

1966

▶ First Speed-the-Light vehicle (bus) is received.

1967

▶ ATBS is renamed American Indian Bible Institute and becomes a regional school of the Assemblies of God.

1968

▶ Dedication of the present ten-acre site on Fifteenth Avenue in north Phoenix on February 28, 1968.

▶ Print shop established; the *Thunderer* becomes the official promotional publication for AIBI.

1971

▶ Dedication of the Washburn building (first building on campus) by Charles W. H. Scott, then national Director of Home Missions of the Assemblies of God on October 1, 1971. This building housed the first dormitory, classrooms, library, chapel, cafeteria, and offices.

1978

▶ Installation of Simon Peter (Choctaw) as AIBI's first Native President on July 1, 1978.

▶ Dedication of the Clyde Henson Memorial Chapel on September 29, 1978.

1979

▶ Vice president Eugene Herd serves as interim president from March to May 1979, succeeding Simon Peter.

▶ Carl E. Collins installed as president of AIBI on May 29, 1979, succeeding Simon Peter.

▶ President Simon Peter passes away after a lengthy illness on November 5, 1979.

1980

▶ AIBI begins offering associate of arts degree as well as bachelor of arts degree to supplement the three year diploma.

1982

▶ Implementation of the Foundational Studies Program (now Learning Resource Department) to provide remedial education to students needing academic assistance.

▶ AIBI granted candidate status for regional accreditation with the North Central Association of Colleges and Schools on June 25, 1982.

▶ AIBI is renamed American Indian Bible College (AIBC) in June 1982.

1983

▶ First associate of arts degrees granted in social work, business management, and secretarial science.

1984

▶ Dedication of the T.E. Gannon dormitory in honor of the former director of Home Missions in January 1984.

▶ Publication of *A Trail of Beauty: A Short History of American Indian Bible College* by Pauline Dunn.

1985

▶ First BA degrees in ministerial studies awarded.

1987

▶ President Carl Collins resigns in January 1987, assumes pastorate of All Tribes Assembly of God in Phoenix, Arizona.

▶ David J. Moore becomes president in March 1987.

1988

▶ AIBC receives regional accreditation as the first Pentecostal Bible college for American Indians in the United States on August 22, 1988.

▶ The Charles Scott Student Center (gymnasium), named in honor of Charles W.H. Scott, former director of the Division of Home Missions, dedicated debt-free on September 13, 1988.

1990

▶ Alta M. Washburn, founder of All Tribes Indian Bible School, passes away after a lengthy illness. Her autobiography, *Trail to the Tribes*, co-authored by Alma F. Thomas, is published posthumously.

1991

▶ The Rodger Cree Student Union completed in February 1991, named in honor of Rodger A. Cree Sr. (Mohawk), successful pastor, educator, elder, and general presbyter.

1992

▶ Special $100,000 gift received from a single individual, allowing completion of the Lee Academic Center in 1993.

▶ Original publication of *Indian Harvest: A History of American Indian Bible College* by Carolyn D. Baker as part of the college's promotion of the Decade of the Harvest theme instituted by the General Council of the Assemblies of God during the 1990s.

1993

▶ Completion and dedication of the Lee Academic Center (LAC) named in honor of Navajo pastor and distinguished artist Charles E. Lee of Shiprock, New Mexico.

1994

▶ American Indian Bible College becomes American Indian College of the Assemblies of God (AIC).

▶ David J. Moore resigns as president in August 1994, becomes the secretary (later director) of Intercultural Ministries for the Division of Home Missions.

1995

▶ Dr. W. Duane Collins becomes president in January 1995.

▶ First BA degrees conferred in elementary education.

▶ Dr. Anthony D. Palma, professor emeritus at American Indian College and long-time AG educator, is one of the first two professors to receive the newly inaugurated Delta Alpha Award, given to a maximum of two distinguished educators, at the General Council of the Assemblies of God biennial gathering.

1997

▶ Rev. Alma F. Thomas, professor emerita at American Indian College, is the second AIC professor to receive the prestigious Delta Alpha Award.

1998

▶ Dr. W. Duane Collins resigns as president in May 1998; alumnus Jim H. Lopez becomes the second Native president (Cocopah/Hispanic) of the college, serving until 2004.

2000

▶ Dedication of the Ramsey Cafeteria, named in honor of President Don (and Virginia) Ramsey, who served as president from 1965 to 1978.

2002

▶ Receipt of first $50,000 grant towards library holdings from the United Parcel Service (UPS) Foundation

2003

▶ Receipt of second $50,000 grant towards additional library holdings and technology from the UPS Foundation

2004

▶ Dr. Larry K. Kelly serves as interim president from June to December 2004

2005

▶ AIC receives official authorization to serve as an approved branch campus for the Assemblies of God Theological Seminary based in Springfield, Missouri. The authorization permits AIC to host courses leading to the master of arts in Christian ministry from AGTS.

▶ AA in Christian ministry degree program approved.

▶ James V. Comer is elected president of AIC at the spring board of regents meeting.

2006

▶ Six (out of eight) BA in Christian ministry graduates from the 2006 class now hold ministerial credentials. This is the first time since 1994 that one graduating class produces that many credential holders during the college's fifty-year history.

2007

▶ August 22, 2007, President James V. Comer declares 2007–2008 to be AIC's Year of Jubilee with the theme "Proclaiming the Lord's Favor." The college's leadership also established a goal of raising over $1 million to cover past student indebtedness.

NOTES

1   See Information gleaned from an unpublished flyer printed in 1957 advertising the opening of the school; Joseph J. Saggio, "Alta M. Washburn: 'Trailblazer' to the Tribes," in *Assemblies of God Heritage* 27:1, 28-33; Carolyn D. Baker, *Indian Harvest: A History of American Indian Bible College* (Phoenix, AZ: 1992); Pauline Dunn, *A Trail of Beauty: A Short History of American Indian Bible College* (Phoenix, AZ: 1984); *2003 A Self-Study Report Submitted to the North Central Association Commission on Higher Education*.

Appendix B
Board of Regents Members
(1984–2008)

(Editors' Note: In *A Trail of Beauty: A Short History of American Indian Bible College*, found in Part Three of this book, Pauline Dunn provided at the end of that work a listing of faculty, staff, administrators, and board members from the school's inception up until 1984. Here we've done our best to update that information, bringing it current to 2008, the year of this work's publication. Accordingly, we have presented only the updated information here.)

Board of Regents
Executive Committee
(Presently Serving)

James V. Comer

Tommy Crider (Secretary)

L. Alton Garrison

R. Kenneth George

Stephen L. Harris (Vice President)

John E. Maracle

T. Ray Rachels (President)

Robert Slaton

Priscilla Taylor

Scott Temple

Lindell Warren

Board
(Presently Serving

Marvin Begay

Tim Black

Donald Bogue

James R. Braddy

Ed Bradford

Frank Cargill

Tommy Carpenter

Gary Chapin

Dave E. Cole

Becky Dickenson

Daniel Fischer

Doyle Fulkes

Gloria Gilson

Joseph Granberry

Duane Hammond

Stephen Harris

Dennis Hodges

Roger Hoffpowier

Samuel Huddleston

Wanda Huie

Carole Ingroum

George Kallappa, Sr.

Tom Lakey

William Lee

Darrell Madsen

Larry Moore

Becky Nenstiel

Charley Odell

Betty Owens

Sandra L. Palmer

Lillie Pearce

Judy Rachels

Keith Smith, Esq.

Howard Spillers

Alvin "Dobie" Weasel

Douglas York

Former Executive Committee Members
(1984–)

Carl E. Collins
W. Duane Collins
Fred Cottriel
Rodger A. Cree
W. E. Cummings
Derwood Dubose
Carolyn Elgin
Elmer D. Geesey
Charles Hackett
Earl Johnson
James Kessler

Charles E. Lee
William Lee
Jim H. Lopez
David J. Moore
Robert Pirtle
Robert Sites
Howard Spillers
James R. Trewern
Stephen Tourville
William Vickery

Former Board Members
(1984–)

Orval Alexander
Donald Annas
Wilbur Balch
Doris Bernard
Anita Bogdan
James Boulware
John Bowersock
James K. Bridges
Howard Burroughs
Debbie Canada
Leroy Cloud
Glen Cole
Linda Crider
Kathleen Cummings
Frances Davis
Derwood Dubose
Mary Fairrington
Donald Farmer
J. W. Farmer
Barbara Forrest
David Gable
Joseph Gerhart
James Girkin

J. K. Gressett
Joe Hanna
Merle Harris
Paul Hodson
Morris Ivey
Donald Keeter
O. W. Killingsworth
Clifton Kornmueller
Duane Johnson
Earl Johnson
Virgil Jones
Paul J. Lanuza
Eric Lee
Jack B. Linney
Mark McGrath
John McPherson
Ralph Morris
Phil Neely
Armon Newburn
Hal Noah
Vernon Nybakken
Jeff Peterson
David Rice

Charlie Roberts
Jerry Roberts
D. Leroy Sanders
Paul W. Savage
Ruth Savage
Roy Schaeffer
Vic Schober
Charles W. H. Scott
Jane Shoults
Manuel Shoults
Robert Sites
Ann Slaton
Everett Stenhouse
Ron Stevens
Jan Trewern
William Vickery
Bob Villa
Leslie E. Welk
Robert Willis
E. Joe Wilmoth
George O. Wood

Honorary Board Members:

T. C. Cunningham
J.K. Gressett
Alpha Henson
Charles E. Lee

Curtis W. Ringness
Irving Terry
James R. Trewern

Appendix C
Administration and Faculty
(1984–2008)

(Editors' Note: In *A Trail of Beauty: A Short History of American Indian Bible College*, Pauline Dunn provided at the end of that work a listing of current administration and faculty from the school's inception up until 1984. Herein we've done our best to update that information, bringing it up to date in 2008, the year of this work's publication. Accordingly, we have presented only updated information here. Some administrators served as classroom instructors and therefore may be listed twice.)

Administration
(Presently Serving)

James V. Comer
(President)

David L. DeGarmo
(Vice-President and Academic Dean)

Jimmy E. Dempsey
(Dean of Institutional Research)

Jerry Stephen Jester
(Executive Director of Institutional Advancement)

Vincent R. Roubideaux
(Dean of Students)

Joseph J. Saggio
(Dean of Institutional Assessment and AGTS Branch Campus Director)

Alvin "Dobie" Weasel
(Non-Resident Vice President, effective: March 2008)

Administration
(1984–2004)

Jack Caudle	(Business Administrator)
Carl E. Collins	(President)
W. Duane Collins	(President)
W. E. Cummings	(Interim President)
Larry K. Kelly	(Interim President)
Robby Jernigan	(Business Manager)
Jim H. Lopez	(Dean of Students, Vice President, President)
Judith A. Mattes	(Academic Dean)
David J. Moore	(Business Administrator, Academic Dean, President)
Charlene Pino	(Business Administrator)
C. Blair Schlepp	(Dean of Students)
Alma Thomas	(Academic Dean)
M. Nadine Waldrop	(Business Administrator)
Norman Wolff	(Business Manager)

Residential Faculty
(Presently Serving)
David Cleaveland (Missions, Bible, Greek, Ministry)
David L. DeGarmo(Bible, Christian Ministry, Music)
Jimmy E. Dempsey (Intercultural Ministry, General Education, Bible)
Sandra M. Gonzales (Registrar, General Education, Learning Resource Dept.)
Glen Gray(Chair, Christian Ministries; General Education)
Peggy Gray(Missions, Bible, Ministry, General Education, Learning Resource)
Betty Hanna (Learning Resource, Elementary Education, Christian Ministry)
Patricia Jackson (Chair, Business)
Jerry Stephen Jester (Missions, Ministry, Bible)
William Kruger (Christian Ministry)
Everett F. Peralta (Chair, Elementary Education; General Education)
John S. Rose (Librarian, Church History)
Vincent R. Roubideaux (General Education)
Joseph J. Saggio (Chair, General Education; Christian Ministry, Elementary Education)

Part-time Faculty
(Presently Serving)
Floyd Allen (General Education)
Henry V. Brown (Business)
Tom Kuyper (Physical Education)
Paul Lanuza (Business, Christian Ministry)
Louisa Lee (Art)
Willis Lewis (Elementary Education)
Kelby Milgrim (General Education)
Harold Partin (General Education)
Sam Prophet (General Education)
Katherine Rose (Assistant Librarian, History)
Nancy J. Saggio (General Education)

Residential Faculty
(1984–2007)
Arden Amenrud (General Education)
Audrey Amenrud (General Education)
Carolyn D. Baker (Bible, Theology, Ministry, Greek)
Leslie E. Bartley (Chair, Elementary Education)
James Boulware (Bible)
Jack Caudle (Chair, Business; General Education)
Donald Coleman (Bible, Theology, Ministry)
W. Duane Collins (Missions)
Pat Dickerson (Bible, Theology)
Timothy Grant (General Education, Men's Basketball and Women's Volleyball Coach)
Marsha Gulfan (Learning Resource, Elementary Education)
Kathleen Haislip Myers (Chair, Business; General Education)
Betty Jernigan (Foundational Studies, General Education, Practical Theology)
Robby Jernigan (General Education, Christian Education)
Edith Kaiser (Bible, Theology)
Otto Kaiser (Bible, Theology)
John H. Knoles (Bible, Theology, Ministry)
Paul J. Lanuza (Chair, Business)
Belinda F. Lopez (Chair, Learning Resource Department;
          Chair, Elementary Education, General Education)
Jim H. Lopez (General Education, Ministry)
Marcia Lyman (Registrar, Business, General Education)

Donna McDougall (General Education)
Judith A. Mattes (Christian Education, Elementary Education)
David J. Moore (General Education)
Robert W. Moore (Librarian, Bible)
Susie Peshlakai (Business)
Dorothy Plake (Chair, Elementary Education; General Education)
Donald R. Ramsey (General Education)
Jim Rivera (Christian Ministry)
Joe Robinson (Chair, Social Work)
R. W. Sanders (Christian Education)
C. Blair Schlepp (General Education)
Boyd R. Tolbert (Chair, Elementary Education; General Education)
Norman Wolff (Business)

Part-time Faculty
(1984–2007)

Chris Aballe (Business)
Joseph Burnsworth (Business)
Alice Collins (Child Evangelism)
Rodger A. Cree (Campus Pastor, Bible, Ministry)
Mary Fischer (General Education)
Diane Garner (Elementary Education)
Donna George (Elementary Education, General Education)
Debra Gerhardt (Elementary Education)
JoAnn Gibbs (General Education)
Christa Grant (Foundational Studies)
Larry Grimmett (General Education)
Eva Lee "Ez" Larson (General Education)
Bonnie Lee (Music)
John E. Maracle (Native American Studies)
Esther Lindfors (Learning Resource Department, Elementary Education)
Lupe Nava (Elementary Education)
Betty Palma (General Education)
Mitchell "Sandy" Parks (General Education)
Loren Raiford (General Education)
Donald R. Ramsey (General Education)
Rick Ricciardi (Business)
Angel Rosa (Ministry, Drug Rehabilitation)
Lucelia Shelton (General Education, Elementary Education)
Don Skipp (Business)
Wayne Soemo (General Education)
James R. Stoll (Biology)
Ludo Vandendriessche (Christian Ministry)
Bob Villa (Music)
Roland Waller (Bible)
John Wenzlau (Business)
Norman Wolff (Church Finance, General Education)
Roger Zimmerman (Elementary Education)

Professors Emeriti
Eugene A. Hunter (Bible, Ministry)
Donald Keeter (Ministry, Bible)
Charles E. Lee (Ministry, Bible)
Anthony D. Palma (Theology, Greek, New Testament)
Alma Thomas (Elementary Education, General Education, Ministry)

Appendix D
Staff (1984-2008)

(Editors' Note: In *A Trail of Beauty: A Short History of American Indian Bible College*, Pauline Dun provided at the end of that work a listing of current staff members at the school from its inception to 1984. We've tried to update this information as best we are able to. Accordingly, we have presented only updated information here. Although we have done our best to provide a complete listing, it is possible that we may have accidentally omitted some individuals. We sincerely apologize if we have done so.

Finally, this college has benefited enormously from MAPS (Mission America Placement Service) and other volunteers who often served on both a short-term and long-term volunteer basis under the auspices of the U.S. Missions Program within the Assemblies of God. Unfortunately, it would be impossible for us to assemble an adequate listing of these folks, but we do want to mention them collectively as a group of individuals who have blessed this institution enormously. To all of our volunteers over the years who have served this institution with faithfulness, loyalty, and excellence—we salute you!)

Staff
(Presently Serving)

Ron Burnette
Nicolas Chvostovsky
Susan Comer
Ryan Gonzalez
Karen Jester
Gay Keeter

Joan Kruger
Lia Lanuza
Pat Merino
Steve Morgan
Sylvia Rivera
Theodore Smith

Sandra Ticeahkie
M. Nadine Waldrop
Dolores Wren
Kenneth Wren

Staff
(1984-2007)

Maria Alexavich
Frances Bartley
Carletta Billy
Mia (Billy) Boyd
Gay Bridges
John Brings
Joe Ann Caudle
Beverly Clindaniel
Steve Clindaniel
Ruth Collins
Dan Copher
Cleo Cordova
Pete Cordova, Jr.
Kristi Deater
Bonnie DeLeon
Linda Dempsey
Clay Dennison
Alexandria Duncan
Mimi Eich
Dorothy Erickson
Billie Fox
Raymond Garcia
Dana Gonzalez
Katrina Guy

Neva Hamilton
Walt Hendrickson
Helen Huffer
Austin Jones
Jennifer Jones
Tonita Keith
Doris Knoles
Kaye Large
Corilee Lee
Carol Lingle
Rick Lingle
Marjorie McPhillips
Frank Marcesa
Alice Martin
Gene Martin
Danette Miller
Steven Miller
Linda Moore
Brenda (Dashna) Morris
Paul Nava
Robin Nez
Charley Odell
Jan Odell
Doris Preston

Linda Rivera
Diane Rodriguez
Randy Rueb
Dorothy Runyan
Danny Sarabia
Joy Sarabia
Patsy Schwanke
Donna Shendo
Doreen Smiley
Nizhoni Smith
William Starkweather
Manny Torres
Carl Vanderpool
Bob Villa
Mazzie Villa
Beverly Wall
Diane Webb
Charlie Williams
Randy Wren
Dennis Young

Appendix E

Graduates

1984–2008

(Editors' Note: At the end of *A Trail of Beauty: A Short History of American Indian Bible College* by Pauline Dunn, contained earlier in this book, a listing of the graduates of All Tribes Bible School, American Indian Bible Institute, and American Indian Bible College up to 1983. Here we have listed the subsequent graduates of American Indian Bible College and American Indian College from 1984 to 2008. Married female graduates are listed by their current last names (if our information is current) with maiden names in parentheses. As editors we have done our best to be as accurate as possible; if there are any mistakes or omissions we sincerely apologize!)

MIN= Ministerial Studies

CE= Christian Education

CM=Christian Ministry

SEC=Secretarial Science

SW= Social Work

BUS=Business

EE= Elementary Education

AA= Associate of Arts

DIP= Diploma

BA= Bachelor of Arts

1984:

Susie (Peshlakai) Alchesay	BA CE
Juanita (Jim) Brooks	AA SEC
Stephanie (Jordan) Coleman	BA CE
Alice Collins	BA MIN/CE
Helen (Harry) Fall	BA CE
Modesta (Scott) Holiday	BA MIN/CE
Julia (Mendoza) Ibarra	BA CE
Paul James Lanuza	BA MS
Eric Lee	BA MIN
Louisa M. Lee	BA CE
Julie Manuel	BA CE
Charlene E. Mendoza	BA CE
Brenda (Dashna) Morris	AA SEC

1985:

Clara Ruth Albert	AA SW
Beverly Kinney	AA SW
	& BA CE
Patricia Morning Gun	AA SEC
Brenda (Dashna) Morris	BA CE
Carlene Myers	BA CE
Geraldine (Moses) Poncho	AA SEC
Carolyn (Norris) Terry	DIP CE
	& AA SW

1986:

Linda (Brown) Charley	DIP CE
Inez Coleman	AA BUS
Rosie (Lee) Jackson	AA SEC

Marguerita John	DIP CE
Marilyn (Zilth) Jones	AA SW
	& BA CE
Stephanie (Gordon) Joseph	AA BUS
Donald Patrick Merino	DIP MIN
Mike Morning Gun	DIP MIN
Marvin Paul	AA BUS
	& BA MIN
Gloria (Pechuli) Smith	AA SW
	&BA MIN
Stanley Tom	AA SW
Corrina Tsosie	AA SEC

1987:

Doreen (Smiley) Baki	AA SW
Elouise Castillo	AA SEC
John Castillo, Jr.	AA SW
Cleo (Dennison) Cordova	AA SW
Daniel Fitts	AA BUS
Renee Fuller	AA SW
Bernita Garcia	AA BUS
Michael L. Jensen	BA MIN
Floyd Lee	BA MIN
Virgil Nez	BA MIN
Darwin Price	BA MIN/CE
Teresa Snider	AA BUS
Marlene (Yazzie) Vallo	AA BUS
Delbert Williams	AA SW
Rhonda Williams	AA BUS

1988:

Shirley Begay	AA	SW
Virnae Buck	AA	SW
Darlene Chischilly	AA	BUS
Sharon (Kee) Clitso	AA	SW
Pete C. Cordova, Jr.	BA	CE
Manfred Duncan	AA	BUS
Clarence Enos	AA	SW
Lucy (Cordova) Fraga	AA	BUS
Estrellita (Fall) Galvan	AA	SW
Rosie (Lee) Jackson	BA	MIN/CE
Myrtle Luna	AA	BUS
Warren Matson	BA	MIN
Patricia Pablo	AA	BUS
Daisy (Jose) Puffer	AA	SW
Jennifer (Smith) Roubideaux	AA	BUS
Roy Stewart	AA	SW
	& BA	MIN
Dale Vallo	AA	BUS
Aaron Williams	AA	SW

1989

Thurman Balchinclowing	AA	BUS
Frederick Billie	AA	SW
Marie (White) Billie	AA	BUS
Joseph D. Clancy	AA	BUS
Joel Cornelius	BA	MIN
Nancy Egan	AA	SW
Daniel Fitts	BA	MIN
Elizabeth (Clancy) Fox	AA	SW
Gloria Gilson	AA	SW
Jeremy Peter Gulfan	AA	SW
	& DIP	MIN
Tamra (Buck) Manuel	AA	BUS
Donna (Arthur) Nez	BA	MIN
Daniel Sarabia	AA	BUS
Donna Shendo	AA	BUS
Leroy Shirley Jr.	AA	SW
Gary Smith	DIP	CE
Geneva Smith	AA	SW
Sarah (Harrison) Tsosie	BA	MIN
Randy J. Wren	BA	MIN
Phelia (Antonio) Yazzie	AA	BUS
Colette (Waconda)Yuzos	AA	BUS

1990

Cynthia Attakai–Clark	AA	BUS
Vina (Topaha) Behn	AA	SW
Frederick Billee	BA	MIN
Pamela (Mosely) Cooper	AA	BUS
Sharon Cornelius	BA	MIN

Catherine Crone	AA	BUS
Jeff Crone	AA	BUS
Lorna Delowe	AA	SW
Matilda Harrison	AA	BUS
Tonita Ann (Yazzie) Keith	AA	SW
Mary Ellen (Loas) Manuel	AA	BUS
Charlene Mendoza	AA	SW
Albert Nez	AA,	SW
	& BA	MIN
Patricia Pablo	BA	CE
Judy Peters	AA	SW
Arlene (Hinton) Pike	AA	SEC
	& BA	MIN
Vincent Roubideaux	AA	SW
Joy L. (Hamilton) Sarabia	BA	CE
Leroy Shirley	BA	MIN/CE
O'Linda Shirley	AA	SW
Sandy (Shane) Stearns	AA	SW
Linda (Alexander)		
White Thunder	AA	BUS
Geneva Yazzie	AA	SW
Genita Yazzie	AA	BUS

1991

Garreth Abbey	AA	BUS
Judy Antone	AA	SW
	& BA	MIN
Sammie Begay, Jr.	BA	MIN
Vina (Topaha) Behn	BA	MIN
Cynthia Burnett	AA	BUS
	& BA	MIN/CE
Benjamin Bert Calvo	AA	BUS
Kevin Drake	DIP	MIN
Michele (Wagoner) Jacobs	AA	BUS
Gene Manuel	BA	MIN
Rose Mary (Tadytin)		
Montour	AA	SW
Armi Pilapil	AA	SW
Loren Raiford	AA	SW
Jennie Reeder	AA	SW
Dawn Terry	AA	BUS
Fannie Ward	BA	CE

1992

Tina (Yazzie) Abbey	AA	BUS
Elmira Hunter	BA	MIN
Betty Morgan	BA	CE
Loren Raiford	BA	MIN
Sandy (Shane) Stearns	BA	CE
Dale Vallo	BA	CE

1993:

Garreth Abbey — BA MIN
Terri L. (Watch) Atcitty — AA BUS
Rachel (Smith) Bedoni — AA BUS
M. Denis Billy — AA BUS
Andrea Bowechop — AA BUS
Monica (Juan) Canizalez — AA BUS
Arcenio Charleston — BA MIN
Abelina Classay — AA BUS
Jeremiah Declay — AA BUS
Janet Gilmore — AA BUS
Lenora (Shorty) Holgate — AA BUS
Michelle (Wagoner) Jacobs — BA CE
Michelle (Antonio) Mix — AA BUS
Bobbi (Hunter) Morego — AA BUS
Rose Mary (Tadytin)
Montour — BA CE
Darryl Noble — BA MIN
Janet Noline — AA BUS
Mary Pina — AA BUS
Scott Pina — AA BUS
M. Nadine Waldrop — AA BUS
Melissa Walts — BA CE
Wade Wilbur — AA BUS
Roy N. Zahney — AA BUS

1994:

Carlos Baki — BA MIN
Marvin Begay — AA BUS
& BA MIN
Pedro Saul Cardenas — BA MIN
Mark Chief — AA BUS
Steven Funston — BA MIN
Jackie Holgate — BA MIN
Bobbi (Hunter) Morego — BA MIN
Lynette Johns — BA MIN
Tonita Ann (Yazzie) Keith — BA CE
Rolanda Rico — AA BUS
Stanley Tom — BA MIN
Aaron Williams — BA CM

1995:

Jerald Bidtah — BA EE
Emanuel Cachon — BA MIN
Evangelina Charles — AA BUS
Pamela (Mosely) Cooper — BA EE
Alexandria (Duncan) Crosby — AA BUS
Manuel Gonzales — AA BUS
Markus Linke — AA BUS
Deborah (Rubio) Ramm — BA EE
Daniel Sarabia — BA MIN

Donna Shendo — BA EE
Bethany (Kessay) Skidmore — AA BUS
Deborah (Lee) Tom — BA EE
Connie Tsosie — BA EE
Fabian Tsosie — AA BUS
Stacie White — AA BUS
Sonya White Mountain — BA MIN
Jessica Wright — AA BUS
Gabriel Yazzie — AA BUS
Michelle Zahn — BA CE

1996:

Delia (Orduno) Begay — BA EE
Jimmie Bidtah — BA MIN
Melody (Fulton) Bidtah — AA BUS
Rewa (Charleston) Blackstar — BA CE
Valerie Boyd — AA BUS
Vadonna (Lupe) Bush — AA BUS
Leonard Chacon — BA MIN
Manfred Duncan — BA EE
Harriette Evans — BA MS
Janet Gilmore — AA BUS
Bryan J. Hall — AA BUS
Lisa (Skeet) Hornsby — BA EE
James Mix — AA BUS
Phenecia Padilla — AA BUS
Alfonso Parga, Jr. — BA EE
Brady Rivers — BA EE
Shirleen (Shorty) Rivers — BA EE
Karla (Shayen) Parga — BA EE
Marvin Slivers — BA EE
Sandra Ticheahkie — BA EE
Irena (Classay) Tsinnie — AA BUS
Randall Tsinnie — AA BUS
Joseph Woodruff — BA CE/MIN

1997:

Marlene Begay — AA BUS
M. Denis Billy — BA MIN
Allison Wayne Boyd, Jr. — BA MIN
Mia (Billy) Boyd — AA BUS
Jason Bryant — BA EE
Monica (Juan) Canizalez — BA EE
Vivian (Tercero) Ehmke — BA EE
Angelica Erosa-Perez — AA BUS
Phillip Fulton — AA BUS
Lucy Gardner — BA EE
Melissa John — AA BUS
Glen Ivanoff — AA BUS
& BA CM
Crescencio S. Juarez — AA BUS

Derryl Long AA BUS
Paula Paul BA CM
Daniel Mark Pechacek AA BUS
Diana Schlepp BA EE
Pamela (Zahney) Shabi BA EE
Elouise Tadytin BA EE
Fabian Tsosie BA EE
Michele Tsosie AA BUS
Gwen Williams AA BUS
Karen Williams AA BUS
Clifford Wolf Black BA MIN
Mary Merasty-Zahney AA BUS

1998:
Andrea Christine Avalos BA CM
Marlene Begay BA CM
Pearlene Benally BA CM
Tammie Bowman BA EE
Donald Campbell AA BUS
Gwen D. (Espinoza) Fox BA EE
Ingrid Gardner BA EE
Sandra (Smith) Gonzales AA BUS
Bryan Hall BA EE
Elena (Fernandez) Hall BA EE
Michael Hall BA CM
Sylvia (Charley) Montoya BA CM
Daniel Mark Pechacek BA CM
Anthony Saldibar BA CM/EE
Karol (Feldhake) Vieux BA CM
Ursula Watchman AA BUS

1999:
Millecent (Thompson) Canales BA EE
Jean Clem AA BUS
Millie Garcia AA BUS
Frances Jackson BA EE
Geraldine Long AA BUS
Darryl Ricker BA EE
Sandra Tsinnie AA BUS
Ronald Van Fleet AA BUS
                    & BA CM
Shari (Caldwell) Williams BA EE

2000:
Mark Abeyta BA EE
Consuelo (Pereida) Berger BA CM
Jean Clem BA CM
Bridget Fominyam BA EE
Ray Garcia BA CM
Nora Lister AA BUS
Valarie Paul AA BUS
Tynisha Pilone-Flores AA BUS

Sean Sloan BA CM
Jonathan Taylor BA CM
Alicia Tsinnie AA BUS
Ruth Wagner BA EE

2001:
Craig Bidtah BA EE
Tonya (Zospah) Bidtah BA EE
Thomas Blackstar III AA BUS
Valencia (Burke) Campbell AA BUS
Leneva George BA MIN
Crescencio Sam Juarez BA EE
Arlene Lang AA BUS
Marcia Lyman BA CM
Tammy Scott BA EE
Ursula Watchman BA CM
Elwanda Williamson BA CM
Matilda Yazzie AA BUS
Lucinda Zospah AA BUS

2002:
Doris Ahlalook BA CM
Dean Doney, Jr. AA BUS
Donald Patrick Merino BA CM
Tynisha Pilone-Flores BA CM

2003:
Emerly Bylene Antonio AA BUS
Jennifer Bahe BA CM
Kent L. Burnette BA CM
Richard Coker BA CM
Millie Garcia BA EE
Sandra (Smith) Gonzales BA EE
Marylita (Fall) Marone BA EE
Christina (Cullen) Olivo BA EE
Alvin Owens BA CM
Amanda Peshlakai-Tracy AA BUS
Joy (Hamilton) Sarabia BA EE
Neil Sellers BA CM
Darlene Vasquez AA BUS
Matilda Yazzie BA CM

2004:
Heather Ayala BA CM
Kristi Begaye BA CM
Crystal (Grass) Doney BA EE
Andrea L. Joe BA EE
Amanda (Van Etten) Johns BA EE
Paul Lent AA BUS
Vince E. Maytubby BA CM
Erica Nozie AA BUS
Irene Lloyd Potter BA CM

Daniel Reed   BA   CM
William Starkweather   BA   CM
Roy N. Zahney   BA   CM

2005:
Arlene Frances Bercier   BA   EE
Emmanuel Dinglas   BA   CM
Daniel Fisher   BA   EE
Jonathan Lanuza   AA   BUS
Benjamin Lee   AA   BUS
Alisha Emily Malone   AA   BUS
Earl P. Matt, Jr.   BA   CM
Dwayne Moolman   BA   CM
Ernie Scott   BA   CM
Miracle (Van Zant) Johnson   BA   CM
Alferda (Malone) Walking Eagle   BA   EE
Sonja (Marks) White   BA   EE
Christina D. Williams   BA   EE
Mary Merasty-Zahney   BA   EE

2006:
James Joseph Bollinger   BA   CM
Alin Calini   BA   CM
Rodale Cooley   BA   EE
Glendon Frank   AA   BUS
Kisha Marie Garcia   AA   BUS
Cheryl Grass   BA   EE
Michael Joseph Johnson   BA   CM
Austin M. Jones   BA   CM
Gayle Marie Large   BA   EE

Paul Lent   BA   CM
Michelle Mix   BA   CM
Manuel Rivera   BA   CM
Vincent R. Roubideaux   BA   CM
Norbert Smith   BA   CM
Colleen Washington   BA   EE

2007:
Marco Burnette   BA   EE
Emmanuel Dinglas   BA   EE
James M. Grisaffe   BA   CM
Jennifer Ann Jones   BA   EE
Doreen Nozie   AA   BUS

2008:
Atcitty, Natasha Lynn   BA   CM
Burnette, Ronald J.   BA   CM
Contreras, Jonathon   BA   CM
Cruse, Seth M.   BA   CM
Declay, Kerrie Virginia   AA   BUS
Frank, Glendon D.   BA   CM
Joe, Pamela R.   BA   EE
Lanuza, David Christopher   BA   EE
Lanuza, Jonathon J.   BA   CM
Lopez, Jameson David   BA   EE
Skeet, Melissa   AA   CM
Skinner, Rev. Lisa A.   BA   CM
Ubaldo, Maurice John   BA   CM

APPENDIX F
Presidential Discretionary Grant

None of the editors, contributors, or graphic artists have received any financial remuneration for their work on this volume. All revenues above actual printing costs are being directed to the *Presidential Discretionary Grant* established here at American Indian College by the Board of Regents to assist worthy students who might otherwise be unable to complete their college education. The grant guidelines are listed below:

▶ The College President will have executive oversight of any and all grant disbursements.

▶ The College President may at his discretion appoint an ad hoc advisory committee to assist with any decision-making.

▶ Grant recipients must be currently enrolled students at American Indian College in good standing both academically (cumulative GPA of 2.0 or higher) and in Student Ministries (cumulative grade of C or higher), and must have a demonstrated financial need.

▶ Student employment responsibilities must be met.

▶ All financial aid paperwork must be completed and submitted by the deadlines.

▶ Funds must be used for tuition, fees, books, dorm costs, or other approved educational expenses.

▶ The amount of the grant is subject to the President's discretion.

▶ The maximum amount of the grant will be equal to the current cost of one semester's tuition, board, books, and fees for a full-time student (fifteen credit hours).

▶ The Scholarship Committee will be consulted in the decision-making of awards.

▶ Any exception(s) to any of these policies will need approval by the Administrative Committee.

▶ Funds awarded will be reported to the Administrative Committee for approval.

If you would like to make an additional tax-deductible contribution to the Presidential Discretionary Grant, please contact the college's Business Office at (602) 944-3335 or contact us via our Web site at www.aicag.edu.

NAMES INDEX

▼▼▼

(Editors' Note: Because of the enormous number of names in the listing of graduates and personnel from 1957 to 1983 found at the end of *A Trail of Beauty: A Short History of American Indian Bible College* in Part Three, and also in Appendices B–G that are listed categorically and include board members, administration, faculty, staff, and graduates from 1984 to 2007, we have chosen not to include those names in this index listing. We refer the reader to those sections for the listings of corresponding names that are organized by category.)

PHOTO INDEX

▼▼▼

PHOTO INDEX

the trail continues...